DATE DUE			

Social Research Methods

SOCIAL RESEARCH METHODS

Random House New York

Perspective, Theory, and Analysis

Kenneth W. Eckhardt
and M. David Ermann

University of Delaware

 All inquiries should be addressed to Random House, Inc., 201 East 50th Street, New York, N.Y. 10022. Published in the United States by Random House, Inc., and simultaneously in Canada by Random House of Canada Limited, Toronto.

Library of Congress Cataloging in Publication Data

Eckhardt, Kenneth W
Social research methods.

Includes bibliographies and index.
1. Social sciences. 2. Social sciences—Methodology. 3. Social science research. I. Ermann, M. David, joint author. II. Title.
H61.E27 300'.1'8 76-57256
ISBN 0-394-31256-2

Manufactured in the United States of America

First Edition
9 8 7 6 5 4 3 2 1

Book design by Karin Batten

ACKNOWLEDGMENTS

Table 2-1: Printed by permission from (Kenneth W. Eckhardt, "Exchange Theory and Sexual Permissiveness") *Behavior Science Notes* 6:8, 1971.

Table 3-1: Shirley Foster Hartley, "The Decline of Illegitimacy in Japan," *Social Problems* 18:1 (Summer 1970), Table 1, p. 80. By permission of The Society for the Study of Social Problems, copyright holder, and the author.

Table 4-1: Karl Taeuber, "Negro Residential Segregation: Trends and Measurement," *Social Problems* 12:1 (Summer 1964), Table 2, p. 46. By permission of The Society for the Study of Social Problems, copyright holder, and the author.

Table 5-1: Reynolds Farley and Albert I. Hermalin, "Family Stability: A Comparison of Trends Between Blacks and Whites," *American Sociological Review,* Vol. 36, 1971, Table 1, p. 3. By permission of The American Sociological Association, copyright holder, and the authors.

Tables 6-1 and 6-2: Charles M. Grigg and Lewis M. Killian, "Negro Perceptions of Organizational Effectiveness," *Social Problems* 11:4 (Spring 1964), Table 1, p. 384, and Table 2, p. 385. By permission of The Society for the Study of Social Problems, copyright holder, and the authors.

Box 7-1: Emory S. Bogardus, "A Social Distance Scale," *Sociology and Social Research* 17(1933):265–271. By permission of the publisher.

Table 7-1 and Figure 7-1: Edward O. Laumann, "Subjective Social Distance and Urban Occupational Stratification," *American Journal of Sociology* 71, 1 (July 1965), Table 1, p. 31, and Figure 1, p. 33. By permission of the University of Chicago Press. © 1965 by The University of Chicago. All rights reserved.

Tables 8-1, 8-2, 8-3, and 8-4: Kenneth W. Eckhardt and Gerry Hendershot, "Transformation of Alienation into Public Opinion," *The Sociological Quarterly* 8 (1967), Table 1, p. 462; Table 3, p. 464; Table 4, p. 465; and Table 5, p. 465. By permission of *The Sociological Quarterly*.

Table 9-10: Harvey Marshall and Ross Purdy, "Hidden Deviance and the Labelling Approach: The Case for Drinking and Driving," *Social Problems* 19:4 (Spring 1972), Table 1, p. 548. By permission of The Society for the Study of Social Problems, copyright holder, and the authors.

Tables 10-2A, 10-2B, 10-2C, 10-3, 10-4, and 10-5: James M. Fendrich, "Perceived Reference Group Support," *American Sociological Review,* Vol. 32 (1967), Tables 1a, 1b, and 1c, p. 965, and Tables 2a, 2b, and 2c, p. 967. By permission of The American Sociological Association, copyright holder, and the author.

Table IV-1 and Table A3-1: Richard P. Runyon and Audrey Haber, *General Statistics,* 2nd ed. (Reading, Mass.: Addison-Wesley, 1973), Table A, pp. 338–339. By permission of Addison-Wesley Publishing Company.

Tables 12-3, 12-4, 12-5, 12-6, and 12-7: Tables from Charles F. Westoff and Raymond H. Potvin, *College Women and Fertility Values* (copyright © 1967 by Princeton University Press), #1 & 2, pp. 11 and 12, and parts of #7, p. 36. Reprinted by permission of Princeton University Press.

Tables 13-1, 13-2, and 13-3: Elton F. Jackson, William S. Fox, and Harry J. Crockett, Jr., "Religion and Occupational Achievement," *American Sociological Review,* Vol. 35, 1970, Table 1, p. 54; Table 2, p. 55; and Table 4, p. 58. By permission of The American Sociological Association, copyright holder, and the authors.

Srole Anomia Scale, p. 221: Leo Srole, "Social Integration and Certain Corollaries: An Exploratory Study," *American Sociological Review,* Vol. 21, 1956, Anomia Scale, pp. 712–713. By permission of The American Sociological Association, copyright holder, and the author.

Tables 14-2 and 14-3: Leslie Carr, "The Srole Items and Acquiescence," *American Sociological Review,* Vol. 36, Table 1, p. 290. By permission of The American Sociological Association, copyright holder, and the author.

Appendix to Chapter 14: Institute for Social Research, University of Michigan, "Quality of Life," interview schedule used in Project 468110 (Summer 1971). By permission of the Institute for Social Research, Ann Arbor, Michigan.

Table 15-1 and parts of Tables 15-3 and 15-4: David Epperson, "A Reassessment of Indices of Parental Influence in the Adolescent Society," *American Sociological Review,* Vol. 36, 1971, Table 1, p. 94, and Table 3, p. 96. By permission of the American Sociological Association, copyright holder, and the author.

Table 15-A: Samuel A. Stouffer, *Communism, Conformity, and Civil Liberties* (Gloucester, Mass.: Peter Smith, 1963), p. 229. Reprinted by permission of the publisher.

Table 15-B: Alan B. Wilson, "Residential Segregation of Social Classes and Aspirations of High School Boys," *American Sociological Review,* Vol. 24, 1959, Table 3. By permission of the American Sociological Association, copyright holder, and the author.

Chapter 18, categories of police-citizen behavior, pp. 273–274, and Figure 18-1: Personal communication to the authors from Richard J. Lundman. Printed by permission of Richard J. Lundman.

Box 18.1, Table A: Julius Roth, "Ritual and Magic in the Control of Contagion," *American Sociological Review,* Vol. 22, 1957, Table 2, p. 312. By permission of The American Sociological Association, copyright holder, and the author.

Table 18-A: Albert F. Wessen, "Hospital Ideology and Communication Between Ward Personnel," in E. Gartly Jaco, *Patients, Physicians, and Illness,* 2nd ed. (New York: Free Press, 1972), table on p. 320. Copyright © 1972, 1958 by The Free Press.

Figure 19-1: James S. Coleman, Elihu Katz, and Herbert Menzel, *Medical Innovation: A Diffusion Study* (Indianapolis: Bobbs-Merrill, 1966), Figure 18, p. 78. By permission of the publisher.

Table 22-2: Richard D. Schwartz and Jerome H. Skolnick, "Two Studies of Legal Stigma," *Social Problems,* 10:2 (Fall 1962), Table 1, p. 137. By permission of The Society for the Study of Social Problems, copyright holder, and the authors.

Tables 23-1 and 23-4: John Colombotos, "Physicians and Medicare: A Before-After Study of the Effects of Legislation on Attitudes," *American Sociological Review,* Vol. 34, 1969, Tables 1 and 2. By permission of The American Sociological Association, copyright holder, and the author.

Figure A1-1: "Notice to Contributors," *American Sociological Review,* 1975, inside cover. By permission of The American Sociological Association, copyright holder.

Figure A2-1: Social Sciences Index, 2 (April 1975–March 1976), p. 678. Copyright © 1976 by the H. W. Wilson Company. Material reproduced by permission of the publisher.

Figure A2-2: *Sociological Abstracts,* Vol. 23, April 1975, p. 243. By permission of Sociological Abstracts, Inc., P. O. Box 22206, San Diego, CA 92122.

Table A3-2: Table C, "Centile Values of the Chi-Square Statistic" (After Pearson and Hartley: *Biometrika Tables for Statisticians,* Cambridge University Press, London), in *Introduction to Applied Statistics* by John G. Peatman. Harper & Row, 1963, pp. 402–403.

Table A3-3: Rand Corporation, *A Million Random Digits with 100,000 Normal Deviates* (Glencoe, Ill.: Free Press, 1955). Reprinted by permission of The Rand Corporation.

Table A3-4: Jack W. Dunlap and Albert K. Kurtz, *Handbook of Statistical Nomographs, Tables and Formulas* (New York: World Book, 1932), Table 72, pp. 72–81. Reprinted by permission of the authors.

Tables A3-5 and A3-6: Taro Yamane, *Elementary Sampling Theory,* © 1967, pp. 398–399. Reprinted by permission of Prentice-Hall, Inc., Englewood Cliffs, New Jersey.

To Marshall B. Clinard and Charles G. Curtis,
Susanne, Toby, and David Eckhardt
and
Marlene, Michael, Natalie, Hertha, and Siegfried Ermann

PREFACE

Our goal in writing this methods text has been to capture the excitement of social research by integrating method with theory and data. In pursuing this objective, we have analyzed studies selected for their substantive and methodological interest. These analyses are focused on topics traditionally covered in the first course in research methods, with a somewhat expanded treatment of data manipulation, analysis, and inference.

The text first exposes students to the interaction of problem finding, theory, method, and data. Processes of concept formation and basic measurement are then explored, followed by discussion of more complex measurement using scaling techniques and cross-classification procedures for analysis of bivariate relationships. Throughout the first half of the text, emphasis is on aggregate or population data.

Issues of sampling, statistical inference, and tests of significance are introduced midway through the text. Problems of reliability and validity for survey data are then raised and various field designs and unobtrusive research studies are examined. This is followed by a consideration of experimental designs. The text concludes with a consideration of values and ethical dilemmas confronted in all types of social research.

The construction of individual chapters likewise follows a clear pattern. Each substantive chapter:

- begins with a concisely stated social science problem of general interest to students;
- presents in a step-by-step fashion the research strategy used in one study to address that problem;
- emphasizes carefully selected issues for each stage of the research;
- presents data relating to the theoretical and methodological issues raised in the research;
- interprets the data in terms of problems posed and methods used, thoroughly discussing issues of reliability, validity, and inference.

In sum, each chapter uses bona-fide research to inductively help students understand theoretical and methodological principles of social research.

Chapters synthesize all stages of the research process in a cumulative fashion, and strengthen and reinforce student interest in social phenomena. For instance, a chapter on the relationship between variables explores whether law enforcement agencies discriminate while enforcing drunk driving laws. A chapter on participant observation examines how individuals handle issues of sexuality in nudist camps. And a chapter on content analysis describes the characteristics stressed by Jewish immigrants in searching for a spouse. Social phenomena such as these structure and guide the learning of research methods.

Students thus learn by being presented with a holistic rather than a fragmented view of research. They discover that scientific inquiry is imperfect, a process in which scientists use their imperfect theory and methods as best they can to answer questions about the empirical world. Those students who pursue graduate studies will have gained an understanding of the strategies, methods, and compromises useful for their own future research undertakings, while those completing their formal schooling with a bachelor's degree will better understand inferences in the research summaries so often cited by the media. Both groups will have a better and more permanent understanding of research because they will have experienced it in approximately two dozen research studies analyzed in this text.

This text is based on a series of readings primarily selected and organized by the senior author. Each chapter is a joint effort resulting from numerous drafts and redrafts. We wish to thank students in Kenneth Eckhardt's methods classes who have commented on various versions of the text over a three year period. We also wish to thank those scholars whose studies were used to present our methods materials. Without their research, this text would have been impossible. Less obvious, without these scholars' comments and suggestions on earlier drafts, and their sharing of experiences not reported elsewhere, it would have been a more imperfect product.

Helen Gouldner and Frank Scarpitti, as colleagues and as former and present chairpersons of our department, provided advice, support, and resources as the occasion demanded. For this, we are grateful. The University of Delaware Center for Teaching Effectiveness provided a summer stipend which freed us from teaching and other responsibilities.

Kirk Elifson, Curtis Krishef, Hanan Selvin, and William Snezak all read the manuscript and offered constructive comments beyond their responsibility as reviewers. Howard Hammerman field tested the manuscript at Cornell University and contributed several useful suggestions. Howard Harlan read the manuscript in its entirety and discussed its strengths and weaknesses. Theresa Haire contributed to the early drafts of several chapters, while Christine Kappas, Daniel Curran, and William Berwick assisted in the construction and assessment of the issues and problems which conclude each chapter. Our colleagues in the department of sociology contributed in numerous ways to the completion of this text.

Karen Druliner reviewed the entire manuscript and frequently made our awkward prose more readable. Diane Iffland was an outstanding typist on each draft of the manuscript, on the teaching manual, and on our voluminous correspondence, while remaining a pleasure to work with through it all. She and Karen deserve our special gratitude. Mary Wood, as executive secretary for our department, has our appreciation for skillful management which allowed us to meet our deadlines.

Finally we are grateful to a number of people at Random House. Former editor Glenn Cowley was our most enthusiastic supporter and critic; his aid and commitment contributed greatly to our effort. Manuscript editor Fred Burns adeptly exercised his professional judgment in guiding the book from unedited manuscript to its current form. Executive editor Barry Fetterolf was our initial contact with Random House, persevered with the manuscript, and has our gratitude.

Newark, Delaware
January 1977

Kenneth W. Eckhardt
M. David Ermann

CONTENTS

PART FIVE Sampling and Sampling Designs

PART SIX Issues in Questionnaire Data

TECHNICAL INSERTS

AMPLIFICATION BOXES

PART ONE

Theory and Research

1

DATA, THEORY, AND RESEARCH

> And then there is the story about the little old lady who, every morning sharply at eight, would walk up and down the street in front of her home shredding a newspaper into small pieces. A neighbor, who had watched her antics for weeks, finally asked what she was doing. The lady replied, "I'm doing this to keep the elephants away." "But there are no elephants," the neighbor exclaimed. "Yes, effective, isn't it?" said the lady.

Social science curricula of most colleges and universities are generally organized along three lines: courses in subject matter, in theory, and in research methods. This organization fosters the unfortunate idea that subject matter, theory, and methods are either independent of one another or that they can be integrated only at the highest level of abstraction. Consequently, students often believe that the study of theory and method is intellectually isolated from the main thrust of the curriculum. They approach courses in theory and methods with reluctance and anxiety because they are convinced these courses are less relevant and more difficult than subject matter courses. Were it not for the fact that such courses are often required, many students would avoid them altogether.

In actuality, however, theory, method, and substance are inseparable. Indeed, as C. Wright Mills once observed, each social scientist must be a theorist and a methodologist.* We maintain that the pursuit of scientific

* C. Wright Mills, "On Intellectual Craftsmanship," in Llewellyn Gross, *Symposium on Sociological Theory* (Evanston, Ill.: Row, Peterson, 1959), pp. 25–53.

information necessitates such an integrated approach. While it is true that theory and method can themselves be objects of study, it is also true that social scientists cannot proceed profitably unless they have fundamental theoretical and methodological skills. Familiarity with these skills is also vital for those who wish to comprehend, evaluate, or make decisions based on the research of others.

This chapter emphasizes the relationships among data, theory, and method as a continual process of interaction. As can be seen from Figure 1-1, there is neither beginning nor end to the interactions of theory, data, and method.

Figure 1-1. Relationships of Theory, Method, and Substance.

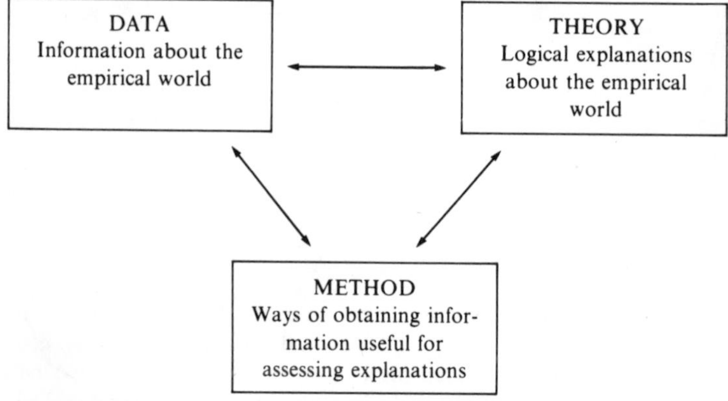

DATA AND THEORY

The recourse of the propagandist is often to argue that facts speak for themselves. Of course, this is false; facts do not speak for themselves. Facts are meaningful only when they are placed in an interpretive framework. They speak only when they are organized, implicitly or explicitly, to fit an explanatory scheme.

Therefore, the task of the social scientist is to organize facts into a framework that provides the best possible explanation. However, even before the facts are assessed, an implicit or explicit theory must be used in deciding which facts are worth examining. Theory and data thus interact in subtle ways. Theory is used to guide the generation of data, and data are used to test and develop theory.

Investigations of suicide provide an excellent illustration of how data and theory interact. For those suicide victims in the United States who have been studied, the empirical evidence indicates

1. men committed suicide more frequently than women,
2. white persons committed suicide more frequently than nonwhites,
3. older persons committed suicide more frequently than younger ones,
4. single persons committed suicide more frequently than married ones, and
5. Protestants committed suicide more frequently than Catholics.

These summary statements about suicide victims studied can be extended as more powerful generalizations. They can be extended to include victims who have not been studied and to understanding future suicides. The restricted and generalized forms of these statements appear in columns A and B below.

Column A: Restricted Generalization	*Column B: Extended Generalization*
Among those persons studied who committed suicide in the United States, men did so more frequently than women.	Among all persons who committed suicide in the United States, men did so more frequently than women (*extended to include cases not studied*). Among all persons who will commit suicide in the United States, men are more likely to do so than women (*extended to the future*).

The extension of statements *beyond* data is often a first step toward developing theory. In this way the construction of theory is essentially an *inductive* reasoning process (also termed *induction*). Inductive reasoning refers to the process by which theories are evolved from a set of particular observations. In inductive reasoning, specific observations are chosen in order to create general explanations about a larger set of phenomena. The observer thus makes general statements about a number of related phenomena from data having a narrower focus.

Inductive reasoning based on the characteristics of suicide victims could lead to the inference that they share a characteristic related to their suicidal behavior. For instance, one might infer that men, whites, older individuals, Protestants, and single persons are not as well integrated into the social networks of friends and relatives as are women, nonwhites, younger individuals, Catholics, and married persons. Consequently, one could hypothesize that more poorly integrated persons are less likely to have their suicidal tendencies restrained by friendship and family than are more integrated ones.

The extension of explanations to cases which have not been studied or to future cases is both common and necessary in social science. However, there is always the risk that the extension may be incorrect and the inferences false. The development of formal theory and methods of research reduces this risk.

THEORY AND METHOD

Observations are a starting point for the development of theory. Ultimately, however, a theory ideally is expressed formally. When it has been expressed formally, its implications can be tested. Determining the implications of a formal theory is a deductive process.

Deductive reasoning (or *deduction*) reverses the processes used in induction. Deductive reasoning begins with general statements. It then uses these to logically derive more specific statements. Using the notion that a lack of integration leads to suicide, it is possible to make the following arrangement of propositions:

Proposition 1: Lack of social integration leads to reduced constraint.

Proposition 2: Reduced constraint leads to deviance.

Therefore,

Proposition 3: Lack of social integration leads to deviance.

This formally stated theory of deviance emerged inductively from data about suicide, since each proposition links two concepts which were inductively formed. Propositions 1 and 2 share the concept of social constraint which permits the derivation of proposition 3.

Theories gain in power when they both explain and predict phenomena beyond those for which they were originally created. Since the theory just discussed emerged from studies of suicide, limited testing would involve examining cases of suicide not previously studied or predicting differences in future suicide rates. A more powerful test of the theory would be to examine its adequacy with respect to other forms of deviance. If the theory can successfully predict other forms of deviance for different categories of individuals, its power and credibility are enhanced.

Figure 1-2. An Illustration of Operationalization.

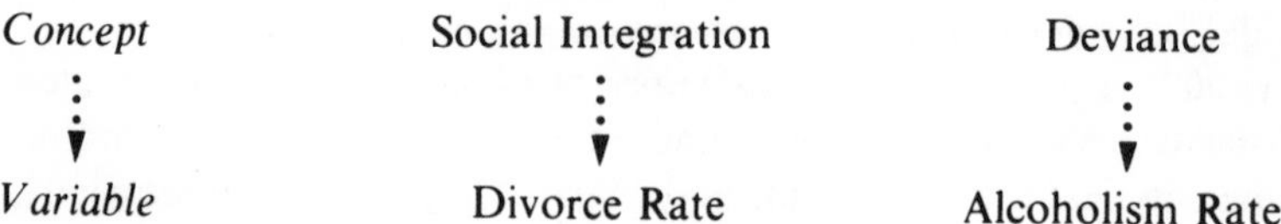

In order to assess the theory, proposition 3 must be transformed through operationalization into a workable hypothesis. To accomplish this, the abstract concepts of social integration and of deviance must be given

1.1 THEORY

Social scientists use the term *theory* inconsistently. As a result, it has multiple meanings. The term theory has been applied to such disparate phenomena as a perspective (e.g., conflict theory); a concept (e.g., alienation); a typology (e.g., bureaucracy); and a process (e.g., social change).

The term also has a more restricted meaning. To signify this, social scientists often modify the term *theory* with the adjective *formal*. A *formal theory* is a closely reasoned set of propositions which explains a group of phenomena. These propositions are arranged so that it is possible to derive a theory statement (called a *hypothesis*) about the empirical world.

A *proposition* consists of a stated relationship between concepts. *Concepts* are mental images of objects or processes. Concepts are neither true nor false. They are simply verbal devices used to express a mental image of some phenomena. They are useful to the extent they assist in creating meaning.

Relationships state the way in which concepts are linked to each other. To the extent that a concept captures some aspect of reality and to the extent that these facets of reality are interrelated, a stated relationship between concepts provides a mental image of the relationship.

For example, if a social group appears to have power and status, then a stated relationship between these concepts might be: As the power of a group increases, its status also increases. A social group may also seem to have solidarity. A stated relationship between status and solidarity might be: As the status of a group increases, its solidarity also increases. Using these two propositions, it is possible to derive a third proposition. As the power of a group increases, so its solidarity increases.

Proposition 1. As the power of a group increases, its status increases.

Proposition 2. As the status of a group increases, its solidarity increases.

Therefore:

Proposition 3. As the power of a group increases, its solidarity increases.

empirical meanings. This linking of an abstract concept with an empirical datum is known as *operationalization* (see Figure 1-2).

Social integration can be operationalized, for example, in terms of a group's divorce rate. Deviance can be operationalized in terms of its alcoholism rate. Divorce and alcoholism rates, the empirical data in this case, are known as *variables*.

Figure 1-3 schematically illustrates the logic of deduction and operationalization. The arrows signify direction, and the signs signify the nature of the relationship. A + sign indicates a *positive relationship*, that is, both variables jointly increase (or both decrease). A − sign indicates a *negative*

Figure 1-3. An Illustration of Operationalization and Deduction.

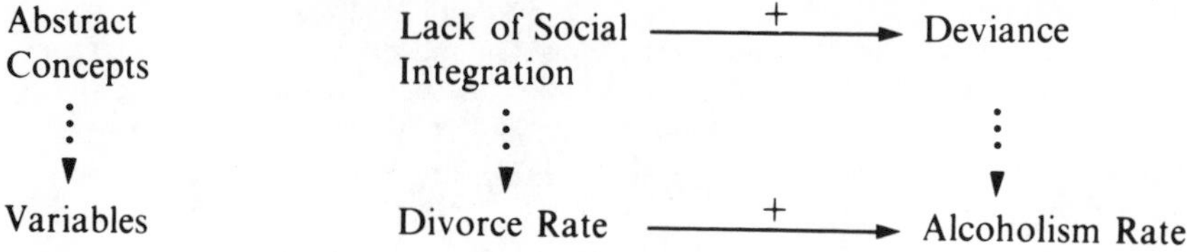

relationship, that is, as one variable increases, the other decreases. Therefore, when the concepts are operationalized, the alcoholism rate is predicted to rise as the rate of divorce rises. Through operationalization, the divorce rate has become an indicator of lack of social integration, and the alcoholism rate has become an indicator of deviance.

1.2 THEORY TESTING AND OPERATIONAL DEFINITIONS

A theory can be evaluated for its logic and for its empirical consistency. It is most important that a theory be logical, that is, that it must not yield inconsistent statements. For this reason, theoretical concepts may have only one definition, and propositions must be arranged systematically. Furthermore, a theory must be empirically adequate. To achieve this, the theory must be interpreted in such a way as to allow for empirical measurement. This can be done through operational definitions in which the measurement procedures are stated.

Although scientists may reach agreement on a concept's theoretical meaning, they often do not reach agreement concerning a concept's measurement. Since a concept may be measured in more than one way, social scientists frequently express doubt whether a concept has been adequately measured. To permit reexamination, a theory should contain clear theoretical definitions, and research utilizing theory should contain clear operational definitions of the procedures employed in measurement.

METHODS AND DATA

Methods (and theory) are intimately involved in the production of data. Methods comprise the procedures used for generating, collecting, and evaluating data. Although many alternative methods are available, all are ultimately reducible to the idea of systematic, disciplined observation. Thus, whether research involves the use of experiments, questionnaires, direct observations, public records, or historical documents, the credibility of the information is ultimately dependent upon the credibility of the initial observations.

It is not possible to separate the procedures for generating, collecting, and evaluating information from either theory or data. Specific methods produce specific types of data. Types of data may, in turn, lead to the development of specific theories, while specific theories may call for unique types of data. Thus, there is a subtle interplay among methods, theory, and data. These interconnections will be a major focus in this text.

SUMMARY

The social sciences, like other sciences, orient their efforts toward providing accurate descriptions and useful explanations of empirical phenomena. Theory, therefore, begins and ends with statements about the real world. From this perspective, it is possible to view research methods as ways of providing useful information for theory building and testing.

Scientific knowledge, however, is continually changing. New data can prompt scientists to form new theories, while new theories can impel them to seek new methods of testing. These new methods can lead to the availability of still newer data and, hence, in turn, to newer theories. For these reasons, scientists accept theories only on a tentative basis. New theories, methods, and data may, at any time in the future, challenge existing ones.

KEY IDEAS AND CONCEPTS

concept
data
deductive reasoning
empirical definition
empirical generalization
formal theory
hypothesis
inductive reasoning
inference
inverse relationship
method
negative relationship
observation
operationalization
positive relationship
proposition
theoretical concept
theoretical definition
theory
variable

ISSUES AND PROBLEMS

1. Discuss at a general level the relationship of theory, method, and data.
2. Locate a set of facts which can be interpreted or explained in more than one way.
3. Provide two different explanations for the observation that men are more likely to commit suicide than women.
4. Complete the following:
   a. Define the concept of physical attractiveness. Define the concept of popularity.
   b. State a positive relationship between these concepts. State an inverse relationship.

c. Using college students as a study population, specify a procedure for measuring physical attractiveness. Using the same population, specify a procedure for measuring popularity.
d. Specify alternative procedures to those just used for measuring physical attractiveness and popularity.
e. Which procedures, those specified in *c* or those specified in *d*, do you consider best for measuring physical attractiveness? for measuring popularity? Explain your answers.

5. List theoretical and measurement problems which may develop from the flexibility researchers have in operationalizing concepts. Offer some suggestions for resolving each of these problems.

RECOMMENDED READINGS

Hammond, Phillip E. (ed.)
1964 *Sociologists at Work.* New York: Basic Books.

Actual, rather than logical, histories of a dozen major social science research efforts. Provides interesting insight into the relationships of theory, methods, and data.

Kaplan, Abraham
1964 *The Conduct of Inquiry.* San Francisco: Chandler.

A thorough and somewhat difficult review of philosophical issues in scientific theory and method. Includes a discussion of such basic notions as concepts, scientific laws, empirical measurement, models, and theories.

Wallace, Walter L.
1971 *The Logic of Science in Sociology.* Chicago: Aldine.

A closely reasoned discussion of the logical relationships among observations, empirical generalizations, theory, and hypotheses.

2

INTERRELATIONSHIP OF THEORY AND RESEARCH: EXPLANATION OF OBSERVED VARIATIONS IN SEXUAL PERMISSIVENESS

THEORETICAL PROBLEM

The idea of comparison has a long tradition in social science. Social scientists early recognized the importance of searching for similarities and dissimilarities among social phenomena in order to find research problems. In his classic work, *The Rules of Sociological Method* (1895), Emile Durkheim distinguished three applications of the comparative approach to problem finding and theory testing.* These involved

1. searching for regularities and variations within one society at a given time,
2. searching for regularities and variations across many societies which are generally alike but differ in specific ways, and
3. searching for regularities and variations across many societies which are generally different but are similar in specific ways.

Numerous social science problems and findings have resulted from use of the comparative approach.

For example, by researching social phenomena within a single society, social scientists discovered that in the United States urban residents are

* Emile Durkheim, *Les Régles de la Méthode Sociologique.* Paris: Alcan, 1895 (8th ed., trans. S. A. Solvay and J. H. Mueller, ed. G. E. G. Catlin, as *The Rules of Sociological Method* [Chicago: Univ. of Chicago Press, 1938], pp. 136–140).

more likely to be members of voluntary associations than rural residents; women are more likely to participate in organized religious activities than men; and blacks are less likely to commit suicide than whites. Each of these intrasocietal empirical variations appears puzzling and therefore calls for a theoretical explanation.

By researching social phenomena across societies which are generally alike but differ in specific ways, social scientists have discovered that class-oriented political parties are likely to be found in societies with rigid stratification systems; that voting turnout varies considerably among Western democratic societies; and that newlyweds among migratory hunting peoples are likely to be required to live with the groom's relatives. Each of these intersocietal empirical variations is also intriguing and begs for a theoretical explanation.

Researching social phenomena among societies which are generally different but share a common dimension, experience, or event has revealed similarly arresting empirical findings. For instance, one-party political governments are likely to emerge as underdeveloped countries industrialize; rural women who migrate to cities in most countries are likely to desire fewer children than women who do not; and the importance of kinship relationships is likely to decline as industrialization increases in most societies. Such variations fairly demand interpretation.

Nevertheless, interpreting these three categories of phenomena frequently results in theoretical explanations which are outwardly in conflict. There may, therefore, be a need for additional studies to reconcile conflicting hypotheses. Such conflicting hypotheses were presented in the form of two letters which appeared serially in a professional journal.

TWO LETTERS

In 1966, two prominent social scientists exchanged views regarding then current explanations of premarital sexual behavior. Their views, in the form of letters to the editor, were published in the *American Journal of Sociology*.

James S. Coleman, in the September issue, expressed dissatisfaction with the prevailing social science perspective on premarital sexual behavior and suggested an alternative.* He wrote:

> Ordinarily, differences in the strictness of premarital sex codes and observance of rigid standards of sexual morality are seen as normative phenomena—that is, deriving from the inculcation of such norms as part of childhood socialization. . . . I would like to suggest that the rigidity of premarital sexual codes varies inversely with female dominance in the determination of family status. Where females are more dominant, that is, where the system is more matriarchal, the sex codes will be less rigid than where the female's ultimate status depends on the status of the husband.

* James S. Coleman, "Female Status and Premarital Sexual Codes," Letter to the Editor, *American Journal of Sociology*, 72(1966):217.

In this passage, Coleman expressed a view sharply divergent from current social science thinking. His thesis suggests that changes in premarital sex codes and behavior will be related to changes in the importance of males and females in the family. He further suggests that accepted explanations of class and race differences in premarital sexual behavior are incorrect. In lieu of relating such differences to childhood socialization and norms, Coleman posits that class variations determine the status of males and females in the family and are responsible for differences in premarital sexual codes and behavior.

Almost predictably, Coleman's view prompted a second social scientist to express his views. In the November issue of the *American Journal of Sociology*, Ira L. Reiss wrote:

> James Coleman's Letter to the Editor (September, 1966, p. 217) raises some interesting questions concerning the explanation of premarital sex codes. Coleman posits the degree of female control over the determination of family status as the key factor in explaining the rigidity of premarital sex codes. . . . I have arrived at some theoretical conclusions relevant to Coleman's view. . . .
>
> The basic theory can be simply stated as follows: The degree of premarital sexual permissiveness which is acceptable among courting individuals varies directly with the degree of autonomy in the courtship roles and with the degree of premarital sexual permissiveness accepted in the social and cultural setting of those individuals.*

Reiss went on to remark about the importance of autonomy in courtship roles among those systems which allow adolescent dating of some sort. In his view, biological sex drives pressure individuals into sexual behavior. Consequently, the greater the autonomy granted courting individuals, the greater the likelihood of premarital sexual behavior. In this way, Reiss believed that Coleman's notion of female power might be important, since it might promote greater autonomy in the role of the female. However, Reiss concluded that Coleman's emphasis on female power was too limited and that an adequate theory of premarital sexual behavior required the consideration of many other factors, including those of social norms.

AN INTEGRATIVE ASSESSMENT OF EMPIRICAL EVIDENCE AND THEORY

In the spring of 1969, Kenneth Eckhardt, teaching a course in social anthropology, had cause to review the literature on sexual behavior. He read the two letters published three years earlier and, as a comparative sociologist, saw the possibility of assessing the Coleman and Reiss arguments through analysis of cross-cultural data. In examining their arguments, he

* Ira L. Reiss, "Some Comments on Premarital Sexual Permissiveness," Letter to the Editor, *American Journal of Sociology*, 72(1967):558–559.

detected what he believed to be a logical flaw in the theory expressed by Reiss. This flaw consisted of tautological reasoning in the statement "... the degree of premarital sexual permissiveness which is acceptable among courting individuals varies directly with the degree of autonomy in the courtship roles and with the degree of premarital sexual permissiveness accepted in the social and cultural settings of those individuals." If the notion of autonomy is deleted, the statement reads ". . . the degree of premarital sexual permissiveness which is acceptable . . . varies . . . with the degree of premarital sexual permissiveness accepted. . . ." Since the second half appears to be a rephrasing of the first half, the statement is a tautology. Consequently, Eckhardt believed that Reiss erred in a portion of his argument. Still, the notion of autonomy appeared to have merit.

2.1 POSSIBILITIES OF TAUTOLOGICAL REASONING IN SOCIAL SCIENCE

The risk of tautological reasoning in social science is high. Two forms of tautology appear frequently. The first form often occurs when norms are used to explain behavior. It is not unusual for social scientists to use behavior to infer the existence of norms and then to cite the same norms to explain the behavior. For instance, by studying behavior, social scientists can determine how often members of different religious groups attend church. When asked to explain why religious groups have different rates of church attendance, it is tempting to say, "Because they have different norms about church attendance."

A second form of tautology occurs when social phenomena are classified and labeled; then the labels are invoked to explain the phenomena. For example, certain forms of mental illness may be labeled schizophrenia. When asked to explain why individuals exhibit certain forms of behavior, it is tempting to say "because they are schizophrenic." Another example might be labeling people who commit suicide as mentally ill. When asked to explain how it is known they were mentally ill, it is tempting to say, "Because they committed suicide."

Such explanations are, of course, not explanations at all but a form of circular reasoning. They must be carefully guarded against since their simplicity and apparent common sense make them appealing.

Using the insights of Coleman and Reiss, Eckhardt constructed a theory based on five assumptions.*

First, biological drives promote sexual intercourse. The implication of this assumption is that when sex drives are strong, intercourse will tend to occur.

* Kenneth W. Eckhardt, "Exchange and Sexual Permissiveness," *Behavior Science Notes*, 1(1971):1–18.

Second, during adolescent years, sex drives among males are stronger than among females. The implication of this assumption is that males will more actively seek sexual intercourse than females during the adolescent years.

Third, opportunity generally promotes sexual intercourse. The implication of this assumption is that when opportunity permits and when biological drives are present, males and females will tend to have sexual intercourse.

Fourth, social relationships are based on exchange. The implication of this assumption is that when individuals possess different goods, they will establish an exchange relationship in order to satisfy personal needs. That is, males and females will exchange sex and other goods in order to satisfy biological drives.

Fifth, individuals seek to maximize their exchanges. The implication of this assumption is that individuals seek more than they give in an exchange relationship.

Using these assumptions, Eckhardt constructed three hypothetical societies.

Hypothetical Society I. Equal Male-Female Dominance

In this hypothetical society, all political, economic, and social resources are distributed equally between males and females. Thus, both sexes share equally the resources of society, and neither is dominant in determining family status.

Since sexual favors will be the primary good which is exchanged, it follows that males and females will engage in sexual intercourse primarily for the social and physical satisfaction it produces. Thus, Eckhardt hypothesized that when biological sex drives are present and opportunity permits, sexual intercourse tends to follow.

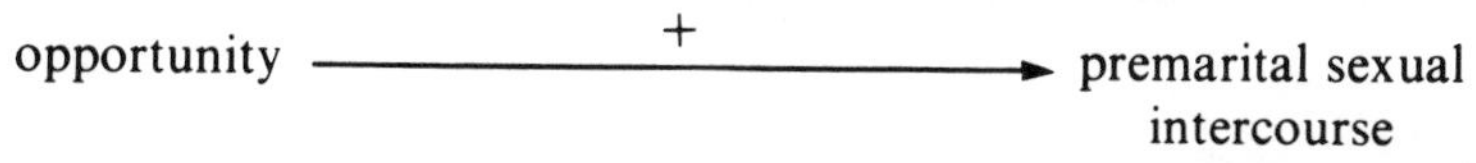

opportunity —(+)→ premarital sexual intercourse

Hypothetical Society II. Male Dominance

In this hypothetical society, political, economic, and social resources are distributed among the males. Thus, males receive more resources than females. Consequently, males will be dominant in determining family status.

Since males control resources, their primary interest is in satisfying other needs, especially biological ones. Since females, on the other hand, lack resources, their interests are twofold: (1) They are interested in obtaining access to the resources controlled by males, and (2) they are interested in satisfying sexual needs. However, because their sexual needs are weaker than males' during the early years, they (and those adults who control their behaviors) withhold sex in the interest of obtaining tangible resources from the male. When their claim to resources becomes legitimate, for example, through marriage, they will have obtained access to the males' resources and have satisfied their biological needs. In such a society, therefore, male dominance will tend to be related to decreased sexual intercourse prior to marriage.

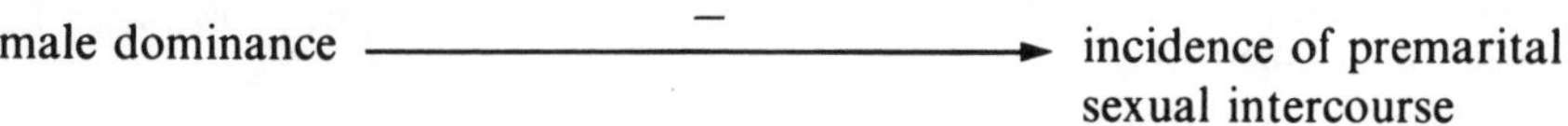

Hypothetical Society III. Female Dominance

In this hypothetical society, political, economic, and social resources are distributed among the females. Thus, females receive more than males. Consequently, women should be dominant in determining family status.

Since females here control resources, their primary interest is in satisfying other needs, especially sexual ones. They have no need to withhold sex in order to obtain resources. In this case, on the other hand, since males lack resources, their interests are twofold: (1) They are interested in obtaining access to the resources controlled by females, and (2) they are interested in satisfying their biological needs. However, because their biological drives are stronger than the females' during the early years, they find it difficult to withhold sex in the interest of obtaining resources from females. Thus, it is hypothesized that female dominance will tend to increase the incidence of sexual intercourse prior to marriage.

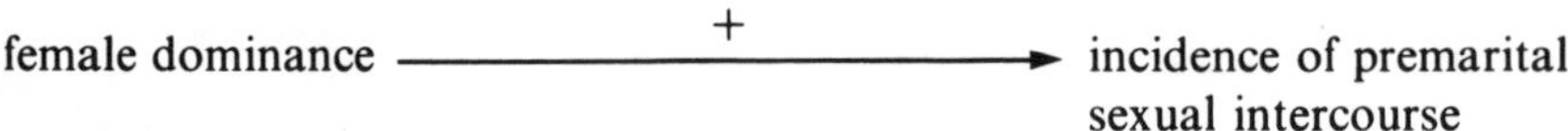

EVALUATING THE THEORY USING ACTUAL DATA

As stated, the three societies Eckhardt constructed were merely hypothetical. Nonetheless, the theory suggests applications to actual behavior. It provides a *logical basis* for hypothesizing that in actual societies sexual dominance is related to premarital sexual freedom. Of course, the theory has simplified societal complexity, and there is no *empirical evidence* that it produces correct statements about actual sexual behavior. Since all theories simplify the structure and processes of the actual world, the primary issue is whether the theory in question has any empirical support. If it shows promise, it can eventually be made more complex to capture additional features of the actual world, and then data can be collected to support or reject the added complexities.

DATA COLLECTION

It is not uncommon for social scientists to collect new data when existing data fail to meet their needs. However, for many research problems, they can resort to information previously made available by other social scientists and by private organizations and various public bodies, such as the federal government. Eckhardt was fortunate that George Peter Murdock and his colleagues at Yale University had been collecting, storing, and indexing information on preliterate societies for a number of years. This collection of information, known as the Human Relations Area File (HRAF), has been made available through libraries to social scientists interested in cross-societal research.

Because sex dominance, autonomy, and premarital sexual freedom were *theoretical concepts*, Eckhardt searched the Human Relations Area File for *variables* which could serve as measurements of these concepts. By operationally defining the concepts, he located three variables which seemed to reflect sexual dominance, one variable which seemed to reflect autonomy or opportunity, and one variable which seemed to reflect premarital sexual freedom.

OPERATIONALLY MEASURING SEX DOMINANCE

The Rule of Descent

Ideally, sexual dominance in determining family status should be measured by direct observation and assessment of the political, economic, and social resources controlled by males and females. Since this was impossible, Eckhardt measured sex dominance by using the rule of descent. The rule of descent refers to the tracing of kinship. In some societies kinship is traced only through the male line—the rule of patrilineal descent. In other societies kinship is traced through the female line—the rule of matrilineal descent. In still others kinship is traced simultaneously through both lines, or through a combination of the two—bi-duolateral descent. Since the distribution and control of resources in preliterate societies are likely to parallel the rule of descent in the society, the rule was selected as an operational measurement of sex dominance. Patrilineal descent is taken as a measurement of male dominance, matrilineal descent is taken as a measure of female dominance, and bi-duolateral descent is taken as a measure of equal or mixed dominance by males and females.

The Rules of Residence

Rules of residence are customs which prescribe where newly married couples will live. In some societies, such couples are expected to live with the groom's relatives—patrilocal residence. In other societies, newly married couples are expected to live with the bride's relatives—matrilocal residence. In still other societies, there is either a combination of patri- and matrilocal customs of residence, or newly married couples may independently establish their residence choice. Since rules of residence are likely to influence sexual dominance in determining family status, the custom of patrilocal residence is taken as a measure of male dominance, while matrilocal residence is taken as a measure of female dominance and varying or nonexistent residence customs are taken as a measure of equal or mixed dominance.

Economic Importance

Families usually depend upon joint contributions of males and females in order to survive. Whereas one popular image is that males concern themselves primarily with nonhousehold economic tasks while females concern themselves primarily with household tasks, the actual economic contributions of males and females vary considerably. In some societies, for example, females bear the responsibility of contributing large shares of food to the family. To do so they cultivate crops, harvest wild fruits, and hunt small animals. Where females contribute a large portion of the food supply, their role in determining family status should be considerably higher than in those societies where their economic role is less important.

OPERATIONALLY MEASURING SEXUAL FREEDOM

An operational measure of the concept of sexual freedom became available through reports of anthropologists and others who commented on the extent of premarital sexual intercourse occurring in a society. These observations were grouped into three categories.

Category	*Definition*
1. Permissive Premarital Sexual Behavior	Premarital sexual relations freely occurred, and societal sanctions were minimal.

2. Somewhat Restrictive Premarital Sexual Behavior	Premarital sexual relations occurred under varying conditions, and societal sanctions were mixed.
3. Restrictive Premarital Sexual Behavior	Premarital sexual relations were prohibited, and societal sanctions were extensive.

OPERATIONALLY MEASURING AUTONOMY

Finding a variable which would reflect the concept of autonomy proved difficult. In some societies, adolescents are free to court one another with only minimal adult supervision. In other societies, however, young males and females are closely supervised and, in some instances, dating is permitted only under the watchful eye of a chaperone. It is quite likely that supervision occurs when families have a direct economic stake in a marriage. When the female's relatives must provide a dowry or when the male's relatives must provide a brideprice, there will be an attempt to supervise courting. This reduces the opportunity for premarital sexual behavior. Eckhardt concluded that where either brideprice or dowry was necessary, the opportunity for premarital sex would be less than in those societies where such transactions did not exist.

OPERATIONAL MEASURES SUMMARIZED

The discussion as outlined leads to the general hypothesis that *societies in which female dominance is high are more likely to be sexually permissive than societies in which male dominance is high.* Since dominance is to be measured in several ways, Figure 2-1 diagrams the relationships expressed between the concept at the abstract level and variables at the empirical level. For purposes of simplicity, the concept of autonomy has not been included.

DATA ANALYSIS

To empirically assess the theory under discussion, Eckhardt required data on five variables: descent, residence, economic contribution of the female, exchange of wealth at marriage, and premarital sexual permissiveness. His research was made easier by previously published studies which provided information on the economic contribution of females and premarital sexual permissiveness for a number of societies. Judith K. Brown had previously researched preliterate societies and had published her analysis of the

Figure 2-1. Graphic Presentation of Eckhardt's Theory at Abstract and Empirical Levels.

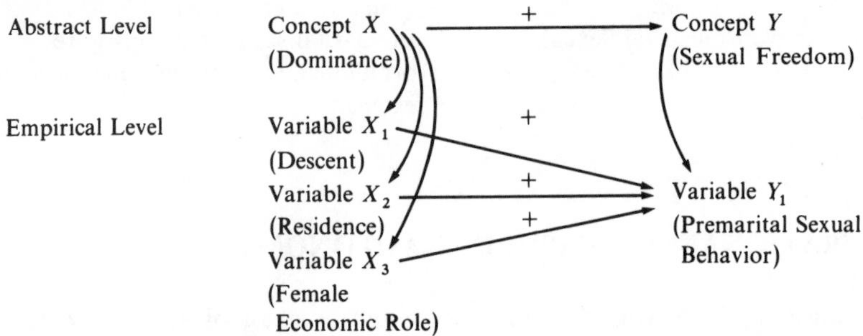

Figure 2-1 portrays the relationships between concepts at the abstract level and variables at the empirical level. At the abstract level, the concepts dominance and sexual freedom are positively related as indicated by the + sign. The direction of the straight arrow signifies a possible causal relationship.

To operationalize the concept dominance, three variables were selected. Curved arrows signify that descent, residence, and female economic role serve as measures of dominance. A curved arrow also signifies that premarital sexual behavior serves as a measure of sexual freedom. The straight arrows signify the direction of possible causal relationships.

economic contribution of females to the household.* Furthermore, John T. Westbrook had researched similar societies and had published his analysis of premarital sexual behavior.†

By systematically searching the HRAF collection and comparing it with the Brown and Westbrook materials, Eckhardt identified 153 societies for which data on all five variables were available. He then cross-classified each of the independent variables with the dependent variable. The dependent variable (the variable to be explained) was hypothesized to be related to the independent variables (the variables doing the explaining). The results appear in Table 2-1.

The data presented in Table 2-1 indicate mixed findings. With respect to descent, 61 percent of the matrilineal societies were permissive, whereas only 40 percent of the bi-duolateral and 30 percent of the patrilineal ones were so. None of the matrilineal societies was restrictive. These findings support the hypothesis; however, the fact that 30 percent of the patrilineal societies were permissive and 39 percent of the matrilineal were somewhat permissive tends to contradict the hypothesis.

With respect to residence, the analysis also provides mixed findings. Forty-seven percent of the matrilocal societies were permissive, compared with 31 percent of the patrilocal societies and 54 percent of the bi-neolocal

* Judith K. Brown, "A Cross-Cultural Study of Female Initiation Rites," *American Anthropologist*, 65(1963):837–853.

† John T. Westbrook, "Norms of Premarital Sex Behavior," *Ethnology*, 2(1963):116.

Table 2-1. Cross-Classification of Four Independent Variables with the Dependent Variable of Premarital Sexual Permissiveness.

INDEPENDENT VARIABLES	DEPENDENT VARIABLE: PREMARITAL SEXUAL PERMISSIVENESS			TOTAL	
	Restrictive	Somewhat Permissive	Permissive		
	%	%	%	%	*N*
Descent					
Patrilineal	27	43	30	100	67
Bi-Duolateral	29	31	40	100	68
Matrilineal	0	39	61	100	18
Total					153
Residence					
Patrilocal	29	40	31	100	97
Bi-Neolocal	21	25	54	100	24
Matrilocal	16	37	47	100	32
Total					153
Economic Importance					
Female highest	16	37	47	100	43
Female higher than male	21	41	38	100	34
Male higher than female	33	31	36	100	36
Male highest	30	40	30	100	40
Total					153
Wealth Exchange					
Brideprice or dowry	28	38	34	100	96
Neither brideprice nor dowry	19	37	44	100	57
Total					153

SOURCE: Eckhardt, "Exchange and Sexual Permissiveness," p. 8, Table 1.

societies. Before explaining some of the reasons possible for this mixture of results, Eckhardt examined the remaining two variables.

The relationship of permissiveness to female economic importance was consistent with the hypothesis. Of those societies in which female economic importance was highest, 47 percent were permissive. As female economic importance declined, the percentage of societies permitting premarital sexual behavior also declined.

The relationship of sexual permissiveness to wealth exchange was also consistent. Of those societies in which customs of wealth exchange existed, only 34 percent were permissive. However, when such customs were absent, 44 percent of the societies were permissive.

COMMENTS AND CONCLUSIONS

An examination of Table 2-1 reveals that the data support the hypothesis that female dominance is related to the likelihood that a society would permit premarital sexual behavior. However, the percentage differences often are small. Even where female dominance was high, some of the societies either prohibited premarital sexual behavior or permitted it only under special conditions.

The inconsistencies between the theory and the data could stem from several sources. Listed below are some of the possibilities.

1. *Invalid Measurement of the Concepts.* It is possible that descent, residence, female economic importance, and wealth exchange served as inadequate measures of the concepts. Thus, while Eckhardt assumed that these variables might serve as appropriate and reliable measures of the concepts, possibly they were measuring other factors instead. Thus, the actual measures may have been invalid.

2. *Unreliable Measurement of the Concepts.* It is possible that some of the societies in the HRAF collection were misclassified with respect to the five variables. Under this circumstance, while the variables potentially may have been valid measures of the concepts, they would have proved inaccurate for specific societies. Thus, the measures of the concepts could be considered unreliable.

3. *Additional Variables May Have Been Operating.* Social phenomena are seldom the result of only one or two forces. Frequently, many forces operate to produce a given effect. Consequently, it is possible that the variables were both valid and reliable measures of the concepts, but that the theory required additional concepts. From this perspective, the theory may have been adequate but incomplete.

4. *The Theory Was Incorrect.* It is also possible that the theory was incorrect. Inasmuch as the theory involved a number of assumptions, perhaps these were inadequate, resulting in a faulty theory that generated an incorrect hypothesis.

Since all of the above are possible explanations for the discrepancy between theory and data, it is impossible to select the best one. Additional research would be necessary to examine and choose among them.

A simplified description of the relationship between theory and research appears in Figure 2-2. Throughout the text, this model of the relationship between theory and research is pursued.

Figure 2-2. The Cycle of Theory and Research (Simplified).

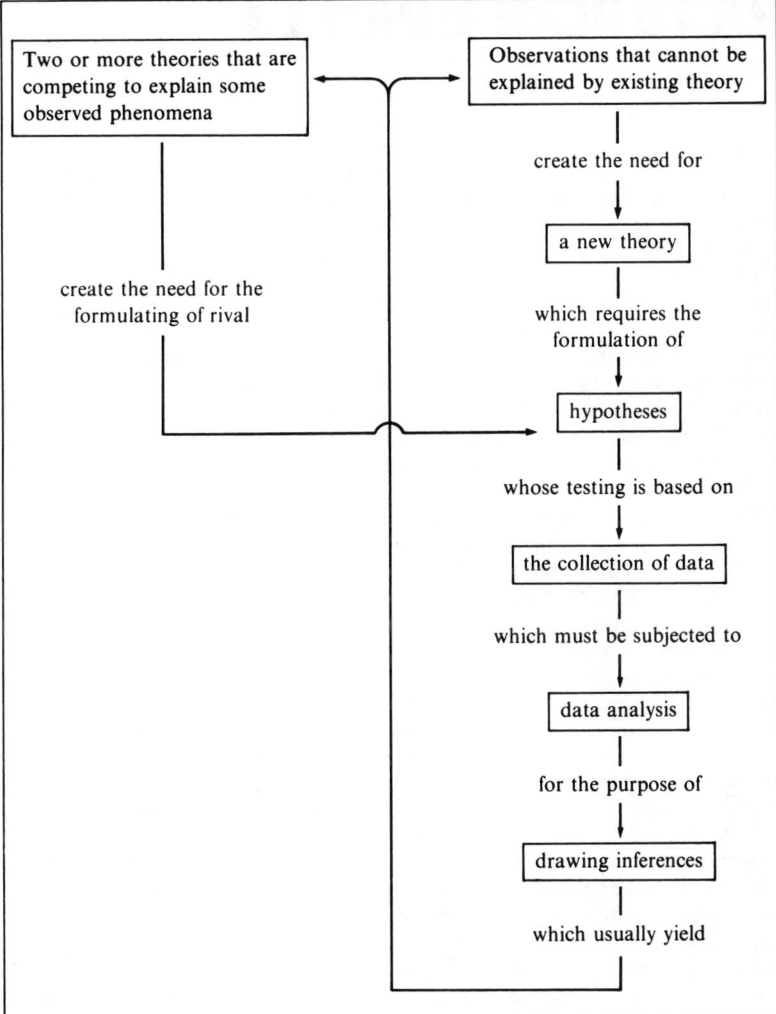

Technical Insert I

Tables

Social scientists frequently use tables for presenting, documenting, and communicating information. Therefore, it is important to understand how to construct and read a table correctly. The four major components of a table are discussed below.

Title Often, readers scan table titles to determine if specific tables warrant careful study. For this reason a table's title should communicate clearly and concisely. Although titles should be brief, they should be as long as necessary to avoid ambiguity or misstatement. Tables should also be numbered. Numbering serves as a quick guide to specific tables.

Heading A table is composed of horizontal rows and vertical columns. Information is therefore organized by rows and columns. Each row and column may require a heading. The heading labels information contained in the column or row.

Body The body of a table consists of the information contained in the rows and columns. Information in the body of tables should reflect the table's title and the row and column headings.

Footnotes Table footnotes provide important information. Footnotes may indicate the original source of the data, may define a heading, or may qualify information in the table. Usually letters or asterisks are used to reference footnotes. Numbers are avoided since they may be confused with numerical information contained in the body of the table.

Table I-1 exhibits several requirements of a properly constructed table. The table is numbered and has a clear and concise title. Each column and each row are labeled. The body of the table reports all cases of murder, and places each case in one and only one row. Footnotes report information which is needed to fully understand the data. Although Table I-1 is useful in its current form, the frequency distribution contained therein is often presented as a percentage distribution. Table I-2 demonstrates the proper construction of a table using percentages.

Like Table I-1, Table I-2 follows conventional rules of table construction. It is numbered and has a clear and concise title. Each row and each column are identified by a heading. The body of the table is organized for easy reading, and footnotes supply additional information which is needed. Table I-2 also illustrates some conventional rules when frequency distributions are presented in the form of percentages. The percent column is labeled in the heading. A percent sign is used for the figure provided in the first row. The total number of cases on which the percentage distribution is based is also provided. Some methodologists recommend eliminating the frequency distribution and providing only the total number of cases since readers can determine for themselves the number of cases in each row. However, when the number of rows is lengthy and space permits, it is frequently desirable to provide both the frequency and percentage distribution. The fact that one of the computed percentages was less than one-tenth of 1 percent is noted but not reported in the body of the table since precision is confined to tenths. Since the percentages do not sum to 100, the discrepancy between the total percentage and 100 is explained in a footnote.

Tables I-1 and I-2 are referred to as *univariate* tables since only one variable

Table Number and title ⟶ **Table I-1. Murder Victims in the United States, by Weapon Used, 1973.**

Headings ⟶

Body ⟶

WEAPON USED	NUMBER OF VICTIMS
Gun	11,249
Cutting or stabbing	2,985
Blunt object[a]	848
Personal weapons[b]	1,064
Poison	8
Explosives	11
Arson	173
Narcotics	24
Strangulation	381
Asphyxiation	41
Other[c]	339
Total	17,123

Footnotes ⟶

SOURCE: U.S. Federal Bureau of Investigation, *Uniform Crime Reports for the United States, 1973,* p. 8, table unnumbered.

[a] Refers to club, hammer.
[b] Refers to beatings by hands, fists, feet.
[c] Refers to weapon unknown or weapon unstated.

Table I-2. Murder Victims in the United States, by Weapon Used, 1973, Reported in Frequency and Percent.

WEAPON USED	NUMBER OF VICTIMS	PERCENT
Gun	11,249	65.7%
Cutting or stabbing	2,985	17.4
Blunt object[a]	848	5.0
Personal weapon[b]	1,064	6.2
Poison	8	[d]
Explosives	11	.1
Arson	173	1.0
Narcotics	24	.1
Strangulation	381	2.2
Asphyxiation	41	.2
Other[c]	339	2.0
Total	17,123	99.9%[e]

SOURCE: U.S. Federal Bureau of Investigation, *Uniform Crime Reports for the United States, 1973,* p. 8, table unnumbered.

[a] Refers to club, hammer.
[b] Refers to beatings by hands, fists, feet.
[c] Refers to weapon unknown or weapon unstated.
[d] Less than one-tenth of 1 percent.
[e] Column does not add to 100 owing to rounding error.

Table I-3. Total Arrest by Type of Crime and Sex, 1973.[a,b]

TYPE OF CRIME	SEX		TOTAL
	Male	Female	
Violent crime[c]	260,800	29,582	290,382
Property crime[d]	851,685	227,157	1,078,842
Total	1,112,485	256,739	1,369,224

[a] Based upon: U.S. Federal Bureau of Investigation, *Uniform Crime Reports for the United States, 1973*, p. 131, Table 32.
[b] Based on the arrest figures provided by 6,004 law enforcement agencies.
[c] Violent crime includes only offenses of murder, forcible rape, robbery, and aggravated assault.
[d] Property crime includes only offenses of burglary, larceny, and auto theft.

is being described (i.e., types of weapons used on victims). If a table contains two variables, with one variable for rows and another for columns, the table is referred to as a *cross-classification* or *bivariate* table. If more than two variables are used, the table is referred to as a *multivariate* table.

Table I-3 illustrates a two by two cross-classification table.

As in earlier tables, Table I-3 is numbered, has a clear and concise title, possesses headings for each row and column, has a well-organized body, and contains footnotes necessary for understanding the table's information. As a cross-classification table, the information is organized simultaneously according to two variables. Information is provided for each *cell* (the intersection of a row and column) as well as for the *marginals* (the separate sums of each row and column). Consequently, where the column Male intersects with the row Violent crime, the table cell provides information for this intersection. Thus, 260,800 of all arrested persons were both male and arrested for committing a violent crime. The information contained in Table I-3 also can be presented in percentage form, as is the case for Table I-4.

Table I-4. Total Arrest by Type of Crime and Sex, Reported in Percent, 1973.[a,b]

TYPE OF CRIME	SEX		TOTAL
	Male	Female	
Violent crime[c]	19.1	2.1	21.2
Property crime[d]	62.2	16.6	78.8
Total	81.3	18.7	100.0
(N = 1,369,224)			

[a] Based upon: U.S. Federal Bureau of Investigation, *Uniform Crime Reports for the United States, 1973*, p. 131, Table 32.
[b] Based on the arrest figures provided by 6,004 law enforcement agencies.
[c] Violent crime includes only offenses of murder, forcible rape, robbery, and aggravated assault.
[d] Property crime includes only offenses of burglary, larceny, and auto theft.

Note that Table I-4 contains all the information necessary for reconstructing Table I-3 approximately. The inclusion of the total number of arrested persons is necessary in order to permit readers to recompute the original data.

Tables often are organized to support assertions about relationships between variables. When this is the case, data are frequently presented in percentage form by either rows or columns. Using arrest data as an operational measure of the types of crimes committed, the data in Table I-5 are organized to support the assertion that sex influences the types of crimes individuals commit. In this assertion, sex (the independent variable) is seen as influencing the type of crime (the dependent variable). By computing percentages in the direction of the independent variable (sex), it is possible to compare the distributions of the dependent variable (type of crime). It can be observed in Table I-5 that males arrested for crimes are more likely than females to have committed a violent crime.

Table I-5. Total Arrest by Type of Crime and Sex Reported in Percent, 1973.[a, b]

	SEX		
TYPE OF CRIME	Male	Female	TOTAL
Violent crime[c]	23.4%	11.5%	21.2%
Property crime[d]	76.6	88.5	78.8
Total	100.0%	100.0%	100.0%
N =	1,112,485	256,739	1,369,224

[a] Based upon: U.S. Federal Bureau of Investigation, *Uniform Crime Reports for the United States, 1973,* p. 131, Table 32.
[b] Based on the arrest figures provided by 6,004 law enforcement agencies.
[c] Violent crime includes only offenses of murder, forcible rape, robbery, and aggravated assault.
[d] Property crime includes only offenses of burglary, larceny, and auto theft.

Table I-6 is organized to support the assertion that, irrespective of the type of crime, males are arrested for a larger percent of crimes than females. Technically, Table I-6 does not contain an independent and a dependent variable since there is no assertion that one variable is influencing the other.

Table I-6. Total Arrest by Type of Crime and Sex, Reported in Percent, 1973.[a, b]

	SEX		
TYPE OF CRIME	Male	Female	TOTAL
Violent crime[c]	89.8%	10.2%	100.0% (*N* = 290,382)
Property crime[d]	78.9	21.1	100.0 (*N* = 1,078,842)
Total	81.2	18.8	100.0 (*N* = 1,369,224)

[a] Based upon: U.S. Federal Bureau of Investigation, *Uniform Crime Reports for the United States, 1973,* p. 131, Table 32.
[b] Based on the arrest figures provided by 6,004 law enforcement agencies.
[c] Violent crime includes only offenses of murder, forcible rape, robbery, and aggravated assault.
[d] Property crime includes only offenses of burglary, larceny, and auto theft.

KEY IDEAS AND CONCEPTS

assumption
bivariate table
column percent
cross-classify
empirical regularities
empirical variations
intersocietal comparisons
intrasocietal comparisons
reliable measurement
rival hypothesis
tautological reasoning
univariate table

ISSUES AND PROBLEMS

1. It has been reported for the 1972 national presidential election that more men voted than women. Extend this observation to include past and future elections. Are there any risks in extending this observation? Explain.
2. Some persons have suggested that men vote more frequently than women because men are more interested in politics. List conditions under which this explanation would be tautological? List conditions under which it would not be tautological.
3. Complete the following:
   a. Identify a phenomenon which varies according to social class in the United States. Suggest a relationship between the social class and the varying phenomenon.
   b. Operationalize the concept social class. Operationalize the varying phenomenon.
   c. Does the above example represent an intrasocietal or an intersocietal variation? Why?
4. Examine Table 2-A and answer the questions below.

Table 2-A. Earned Advanced Degrees in the Physical and Social Sciences for 1,617 Institutions, July 1, 1969, Through June 30, 1970.

FIELD	MASTER'S DEGREE	DOCTOR'S DEGREE	TOTAL ADVANCED DEGREES
Physical Sciences[a]	5,948	4,313	10,261
Social Sciences[b]	23,580	3,778	27,358
Total	29,528	8,091	37,619

SOURCE: Data from National Center for Educational Statistics, *Higher Education: Earned Degrees Conferred: Part A-Summary Data, 1969-70.* DHEW Pub. No. (OE) 72-65. Office of Education, U.S. Department of Health, Education, and Welfare. Washington, D.C.: Government Printing Office, 1972. Data for United States, Guam, and Puerto Rico.

[a] Includes chemistry, pharmaceutical chemistry, and physics.

[b] Includes anthropology, economics (excluding agricultural economics), sociology, social work, and social administration.

   a. What percent of those earning advanced degrees in the physical and social sciences earned them in the physical sciences?

b. What percent of those earning master's degrees earned them in the social sciences?
c. What percent of those earning advanced degrees in the social sciences earned a doctor's degree? What percent of those earning advanced degrees in the physical sciences earned a doctor's degree?
d. Create two different explanations to account for the observation that the percentage of persons who earned a master's degree in the social sciences is much larger than the percentage who earned a doctor's degree. Discuss the assumptions and strengths and weaknesses of each explanation.

RECOMMENDED READINGS

Davis, James H., and Ann M. Jacobs
1968 "Tabular Presentation," in *International Encyclopedia of the Social Sciences*, Vol. 15, pp. 497–509. New York: Macmillan.

Presents the basic principles involved in constructing bivariate or two by two cross-classification tables. Provides interesting variations for simplifying the presentation of complex data.

Glaser, Barney M., and Anselm M. Strauss
1967 *The Discovery of Grounded Theory: Strategies for Qualitative Research.* Chicago: Aldine.

Discusses the need for, and strategies of, inductively discovering and constructing theory from data. The result, known as grounded theory, provides an alternative to deductively created theory.

Murdock, George P.
1971 *Outline of Cultural Materials.* New Haven, Conn.: Human Relations Area Files, Inc.

Describes the conceptual contents of Human Relations Area Files and presents aids in their location and use as a data source.

Zetterberg, Hans
1963 *On Theory and Verification in Sociology.* Totawa, N.J.: Bedminister Press.

Presents a deductive approach to theory building and testing. The result, known as deductive axiomatic theory, provides an alternative to grounded theory.

PART TWO

Fundamentals of Measuring and Comparing Variables

3

PERCENTAGES, RATIOS, AND RATES AS NORMED MEASURES OF VARIABLES: MODERNIZATION THEORY AND JAPANESE ILLEGITIMATE BIRTH RATES

GENERAL ISSUE

International bodies, national governments, and private organizations frequently collect and publish quantitative information. Often, however, these data appear in raw form. For the most part, they are frequency counts of characteristics, events, or processes occurring during a specified period of time. This published information provides scientifically useful data on subject matter as diverse as total population, number of marriages, divorces, deaths, automobiles purchased, electric power generated, and gallons of milk produced.

While raw frequency counts themselves can be scientifically valuable, social scientists frequently find it necessary to convert the numbers into more useful forms, sometimes by converting the frequencies to percentages. At other times, two numbers are converted to a ratio: a quantity of one thing expressed as a multiple of another. And, at still other times, a ratio is conceptually expressed as a rate: the average magnitude of one thing per unit of another over a specified time interval.

These conversions serve several purposes. By converting frequencies into percents, the numbers are standardized or *normed* to a common decimal base of one hundred. By converting numbers into ratios or rates, it is possible to develop an understanding of the relationship between variable quantities. Furthermore, it is feasible to arrive at empirical measures of theoretical variables by converting raw frequency counts into new forms.

Converting frequencies into percents, ratios, and rates is a complex conceptual process. As an illustration, consider the task of constructing an automobile theft rate. The rate might be determined by calculating the frequency of automobiles stolen per 1,000 automobiles purchased or by calculating the frequency of automobiles stolen per 1,000 automobiles registered, or by calculating the frequency of automobiles stolen per 1,000 persons fifteen years of age or older. It is clear that the meaning of an automobile theft rate varies with the base quantity involved.

Additional complications emerge in comparing percentages, ratios, or rates. For instance, since a rate is defined in terms of the average magnitude of one thing per unit of another thing, changes in the frequency of either the first or second quantity produce changes in the rate. Thus, either an increase in the number of automobiles stolen *or* a decrease in the number of automobiles registered could yield an increase in the automobile theft rate.

This chapter introduces the conceptual and mathematical considerations involved in converting raw frequency counts into percentages, ratios, or rates. It will also explore the relationship between the intended meaning of a concept and its operational measurement.

THEORETICAL PROBLEM

All societies distinguish between legitimate and illegitimate births. This distinction is reflected in the public ridicule and ostracism directed toward unwed mothers and in the legal codes defining the rights or lack thereof of illegitimate children. The severity and extent of a society's reaction to illegitimate births vary from society to society.

These circumstances offer a context for creating interesting theoretical questions. For instance, why are some societies tolerant of illegitimacy while other societies are not? Or why does the level of tolerance within a given society vary according to the class or to the ethnic or cultural background of the unwed mother? Further, why is there an increase in illegitimacy rates when underdeveloped societies modernize?

The last question has received a great deal of attention from social scientists. They generally argue that the forces of modernization weaken traditional values governing individual freedom and sexual conduct. As societies become more urban, industrial, and literate, that is, as they modernize, a number of social changes can be readily observed. First, as individuals seek economic and social opportunities beyond the boundaries of local towns and villages, there is an increase in their geographic mobility. Second, as they pursue occupations different from those of their parents, there is an increase in their social mobility. Third, as they conserve resources for private use or for use by their immediate families, there is a marked decline in the strength of kinship bonds. Social scientists argue that these changes reduce the effectiveness of traditional values with respect to the regulation of personal conduct.

In Western societies, the weakening of traditional values is termed increased personal freedom. This personal freedom may be expressed in changed sexual behavior. As young people are freed of traditional controls, they presumably engage in more sexual experimentation, which, in turn, presumably produces increased illegitimacy.

This theory, widely accepted and supported by social scientists, appears to explain the observed relationship between modernization and increased illegitimacy. Japan appears to be the exception to this theory. Thus, although Japan has experienced rapid modernization since 1900, the rate of illegitimacy has decreased rather than increased.

Using already published data, Shirley Hartley undertook to investigate this problem.* Like many social scientists, she was puzzled by Japan's differing in this respect from the rest of the rapidly changing societies.

3.1 OPERATIONAL DEFINITIONS

The relationship of a theoretical concept to the procedures for its measurement has a long history of intense philosophical and scientific debate. Scientists now accept the conclusion that it is impossible to prove that the meaning of a concept is fully captured by the procedures used in its measurement. The classic case of intelligence as a theoretical concept and intelligence tests as a procedure for measurement illustrates this point. Since for the same individual different intelligence tests produce different intelligence scores, the relationship between concept and test is problematic. If, on one hand, we select one intelligence test score and ignore others, how do we know which test to select? Or if we permit the use of many tests, does this imply that an individual has many intelligences?

There is no known solution to this problem. Scientists recognize that it is a matter of belief that measurement procedures appropriately measure a theoretical concept. They further recognize that alternative procedures may yield equally appropriate measures. Although the gap between concept and measurement appears to be empirically insurmountable, scientists accept the responsibility of clearly specifying theoretical definitions and operational definitions of measurement in order to professionally judge whether such definitions and procedures are consistent with those used by other scientists.

* Shirley F. Hartley, "The Decline of Illegitimacy in Japan," *Social Problems*, 18(1970):78–91.

3.2 PERCENTAGES, RATIOS, AND RATES AS NORMING OPERATIONS

As suggested in Chapter 1, facts do not speak for themselves. Facts are always interpreted in terms of a norm or standard. An important contribution of the statistical method is to furnish procedures for developing quantitative norms or standards which permit proper interpretation of single measures or meaningful comparisons of two or more measures. Conversions of numbers into percentages, ratios, or rates are common statistical norming operations.

Percentages Social scientists frequently report quantities of things in terms of subcategories. Thus, they may report that an organization contains 1,334 men and 666 women. Converting these numbers to a common base of 100 permits the statement that 66.7 percent of the members of an organization are men and 33.3 percent are women. If another organization has 889 men and 444 women, converting these numbers to percentages would reveal that both organizations had the same distribution (i.e., 66.7 percent men and 33.3 percent women). Converting frequencies to percentages permits both a more comprehensive understanding of single measures and a comparison of distributions within different totals.

Ratios Values may be compared by expressing one value as a multiple of another. Thus, the number of illegitimate births may be expressed as a multiple of the number of legitimate births: a ratio of two subfrequencies. Or the number of illegitimate births may be defined as a multiple of the total number of births. Births may be expressed as a multiple of the number of unmarried females aged 15 through 44, a ratio of a quantity of one thing to the quantity of another thing. Calculating a ratio frequently results in a decimal fraction, for example, .682 or .4382. These decimal fractions are frequently cleared through multiplying by a base number such as 100, 1,000, or 10,000. The choice of a base is arbitrary; it is selected for its comprehensibility. Thus, there were 96,900,000 males in the United States and 99,942,000

MEASURING THE ILLEGITIMATE BIRTH RATE

So far, the concept *illegitimate birth rate* has been used without either a clear theoretical or operational definition. To some readers, it may have meant the frequency of illegitimate births per 100 total births. To other readers, it may have meant the frequency of illegitimate births per 100 legitimate births. And to still others, it may have conveyed other meanings. Conceptually, an illegitimate birth refers to a birth out-of-wedlock. The conceptual and operational meanings of an illegitimate birth rate are more complex.

Researcher Shirley Hartley operationalized the illegitimate birth rate in two ways. Each method involved calculating a rate. Her operational definitions and procedures are provided below.

females in 1966. The ratio of males to females is .96956 (i.e., .96956 males per 1 female). Since this number is both cumbersome and repugnant, it has become conventional to multiply the ratio by 100 and round the result. Consequently, the 1966 ratio of males to females is 97 males per 100 females. The decision to clear the decimal by a given base is dependent upon the desired meaning. For some ratios, such as the sex ratio of males to females, it has become conventional to use a base of 100.

Rates Basically all rates are ratios. However, there is a verbal distinction between the two concepts. A rate is defined as the average quantity of one thing per unit quantity of another over a specified time interval. Thus the illegitimacy rate may be defined as the average number of illegitimate children per unmarried women. For Japan in 1964, there were 17,000 illegitimate births and 10,482,000 unmarried women aged 15 through 44. Dividing the first quantity by the second quantity yields an average .00162 illegitimate births per unmarried women. Since this number is also cumbersome, multiplying by 1,000 and rounding yield an average of 2 illegitimate births per 1,000 unmarried women, a number much easier to comprehend.

Since a rate is the statistical result of two variables, a *criterion variable,* whose variation is in doubt, and a *norming variable,* whose variation is to be eliminated, the selection of the norming variable is crucial. In calculating the illegitimate birth rate, the criterion variable is the number of illegitimate births. The norming variable for rate 1 was the total number of births, but for rate 2 it was the number of unmarried females aged 15 through 44. The selection of a norming variable whose variation is to be eliminated is crucial if the operational definition is to correspond closely to the intended meaning of the concept.

This discussion is indebted to the material presented in J. F. Mueller, K. Schuessler, and H. Costner, *Statistical Reasoning in Sociology,* 2d ed. (Boston: Houghton Mifflin, 1970), pp. 180–184.

Rate 1. Operational Definition

First, Hartley operationalized the illegitimate birth rate as the frequency of illegitimate births per hundred annual births. Thus:

$$\text{Illegitimate birth rate 1} = \frac{\text{number of illegitimate annual births}}{\text{number of total annual births}} \times 100$$

Since she defined illegitimate birth rate in terms of the quantity of illegitimate births to the quantity of total births, a change in either quantity produces a difference in the rate:

A. $$\frac{\text{Increase in number of illegitimate births}}{\text{Smaller increase in total births}} = \text{rate increase}$$

(Since total annual births means legitimate and illegitimate births combined, an increase in the number of illegitimate births also increases the number of total births, but the incremental change is smaller.)

However, a rate increase can also occur if the total number of legitimate births declines but the number of illegitimate births remains the same:

B. $$\frac{\text{Stable number of illegitimate births}}{\text{Decrease in total births}} = \text{rate increase}$$

(Since total births means legitimate and illegitimate births combined, stable illegitimate births accompanied by a decrease in legitimate births produces a decrease in total annual births.)

Although the illegitimate birth rate increased in examples A and B, it is evident that the rate changed for different reasons. In example A, the rate changed because the number of illegitimate births increased. However, in example B, the rate changed because the number of legitimate births decreased. Quite clearly, if rates are to be compared, it is necessary to understand both the quantities used in their calculations and possible variations in those quantities over time.

It is also true that a rate may change for reasons unrelated to the intended theoretical use of the concept. For instance, although the illegitimate birth rate may decrease over a period of time, this does not necessarily mean that there has been a reduction in premarital sex. The increased availability of abortion, which reduces the number of both legitimate and illegitimate births, would increase the illegitimate birth rate even if the number of illegitimate births remained unchanged.

Rate 2. Operational Definition

Second, Hartley operationalized the illegitimate birth rate as the frequency of illegitimate births per 1,000 unmarried females aged fifteen through forty-four. Thus:

Illegitimate birth rate 2 =

$$\frac{\text{number of annual illegitimate births}}{\text{number of unmarried females aged 15 through 44}} \times 1{,}000$$

Rate 2, like rate 1, is subject to change for a number of reasons. For instance, if the number of unmarried females (15 through 44) decreases, rate 2 increases. Or, if the number of illegitimate births increases, rate 2 again increases. It is essential to understand the operational definition of a concept and possible changes in the quantities used to determine a specified rate if the rate is not to be misunderstood.

SELECTING AN OPERATIONAL DEFINITION

Faced with two operational definitions, it is reasonable to ask: Which definition leads to the correct procedure for measuring the illegitimate birth rate? When the question is phrased this way, it is unanswerable. There is no one correct procedure. Various procedures provide different types of information. Thus, researchers must decide which measurement best represents the concept they are attempting to measure. In this study, it appears useful to calculate the illegitimacy rate by using both procedures because they reveal different aspects of the phenomenon.

JAPANESE ILLEGITIMATE BIRTH RATES

Table 3-1 presents the available crude illegitimate birth rates (computed two ways) for Japan between 1900 and 1964. They are labeled as crude rates since they are computed for all unmarried women aged 14 to 44 combined.

Table 3-1. Illegitimate Birth Rates, Japan, 1900–1964.

DATE	RATE 1[a]	RATE 2[b]
(A)	(B)	(C)
1900	8.8	Data not available
1920	8.2	"
1940	4.1	14
1950	2.5	7
1964	1.0	2

SOURCE: The original data from which Hartley computed these rates appeared in the *United Nations Demographic Yearbook,* 1954, 1959, and 1965, and in data published by Japan Bureau of Statistics (1964), and Japan Division of Health and Welfare (1940). The data for this table are from Hartley, "Decline of Illegitimacy," p. 80, Table 1.

[a] Rate 1 = Frequency of illegitimate births per 100 annual births.

[b] Rate 2 = Frequency of illegitimate births per 1,000 unmarried females, 15 through 44.

An examination of this table discloses that illegitimate birth rates, however calculated, have dramatically declined over the time period covered. Illegitimate birth rate 1 has fallen steadily since 1900. In 1900, there were 8.8 illegitimate births per 100 total births; in 1940, the rate was 4.1; in 1950, 2.5; and, in 1964, 1.0.

Similarly, illegitimate birth rate 2 has fallen steadily since 1940, the first year for which data are available. In 1940 there were 14 illegitimate births per 1,000 unmarried females, 15 through 44; a decade later, in 1950, the rate was 7, and, by 1964, it had fallen to 2. The pace of the decline was indeed dramatic.

Thus, both measures indicate that Japanese illegitimate birth rates have declined rather than increased during this half-century of modernization. Does this mean that the theory which proposed a relationship among modernization, personal freedom, and sexual conduct is not applicable to Japan? And does the theory remain applicable if other variables are considered? The goal for the remainder of this chapter is to answer these two key questions.

ONE POSSIBLE EXPLANATION: DEMOGRAPHIC CHANGES IN JAPAN

Using the two alternative procedures for measuring the illegitimate birth rate, Hartley established that the illegitimate birth rate in Japan has been declining steadily. Table 3-2 reports some of the data on which this finding is based. It contains the number of illegitimate births, legitimate births, and total annual births used to calculate illegitimate birth rate 1 for selected years since 1940.

Table 3-2. Number of Legitimate, Illegitimate, and Total Births, Japan, 1940, 1950, and 1964.[a]

YEAR	ILLEGITIMATE BIRTHS	LEGITIMATE BIRTHS	TOTAL BIRTHS	ILLEGITIMATE BIRTH RATE 1 (B/D × 100)
(A)	(B)	(C)	(D)	(E)
1940	86,000	2,004,000	2,090,000	4.1
1950	58,000	2,268,000	2,326,000	2.5
1964	17,000	1,703,000	1,720,000	1.0

[a] All frequencies have been rounded to the nearest 1,000.

By examining each column and then examining the relationship between columns, it is possible to obtain a more accurate picture of the change in illegitimate birth rates. Column B reveals that the number of illegitimate births fell precipitously from 86,000 in 1940 to 17,000 in 1964. Column C shows that the number of legitimate births fell from 2,004,000 in 1940 to 1,703,000 in 1964. This also was a fairly steady decline, except for the expanded frequency of births in 1950 following the end of World War II. Column D reveals that total births declined from 2,090,000 in 1940 to 1,720,000 in 1964, with the same pattern as column C, because total births consist primarily of legitimate births.

These data establish a basis for determining why illegitimate birth rate 1 fell from 4.1 (1940) to 1.0 (1964), a decline of 76 percent (4.1 − 1.0/4.1 = .76). A more rapid decline had occurred in the frequency of illegitimate births (80 percent) than in the frequency of legitimate births (15 percent). Thus, a more rapid decline in the frequency of illegitimate births than in the frequency of legitimate births caused a drop in the calculated illegitimacy rate.

Hartley also examined the second procedure for calculating the illegitimate birth rate:

Illegitimate birth rate 2 =

$$\frac{\text{number of annual illegitimate births}}{\text{number of unmarried females aged 15 through 44}} \times 1{,}000$$

Table 3-3 reports the number of unmarried and married females (aged 15 through 44) and the frequency of legitimate and illegitimate births for selected years. It permits an examination of demographic changes that may have influenced the illegitimacy rate.

Table 3-3 shows, first, that the total number of females 15 through 44 has increased since 1940 (read down column B). Although there are more potentially fertile females, the total number of births has decreased since 1940 (read down column C). By comparing 1940 and 1964, it is obvious that in 1964 there were more females in the fertility years but fewer births. Similarly, it can be observed by comparing columns D and E that the number of unmarried females in the fertility years increased while the number of illegitimate births decreased.

Table 3-3 reveals two factors which should have produced an increase in the illegitimacy rate: an increase in the number of potential mothers of illegitimate children (column D) and a decrease in the number of legitimate births (column G). It is important to note that the formula for rate 1 does not use the information about the number of potential mothers and so remains unaffected by an increase or a decrease in these numbers. However, the formula for rate 2 does not use the information about the frequencies of both kinds of births (legitimate and illegitimate) and so is unaffected by variations in the number of legitimate births.

Examining all available information results in the conclusion that, however measured and considering whatever changes in variables may have distorted the rates, the illegitimate birth rate has declined.

A SECOND POSSIBLE EXPLANATION: BIRTH CONTROL

The decline of both legitimate and illegitimate birth rates from 1940 to 1964, by age groups, appears in Table 3-4. These rates are *age-specific* since they are calculated for specific age groupings.

Table 3-3. Illegitimate Birth Rate 2 and Total Unmarried and Married Females 15 Through 44, Japan, 1940, 1950, and 1964.[a]

YEAR	TOTAL FEMALES	TOTAL BIRTHS	UNMARRIED FEMALES	ILLEGITIMATE BIRTHS	MARRIED FEMALES	LEGITIMATE BIRTHS	ILLEGITIMATE BIRTH RATE 2 (E/D × 1,000)
(A)	(B)	(C)	(D)	(E)	(F)	(G)	(H)
1940	15,617,000	2,090,000	6,339,000	86,000	9,278,000	2,004,000	14
1950	19,266,000	2,326,000	8,389,000	58,000	10,877,000	2,268,000	7
1964	24,689,000	1,720,000	10,482,000	17,000	14,207,000	1,703,000	2

[a] All frequencies have been rounded to the nearest 1,000.

Table 3-4. Legitimate and Illegitimate Birth Rates for Japan, 1940–1964.

AGE OF MOTHER (A)	ILLEGITIMATE BIRTH RATE 2[a] 1940 (B)	1964 (C)	% Change (D)	LEGITIMATE BIRTH RATE 1940 (E)	1964 (F)	% Change (G)
15–19	2.4	.2	−92	274.7	271.2	−1
20–24	14.8	1.5	−90	314.9	337.0	+7
25–29	46.5	6.5	−86	284.9	240.1	−16
30–34	59.9	8.3	−86	230.5	92.7	−60
35–39	43.8	4.0	−91	161.6	21.1	−87
40–44	17.9	1.1	−94	70.7	3.7	−95
Average:	13.5	1.6	−88	216.0	120.9	−45

SOURCE: Hartley, "Decline of Illegitimacy," p. 83, Table 2, and p. 84, Table 3.
[a] Illegitimate birth rate = frequency of births per 1,000 females in age bracket.

This table demonstrates that the average legitimate and illegitimate birth rates (columns D and G) dropped drastically, with the average illegitimate rate dropping much faster (down 88 percent) than the legitimate rate (down 45 percent). Furthermore, grouping the women by age permits one interpretation of the reason for the decline in birth rates.

While the youngest (15 through 19) and the oldest (40 through 44) age groups have the largest decline in illegitimate rates as reported in column D (down 92 percent and down 94 percent), the decline in the illegitimate birth rate was large in all age groups. Column G, on the other hand, shows that legitimate births had their greatest rate decrease in the three older age groups (down 60 percent, down 87 percent, and down 95 percent), with little decrease among young women (down 1 percent, up 7 percent, and down 16 percent).

Hartley concluded that women under thirty years old who could bear children legitimately have not changed their pregnancy patterns. Presumably this is because they wish to bear children while they are young. Unmarried young women, however, were dramatically reducing the number of children they had. How? Most likely by use of birth control techniques which became more available and more effective in the years between 1940 and 1964.

ABORTION AS A METHOD OF BIRTH CONTROL

Indirect data for assessing the impact of birth control techniques are available in the specific case of abortion, an important birth control method in Japan. Between 1955 and 1964, approximately 8 percent of all fetal deaths in the last three months of pregnancy were classified as being connected with illegitimacy. It seems reasonable to assume that intentional abortions during the previous six months of pregnancy would also be at least 8 percent, for most unwed mothers probably would not wait until the seventh, eighth, or ninth month before undergoing abortion.

Conservatively, therefore, it can be assumed that at least 8 percent of the abortions in 1955 (a sample year) were to unwed mothers. As reported by Hartley, there were 1,250,000 abortions in Japan in 1955; so 8 percent, or 100,000 of those abortions, would have been to unwed mothers. Since Japan recorded an additional 29,000 births as illegitimate that year, there would have been a minimum total of 129,000 illegitimate births had the abortions not occurred.

To determine the illegitimate birth rate for 1955 (had these abortions not occurred) the following calculations are performed:

$$\text{1955 Rate 1} = \frac{\text{number of annual illegitimate births}}{\text{number of annual births}}$$

$$= \frac{\text{100,000 illegitimate births hidden by abortion + 29,000 recorded illegitimate births}}{\text{100,000 illegitimate births hidden by abortion + 1,731,000 actual births}} \times 100$$

$$= \frac{129{,}000}{1{,}831{,}000} \times 100 = 7\%$$

Employing the formula for rate 2:

$$\text{1955 Rate 2} = \frac{\text{number of annual illegitimate births}}{\text{number of unmarried females, 15 through 44}} \times 100$$

$$= \frac{\text{100,000 hidden illegitimate births + 29,000 recorded illegitimate births}}{\text{9,425,000 unmarried females, 15 through 44}} \times 100$$

$$= \frac{129{,}000}{9{,}425{,}000} \times 1{,}000 = 14\%$$

The estimated 1955 rates are similar to rates in earlier periods when modernization was beginning and abortion was unavailable. The 1955 no-abortion rate 1 of 7 percent was calculated conservatively. Nevertheless, it is comparable to the actual 1900 rate of 8.8 percent (see Table 3-1, column B). The no-abortion 1955 rate 2 of 14 percent is exactly equal to the actual 1940 rate of 14 percent (see Table 3-1, column C). Thus, if the assumptions are correct, abortion as a birth control technique could have been a major cause of the decline in the illegitimate birth rate. Without abortion, the illegitimacy rate might have remained relatively consistent.

EVALUATING MODERNIZATION AS APPLIED TO JAPAN

It has not been proven that abortion was the cause of declining illegitimacy, only that it could have been. However, rather convincing evidence exists to suggest that abortion as well as other methods of birth control could have been primary causes of the decline. But there is no certainty that this is indeed what happened. Lacking direct information about birth control, it cannot be ascertained that a causal relationship has been established.

One thing is known, however: Sexual activity outside of marriage need not have declined for the decrease in the illegitimacy rate to have occurred. Rather, behavior related to such activity (e.g., marriage, abortion, contraception, etc.) may have changed. While there is evidence suggesting that linking modernization theory with an increase in sexual freedom may be applicable to Japan, it has not been established with certainty.

It has been necessary to address the theoretical question indirectly because there are no data indicating the frequency of extramarital sexual activity. Until such data become available, it can only be inferred that the incidence of sexual activity outside of marriage could have remained concealed by the availability of birth control techniques in Japan. Thus, the theory suggesting a relationship between modernization and individual freedom cannot be rejected. Increased personal freedom and the weakening of traditional taboos in Japan may have led to increased but undetected extramarital sexual activity.

SUMMARY

This chapter's study of illegitimacy in Japan has illustrated the importance of careful use and interpretation of data. Raw data usually must be converted into other more useful forms. However, there are many possible conversions, each with its own strengths, weaknesses, and alternative interpretations. In this study, two different methods for operationalizing illegitimate birth rates were used. Both methods suggested a decline in illegitimacy rates. The data were then further analyzed to evaluate the impact of demographic change and birth control on the decline in illegitimacy rates.

As a result of such data manipulations, what at first appeared to be a clearcut contradiction of the theory of the effect of modernization turned out to be only indirect evidence of a possible contradiction. Rates may have changed for reasons unrelated to the issues of modernization and personal freedom. Nevertheless, the use of rates was crucial in drawing some meaning from the millions of births occurring in Japan during the last half century.

KEY IDEAS AND CONCEPTS

age-specific rate
crude rate
illegitimate birth rate
legitimate birth rate
normed measure
operational definition
percentage
rate
ratio
raw frequency count
standardize
units per thousand

ISSUES AND PROBLEMS

1. What is a crude rate? An age-specific rate? List the advantages of an age-specific rate.
2. Identify a variable which you think should be measured on an age-specific basis. What are the disadvantages of using age-specific measures?
3. List the advantages of norming or standardizing a set of observations. List the disadvantages.
4. Distinguish between a rate and a ratio.
5. Examine Table 3-A below and complete the questions following.

Table 3-A. Marriages and Divorces in the United States for Selected Years.

MARRIAGE AND DIVORCE	1940	1950	1960	1970
Marriages				
Total (in 000's)	1,596	1,667	1,523	2,163
Rate per 1,000 population	12.1	11.1	8.5	10.6
Divorces[a]				
Total (in 000's)	264	385	393	708

SOURCE: U.S. Bureau of the Census, *Statistical Abstract of the United States: 1974,* 95th ed. (Washington, D.C.: Government Printing Office, 1974). Adapted from Table No. 93, p. 66.
[a] Includes annulments.

a. Calculate the total U.S. population for 1940, 1950, 1960, and 1970.
b. Calculate the divorce rate per 1,000 population for 1940, 1950, 1960, and 1970.
c. Calculate the ratio of marriages to divorces for 1940, 1950, 1960, and 1970.
d. What was the percentage decline in the marriage rate between 1950 and 1960? What was the percentage increase in the marriage rate between 1960 and 1970?
e. Offer an explanation for the decline in the marriage rate between 1950 and 1960.

6. Examine the tables below and answer the questions pertaining to each.

Table 3-B. Population Distribution by Sex, United States, 1960, 1970.

YEAR	MALES	FEMALES	TOTAL
1960	88,331,000	90,992,000	179,323,000
1970	98,926,000	104,309,000	203,235,000

SOURCE: U.S. Department of Commerce, Bureau of the Census, *Statistical Abstract of the United States 1975,* 96th ed. (Washington, D.C.: Government Printing Office), p. 26, Table 26.

a. Calculate the sex ratio for 1960. (Sex ratio is number of males per 100 females.)
b. Which group had the greater numerical increase?

Table 3-C. Homicide Victims, United States, 1960, 1965, 1970.

YEAR	MALES	FEMALES	TOTAL
1960	6,269	2,195	8,464
1965	8,148	2,564	10,712
1970	13,278	3,570	16,848

SOURCE: U.S. Department of Commerce, Bureau of the Census, *Statistical Abstract of the United States 1975,* 96th ed. (Washington, D.C.: Government Printing Office), p. 155, Table 257.

a. Calculate the percent of male victims for 1960, 1965, and 1970.
b. Calculate the ratio of male to female victims for 1960, 1965, and 1970.
c. What were the rates of female victims per 1,000 females in 1960 and 1970?

7. Two possible explanations for the declining illegitimacy rate in Japan were given in this chapter. Review these and indicate the authors' findings in regard to both.

RECOMMENDED READINGS

Durkheim, Emile
1951 *Suicide: A Study in Sociology.* New York: The Free Press.

A classic intra- and intersocietal analysis of suicide using percentages, rates, and ratios. Presents cross-national comparisons with many examples of imaginative operationalization.

Hartley, Shirley F.
1975 *Illegitimacy.* Berkeley, Calif.: Univ. of California Press.

A book-length exploration of differences in illegitimacy. Provides further illustrations of the use of rates and ratios.

Loether, Herman J., and Donald G. McTavish
1974 *Descriptive Statistics for Sociologists: An Introduction.* Boston: Allyn and Bacon.

A readable statistics text describing the use of rates and ratios, comparisons, and univariate distributions. See especially chapters 2, 3, and 5.

Mueller, John H., Karl F. Schuessler, and Herbert L. Costner
1970 *Statistical Reasoning in Sociology.* Boston: Houghton Mifflin.

An excellent introductory statistics text. See especially chapter 7 for a discussion of norming operations involving percentages, rates, and ratios.

Stouffer, Samuel A.
1963 *Communism, Conformity, and Civil Liberties.* Gloucester, Mass.: Peter Smith.

An illustration in the power of percentages for presenting data in bivariate tables.

United Nations
(annual) *Demographic Yearbook.* New York: Publishing Service of the United Nations.

An annual publication containing worldwide and individual nation data on births, deaths, divorces, migration, and similar population-relevant information. Useful for comparative research.

4

USING A BASELINE TO CONSTRUCT AN INDEX: RESIDENTIAL SEGREGATION IN THE UNITED STATES

GENERAL ISSUE

Social scientists frequently norm data to a common base in order to facilitate meaningful comparisons. For instance, in Chapter 2 the number of patrilineal, bilateral, and matrilineal societies which were sexually permissive were normed to a common base of 100. Meaningful comparisons of sexual permissiveness among the different types of societies were then possible. Similarly, in Chapter 3 the frequency of illegitimate births in Japan were normed to the common base of 1,000 unmarried women. This norming made possible meaningful comparisons of the illegitimate birth rates among different age groups.

Sometimes, rather than using a common base, social scientists use the distribution of one population as a basis for comparing the distribution of another. For example, the income distribution of whites might be used as a standard for comparing the distribution among blacks. This technique makes possible an evaluation of the black income distribution *in terms of* the white.

All of the previous examples illustrate a norming procedure using existing data. Often, however, social scientists wish to norm data in terms of a hypothetical standard. Such standards are useful for interpreting discrepancies between actual and potential distributions. Therefore, they frequently involve assumptions. For example, in matters of school desegregation, the federal courts often assume a hypothetical race-mix distribution of students for determining the discrepancy between existing racial distribution and a potential distribution were the schools integrated.

Similarly, a hypothetical distribution can be used to determine whether parents continue to have children in order to have sons. Since there is approximately a fifty-fifty chance that a newborn child will be a female, this means that approximately 50 percent of the last-born children for all families would be female. By comparing this hypothetical percentage with the actual percentage of last-born females, it should be possible to determine if cultural values influence whether parents continue having children until they achieve a last-born child who is male. (Of course, in developing a research project the sex of previously born children would have to be considered.)

In each of the above examples, one distribution was selected as a standard and was used as the basis for comparison with another. The distribution used as the standard is often referred to as a *baseline distribution.* This chapter illustrates the usefulness of a baseline distribution for comparing the residential segregation of white and black households in American cities.

THEORETICAL PROBLEM

In most American cities, members of ethnic and racial groups tend to be residentially segregated from each other. Hence, neighborhoods frequently develop an identification in terms of ethnic or racial characteristics. Some neighborhoods are predominantly Italian, some are Polish, and many are black. These clusterings necessarily influence the lives of neighborhood inhabitants. The kinds of stores where people shop, their access to recreational activities, and the types of schools children attend depend to a large degree on where and how they live. In addition, people who live close physically are more likely to be friends than are people who live further apart; for instance, next-door neighbors are more likely to be friends than are people who live two or three blocks apart.

Thus, even if attention is focused on the social relationships between groups, their physical spacing within the larger community is important. Where people live—that is, their residential clustering—seems to be an important influence on, and a reasonable indicator of, the extent of their social segregation.

MEASURING RESIDENTIAL SEGREGATION

In 1964, Karl Taeuber proposed a procedure for measuring residential segregation in American cities.* Since his procedure yielded a measure which was intended as an indicator of the more general phenomenon of social segregation, it was termed a *segregation index.*

* Karl Taeuber, "Negro Residential Segregation: Trends and Measurements," *Social Problems,* 12(1964):42–50.

4.1 THE IDEA OF AN INDEX

Because theoretical concepts can never be measured directly, scientists link operational definitions to them. These operational definitions provide procedures for indirect measurement of the concepts.

For example, social status may be theoretically defined as an individual's prestige position within a social group. Operationally, the same concept might be defined and measured in terms of the frequency with which other members of the group defer to his or her wishes.

Often, however, a theoretical concept is too abstract or complex to permit a relatively straightforward operational definition. When this occurs, social scientists often obtain measurements which they believe are indicative of the theoretical concept. Frequently, they refer to such measurements as an *index* of the concept. Furthermore, an index may consist of a single measurement or a combination of measurements. Economists, for instance, use a series of measurements to obtain a *cost of living* index.

Taeuber's procedure involved comparing the distribution of black households with a baseline distribution. He reasoned that the distribution of white households would serve as an effective baseline for this purpose. *If* the actual distribution of black households were similar to the white baseline, then the city could be considered integrated in terms of household distribution. On the other hand, any difference between the two distributions could serve as an index of the city's segregation.

According to Taeuber's procedure, there would be no difference between the black distribution and the white baseline distribution if a city were completely integrated (segregation index = 0). On the other hand, if there were no similarity between the two distributions (segregation index = 100) the city would be completely segregated. Segregation indices falling between 0 and 100 would indicate the degree of segregation in the given city. (For an explanation of the procedure used in calculating a segregation index, see Technical Insert II, page 54.)

Taeuber used Bureau of the Census data for 1940 and 1960 to determine the extent of segregation and to measure change over these two decades. Census data were available for all urban areas (defined as cities over 50,000 population including contiguous counties). Taeuber, however, restricted his research to those cities for which block level data were available in 1940 and 1960, and which in 1940 contained more than 1,000 black households.

His findings on the 109 cities which met his criteria appear in Table 4-1. The top row of this table reports the average indexes of all 109 cities for 1940 and 1960. In both years, the average segregation index values are high: 85.2 for 1940 and 86.1 for 1960. Further, there was a slight increase in the segregation index from 1940 to 1960.

Table 4-1. Average Values of Segregation Indexes of U.S. Cities, 1940, 1960, and Change 1940-1960.

		AVERAGE VALUE OF SEGREGATION INDEXES		
CITY GROUPING	NO. OF CITIES	1940	1960	Change 1940–1960
All cities	109	85.2	86.1	+ .9
Region				
Northeast	25	83.2	78.9	−4.3
North Central	29	88.4	88.4	0.0
West	10	82.7	76.4	−6.3
South	45	85.0	90.7	+5.7
Percentage black				
1940				
1.2–4.1	22	84.8	80.8	−4.0
4.2–8.0	22	84.6	81.9	−2.7
8.1–12.9	22	84.8	84.8	0.0
13.0–27.5	22	86.4	91.1	+4.7
27.6–48.6	21	85.5	92.0	+6.5
City size (in thousands), 1940				
46–69	22	83.8	86.8	+3.0
70–111	22	83.7	85.6	+1.9
112–178	22	86.6	86.1	−0.5
179–368	22	84.9	86.5	+1.6
369–7455	21	87.2	85.3	−1.9

SOURCE: Taeuber, "Residential Segregation," p. 46, Table 2.

Since patterns of segregation may vary by region, percent black, and city size, indexes are reported separately for these categories. First, using four regions defined by the Bureau of the Census, one can observe that there were only small regional differences in 1940, while the variations between regions were somewhat larger in 1960. The segregation index decreased slightly in the Northeast and West, remained the same in the North Central region, and increased slightly in the South. Of course these are average segregation indexes for cities within these regions. Specific cities may have increased, decreased, or experienced no change in their segregation indexes.

Similar observations can be made for cities when categorized by percent black or population size. In both cases, segregation indexes were high in 1940 and 1960, and changes over twenty years were small and irregular. Still, the changes may represent trends which might be clarified by an examination of 1970 data.

SUMMARY AND CONCLUSIONS

Taeuber's segregation index showed that American cities had a high degree of segregation both in 1940 and 1960. The average level of the index actually increased slightly from 1940 to 1960. Further data are needed in order to interpret these small changes.

Of course, the study of segregation cannot be reduced to construction of a single index. The index provides no information about social relationships between whites and blacks, nor does it address the causes or effects of segregation. Further, the index presented, as originally calculated, was limited by the fact that it focused only on the cities as they were defined by their political boundaries. Segregation between cities and their suburbs, for example, was not reflected.

It should also be noted that the given index measures residential segregation at the block level but does not measure residential variations within a block. For instance, a city block may be completely segregated by an alley so that blacks occupy one half of the block and whites occupy the other half. Therefore, the index, while valuable, has obvious limitations.

For this reason, research studies frequently build on and complement one another. Taeuber's findings should be synthesized with the findings of other social scientists studying such topics as school segregation, job segregation, and income distribution, in order to obtain a more complete picture of racial segregation.

Technical Insert II

Dissimilarity: A Procedure for Calculating a Segregation Index*

To calculate a segregation index, Taeuber compared the residential distribution of blacks in a city with that of whites; the difference between the two distributions provided the basis for his index. As stated, the greater the dissimilarity in the two distributions, the greater the segregation.

Figure II-1 is a partial reproduction of a census map containing blocks and census tracts for an area of Milwaukee. For purposes of identification, the Bureau of the Census numbered each tract, and each block within a given tract, according to the definitions used by the Bureau:

> Census tracts are small areas into which large cities and metropolitan areas are divided for statistical purposes. Tract boundaries are established cooperatively by a local committee and the Bureau of the Census and are generally designed to achieve some uniformity of population characteristics, economic status, and living conditions. Initially, the average tract had about 4,000 residents. Tract boundaries are established with the intention of being maintained over a long time so that comparisons can be made from census to census. A block is usually a well-defined rectangular piece of land bounded by streets or roads. However, it may be irregular in shape or bounded by railroad tracks, streams or other features. The block is the specific numbered area shown on the map.†

To illustrate Taeuber's procedure and to simplify calculations, a residential segregation index for tracts 103 and 108 in an area known as West Milwaukee is calculated on page 58. Of course, in calculating a segregation index for the entire city of Milwaukee it would be necessary to use all census tracts.

Table II-1 on page 56 is an adaptation of block level statistics published by the Bureau of the Census for the city of Milwaukee.* It contains the information necessary for calculating a segregation index for census tracts 103 and 108. The appendix at the end of this chapter contains additional information on these and other census tracts in the West Milwaukee area.

Columns (1) and (2) of Table II-1 identify the tracts and blocks used in this example. Columns (3), (4), and (5) report the number of occupied dwelling units in each block, the number of units occupied by whites, and the number occupied by blacks. Column (6) gives the distribution by percentage of all white-occupied dwelling units over the forty-four blocks in the two census tracts. Similarly, column (7) shows the percentage distribution of all black-occupied dwelling units over the same forty-four blocks. Column (8) gives the percentage of difference or dissimilarity per block for the two distributions.

In this illustration, the white distribution is the baseline against which the black distribution is compared. The operational approach to developing a segregation index is based on the idea that, if the census tracts were integrated at the block level, the black distribution would be the same as the white.

The percentage of difference (dissimilarity) per block represents either a surplus or shortage of one group's distribution in comparison to the other group. For example, block 105 (census tract 103) has 10.5 percent of all black households in the two tracts but zero percent of the nonblack households. Using

* For an interesting discussion of indexes, see Otis Dudley and Beverly Duncan, "A Methodological Analysis of Segregation Indices," *American Sociological Review*, 20(1955): 210–217.

† *Block Statistics, Milwaukee, Wisconsin, Urbanized Area, 1970*, U.S. Department of Commerce, Bureau of the Census (Washington, D.C.: Government Printing Office).

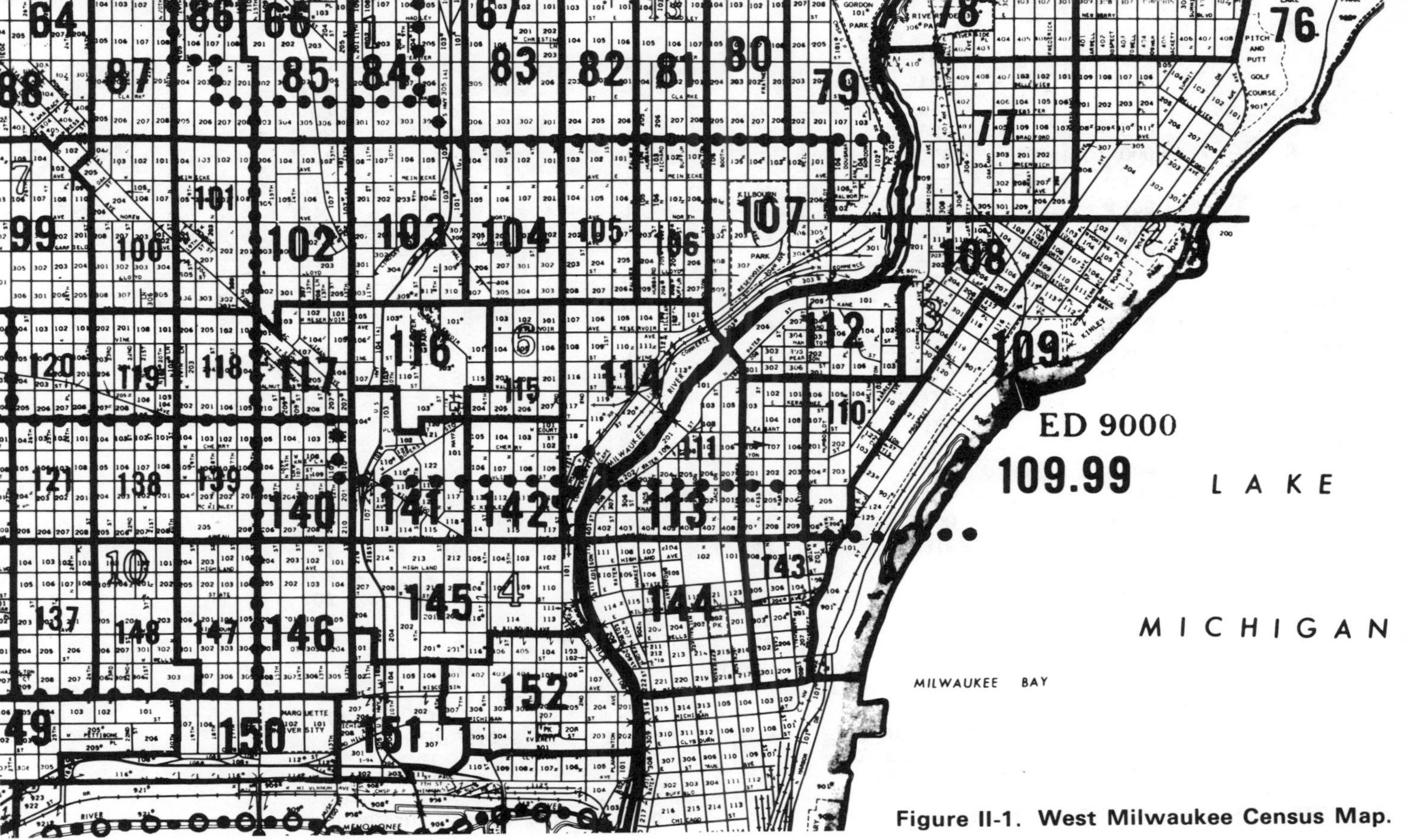

Figure II-1. West Milwaukee Census Map.

Table II-1. Household Distribution by Race per Block, Milwaukee Census Tracts 103 and 108, 1970.*

TRACT	BLOCK	TOTAL OCCUPIED HOUSING UNITS	NON-NEGRO UNITS	NEGRO UNITS	PERCENT DISTRIBUTION OF NON-NEGRO HOUSEHOLDS	PERCENT DISTRIBUTION OF NEGRO HOUSEHOLDS	PERCENT DIFFERENCE (6)–(7)
(1)	(2)	(3)	(4)	(5)	(6)	(7)	(8)
103	105	68	0	68	.000	10.526	−10.526
	106	68	0	68	.000	10.526	−10.526
	107	68	3	65	.189	10.063	−9.874
	108	56	0	56	.000	8.669	−8.669
	201	53	5	48	.315	7.430	−7.115
	202	41	0	41	.000	6.347	−6.347
	203	8	0	8	.000	1.238	−1.238
	204	64	4	60	.252	9.288	−9.036
	205	20	4	16	.252	2.477	−2.225
	206	10	2	8	.125	1.238	−1.113
	207	23	2	21	.125	3.251	−3.126
	301	36	5	31	.315	4.799	−4.484
	302	23	1	22	.063	3.406	−3.343
	303	10	1	9	.063	1.393	−1.330
	304	3	0	3	.000	.464	−.464
	307	3	0	3	.000	.464	−.464
	308	4	0	4	.000	.619	−.619
	309	36	2	34	.125	5.263	−5.138
	310	32	1	31	.063	4.799	−4.763
	311	35	2	33	.125	5.108	−4.983
108	101	1	1	0	.063	.000	+.063
	102	47	47	0	2.956	.000	+2.956
	103	22	22	0	1.384	.000	+1.384
	104	3	3	0	.189	.000	+.189
	106	4	4	0	.252	.000	+.252

TRACT	BLOCK	TOTAL OCCUPIED HOUSING UNITS	NON-NEGRO UNITS	NEGRO UNITS	PERCENT DISTRIBUTION OF NON-NEGRO HOUSEHOLDS	PERCENT DISTRIBUTION OF NEGRO HOUSEHOLDS	PERCENT DIFFERENCE (6)–(7)
(1)	(2)	(3)	(4)	(5)	(6)	(7)	(8)
	107	19	19	0	1.195	.000	+1.195
	109	19	19	0	1.195	.000	+1.195
	110	23	23	0	1.447	.000	+1.447
	111	44	44	0	2.767	.000	+2.767
	201	95	90	5	5.660	.774	+4.886
	202	47	47	0	2.956	.000	+2.956
	203	7	7	0	.440	.000	+.440
	204	25	25	0	1.572	.000	+1.572
	205	9	9	0	.566	.000	+.566
	206	102	102	0	6.415	.000	+6.415
	207	75	75	0	4.717	.000	+4.717
	208	78	77	1	4.843	.155	+4.688
	301	41	41	0	2.579	.000	+2.579
	302	75	75	0	4.717	.000	+4.717
	303	17	17	0	1.069	.000	+1.069
	304	545	535	10	33.648	1.548	+32.100
	305	93	93	0	5.849	.000	+5.849
	306	83	83	0	5.220	.000	+5.220
	307	101	100	1	8.289	.155	+6.134
Total		2236	1590	646	100.000[a]	100.000[a]	

Segregation Index = 95.356: the percentage of Negro households which would be required to relocate in order to obtain the same block percentage distribution as non-Negro households.

SOURCE: U.S. Department of Commerce, Bureau of the Census, 1970, *Block Statistics, Milwaukee, Wisconsin, Urbanized Area,* Table 2 (Washington, D.C.: Government Printing Office).

[a] Percentages rounded to equal 100.

the nonblack distribution as the baseline and subtracting the black distribution from it discloses a dissimilarity of −10.5 percent. This figure means that block 105 has a surplus of 10.5 percent of black households (or, a shortage of 10.5 percent white households). To eliminate this difference would require 10.5 percent of the black households in this block to relocate (or, 10.5 percent of white households living elsewhere to move into this block).

A block by block comparison for the two census tracts discloses that the two tracts have few blocks which are racially mixed. To obtain an overall segregation index, or index of dissimilarity, requires only the summing of the percentage differences for those blocks in which there is a percentage surplus of black households. This sum yields an index which can be interpreted as meaning that a given percent of black households would have to relocate in order to achieve a distribution similar to the white. For the two census tracts, the summary index is 95.4. This means that 95.4 percent of all black households would have to relocate in order to achieve the same percentage distribution as whites. (If the percentages showing a shortage of whites had been summed, the index value would have been the same—95.4—and could be interpreted as meaning that 95.4 percent of all white households would have to relocate in order to achieve the same percentage distribution as blacks.)

Using this procedure for all blocks within a city, Taeuber calculated a city segregation index for each of the 109 cities in his study.

The index of dissimilarity, as illustrated here, is useful whenever it is desirable to obtain a measure of the difference between two distributions.

KEY IDEAS AND CONCEPTS

baseline distribution
dissimilarity
empirical distribution
hypothetical distribution
index
range
segregation index
standard distribution

ISSUES AND PROBLEMS

1. Define an index.
2. Define a baseline.
3. Provide an example involving the use of a hypothetical distribution as a baseline distribution.
4. Define an *index of dissimilarity*.
5. Examine Table 4-A and answer the following questions.
   a. Calculate an income dissimilarity index for white and black and other families.
   b. What percent of all black and other families would have to change their income in order to achieve the same distribution as white families?
   c. What percent of all families in the United States earned less than $5,000 in 1970?

Table 4-A. Money Income: Percentage Distribution by Income Level for Families in 1970.

MONEY INCOME	WHITE FAMILIES	NEGRO AND OTHER FAMILIES
Less than $3,000	6.7	18.2
$3,000–$4,999	8.6	16.1
$5,000–$6,999	10.1	15.5
$7,000–$9,999	18.2	18.2
$10,000–$11,999	13.0	9.4
$12,000–$14,999	15.7	9.5
$15,000 and over	27.7	13.1
Total	100.0	100.0
(*N*)	46,022,000	5,215,000

SOURCE: U.S. Bureau of the Census, *Statistical Abstracts of the United States 1974,* 95th ed. (Washington, D.C.: Government Printing Office, 1974). Adapted from Table No. 615, p. 382.

RECOMMENDED READINGS

Duncan, Otis D., and Beverly Duncan
1955 "Residential Distribution and Occupation Stratification," *American Journal of Sociology*, 60: 493–503.

Provides an interesting use of an index of dissimilarity by residence and occupation.

Duncan, Otis D., and Beverly Duncan
1957 *The Negro Population of Chicago: A Study of Residential Succession.* Chicago: University of Chicago Press.

Presents the first formal development of the index of dissimilarity.

Lazarsfeld, Paul F.
1972 "Concepts, Indices, Classification, and Typologies," pp. 9–16 in *Continuities in the Language of Social Research.* Paul F. Lazarsfeld, Ann. K. Pasanella, and Morris Rosenberg (eds.). New York: Free Press.

Provides an insightful discussion into the theory of indices. Other sections of this volume are recommended for future reading on issues of social research.

Schnore, Leo F.
1964 "Urban Structure and Suburban Selectivity," *Demography*, 1:164–176.

Illustrates the development of an index using different procedures.

Schnore, Leo F., and Philip C. Evenson
1966 "Segration in Southern Cities," *American Journal of Sociology*, 72:58–67.

Provides another application of an index of dissimilarity.

APPENDIX TO CHAPTER 4

CHARACTERISTICS OF HOUSING UNITS AND POPULATION, BY BLOCKS, 1970

The following pages contain a partial reproduction of statistical data at the block level published by the U.S. Bureau of the Census. Definitions for concepts and column headings are provided in the series of publications entitled *Block Statistics, Urbanized Areas, U.S. Department of Commerce, Bureau of the Census* (Washington, D.C.: Government Printing Office). Percents which round to less than 0.1 are not shown but are indicated as zero.

This table uses the following symbols which are defined by the census bureau as follows:

> The # next to a block number indicates the contract rent was allocated for 20 percent or more of the renter-occupied units.
>
> Three dots [. . .] indicate that the data are being withheld to avoid disclosure of information for individual housing units, or the base for an average, percentage, or ratio is too small for it to be shown.
>
> The dagger [†] identifies blocks for which tabulations are not available because of processing errors.

able 2. **Characteristics of Housing Units and Population, by Blocks: 1970**—Con. **Milwaukee County, Wis.**

[Data exclude vacant seasonal and vacant migratory housing units. For minimum base for derived figures (percent, average, etc.) and meaning of symbols, see text]

locks within ensus racts	Total population	Percent of total population				Year-round housing units				Occupied housing units														
								Units in—		Owner					Renter					1.01 or more persons per room				
		Negro	In group quarters	Under 18 years	62 years and over	Total	Lacking some or all plumbing facilities	One-unit structures	Structures of 10 or more units	Total	Lacking some or all plumbing facilities	Average number of rooms	Average value (dollars)	Percent Negro	Total	Lacking some or all plumbing facilities	Average number of rooms	Average contract rent (dollars)	Percent Negro	Total	With all plumbing facilities	One-person households	With female head of family	With roomers, boarders, or lodgers
404	201	21	–	35	17	73	–	22	–	29	–	6.2	10800	14	36	–	4.7	74	19	6	6	14	15	3
405	248	17	4	44	13	71	3	18	–	29	–	6.3	10800	17	40	3	5.0	82	10	9	9	12	14	4
406	27	–	–	30	4	13	–	4	–	1	...	...	...	–	10	–	4.5	78	–	1	1	2	2	–
407	538	18	–	44	10	189	4	42	–	55	–	6.2	10300	9	110	4	4.2	77	19	22	22	43	24	6
0	2323	82	–	49	6	690	17	222	13	170	4	6.0	7700	61	465	10	4.9	75	79	101	100	113	172	31
101	217	82	–	51	4	61	2	34	–	16	–	6.3	7000	69	39	2	5.1	69	87	8	7	5	15	1
102	273	88	–	50	6	80	2	27	–	25	1	6.2	9100	72	47	–	4.9	73	87	12	12	11	18	3
103	221	88	–	51	7	59	2	31	–	29	1	6.9	8700	72	28	1	4.8	79	75	3	3	10	21	3
104	102	87	–	40	6	36	–	8	1	8	–	5.4	...	63	22	–	5.3	87	86	3	3	4	5	3
105	28	64	–	29	14	15	–	–	12	–	–	–	–	–	15	–	3.5	77	47	1	1	8	2	–
106	8	100	–	50	–	3	...	...	...	...	...	...	...	...	...	...	...	...	...	...	...	...	...	...
107#	120	69	–	40	20	38	–	19	–	17	–	5.2	7400	41	21	–	5.0	70	67	4	4	8	7	2
201	37	54	–	27	14	17	–	1	–	–	–	–	–	–	17	–	3.9	74	53	1	1	9	1	–
202	88	77	–	41	10	33	1	8	–	2	...	...	...	...	30	1	4.5	75	80	3	3	9	8	1
203#	9	89	–	–	11	5	–	–	–	–	–	–	–	–	5	–	3.0	95	80	–	–	1	–	–
204	25	48	–	4	12	11	–	–	–	–	–	–	–	–	11	–	4.9	105	27	–	–	4	–	3
205	52	2	–	27	21	23	–	7	–	7	–	5.0	...	–	12	–	5.5	80	8	1	1	4	2	–
207	18	–	–	44	22	6	1	3	–	2	...	...	...	–	3	...	...	...	–	1	1	–	2	–
208	2	...	...	...	...	1	...	...	...	...	...	...	...	...	...	...	...	...	...	...	...	...	...	...
301	255	95	–	52	4	68	–	7	–	14	–	6.1	9800	79	49	–	5.2	75	94	16	16	8	18	3
302	162	79	–	56	3	40	–	11	–	5	–	5.0	...	60	33	–	5.2	73	82	10	10	3	19	–
303#	71	100	–	58	–	20	2	9	–	1	...	...	...	...	16	2	4.4	77	100	4	4	2	6	1
306	208	80	–	51	5	61	4	23	–	20	2	6.2	6900	55	33	2	5.3	73	91	13	13	12	12	3
307	215	92	–	54	4	58	1	17	–	11	–	6.0	...	82	41	–	5.2	70	88	12	12	7	18	4
308	212	89	–	57	3	55	2	17	–	13	–	5.6	5800	46	39	1	5.3	76	85	9	9	8	16	4
01	2319	95	1	46	7	749	35	123	32	161	2	6.0	9100	81	511	22	5.0	73	94	88	85	144	213	43
101#	201	96	7	44	10	57	–	14	–	13	–	6.0	12200	85	40	–	5.2	74	98	8	8	10	21	5
102	226	98	–	43	6	77	2	15	10	13	–	6.2	11300	77	59	2	4.7	78	100	8	8	18	28	2
103	272	95	–	44	6	80	4	10	–	24	1	5.9	9800	88	53	3	5.1	73	93	7	7	17	21	3
104	7	–	–	57	–	1	...	...	...	...	...	...	...	–	...	...	...	...	–	...	...	...	...	...
105	190	87	–	41	12	81	19	16	22	19	–	5.4	7300	68	44	8	4.0	66	75	9	8	14	14	4
106	136	98	–	47	7	45	–	9	–	14	–	5.8	6800	86	26	–	5.1	72	100	6	6	9	15	2
107	191	96	–	47	4	56	–	9	–	12	–	6.0	7500	75	41	–	5.2	70	98	10	10	9	20	2
108	199	96	–	49	7	56	1	10	–	17	–	5.8	...	71	34	1	5.4	74	97	10	9	10	9	4
201	278	99	3	43	9	94	3	9	–	19	–	6.7	...	100	64	3	5.0	76	98	7	7	16	31	9
202	310	96	–	46	10	95	1	14	–	19	1	6.1	...	84	64	–	5.6	76	95	9	9	8	28	8
203	60	100	–	67	2	17	–	2	–	–	–	–	–	–	15	–	5.3	74	100	3	3	4	8	–
205	112	88	–	43	5	40	2	7	–	6	–	7.3	...	50	33	2	4.5	65	85	3	2	16	10	3
207	68	100	–	49	3	21	1	4	–	3	...	...	...	...	15	1	4.5	72	100	5	5	5	4	1
208	1	...	...	...	...	6	1	–	–	–	–	–	–	–	1	...	...	...	...	...	...	...	...	...
209	5	100	–	20	40	2	...	...	...	...	...	...	...	...	...	...	...	...	...	...	...	...	...	...
304	2	...	...	...	...	2	...	...	...	...	...	...	...	...	...	...	...	...	...	...	...	...	...	...
305	4	...	...	...	...	1	...	...	...	...	...	...	...	...	...	...	...	...	...	...	...	...	...	...
306	57	100	–	51	4	18	–	4	–	1	...	...	...	...	17	–	5.1	78	100	2	2	5	4	–
02	2599	96	–	47	7	785	26	191	11	149	5	5.8	8100	87	580	19	4.9	72	95	111	110	133	213	52
101	61	100	–	66	2	13	–	3	–	2	...	...	...	...	8	–	6.3	94	100	4	4	–	3	–
102	153	98	–	48	6	40	3	11	–	13	–	6.0	9800	100	27	3	4.4	71	93	10	10	5	10	3
103	149	94	–	42	6	47	2	6	–	10	1	5.3	...	70	34	1	4.6	88	97	6	5	9	14	1
104	199	99	5	37	8	56	1	16	–	14	1	5.8	9800	100	41	–	5.0	78	100	6	6	7	13	6
105	286	96	–	47	7	84	4	23	–	15	1	5.9	9200	93	64	3	4.9	68	95	11	11	9	31	9
106	175	94	–	46	11	63	2	12	–	10	1	4.8	5700	60	46	1	4.6	73	94	8	8	14	16	3
107	143	99	–	42	6	49	7	16	–	5	–	6.4	...	80	38	5	4.3	58	100	9	9	14	6	3
201	28	89	–	50	–	9	–	2	–	2	...	...	...	...	7	–	4.4	72	100	2	2	4	2	–
202	175	98	–	48	11	64	2	15	–	7	–	5.7	7200	71	51	2	4.7	67	100	8	8	20	16	3
203	7	100	–	29	–	2	...	...	...	...	...	...	...	...	...	...	...	...	...	...	...	...	...	...
207	27	100	–	59	–	8	1	1	–	1	...	...	...	...	7	1	3.4	54	100	1	1	4	2	–
301#	46	100	–	52	–	13	–	2	–	2	...	...	...	...	11	–	4.5	64	100	2	2	2	6	1
302#	91	74	–	42	15	34	–	6	11	4	...	...	...	...	27	–	4.6	68	52	5	5	9	4	1
303	395	98	–	54	6	104	–	23	–	11	–	6.4	...	91	85	–	5.4	73	97	14	14	7	39	6
304	316	98	–	48	5	92	1	27	–	21	–	5.6	7000	95	66	1	4.9	72	99	11	11	12	25	5
305	168	90	–	49	8	49	2	7	–	10	1	6.7	...	70	35	1	5.1	76	91	8	8	9	11	5
306#	180	98	–	40	7	58	1	21	–	21	–	5.5	6700	95	32	1	5.3	79	100	6	6	8	13	6
103	2221	97	–	42	9	751	38	183	14	160	4	6.0	8400	94	500	28	4.6	67	96	117	117	153	142	61
105	255	100	–	50	4	75	1	33	–	14	1	6.4	7300	100	54	–	4.3	67	100	16	16	11	18	7
106	245	100	–	44	5	78	4	23	–	14	1	7.1	8400	100	54	2	5.0	69	100	12	12	22	8	5
107	240	98	–	44	9	74	2	21	–	15	–	5.5	8300	93	53	1	5.1	67	96	15	15	12	17	2
108	202	98	4	44	6	59	1	15	–	13	–	6.2	7900	92	43	1	4.7	71	98	9	9	12	14	1
201	178	94	–	46	11	68	2	19	–	14	1	5.6	7500	86	39	1	4.8	68	92	9	9	13	7	10
202	150	99	–	43	11	43	–	12	–	13	–	6.9	8800	100	28	–	5.0	71	100	8	8	5	9	5
203	30	97	–	40	–	9	–	1	–	–	–	–	–	–	8	–	3.8	66	100	3	3	2	1	3
204	179	97	–	33	6	66	5	8	–	14	1	6.1	...	100	50	4	3.9	72	92	9	9	19	16	2
205#	64	89	–	48	9	21	–	7	–	5	–	5.0	...	80	15	–	4.8	71	80	1	1	3	7	2
206	37	95	–	46	3	12	1	–	–	1	...	...	...	...	9	1	4.9	64	89	3	3	1	2	–
207#	77	100	–	51	5	28	9	3	13	2	...	...	...	...	21	9	3.9	68	100	5	5	11	5	1
301	103	88	–	26	19	45	5	10	–	9	–	5.6	8700	67	27	2	4.9	60	93	4	4	8	5	7
302	98	97	–	47	10	31	–	3	–	6	–	5.0	...	100	17	–	4.6	64	94	6	6	3	7	4
303	31	100	–	52	13	12	–	5	–	1	...	...	...	...	9	–	5.4	65	100	1	1	2	3	–
304	12	100	–	42	–	3	...	...	...	...	...	...	...	...	...	...	...	...	...	...	...	...	...	...
307	5	100	–	20	–	3	...	...	...	...	...	...	...	...	...	...	...	...	...	...	...	...	...	...
308	6	100	–	17	33	4	...	...	...	...	...	...	...	...	...	...	...	...	...	...	...	...	...	...
309	106	88	–	36	13	41	2	6	–	8	–	5.8	...	100	28	2	4.6	67	93	5	5	9	5	2
310	101	99	–	29	20	37	1	7	–	19	–	5.4	9200	100	13	–	4.4	63	92	5	5	10	9	4
311	102	98	–	36	18	42	2	8	1	10	–	6.7	5700	80	25	2	4.6	57	100	5	5	8	6	6

Table 2. **Characteristics of Housing Units and Population, by Blocks: 1970**—Con. **Milwaukee County, Wis.**

[Data exclude vacant seasonal and vacant migratory housing units. For minimum base for derived figures (percent, average, etc.) and meaning of symbols, see text]

Blocks Within Census Tracts	Total population	Percent of total population: Negro	Percent of total population: In group quarters	Percent of total population: Under 18 years	Percent of total population: 62 years and over	Year-round housing units: Total	Year-round housing units: Lacking some or all plumbing facilities	Year-round housing units: Units in— One-unit structures	Year-round housing units: Units in— Structures of 10 or more units	Occupied, Owner: Total	Occupied, Owner: Lacking some or all plumbing facilities	Occupied, Owner: Average number of rooms	Occupied, Owner: Average value (dollars)	Occupied, Owner: Percent Negro	Occupied, Renter: Total	Occupied, Renter: Lacking some or all plumbing facilities	Occupied, Renter: Average number of rooms	Occupied, Renter: Average contract rent (dollars)	Occupied, Renter: Percent Negro	1.01 or more persons per room: Total	1.01 or more persons per room: With all plumbing facilities	One-person households	With female head of family	With roomers, boarders, or lodgers
104	2731	96	1	45	8	863	54	232	14	153	8	5.9	8800	90	625	37	4.8	67	93	121	120	184	190	72
101	153	95	-	42	11	53	4	14	-	4	...	...	...	...	44	4	4.5	67	86	7	7	14	10	7
102	189	98	-	40	9	65	-	15	-	16	-	5.8	12500	94	46	-	4.6	74	96	8	8	17	15	5
103	180	98	-	47	4	54	1	22	-	8	-	6.9	...	100	44	1	4.5	74	100	4	4	16	8	1
104	226	99	-	44	6	72	4	20	-	21	2	5.6	9700	86	45	2	5.0	71	100	8	8	14	17	12
105	215	93	-	42	7	71	1	27	-	18	-	6.2	5800	78	44	1	4.8	69	91	8	8	10	16	4
106#	190	85	-	40	5	78	14	18	3	12	-	5.5	...	92	53	8	4.4	70	89	8	8	23	13	8
107#	195	97	3	51	7	53	2	10	-	10	-	6.3	...	90	37	2	5.1	72	92	12	12	5	19	6
201	11	46	-	27	9	15	7	-	-	1	...	...	...	...	6	5	1.7	62	17	1	1	6	-	-
202	3	...	...	...	...	2	...	...	...	...	...	...	...	...	...	...	...	...	...	...	...	...	...	...
203#	54	96	-	65	7	12	-	5	-	1	...	...	...	...	10	-	5.4	61	80	4	4	2	2	-
204#	87	89	-	38	16	28	3	10	-	8	3	5.9	...	63	17	-	4.9	58	88	4	4	4	6	7
205	168	100	-	48	9	53	-	15	-	6	-	5.0	...	100	41	-	4.5	62	100	9	9	9	12	1
206	128	98	-	52	11	34	2	8	-	6	-	5.3	...	100	25	2	5.2	65	96	5	5	5	6	1
207	222	97	6	48	5	52	4	16	-	10	-	6.4	6200	100	39	4	5.4	62	97	12	12	6	13	6
301	142	94	-	40	14	43	-	14	-	6	-	6.7	...	67	34	-	5.6	69	94	2	2	6	12	3
302	42	74	-	14	17	24	1	1	11	1	...	...	...	...	20	1	3.8	71	75	-	-	9	1	1
303	17	88	-	41	24	6	-	3	-	1	...	...	...	...	4	...	...	...	...	1	1	1	2	1
304	247	98	-	51	6	73	1	11	-	9	-	5.4	...	100	58	-	4.9	60	98	15	15	16	22	6
305#	164	98	-	45	9	49	8	14	-	7	1	6.1	...	100	39	7	4.8	64	92	8	7	18	8	2
307	98	100	-	49	15	26	2	7	-	8	2	5.4	6200	100	17	-	5.1	61	100	5	5	2	7	1
105	2176	90	3	44	10	699	63	191	26	131	2	6.4	8300	73	506	54	4.7	72	88	82	80	177	144	43
101	198	88	4	47	8	48	-	12	4	17	-	6.4	11400	82	27	-	5.5	84	74	7	7	10	13	5
102#	210	78	9	32	20	79	7	10	-	9	1	7.0	...	67	65	6	3.9	71	79	6	6	30	13	4
103	133	89	4	56	10	47	-	7	-	7	-	5.0	...	57	32	-	4.6	70	75	7	7	16	8	4
104	13	77	-	-	23	10	4	1	-	1	...	...	...	...	9	4	4.8	72	67	-	-	7	-	-
105	215	92	-	46	6	67	3	15	6	15	-	6.4	7200	73	45	3	4.5	90	96	8	7	11	13	2
106	268	87	10	45	14	76	3	17	-	14	-	7.1	10300	57	56	2	5.0	76	88	8	7	12	22	3
107	128	80	6	43	10	39	7	17	1	9	-	6.4	6200	44	27	6	4.1	64	85	5	5	9	10	5
201	117	91	-	47	9	40	1	13	1	8	-	6.4	7100	63	29	1	5.3	80	86	5	5	9	8	4
202	8	75	-	-	-	6	1	-	-	-	-	-	-	-	6	1	3.8	70	83	-	-	4	-	1
203	7	100	-	-	-	5	-	2	-	1	...	...	...	...	2	...	...	...	...	...	...	...	...	...
204	177	95	-	36	15	73	17	23	2	16	-	6.4	8400	88	48	15	4.2	65	92	6	6	21	15	5
205	267	98	-	55	4	70	3	29	-	8	-	5.6	6100	75	59	2	5.2	69	98	10	10	11	17	2
206	165	95	-	38	13	64	14	18	12	12	1	6.3	7300	83	47	11	4.5	65	94	4	4	18	11	5
207	182	99	-	50	7	48	3	16	-	8	-	6.0	...	86	39	3	4.8	63	97	12	12	14	9	2
208	88	98	8	39	11	27	-	11	-	6	-	6.8	9200	67	15	-	5.7	73	100	3	3	3	5	1
106	2818	68	2	48	7	769	28	263	4	207	3	6.0	8100	45	506	23	5.0	74	72	126	123	126	163	29
101	162	47	-	37	14	60	3	21	2	22	-	5.5	7400	5	36	3	4.4	72	67	5	4	12	9	1
103	194	82	7	55	3	43	1	15	-	10	1	6.1	8000	50	30	-	5.4	77	87	9	9	7	9	1
104	178	95	-	56	6	42	-	15	-	9	-	6.6	13500	67	29	-	5.6	80	100	9	9	3	15	2
105	140	89	4	42	6	50	5	6	-	9	-	7.0	...	56	33	5	4.7	76	91	3	3	13	12	1
106	167	78	2	53	8	38	2	18	-	17	-	6.7	9800	82	18	2	5.6	75	72	5	5	6	11	1
107	197	53	-	46	9	61	1	23	-	18	1	6.0	8200	33	34	-	5.4	78	56	6	6	8	5	2
108	213	21	-	39	13	64	2	24	2	20	-	6.1	8000	20	42	2	4.8	80	17	6	6	12	11	3
201	97	44	7	46	10	33	-	15	-	10	-	5.4	6200	30	18	-	5.6	75	50	2	2	8	7	-
202	219	84	-	48	5	53	4	23	-	12	-	5.6	7800	50	39	3	4.8	74	95	12	12	5	7	4
203	167	69	-	53	2	48	-	31	-	12	-	5.4	9100	67	33	-	4.7	79	70	7	7	8	19	2
204	174	86	-	45	5	54	2	21	-	12	1	5.6	4000	58	39	1	5.2	73	95	11	10	11	18	3
205	200	69	1	56	3	47	-	12	-	17	-	5.2	5500	47	29	-	4.7	71	76	14	14	10	7	2
206	180	46	6	47	8	40	2	11	-	12	-	7.2	8100	33	24	2	4.8	77	50	10	9	4	3	2
207	150	46	-	45	1	42	5	12	-	10	-	6.7	...	40	31	4	4.8	76	42	4	4	6	9	3
208#	185	80	-	52	8	39	-	12	-	10	-	6.4	9800	60	25	-	5.2	69	92	11	11	5	8	-
209	195	93	-	46	5	55	1	4	-	7	-	5.9	...	100	46	1	4.8	65	91	12	12	8	13	2
107	2897	14	-	35	12	1007	63	258	11	297	11	5.6	8600	7	639	48	4.7	74	12	95	94	217	122	45
101	209	1	-	24	14	80	5	12	-	20	1	5.3	11700	-	57	4	4.5	83	2	2	2	14	7	5
102	222	6	-	27	15	96	5	25	-	26	2	5.3	9800	8	59	2	4.7	70	-	4	4	26	9	5
103	252	3	-	45	9	83	6	25	-	24	1	5.2	8300	4	53	5	4.7	67	2	11	11	19	14	1
104	230	-	-	29	16	85	4	21	-	28	1	5.5	9300	-	48	2	4.4	70	-	6	6	18	7	2
105	248	4	-	38	11	79	3	33	-	30	1	5.7	6900	-	43	2	5.0	68	5	8	8	15	10	2
106	211	28	-	43	8	67	3	22	-	21	-	6.1	5700	14	41	3	4.8	65	22	7	7	12	9	-
201	225	34	2	38	13	71	3	17	-	22	-	5.6	8800	9	45	3	5.2	72	31	10	10	16	12	1
202#	177	33	-	37	10	58	10	12	-	5	-	8.0	...	20	50	9	4.0	71	26	8	8	16	5	6
203#	113	26	-	43	8	34	-	6	-	8	-	6.0	...	38	25	...	5.2	78	16	4	4	5	5	5
204	92	10	-	37	17	36	2	12	-	13	-	6.4	8100	15	17	2	4.6	70	-	3	3	8	4	2
205	145	5	-	29	10	60	2	10	-	16	1	4.9	...	6	43	1	4.4	75	5	-	-	19	8	1
206	166	-	-	28	12	63	-	13	-	22	-	5.3	7400	-	37	-	5.0	79	-	5	5	9	8	5
301	5	-	-	-	40	2	...	...	...	...	...	...	...	-	...	...	...	...	-	...	...	...	...	...
305#	46	-	-	39	4	17	-	7	-	6	-	5.0	-	-	9	-	4.7	77	-	2	2	4	1	2
306	65	9	-	37	17	22	1	6	-	8	1	5.5	...	13	13	-	4.4	91	8	2	2	4	3	1
307#	167	37	-	38	14	57	13	13	11	10	1	6.0	...	40	45	12	4.1	74	31	9	8	21	5	4
308	108	15	-	34	9	35	3	3	-	11	-	5.5	...	-	20	2	5.1	80	15	6	6	5	5	-
309	216	26	-	40	9	62	3	19	-	25	2	5.6	7600	8	34	1	4.9	79	32	8	8	6	10	3
108	2977	1	-	17	18	1684	149	150	905	194	7	5.9	13000	-	1380	124	3.1	102	1	65	60	833	113	88
101	1	...	...	...	...	1	...	...	...	...	...	...	...	...	...	...	...	...	...	...	...	...	...	...
102	56	-	-	2	36	49	-	1	48	-	-	-	-	-	47	-	2.6	91	-	-	-	38	2	-
103	35	-	-	-	26	23	1	1	12	2	...	...	...	-	20	1	3.3	92	-	-	-	10	-	1
104	7	-	-	14	57	3	...	...	...	...	...	...	...	-	...	...	...	...	-	...	...	...	...	...
106	11	-	-	36	27	4	...	...	...	...	...	...	...	-	...	...	...	...	-	...	...	...	...	...
107	57	-	-	33	11	20	-	6	-	7	-	6.9	...	-	12	-	5.8	83	-	1	1	2	2	-
109	62	-	-	36	15	21	3	12	-	9	-	5.6	13200	-	10	3	4.5	71	-	3	3	5	3	-
110	82	-	-	44	16	23	-	7	-	11	-	5.8	11600	-	12	-	5.8	83	-	3	3	4	1	-
111	155	-	-	36	14	44	2	13	-	18	1	6.8	10300	-	26	1	5.2	99	-	4	4	7	7	2
201	170	4	-	12	7	102	2	6	65	5	-	6.4	...	-	90	2	3.2	129	6	2	2	46	8	3
202	131	-	-	29	20	48	1	8	-	20	-	5.7	12700	-	27	-	4.3	95	-	5	5	13	6	1
203	20	-	-	25	30	7	1	2	-	1	...	...	...	-	6	1	4.7	105	-	-	-	2	-	-

BLOCK STATISTICS MILWAUKEE URBANIZED AREA WIS.—39

Table 2. **Characteristics of Housing Units and Population, by Blocks: 1970**—Con. **Milwaukee County, Wis.**

[Data exclude vacant seasonal and vacant migratory housing units. For minimum base for derived figures (percent, average, etc.) and meaning of symbols, see text]

Blocks within census tracts	Total population	Percent of total population: Negro	In group quarters	Under 18 years	62 years and over	Year-round housing units: Total	Lacking some or all plumbing facilities	Units in—: One-unit structures	Structures of 10 or more units	Occupied housing units: Owner: Total	Lacking some or all plumbing facilities	Average number of rooms	Average value (dollars)	Percent Negro	Renter: Total	Lacking some or all plumbing facilities	Average number of rooms	Average contract rent (dollars)	Percent Negro	1.01 or more persons per room: Total	With all plumbing facilities	One-person households	With female head of family	With roomers, boarders, or lodgers
204	97	-	-	36	7	27	-	9	1	10	-	6.1	15000	-	15	-	6.3	112	-	-	-	3	6	5
205	30	-	13	40	-	9	-	1	-	-	-	-	-	-	9	-	4.4	83	-	1	1	5	-	-
206	159	-	-	6	9	107	26	2	45	2	...	...	...	-	100	21	2.8	110	-	1	1	63	4	3
207	122	-	-	6	34	78	3	4	38	3	...	...	...	-	72	3	4.1	110	-	-	-	36	6	1
208	123	1	-	15	29	89	13	7	59	9	-	5.4	...	-	69	10	3.3	95	1	3	3	55	1	1
301	95	-	-	16	8	46	1	3	16	9	-	6.4	...	-	32	1	3.5	110	-	1	1	13	3	5
302	167	-	-	25	11	82	10	7	35	16	-	6.5	12900	-	59	5	3.3	105	-	6	6	36	5	5
303#	50	-	-	32	16	19	1	13	-	11	1	6.5	13500	-	6	-	6.3	87	-	-	-	5	1	1
304	860	2	-	9	24	584	36	29	407	34	4	5.3	12700	-	511	30	2.5	105	2	23	21	330	38	52
305	176	-	-	21	7	95	2	5	54	8	-	5.0	...	-	84	2	2.8	87	-	3	3	53	6	2
306	143	-	-	9	16	95	18	9	63	14	-	5.5	13300	-	69	17	3.0	98	-	2	2	48	4	4
307	168	1	-	14	20	108	28	4	62	3	...	...	...	...	98	27	2.9	82	1	7	4	57	10	2
109	5061	1	8	5	32	3247	244	101	2658	155	3	5.7	36500	-	2894	221	3.3	157	1	54	40	1839	130	90
102	79	1	-	9	11	44	-	1	21	3	...	...	...	...	38	-	5.1	157	-	-	-	16	4	3
103	118	-	-	11	30	66	3	4	40	5	1	5.2	...	-	60	2	3.6	93	-	1	1	35	2	-
104	48	2	17	10	6	20	-	5	-	4	...	...	...	...	16	-	4.2	141	6	-	-	11	1	5
105	34	-	-	18	27	13	-	4	-	6	-	9.5	...	-	7	-	4.0	142	-	-	-	3	2	1
106	35	-	-	9	37	15	-	10	-	4	...	...	...	-	9	-	7.0	223	-	-	-	4	-	1
107	49	-	-	22	12	18	-	7	-	6	-	7.8	35500	-	11	-	5.0	127	-	-	-	4	1	1
108	168	2	-	4	23	114	4	4	104	3	...	...	...	...	110	4	3.3	163	2	-	-	69	3	4
109	81	1	-	5	14	47	-	-	30	1	...	...	...	...	46	-	4.4	202	2	1	1	24	3	4
110	57	-	-	25	25	25	1	2	3	3	...	...	...	-	20	-	4.4	180	-	-	-	4	1	2
111	38	-	-	34	16	14	-	7	-	4	...	...	...	-	9	-	6.3	322	-	-	-	2	-	-
112	27	-	-	-	52	18	-	3	-	7	-	7.6	...	-	9	-	6.1	287	-	-	-	7	2	-
113	39	-	-	-	44	24	-	2	4	3	...	...	...	-	19	-	5.7	184	-	-	-	8	1	2
114	169	3	4	4	18	100	-	3	82	4	...	...	...	...	94	-	4.1	172	4	-	-	48	5	8
115	39	-	15	28	13	13	4	5	-	2	...	...	...	-	11	4	4.6	89	-	-	-	6	-	-
116	614	-	-	2	45	429	4	-	386	3	...	...	...	-	391	4	4.2	192	-	1	1	218	23	5
117	98	-	-	32	13	40	4	2	4	4	...	...	...	-	35	4	4.3	104	-	-	-	12	6	1
118	294	-	-	6	19	195	35	4	163	4	...	...	...	-	163	29	3.2	129	-	2	2	105	14	6
119	284	2	45	5	56	92	-	2	63	3	...	...	...	...	82	-	4.3	152	-	-	-	33	6	1
120	348	1	13	1	33	248	16	3	218	3	...	...	...	...	230	15	2.8	144	-	2	1	174	7	2
121	633	2	-	2	13	521	143	8	480	5	-	2.6	...	-	467	135	2.1	118	2	29	17	341	13	19
122	141	-	65	1	60	36	10	2	12	3	...	...	...	-	29	9	3.2	98	-	2	1	20	-	2
123	145	-	-	1	11	125	11	1	111	3	...	...	...	-	109	8	1.8	134	-	10	10	82	2	4
124	18	-	-	6	-	13	-	-	8	-	-	-	-	-	12	-	1.8	136	-	1	1	6	-	-
901	1363	2	2	2	36	993	6	17	929	68	-	4.7	-	-	879	6	3.2	173	2	5	5	600	34	19
904	142	1	65	7	66	24	3	5	-	4	...	...	...	...	18	1	4.8	205	-	-	-	7	-	-
110	4037	2	9	10	22	2426	140	157	1748	151	3	5.7	15000	1	2130	111	2.8	97	2	80	73	1423	105	92
101	499	2	-	9	8	340	6	31	275	19	-	5.5	14700	-	294	5	2.6	119	2	12	12	182	16	4
102	103	-	-	25	18	38	1	23	-	13	-	5.5	10500	-	25	1	4.4	72	-	3	3	8	6	4
103	209	2	4	8	20	140	16	12	66	3	...	...	...	...	121	8	3.4	95	3	5	3	72	7	1
104	512	1	-	14	49	340	4	18	255	19	1	5.3	...	-	311	2	3.3	61	1	4	4	237	14	8
105	193	1	-	18	21	111	6	7	62	11	1	5.5	...	-	95	4	3.2	83	1	5	4	60	7	3
106	130	-	6	19	12	65	24	4	18	13	-	5.8	...	-	45	18	3.2	76	-	1	-	25	6	3
107	417	2	-	24	12	198	6	23	103	34	-	5.7	11800	-	159	6	2.8	98	3	15	14	91	14	5
201	204	2	-	7	25	134	21	7	78	8	-	5.9	9200	-	122	18	2.8	90	3	5	5	82	6	4
202	251	1	-	4	21	195	6	4	165	4	...	...	...	...	183	6	2.5	95	1	-	-	135	6	-
203	147	6	-	6	15	113	3	6	83	5	1	4.8	...	-	91	1	2.7	93	8	1	1	60	2	15
204	225	3	4	9	13	165	3	7	148	4	...	...	...	...	148	3	2.3	86	4	7	7	114	5	11
205	558	1	40	3	12	246	15	9	206	10	-	7.9	...	-	221	14	2.6	120	3	3	3	144	10	15
206	589	2	21	2	32	341	29	6	289	8	-	4.3	...	-	315	25	2.3	116	2	19	17	213	6	19
111	2099	1	9	14	28	1302	365	75	732	93	7	5.5	11700	-	1061	300	2.6	89	1	62	47	750	65	35
101	113	-	-	14	20	61	4	13	12	19	2	5.8	9700	-	37	2	3.2	97	-	2	1	23	6	4
102	144	1	-	35	11	61	4	7	2	16	1	5.5	8700	-	40	3	3.9	79	3	6	5	22	5	3
103	151	-	5	28	14	62	10	7	-	11	1	5.2	...	-	44	5	4.5	83	-	2	2	16	9	1
105	158	3	-	12	15	99	45	3	61	11	1	5.1	...	-	78	38	2.5	82	3	10	5	48	7	8
106	160	3	-	18	14	68	6	6	29	14	-	6.6	...	-	52	6	3.6	123	4	3	3	18	8	7
107	196	1	-	29	15	105	32	12	42	10	1	5.0	...	-	80	24	2.8	73	-	10	9	49	9	5
108	200	2	-	19	19	137	59	9	56	4	...	...	...	...	116	50	2.4	65	3	9	5	85	8	1
201	38	3	-	13	21	35	15	1	30	-	-	-	-	-	26	11	2.3	68	4	2	2	20	-	-
202	25	-	8	24	-	13	7	1	-	-	-	-	-	-	12	6	2.4	76	-	2	1	7	-	-
203	110	1	-	5	24	115	57	2	67	-	-	-	-	-	93	46	1.6	63	1	1	1	80	1	-
204	124	-	44	-	40	65	7	6	45	3	...	...	...	-	53	5	2.3	75	-	1	1	45	1	2
206#	217	-	9	6	26	173	53	-	145	1	...	...	...	-	161	45	1.7	67	-	8	8	136	5	1
207	137	-	7	3	24	90	46	6	57	2	...	...	...	-	84	43	2.7	83	-	2	2	55	1	3
208	156	-	56	-	75	55	11	-	34	1	...	...	...	-	49	9	2.4	91	-	3	2	37	1	-
209	170	-	-	3	73	163	9	2	152	1	...	...	...	-	136	7	2.9	170	-	1	-	109	4	-
112	2473	-	-	26	19	1109	101	207	170	225	12	5.4	8700	-	808	60	4.2	65	1	48	44	401	122	43
101	307	2	-	8	64	241	14	9	159	8	3	5.5	...	-	221	7	3.1	48	2	2	1	187	7	3
102	180	-	-	24	16	81	8	21	-	22	1	5.0	8200	-	51	3	4.6	75	-	4	4	18	11	5
103	93	-	-	25	12	43	5	8	-	10	-	4.6	...	-	28	4	4.2	70	-	3	3	10	6	2
104	380	-	-	31	11	159	11	32	-	31	2	5.2	6900	-	111	4	4.5	72	-	10	9	44	17	13
105	209	-	-	25	16	79	4	18	-	14	-	5.9	...	-	64	4	4.5	75	-	7	7	21	8	4
106	212	-	-	23	12	95	19	15	-	20	2	4.7	...	-	67	12	4.6	66	-	4	3	25	9	3
107	119	-	4	29	13	41	3	13	-	13	-	5.5	6200	-	26	3	5.0	77	-	2	1	7	9	5
201	82	-	-	32	16	33	1	7	-	12	1	5.8	8800	-	19	-	4.3	77	-	1	1	7	5	-
202	134	-	-	34	13	43	3	11	-	12	1	4.9	8200	-	31	2	5.3	88	-	3	3	6	7	2
203	94	-	-	33	11	34	1	11	-	12	-	5.6	10500	-	21	1	4.6	69	-	1	1	9	7	-
204	127	-	5	28	6	55	5	4	-	8	-	5.4	-	-	40	3	4.3	64	-	1	1	14	7	3
207	60	-	-	22	13	29	7	10	-	8	-	5.9	...	-	19	5	3.9	67	-	-	-	11	5	-
208	29	-	-	45	14	20	15	2	11	1	...	...	...	-	13	9	2.6	45	-	1	1	9	2	-
301	30	-	-	10	20	13	-	5	-	4	...	...	...	-	9	-	4.6	59	-	-	-	5	1	-
302	138	-	-	33	12	43	-	14	-	18	-	5.8	10000	-	24	-	5.0	70	-	4	4	4	8	1

5

STANDARDIZATION AS A NORMING TECHNIQUE FOR GROUP COMPARISONS: FAMILY STABILITY OF U.S. WHITES AND BLACKS

GENERAL ISSUE

As already mentioned, a fundamental process in scientific research is the comparison of phenomena. Comparisons can be made in many ways. Phenomena can be compared according to a common dimension, as we saw earlier when preliterate societies were compared as to their sexual permissiveness. They can be compared with themselves over time, as was done in the study of changing Japanese illegitimacy rates. They also can be compared to a standard, as in the case of actual urban racial distributions being compared to the expected distribution.

These types of comparisons often require a researcher to use statistical procedures to make the phenomena comparable to one another. For instance, comparing the characteristics of two populations, where one is larger than the other, would be difficult unless the two were normed to a common base. Converting the characteristics of both populations to percentages would alleviate this difficulty because the sizes of both would then be normed to a common base of one hundred.

Norming is often accomplished by *subclassification.* In subclassification, a researcher divides a population into a series of subgroups, and then calculates measures for each. For instance, a population of women may be subclassified by age and marital status. The number of births that are illegitimate in each age group can then be compared to the number of unmarried women in the group. In this case, the resulting data are known as age-specific illegitimate birth rates.

In addition to permitting internal comparisons, subclassification often reveals whether concealed factors are operating. For example, Japan's illegitimate birth rate fell between 1940 and 1964, but one could not know from this summary measure whether the decline resulted from a decline in illegitimate fertility or a change in the proportion of married and unmarried women until births were subclassified for both types. Subclassification revealed whether or not a concealed factor was operating.

Although there are many advantages to norming through subclassification, these advantages come at the expense of convenience, because there is no longer a single summary measure. For instance, the data may indicate a different *age-specific* illegitimate birth rate for each of several age groups in a population. Under many conditions, however, researchers desire to compare two or more populations using a single summary measure rather than a series of subgroup measures. For example, researchers often wish to calculate and compare single measures for rates of fertility, marriage, crime, or suicide for entire societies, rather than compare the subgroup measures for each society. However, if they compare unadjusted *crude rates* (rates which ignore subgroup differences), there is the possibility that concealed factors will lead them to false inferences.

In order to eliminate concealed factors and simultaneously compare populations using summary measures, researchers often norm the populations on subgroup differences. By adjusting for unwanted differences, the effects of these are removed.

The procedure for norming populations on subgroup differences is known as *standardization.* This procedure has found frequent use among demographers interested in comparing population properties of total societies and among economists calculating rates of inflation. Standardization is useful whenever two objects possess subgroup differences which have an undesirable influence on the calculation of an overall summary measure.

This chapter illustrates the usefulness of standardization as a procedure for determining family stability patterns among American whites and blacks from the 1800s to the present.

THEORETICAL PROBLEM

In their effort to understand stratification, social mobility, and the development of social classes, social scientists have frequently researched the relationship between family structure and social inequality. The importance of this relationship was highlighted by a controversial 1965 report of the Department of Labor.* This study, which reported important differences between the family structures of whites and blacks, concluded that:

* *The Negro Family: The Case for National Action.* U.S. Department of Labor, Office of Policy Planning and Research (Washington, D.C.: Government Printing Office, 1965).

1. black families were less stable than white,
2. black families were becoming increasingly unstable, and
3. black-family instability was a major cause of the economic gap between blacks and whites.

Not all social scientists agreed with these conclusions.

Some social scientists believed that the Department of Labor used an unwarranted definition of family stability. Others believed that social inequality caused family instability and not, as the report concluded, that family instability caused social inequality. Still others believed that the report's conclusions were inadequately supported by the data.

To resolve some of these issues, Reynolds Farley and Albert Hermalin examined census data published since 1890. Their objectives were to determine: (1) if there were in fact any differences in family stability between blacks and whites, (2) if there was evidence of change between 1890 and 1969, and (3) if any changes could be explained through differences in the population composition of these two groups. Their study was published in 1971.*

Defining and Measuring Family Stability

By systematically searching the literature, Farley and Hermalin discovered that social scientists conceptualized and measured family stability in different ways. Thus, there was no consensus regarding the concept's theoretical meaning or about the procedures of measurement. Family stability appeared to be a *multidimensional concept* involving four dimensions: (1) the extent and stability of marriages, (2) the living arrangements of adults, (3) the living arrangements for children, and (4) the frequency of illegitimate births. To operationalize these dimensions, Farley and Hermalin constructed a series of measures employing census data.

Dimension of Family Stability	*Measure*
Extent and stability of marriage	Percent married
	Percent divorced
	Percent single
	Percent widowed
Living arrangements of adults	Percent spouses living together
Living arrangements of children	Percent children living with both parents
Extent of illegitimacy	Illegitimate birth rate

* Reynolds Farley and Albert I. Hermalin, "Family Stability: A Comparison of Trends Between Blacks and Whites," *American Sociological Review*, 36(1971):1–17.

Data Analysis

Comparing blacks and whites along the above dimensions for different years posed special problems for Farley and Hermalin. Since the measures they sought to use were either percentages or rates, changes from year to year in either the numerator or denominator would influence the measure. Thus, a decline in the percent married from one year to the next might be due to a decrease in the proportion of persons eligible for marriage, or to a true decline in the proportion of eligible persons marrying.

Problems of this sort plagued all their measures. Changes in the age or sex composition of blacks or whites could influence each of the measures independently of any true changes in behaviors. The calculation of crude measures unadjusted for changes in age and sex composition would conceal the influence of changes in important population subgroupings.

One solution would have been to subclassify the population by age and sex, and examine measures calculated for each subgroup. However, the number of internal and cross-group comparisons required would have been intolerably large. Consequently, Farley and Hermalin decided to standardize the white and black distributions on age and sex composition. In this manner, they sought to eliminate any concealed influence of age and sex on their rates.

Farley and Hermalin chose to standardize all data to the age and sex distribution of the 1960 U.S. population. Thus, they presented data for each year as if the two groups had the same age and sex distribution as the total 1960 population. Any reported racial differences in percentages of married spouses living together, children living with both parents, and illegitimate birth rates, therefore, would not result from variations in the age or sex composition of the two groups.

Table 5-1 provides the standardized distribution of marital status for white and black women for selected years from 1890 to 1969. By examining black and white data for each marital category, the following observations may be made:

Table 5-1. Percentage Distribution of Black (*B*) and White (*W*) Women, Age Fifteen and Over—by Current Marital Status, for Selected Years, 1890–1969.

	SINGLE		MARRIED		WIDOWED		DIVORCED	
YEAR	*B*	*W*	*B*	*W*	*B*	*W*	*B*	*W*
1890	18	23	56	60	25	17	1	—
1910	17	23	57	60	25	16	1	1
1930	16	23	56	61	26	15	2	1
1950[a]	16	19	61	66	20	13	3	2
1969	20	17	58	68	17	12	5	3

SOURCE: Farley and Hermalin, "Family Stability," page 3, Table 1.
[a] 1950 data refer to all nonwhites.

5.1 STANDARDIZING A POPULATION

Table A presents the crude death rates for three southern states: South Carolina, Georgia, and Florida. It is evident that the crude death rate is lowest in South Carolina and highest in Florida. Since death is age-linked, however, it is possible that these data are concealing important differences in age composition in these states and that, in fact, Florida is not as "unhealthy" as these data suggest.

Table A. Death Rates: South Carolina, Georgia, Florida, 1971.

STATE	POPULATION	TOTAL DEATHS	DEATH RATE[a]
S. Carolina	2,625,624	22,819	869
Georgia	4,664,057	41,706	894
Florida	7,040,457	75,504	1,072

SOURCE: Based on population data provided by the Bureau of the Census (1970) and U.S. Department of Health, Education and Welfare, *Vital Statistics of the United States:* 1971, Vol. II, Table 1–12.
[a] Death rate per 100,000.

Table B presents the *age-specific death rates* for South Carolina and Florida. This table reflects some fascinating findings. By comparing the age-specific death rates it can be observed that, for each subgrouping, Florida has a *lower* death rate than South Carolina. Yet, the crude death rate for Florida is *higher* than South Carolina's.

Table B. Age-Specific Death Rates for South Carolina and Florida, 1971.

	FLORIDA			SOUTH CAROLINA		
AGE	Population	Deaths	Death Rate	Population	Deaths	Death Rate
Under 5	517,403	2,804	542	236,700	1,335	564
5–19	1,902,050	1,426	75	852,251	690	81
20–44	2,069,261	5,049	244	849,547	2,447	288
45–64	1,523,132	18,415	1,209	492,672	7,267	1,475
65+	1,028,611	47,810	4,648	194,454	11,080	5,698
	7,040,457	75,504	1,072	2,625,624	22,819	869

This anomaly is caused by the different age compositions of Florida and South Carolina. Florida has a much higher proportion of its population in the older age brackets than South Carolina. Since the death rate is highest for these groups, the result is a higher crude death rate. The difference in population proportions is presented in Table C.

Table C. Proportional Distribution of Population: Florida and South Carolina, 1971.

AGE	FLORIDA		SOUTH CAROLINA	
	Population	Proportion	Population	Proportion
Under 5	517,403	.074	236,700	.090
5–19	1,902,050	.270	852,251	.325
20–44	2,069,261	.294	849,547	.323
45–64	1,523,132	.216	492,672	.188
65+	1,028,611	.146	194,454	.074
Total	7,040,457	1.000	2,625,624	1.000

To remove the effects of differences in the age composition of Florida and South Carolina, it is necessary to calculate death rates as if the two states had identical age distributions. This is accomplished by adopting one of the state populations as the standard, and calculating a hypothetical death rate as if the remaining state had the same population distribution. The statistical procedure consists of linking the death rate of one state to the age composition of the other. Table D reflects this procedure.

The data indicate that if South Carolina had the same age distribution as Florida, the death rate would have been 1,300 instead of 869. In other words, the initial lower death rate of South Carolina was the result of a younger population rather than a true difference in health. Through standardization, the concealed factor of age distribution was eliminated.

Table D. Standardized South Carolina Death Rate, 1971.

AGE	FLORIDA POPULATION AS THE STANDARD POPULATION	SOUTH CAROLINA DEATH RATES	EXPECTED DEATHS (A) × (B)/100,000
	(A)	(B)	(C)
Under 5	517,403	564	2,918
5–19	1,902,050	81	1,541
20–44	2,069,261	288	5,959
45–64	1,523,132	1,475	22,466
65+	1,028,611	5,698	58,610
Total	7,040,457		91,494

$$\text{Standardized S. Carolina Death Rate} = \frac{91{,}494}{7{,}040{,}457} \times 100{,}000 = 1300$$

1. The percentage of black women who are single steadily decreased from 1890 to 1950 but showed a sharp increase in 1969. The percentage of white women who are single, however, has steadily decreased since 1890.
2. The percentage of black women who are married remained at approximately the same level from 1890 to 1930 but showed an increase in 1950 and then a decrease in 1969.
3. The percentage of black women who are widowed decreased since 1930. However, the percentage of white women who are widowed has steadily decreased since 1890.
4. The percentage of women who are divorced has increased for both black and white women in recent decades.

Some conclusions with respect to family stability can be drawn from these data. First, there are racial differences for each year on all measures. White families show greater stability than black families. Second, although the percentage differences are meaningful, the percentage differences exceed 7 percent only in the case of widows. Third, the experience of the majority of black women is similar to the experience of the majority of white women.

It is difficult, however, to draw conclusions about these measures with respect to racial trends in family stability. Some measures indicate greater instability while other measures indicate greater stability. In terms of marriages and related marital states, therefore, it is probably best to withhold judgment concerning any trends.

Table 5-2 presents the standardized distribution of currently married adults living with a spouse in 1960, 1964, and 1969. The data in this table indicate that white men and women who are currently married are more likely to be living with their spouse than are currently married blacks. Racial differences are present for each year. With respect to trends, only black women indicate any change, the percentage of black women living with spouses having decreased. Thus, for this measure there is some evidence of increased family instability. This conclusion is supported by data in Table 5-3. The latter shows that the percentage of nonwhite women

Table 5-2. Percentage of Currently Married Adults Who Had a Spouse Present, 1960, 1964, 1969.

	MEN		WOMEN	
YEAR	Black	White	Black	White
1960[a]	85	96	80	95
1964	88	97	78	96
1969	86	97	77	96

SOURCE: Farley and Hermalin, "Family Stability," p. 4, Table 2.
[a] Data refer to all nonwhites.

Table 5-3. Percentage of Females (25 to 64 Years Old) Who Are Family Heads—by Race for 1950, 1960, 1969.

RACE	1950	1960	1964
White	6	6	7
Nonwhite[a]	13	16	22

SOURCE: Farley and Hermalin, "Family Stability," p. 7, Table 4.
[a] Data unavailable for blacks only.

serving as primary heads of households increased markedly from 1950 to 1964, while there was only a slight increase among whites. Table 5-4 presents the distribution of children under seventeen living with both parents, one parent only, or neither parent for 1960 and 1968. Racial

Table 5-4. Distribution of Children Seventeen Years of Age and Under by Living Arrangements for 1960 and 1968 in Percentages.

LIVING ARRANGEMENTS	1960		1968	
	Whites	Nonwhites	Whites	Nonwhites
	(A)	(B)	(C)	(D)
Both parents	90	66	90	60
One parent	7	22	8	30
Neither	3	12	2	10
Total	100	100	100	100

SOURCE: Farley and Hermain, "Family Stability," p. 14, Table 8.

differences are evident in all categories. For 1960 and 1968, white children were more likely to be living with both parents than were nonwhite. Further, there was evidence of a downward trend among nonwhite children (from 66 percent in 1960 to 60 percent in 1968).

Table 5-5 shows the white and nonwhite illegitimate birth rates for 1940, 1950, 1960, and 1968. The data indicate that the illegitimate birth rate for both groups has been increasing since 1940. There was a greater change in the white rate

$$\left(\frac{1968}{1940} \times 100 = \frac{53}{19} \times 100 = 279\%\right)$$

than the nonwhite

$$\left(\frac{312}{168} \times 100 = 186\%\right).$$

There remain, however, large differences in the rates between nonwhites and whites.

Table 5-5. White and Nonwhite Illegitimate Birth Rates: 1940, 1950, 1960, 1968.

YEAR	WHITE[a]	NONWHITE[a]
1940	19	168
1950	18	180
1960	23	216
1968	53	312

SOURCE: Farley and Hermalin, "Family Stability," p. 8, Table 5.
[a] Illegitimate birth rate per 1,000 total births.

SUMMARY AND CONCLUSIONS

Data provided by Farley and Hermalin have permitted a number of comparisons between blacks and whites on several measures of family stability for recent and earlier years. Comparisons such as these can be complicated, since blacks and whites differ in ways other than as to family stability. Nevertheless, the data in this chapter eliminated one reason such comparisons are complicated. All data were based on the proportional age and sex distribution of the 1960 population. In this way, differences due to the changing compositions of the two groups, with respect to age and sex, were eliminated. The data, therefore, must be explained in terms of factors other than age and sex composition.

With respect to family stability and racial differences, Farley and Hermalin drew these conclusions:

1. There are racial differences in each of the family stability dimensions examined. In each case, a higher percent of whites was in a status considered indicative of family stability. However, among both whites and blacks, a larger percentage of the total families was stable than unstable.
2. The data on trends were mixed. On some measures, both whites and blacks showed evidence of increased instability.
3. The causal relationship between family stability and social inequality could not be answered conclusively by currently available data. More extensive research was required, but family stability by itself did appear to go far in accounting for racial inequality.

KEY IDEAS AND CONCEPTS

age-specific
concealed influence
cross-group comparison
crude rate
dimension
internal comparison
multidimensional concept
norming
population composition
removing the effects of composition
standardization
subclassification
summary measure
trend
unadjusted crude rate

ISSUES AND PROBLEMS

1. Many social phenomena are age- or sex-related. As a result a comparison of crude rates for different populations may be misleading. Suggest some social phenomena which are age- or sex-related and discuss how age-specific or sex-specific rates would be useful.
2. Discuss the differences in norming by subclassification versus norming by standardization.
3. Identify three multidimensional concepts commonly used by social scientists. Select one of the concepts and list its dimensions. Suggest measures for each of the dimensions identified.
4. Examine Table 5-A below and answer the accompanying questions.
   a. Calculate the total population of the United States for 1940 and 1960.
   b. Calculate the crude death rates for 1940 and 1960.
   c. Standardize the 1940 population to the 1960 U.S. distribution and calculate the standardized 1940 death rate.

Table 5-A. Death Rates by 5-Year Age Groups, United States, 1940 and 1960.

	1940		1960	
AGE DISTRIBUTION	Population[a]	Death Rate[b]	Population[a]	Death Rate[b]
Under 1 year	2,020	54.9	4,112	27.0
1–4 years	8,521	2.9	16,209	1.1
5–9 years	10,685	1.1	18,692	0.5
10–14 years	11,746	1.0	16,773	0.4
15–19 years	12,334	1.7	13,219	0.9
20–24 years	11,588	2.4	10,801	1.2
25–29 years	11,097	2.8	10,869	1.3
30–34 years	10,242	3.4	11,949	1.6
35–39 years	9,545	4.4	12,481	2.3
40–44 years	8,788	6.1	11,600	3.7
45–49 years	8,255	8.7	10,879	5.9
50–54 years	7,257	12.8	9,606	9.4
55–59 years	5,867	18.5	8,430	13.8

Table 5-A ***(Continued)***

AGE DISTRIBUTION	1940		1960	
	Population[a]	Death Rate[b]	Population[a]	Death Rate[b]
60–64 years	4,756	26.7	7,142	21.5
65–69 years	3,756	39.7	6,258	31.4
70–74 years	2,570	61.1	4,739	47.2
75–79 years	1,504	94.8	3,054	72.0
80–84 years	744	145.6	1,580	117.2
85 years plus	365	235.7	929	198.6

SOURCE: *Vital Statistics Rates in the United States 1940–1960.* National Center for Health Statistics. U.S. Department of Health, Education, and Welfare (Washington, D.C.: Government Printing Office, 1968). Adapted from Tables 55 and 69.
[a] Population in 1,000s
[b] Death rate per 1,000

5. Examine Figure 5-A for a graphic profile of changes in the U.S. population distribution for the years 1900, 1940, and 1960. Discuss how 1940 differs from 1900.

RECOMMENDED READINGS

Barclay, George W.
1958 *Techniques of Population Analysis.* New York: Wiley.

Provides a useful overview of techniques available for the manipulation and analysis of population data.

Glenn, Norval
1975 "Trend Studies with Available Survey Data: Opportunities and Pitfalls," in Philip K. Hastings and Jessie Southwich (eds.), *Survey Data for Trend Analysis: An Index to Repeated Questions in U.S. National Surveys Held by the Roper Public Opinion Center.* Williamstown, Mass.: Roper Public Opinion Research Center.

Provides a discussion of the use of time series data and standardization.

Jaco, E. Gartly
1960 *The Social Epidemiology of Mental Disorders.* New York: Russell Sage Foundation.

Part One on demographic aspects of mental disorders and Appendix B, which demonstrates a standardization approach to calculating incidence rates, are informative.

U.S. Bureau of the Census
1971 *The Methods and Materials of Demography: Volumes I and II.* Washington, D.C.: U.S. Department of Commerce.

An authoritative discussion in two volumes (approx. 1,200 pages) of various techniques available to social scientists. Selective reading is required.

Figure 5-A. Population of the United States: Percentage Distribution by Age and Sex.

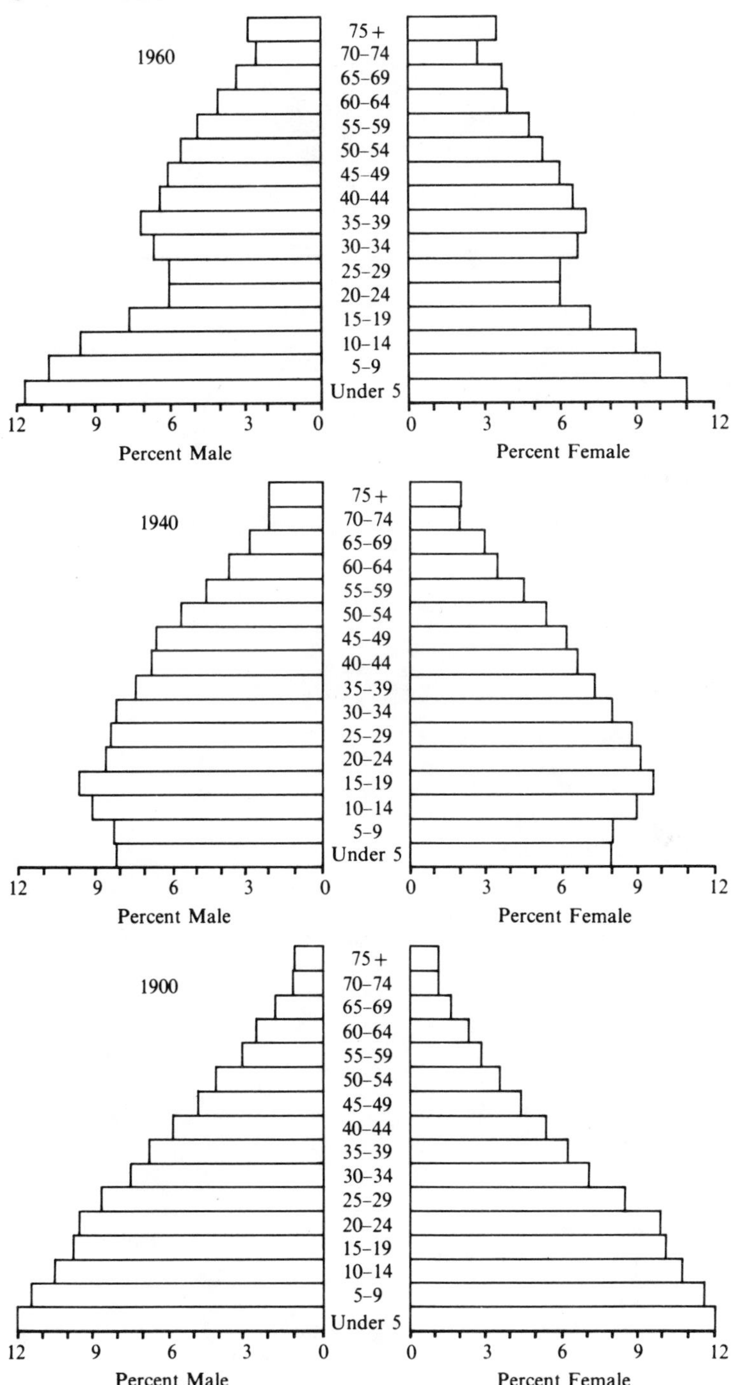

SOURCE: *Vital Statistics Rates in the United States 1940–1960,* p. 20.

PART THREE

Measuring Variables Through Scaling

6

ORDINAL SCALING USING ARBITRARY WEIGHTS: BLACK PERCEPTIONS OF ORGANIZATIONAL EFFECTIVENESS

GENERAL ISSUE

Scientists are interested in the properties of objects, and in the relationship of the properties to one another. For instance, they are interested in intelligence, education, and income as properties of individuals and membership size, use of written rules, and sex composition as properties of groups. They are interested in the relationship of intelligence to education and the relationship of membership size to the use of written rules.

To measure properties such as these, social scientists have developed a variety of techniques. These techniques are directly related to the scientist's conception of the property under consideration. Certain properties are conceived as being either present or absent. For instance, a person is either a male or not a male, a student or not a student, a Protestant or not a Protestant, and so forth. Properties such as these are sometimes called *attributes*.

Since an attribute is a property conceived of as being either present or absent, one cannot measure its depth. It is possible only to record the number of objects which either have or do not have it. Therefore, in order to determine whether the attribute is present or absent, it is first necessary to agree on a precise definition of it. Then, by comparing an object to the definition it is possible to determine whether the attribute is present or absent. Repeated comparison of objects to definitions permits a determination of the incidence of objects which either have or do not have the attribute.

This process is called *nominal scaling*. There are several rules or requirements for forming a nominal scale. Objects which have the same properties are placed in the same class, while objects which do not share the property are placed in a different class. A nominal scale has at a minimum two classes (present or absent) but may have as many as necessary in order to exhaust the kind of property under consideration. For example, one might consider the property of the marital state. A two-class nominal scale might consist of (1) persons who are currently married and (2) persons who are not currently married. A three-class nominal scale might consist of (1) persons who are currently married, (2) persons currently divorced, and (3) persons who are neither currently married nor currently divorced. A nominal scale permits every object to be placed in one and only one class. If an object can be placed in more than one class, the classification scheme does not result in a nominal scale. On the other hand, if an object cannot be placed in *any* class, the nominal scale is incomplete.

In the above example, we used numbers to refer to a class of objects: class 1, class 2, and class 3. Letter symbols can be also used to refer to classes of objects. Thus, those currently married could have been labeled class A, those currently divorced labeled class B, and those neither currently married nor divorced as class C.

The use of number symbols as labels for nominal classes occasionally causes data-analysis confusion. The confusion stems from the tendency to impute the properties of numbers to the properties of nominal values. Since the numbers used in a nominal scale are arbitrary and do not imply a quantity of property, the number labels should not be manipulated by adding, subtracting, multiplying, or dividing.

Other properties of objects vary in quantity rather than by attribute. The concept of a *variable* is used to refer to object properties conceived as varying in quantity or magnitude. Thus, an individual can have more or less education or more or less income and an organization can have many or few members, a large or small budget, and so on. When properties of objects are conceived of as varying in magnitude, using numbers to represent the extent of a property becomes more tempting and reasonable. However, it is easier to conceive of such a property as varying in magnitude than to measure it.

Consider, for example, the concept of power: the ability to impose one's will on others. It is not difficult to conceive of a continuum of power in which some organizations have more power than others. For instance, a federal district court may be conceived of as being more powerful than a local state court which, in turn, may be conceived of as being more powerful than a municipal court. However, the power of a court may defy numerical quantification. It might appear self-evident that one court is more powerful than another, yet impossible to conceive of a procedure which permits measuring the magnitude of the power difference. Thus, in this case, it is possible to rank objects in terms of their possession of a property, but impossible to specify the magnitude of the differences. The objects in this case form an *ordinal scale.*

Four important rules govern the development of an ordinal scale. First, the rules which govern nominal scaling apply. Objects which have the same quantity of property are placed in the same class, while objects having unlike quantities are placed in different classes. Second, ordinal scaling requires comparing the objects as to a common property. Examples of a common property might be power, social status, or alienation. Third, the rule of asymmetry applies. Obviously, if object A has more of a property than object B, then object B cannot have more of the property than object A. In other words, the order of objects cannot be reversed. Finally, the rule of transitivity applies. If object A has more of a property than object B and if object B has more of the property than object C, then object A has more of the property than object C. It should be clear that the rank order of relationships is preserved throughout the scale.

Numbers are frequently used to rank objects in terms of their possession of a common property. Thus, the number 1 represents the object which possesses more of the property than other objects. The number 2 represents the object which possesses less of the property than objects coded 1 (first) but more of the property than the remaining ones. This process continues until all objects have been ordered.

Again, the use of numbers to signify rank may lead to confusion in data analysis. The difference in quantity of property between an object ranked 1 and an object ranked 2 is *not* one unit. Nor is the difference between second-ranked objects and third-ranked objects one unit. With ordinal scales, scientists are limited to the statement that an object possesses more of the property than another object, but the magnitude of difference is an unknown.

Ordinal measurement scales are extremely important in social science research since, as suggested, it is often possible to conceive of properties varying in degree, but simultaneously impossible to conceive of ways of measuring the magnitude of difference. It is also difficult to translate the conception of rank differences into procedures which yield an acceptable ordinal scale. This chapter, as well as the next two, present three procedures social scientists use to obtain ordinal scales.

Two other measurement scales used later in this text should also be mentioned: *interval scales* and *ratio scales.* Both meet the requirements of an ordinal scale. They have the extra advantage of specifying the degree of difference between objects. This advantage results from a correspondence between the properties of the mathematical scale of numbers and the properties of the objects under measurement.

The number system is based upon the idea of equal intervals between adjacent numbers. Thus, the difference between 1 and 2 is taken to be equal to the difference between 2 and 3, and so forth. Therefore, one can manipulate the number used to represent the quantity of the property. For instance, scientists can calculate the per capita income in the United

States by adding all individual incomes and dividing by the total population. They are manipulating only the numbers representing income, not the income per se; that is, they are not really physically redistributing the income in order to obtain the average. Since they measure the variable property in terms of equal units, the outcomes of such manipulations are meaningful.

The preceding paragraphs illustrate that interval and ratio scales are quite similar to each other. The important difference between them is the idea of a zero point. A ratio scale has a true zero point; for example, zero years of formal schooling, zero dollar income, or zero children. Ratio scales are quite common in social science.

In an interval scale, the zero point is an arbitrarily selected point on a continuum. The Fahrenheit temperature scale exhibits this feature. While the scale is calibrated in terms of equal distance intervals (i.e., degrees), the zero point on the scale is arbitrary. It does not signify the total absence of the property of heat. It is merely a conventional zero point. Interval scales are rarely encountered in social science, for it has been difficult to imagine properties which might vary along a continuum of equal intervals yet lack a true zero point.

It is to the problem of developing ordinal scales to which this chapter now returns.

THEORETICAL PROBLEM

Social movements often contain a number of groups each claiming to represent the movement's true supporters. Frequently, these groups present conflicting demands. As a result, it is difficult to determine the movement's precise objectives or the extent to which movement members endorse them.

This was the situation during the 1960s, when CORE, SCLC, NAACP, and many other groups supported and acted on behalf of the civil rights movement. Differences in organizational goals, strategies, and demands blurred the priorities of the movement. Of course, the movement was characterized by such general values as "equal opportunity," "first class citizenship," and "full participation in American life," but these general values were of little practical use in determining the priorities of such matters as housing, education, or employment.

Whereupon, Lewis Killian and Charles Grigg undertook research to develop a procedure by which they could rank the priorities of the movement.* Their starting point was the perception of individual participation in a mass society. In a mass society such as that of the United

* Lewis M. Killian and Charles M. Grigg, "Negro Perceptions of Organizational Effectiveness," *Social Problems*, 11(1964):380–388.

States, many citizens have positive attitudes about specific goals and objectives but do not actively participate in supporting them. Instead, many support the activities of those who act on their behalf.

Thus, many people are casual members of large organizations. They pay dues and attend occasional meetings. Equally important to an organization, however, is the voluntary contribution of money and the emotional support of individuals who endorse the organization's actions but who are not formal members. Emotional support may be especially important for organizations that seek to represent the poor, since many of the latter have neither the time nor money to support the organization in a more active way.

Killian and Grigg decided to rank the priorities of a black community by determining which organizations received the greatest emotional support from that community.

Research Site

Killian and Grigg conducted their study in "Florida City," a Florida city with a population of approximately 200,000 in 1960. Census data indicated that approximately 40 percent (80,000) of the city's residents were black. In 1962, approximately 1,700 black families in Florida City were relocated because of an expressway project. A sample of 549 heads of households from these 1,700 family units was selected for interviews. Data for comparing characteristics of the sample with characteristics of the general Florida City population appear in Table 6-1.

The data in Table 6-1 demonstrate slight differences between the 1962 sample and the 1960 black population of Florida City with respect to education, income, and age. Some of these differences might be due to sampling from relocated families rather than sampling from all families. Other differences are probably due to the selection of only heads of households for inclusion in the research.

Constructing an Ordinal Scale of Perceived Organizational Effectiveness

To construct an ordinal scale of organizational effectiveness, the 549 heads of households were given a list of 16 organizations and asked to rate each organization according to the question: "How much do you think each of the following groups is doing things in Florida City that are in the best interests of people like you?" An ordered set of response choices was given to each respondent. Respondents were asked to choose the response which best reflected their perception of effectiveness: a lot, some, a little, or none. A "don't know" response was also provided for those who could not make a choice. By forcing respondents to select one of a set of ordinally ranked, forced-choice alternatives, Killian and Grigg sought to generate information for constructing an ordinal ranking of the sixteen organizations.

Table 6-1. Comparison of Selected Characteristics of 1962 Black Sample and 1960 U.S. Census of Florida City Black Residents.

	1962 SAMPLE[a] %	1960 CENSUS %	% DIFFERENCE
Education			
None	.6	5.1	−4.5
Some or completed G.S.	87.2	88.4	−.8
Some or completed college	12.0	6.4	+5.6
No response	.2		
Individual Annual Income			
Under $3,000	61.4	79.9	−18.5
$3,000–$5,000	30.2	15.9	+14.3
Over $5,000	5.6	4.2	+1.4
No response	2.7		
Age			
20–29	26.1	21.5	+.6
30–39	33.7	22.5	+11.2
40–49	23.1	22.0	+1.1
50–59	10.6	17.4	−6.8
60–69	4.4	10.4	−6.0
70+	1.8	6.2	−4.4
No response	.4		

SOURCE: Killian and Grigg, "Negro Perceptions," p. 384, Table 1.
[a] Column percentage totals do not add to 100 due to rounding.

Although Killian and Grigg obtained a separate rating for each of the sixteen organizations, they still needed a procedure by which the separate ratings could be combined to yield a scale of organizations. To create this scale, they assigned a numerical value or weight to each choice. The numerical weights they selected were as follows:

Rating Category	*Numerical Value or Weight*
A lot	5
Some	2
A little	1
None	0
Don't know	0

The rating categories, you may recall, were ordinal. Therefore, the selection of numerical weights was arbitrary. Such selection is defensible only on the grounds of professional judgment. Killian and Grigg intuitively believed that "a lot" meant approximately two and one-half times more

6.1 FORCED-CHOICE RESPONSES AND RATING SCALES

In interview or questionnaire design, social scientists frequently use the technique of forced choices. Respondents are provided with a question and set of responses from which they must select their answer. Responses may be at a nominal-scale level, for example, are you a homeowner? (1) Yes, (2) No. Or at an ordinary level, for example, how often do you go to the movies? (1) Very often, (2) Somewhat often, (3) Not too often, (4) Don't go.

In theory, forced-choice questions seem simple but they are actually conceptually complex. First, such questions require that the range of potential responses be clearly conceptualized and reflected in the choices provided. If not, refusal to select a choice will be high. Second, forced-choice responses must be mutually exclusive. If not, respondents will be unable to select only one.

When forced-choice questions use ordinal responses, it is essential that the responses be distinguishable from one another (e.g., will "somewhat often" be interpreted by the respondent to mean more than "not too often"?) and the responses should reflect the full range of rank orders the researcher needs.

Often the choices or ordinal responses are based on face validity or professional judgment, and there is little empirical evidence to demonstrate why the researcher adopted the responses. It is common, however, to use such ordinal responses as: very frequently, somewhat frequently, infrequently, and not at all; or like a greal deal, like somewhat, like a little, like not at all.

The use of ordinal responses constitutes one form of a rating scale. Respondents are usually asked to rate an object according to some standard. It is desirable to clearly specify the standard in order to provide a basis for response and to avoid misunderstanding.

Rating scales have many forms. Sometimes the rating scale is provided graphically as in this example:

In social conversation are you:	____ talkative	____ somewhat talkative	____ primarily a listener

organizational effectiveness than "some," that "some" was one unit more than "a little," and that "none" and "don't know" meant zero effectiveness. Other researchers, using their own judgment, might well have chosen different numerical values. In the absence of interval or ratio measurement, the use of numerical values has its basis solely in informed judgment. Such judgments are always open to question.

Once they had assigned weights, Killian and Grigg were able to produce a numerical score of effectiveness for each organization. This they accomplished by multiplying the percent of respondents who selected a given choice by the arbitrary weight assigned that response. Using CORE as an illustration, the procedure was implemented as follows:

Organization: CORE

RATING CATEGORY	NUMBER OF INDIVIDUALS SELECTING THE RESPONSE	PERCENT OF TOTAL RESPONSES	WEIGHT	WEIGHT × PERCENT
A lot	40	7.3	5	36.5
Some	190	34.6	2	69.2
A little	100	18.2	1	18.2
None	40	7.3	0	0.0
Don't know	179	32.6	0	0.0
Total	549	100.0		123.9

Composite Score: 123.9 or 124 (rounded)

They followed this procedure for each of the sixteen organizations, which were ranked from high to low score. This ranking appears in Table 6-2.

In this manner, Killian and Grigg used a numerical weighting system to translate verbal responses (a lot, some...) into quantitative scores (5, 2...) in order to achieve a composite score (364, 214...). The composite score

Table 6-2. Composite Scores and Ranks of Sixteen Organizations by Perceived Organizational Effectiveness Score.

ORGANIZATION	COMPOSITE SCORE	RANK
NAACP	364	1
Democratic party	214	2
Federal government	208	3
Urban League	202	4
Negro churches	198	5
Labor unions	184	6
State government	156	7
Negro businesses	153	8
City government	138	9
Council on Human Relations	133	10
CORE	124	11
Chamber of Commerce	113	12
White businesses	92	13
Republican party	81	14
White churches	56	15
Black Muslims	25	16

SOURCE: Killian and Grigg, "Negro Perceptions," p. 385, Table 2.

represents the weighted overall score for an organization. Although technically the use of numerical weights violates the meaning of an ordinal scale, it is an approximating procedure social scientists often employ.

To restore their data to an ordinal scale, Killian and Grigg used the composite scores only to obtain a ranking of organizations. They discarded the composite scores and substituted numbers which represented only rank position. Thus, NAACP was given a rank of 1 (composite score 364), the Democratic party was given a rank of 2 (composite score 214), and the federal government was given a rank of 3 (composite score 208). The composite scores were not interpreted as interval or ratio measures reflecting the quantity of difference between organizations.

6.2 PAIRED COMPARISONS AS A TECHNIQUE FOR ORDINAL SCALING

Social scientists often use a paired comparison technique for ranking objects. As an example, one might assume that a researcher wished to rank three persons according to their influence in the community. A respondent might be asked: "Who has more influence, Person A or Person B?"; "Who has more influence, Person B or Person C?"; "Who has more influence, Person A or Person C?" Based on the respondent's choices, it is possible to obtain a ranking of Persons A, B, and C according to perceived social influence.

One practical problem in using this procedure is the number of paired comparisons which must be made if the list is long. Statisticians have developed a formula for determining the number of pairs which must be compared. This formula is as follows: given N objects, there are $N(N-1)/2$ pairs. Thus, if there are three objects, there are $3(3-1)/2$ pairs or 3 pairs. If there are ten objects, there are $10(10-1)/2$ pairs or 45 pairs. Consequently, the number of pairs in a lengthy list soon becomes unwieldy and consumes more time than is desired.

There is an additional problem in that respondents frequently find it difficult to maintain a single standard for comparison. Thus, objects A and B may be compared according to one dimension, while objects B and C may be compared as against a different dimension. When this occurs, the transitive rule of an ordinal scale is violated. That is, a person may rank object A over object B, and object B over object C—but rank object C over object A. It is possible to avoid this problem by continuously making the respondent aware of the standard of comparison being used.

COMMENTS ON THE ORDINAL RANKING

Assuming that the approximate weights employed in the ordinal rating scale did not severely distort "true" organizational ratings, it is possible to draw several inferences from Table 6-2.

First, for the sample of blacks drawn from Florida City residents, the racial characteristics of the organization prove not as important as might have been expected. Some of the top-ranked organizations are predominantly white (Democratic party, labor unions), while others are predominantly black (NAACP, Urban League).

Second, the scope of the organization appears to be important. Of the top four organizations, all derived their primary revenues and executed their policy functions nationally. On the other hand, local organizations, especially local white ones, fared poorly. Of organizations in the lower six ranks, five were controlled locally and were primarily white.

Based on knowledge of these organizations, Killian and Grigg also inferred that their policies were important. All predominantly black organizations in the top ten ranks had compromising and conciliatory strategies. CORE, on the other hand, which placed primary emphasis on direct action, occupied the eleventh rank and was lower in support than such organizations as the Council on Human Relations and city and state governments.

SUMMARY

This chapter was the first of three on the techniques of scaling. Its focus has been on ordinal scaling where researchers used their judgment to translate verbal responses into quantitative scores. The use of arbitrary weights, while technically violating the principles of an ordinal scale, has a practical value when more suitable measurement procedures are unavailable. However, these violations of measurement rules should be undertaken with caution and with recognition of possible distortions that could result.

The goal of the research was to determine support for civil rights organizations by black residents of one community during the early 1960s. The researchers used a rating scale and an arbitrary weighting system to compare the perceived effectiveness of sixteen different organizations. Their data indicated the highest ratings for organizations that were national and compromising.

KEY IDEAS AND CONCEPTS

absolute zero
arbitrary zero
asymmetry
attribute
class
equal intervals
fixed choice
forced choice
interval scale
nominal scale

numerical weight
ordinal scale
paired comparison
property
rank
rating scale
ratio scale
scale
symmetry
variable
variation

ISSUES AND PROBLEMS

1. Define the concept of property.
2. List three properties of groups. List three properties of individuals. Identify one property which can belong to a group but not to an individual. Identify one which can belong to an individual but not a group.
3. List three examples of properties which are attributes. List three examples of properties which are variables.
4. We sometimes say that a person is very educated. Create an equal-interval-based scale for measuring "educated." Is the scale a ratio scale or an interval scale? Create an ordinal scale for measuring the same property. Create a nominal scale for measuring the same property.
5. Universities often use letter grades such as A, B, C, D, and F to represent a person's course performance. Do the letter grades constitute a nominal or an ordinal scale? Why? For purposes of calculating a grade point average, number values are often assigned to letter grades such as A = 4, B = 3, C = 2, D = 1, and F = 0. What assumptions are made in assigning these values and in calculating an overall grade point average?
6. Specify the conditions which must be met for obtaining:
   a. a nominal scale
   b. an ordinal scale
   c. an interval scale
   d. a ratio scale
7. Some people are more active in politics than others. Endorsing a candidate may range from displaying a bumper sticker, contributing money, distributing literature, etc. Using five items and assigning arbitrary weights, create a scale which measures political activity over a range from not very active to very active.

RECOMMENDED READINGS

Guilford, J. P.
1954 *Psychometric Methods.* New York: McGraw-Hill.

Chapter 1 on a general theory of measurement can be profitably read by those with and without a mathematical background. The remainder of this work requires a mathematical background but can be read selectively by a discerning reader.

Stevens, S. S.
1946 "On the Theory of Scales of Measurement," *Science*, 103:677–680.

Discusses the four levels of measurement (nominal, ordinal, interval, and ratio) in detail and provides an understanding of the mathematical operations permitted with each level of measurement.

Summers, Gene F. (ed.)
1970 *Attitude Measurement.* Chicago: Rand McNally.

A collection of articles dealing with various aspects of the problems of scale measurement.

7

ORDINAL SCALING USING A LIKERT TECHNIQUE: MEASURING SOCIAL DISTANCE

GENERAL ISSUE

Social scientists use scaling procedures to achieve one of two objectives. One objective is to rank stimuli or external objects along a given continuum. The other objective is to rank respondents or responses along a hypothetical continuum. An example of the first objective is the ranking of civil rights organizations by how effective the public perceives them to be, as was done in Chapter 6. An example of the second objective is the ranking of respondents by the degree of racial prejudice they express.

In 1932, Rensis Likert introduced a procedure for ranking respondents in terms of a hypothetical attitude continuum.* His procedure, while still widely used for scaling attitudes, has been used for many other purposes as well.

Sometimes referred to as the *method of summated ratings*, the Likert technique involves the summing of responses to a set of items. It is like a test score obtained by summing correct answers. Of course, in scaling attitudes or other social phenomena there is not always a *correct* answer, so a criterion other than that of correctness is used in determining the score. In the opinion of many social scientists, the Likert technique is efficient, for it has many features which allow assessing a scale's *validity* and *reliability*.

* Rensis Likert, "A Technique for the Measurement of Attitudes," *Archives of Psychology*, 1932, No. 140.

A scale's validity indicates how well it measures what it is intended to. Thus, scaling procedures designed for measuring alienation should produce a measure consistent with the conceptual definition of alienation. A scale's reliability is determined by its ability to produce the same score consistently. That is, different scientists using the same scaling procedures should arrive at the same measurements for the same objects.

However, demonstrating a scale's validity and reliability is a difficult task, and several procedures for assessing these are discussed in connection with the Likert technique presented.

THEORETICAL PROBLEM

In examining America's social stratification system, social scientists frequently have observed a relationship between occupation, life-style, and prestige. Occupation, for instance, affects income, which in turn influences ability to pursue a socially desired life-style, which then helps determine prestige. Because of the importance of occupations and their visibility, individuals often use people's jobs in evaluating whether their life-styles and social statuses make them desirable persons.

The nature of one's work, then, serves as a condensed piece of information frequently used by Americans in their relationships with others. It is often the link by which patterns of social interaction (e.g., marriage, friendship, group membership, etc.) become associated with patterns of stratification (e.g., differences in class). As such, occupation influences the character of American social stratification and the degree to which social classes do or do not form distinct entities. The more readily Americans determine social interactions on the basis of class, the more likely it is that social class distinctions will remain. However, since Americans are socially mobile, two alternate hypotheses regarding interaction are intuitively credible.

One suggests that persons of similar social status prefer to interact with each other. This, the *similar status hypothesis*, is reflected in the adage "birds of a feather flock together." It comes from the assumption that an individual feels most comfortable with persons of similar status, since they are likely to share common motivations, interests, goals, and perspectives. According to this assumption, in the absence of other information, individuals prefer to interact with persons holding occupational statuses similar to their own.

A second hypothesis suggests that individuals prefer to interact with persons of higher status. This, the *higher status hypothesis*, has foundations in the idea of social mobility or "social climbing." It is based on the assumption that individuals prefer interacting with persons of higher status because of personal satisfactions or because of the possibility of enhancing their own social positions. According to this assumption, individuals prefer to interact with persons holding occupational statuses higher than their own.

These hypotheses were the basis of a study conducted by Edward O. Laumann in the early 1960s.*

Study Design

Using information provided by the Bureau of the Census for 1960, Laumann grouped census tracts in Cambridge and Belmont, Massachusetts, into three categories: (1) low-income (median family income below $5,500), (2) middle-income (median family income between $5,500 and $7,499), and (3) high-income (median family income $7,500 or higher). He then randomly selected three tracts from each income category, for a total of nine.

Using lists of all adults occupying legal residences in these nine tracts, Laumann then drew a sample of 50 males from each tract. The sample thus totaled 450 adult males. Since Laumann was aware that race can be a factor in social interaction, he had deliberately focused on white males. His interviewers successfully interviewed 422 white males in the original sample of 450. Of the 442 men, 327 provided information needed to construct a scale of occupational social distance.

Constructing a Scale of Social Distance

Social distance scales have existed for many years. In the early thirties, Emory S. Bogardus developed a scale for measuring the social distance individuals prefer to maintain between themselves and members of other racial or ethnic groups.† While the original Bogardus Social Distance Scale has undergone many modifications and is somewhat dated, it was important in stimulating research into the problem of measuring social distance. Bogardus based his scale on a continuum of social relationships, with one end of the continuum being intimate (for example, willingness to marry) and the other end being impersonal (for example, prohibiting immigration). An abbreviated form of his scale appears in Box 7.1.

As can be observed, the Bogardus Social Distance Scale contains items ordered along an intuitive continuum of social intimacy. Bogardus believed that this scale accurately measured the social distance between groups of different ethnic, racial, or national backgrounds. Since his research was conducted when such identities were still strong, his scale was viewed as an important tool for measuring the probability of migrant assimilation.

A variety of scoring methods for using the Bogardus Scale were later developed. One of the most convenient and simplest methods consisted of summing the lowest or "nearest" column of a specific group for all respondents and dividing by the number of respondents. For instance, if a sample of five respondents had each indicated "would marry into the group" for Canadians, the social distance score would be 1.0 (1 + 1 + 1 + 1 + 1 = 5;

* Edward O. Laumann, "Subjective Social Distance and Urban Occupational Stratification," *American Journal of Sociology*, 71(1965):26–36.

† See Emory S. Bogardus, *Social Distance* (Yellow Springs, Ohio: Antioch Press, 1959).

7.1 THE BOGARDUS SOCIAL DISTANCE SCALE

The Bogardus Scale* contained the following directions and form:

"You are urged to give yourself as complete freedom as possible. In fact, the greater the freedom you give yourself, the more valuable will be the results. Use only checkmarks or crosses.

"Seven kinds of social contacts are given. You are asked to give in every instance your first feeling reactions. Proceed through the tests without delaying. . . . Remember to give your first feeling reactions in every case. Give your reactions to each race as a group. Do not give your reactions to the best or worst members that you have known.

"Put a cross after each race in as many of the seven columns as your feeling reactions dictate."

* Emory S. Bogardus, "A Social Distance Scale," *Sociology and Social Research*, 17 (1933):265–271. Copyright 1933 by Sociology and Social Research, Los Angeles, California.

5/5 = 1.0). For Turks, if three of the five respondents had checked "would have as close friends" and two had checked "would have as next door neighbors" the social distance score would be 2.4 (2 + 2 + 2 + 3 + 3 = 12; 12/5 = 2.4).

Although the Bogardus Social Distance Scale appears to have acceptable levels of reliability and validity, there are a number of methodological objections to its use. Assigning numerical weights to "social distance columns," and then summing the values and dividing by the total number of respondents, violates the principle of ordinal scaling. Since the distances between positions on the scale are unknown and likely to be of different widths, the resulting score is likely to be misleading. For instance, the distance between *marrying* someone and having him as a *neighbor* is intuitively greater than the distance between having someone as a *neighbor* and knowing him only as a speaking acquaintance. Thus, the response categories do not reasonably permit the assignment of equal weights. In addition, the use of extreme categories probably encourages respondents to select choices toward the middle of the scale. The likely result is a distribution which inaccurately reflects the feelings of respondents.

Although indebted to Bogardus for the concept of social distance, Laumann elected to use a Likert technique for developing an occupational social distance scale. The Likert technique for constructing scales avoids the use of extreme items, since the latter distort responses in one direction or the other. The avoidance of extreme items is frequently practiced in test construction. For instance, college instructors may eliminate test questions which are either too easy or too difficult for the majority of students. Since extremely easy or extremely difficult questions do not discriminate between students who have learned the material and students who have not, such questions are not very useful.

Laumann used the following procedures to select questions. First, he

	1	2	3	4	5	6	7
	Would marry into group	Would have as close friends	Would have as next-door neighbors	Would work in same office	Have as speaking acquaintances only	Have as visitors only to my nation	Would debar from my nation
Armenians							
Americans (U.S. white)							
Canadians							
Chinese							
Czechs							
English							
Filipinos							
Finns							
French							
Germans							
Greeks							
. . .							
Spanish							
Swedish							
Turks							

assembled a large pool of items judged to measure social distance. Second, he removed the extreme ones. Finally, he included in the questionnaire the items he judged best. For a given occupation, interviewers requested respondents to rate that occupation according to a continuum of five choices. Using carpenter as an example, the seven items and five response categories are provided below. Respondents were instructed to rate the occupation on each item.

I believe I would like to have a carpenter (specific occupation) as:

	Strongly agree	Agree	Undecided	Disagree	Strongly disagree
My son-in-law	_____	_____	_____	_____	_____
My father-in-law	_____	_____	_____	_____	_____
My closest personal friend	_____	_____	_____	_____	_____
A person I would have over for supper in my home	_____	_____	_____	_____	_____
A person I might often visit with	_____	_____	_____	_____	_____
A member of one of my social clubs, lodges, or informal social groups	_____	_____	_____	_____	_____
My next-door neighbor	_____	_____	_____	_____	_____

Laumann manipulated the responses to social distance items by assigning numerical values to each response category and then summing scores. The values used were:

Strongly agree	= 1.0
Agree	= 2.0
Undecided	= 3.0
Disagree	= 4.0
Strongly disagree	= 5.0

These numerical weights are arbitrary, but represent the assumption of most social scientists that between each category there is about one unit of distance.

Since seven items appear in the scale, a respondent's social distance score for the occupation could range from 7.0 to 35.0, if each item were answered. These scores are obtained by summing the respondent's choices. To obtain a mean occupational social distance score, the scores of all respondents for an occupation are summed and divided by the total number of respondents.

By using the same procedure for a list of occupations, Laumann obtained a social distance score for each occupation. The occupations examined by Laumann are listed below in order of occupational prestige (Laumann reordered the list to avoid having the order of presentation influence respondents.):

physician
college professor
top executive
electrical engineer
high school teacher
garage mechanic
salesclerk
machine operator
truck driver
banker
owner-manager
bank teller
factory foreman
carpenter
unskilled construction worker
janitor
street sweeper

It should be noted that Laumann used the same Likert-based Occupational Social Distance Scale for each of the seventeen occupations.

Measuring Respondent Status

Laumann used two procedures for measuring a respondent's status. In the first procedure, he asked each respondent to state his occupation. Expert coders then classified these occupations according to an ordinal scale of nine occupational categories which were later recombined to yield five categories. These were

1. Professional and top business occupations
2. Semiprofessional and middle-level business occupations
3. Clerical and sales occupations, small-business owners, and managerial occupations
4. Skilled craft occupations and foremen
5. Semiskilled and unskilled occupations

In the second procedure, Laumann requested that respondents state their social class identification. Respondents were allowed to choose from five social classes. These were

1. Upper class
2. Upper middle class
3. Middle class
4. Upper working class
5. Working class

Laumann's measures of social class therefore were based on objective occupational evaluations and subjective self-identification.

7.2 DETERMINING RELIABILITY AND VALIDITY

RELIABILITY

The term "reliability" generally has two meanings: stability and internal consistency.

Stability As suggested, the notion of stability is based on the idea that different researchers using the same scaling procedures should obtain identical measurements for the same object. Consequently, according to this definition at least two measurements are required in order to determine a scale's reliability. These are necessary for comparison. If the two are identical, the scale is reliable; if they are different, it is unreliable. An ordinary bathroom scale illustrates this point. If an object is weighed and its weight recorded at 50 pounds, its next weighing also should be 50 pounds. If it is, the scale is reliable; if it is not, the scale is unreliable. Since the difference in weighings may be large or small, statisticians have developed a number of procedures for determining the extent of a scale's reliability.

Internal Consistency The notion of internal consistency is based on the idea that the items involved in a scale are but a sample of all items which could have been used. The Bogardus Social Distance Scale used seven items in its construction, but others could have been employed. Internal consistency focuses on the interrelationship of all such items. A true-false examination illustrates this point. Since an instructor might have used many test questions, the ones used are but a sample of all possible ones. If a test score is to be reliable, then a score obtained on a randomly selected half of the items should be similar to a score obtained on the remaining half. This method of determining a scale's reliability is known as a "split-half" technique. As in the case of a scale's stability, the differences between scores on the two halves of the test may be large or small. For this reason, statisticians have developed a number of procedures for measuring a scale's internal consistency.

VALIDITY

As suggested, from the standpoint of theory, a scale's validity is determined by how well it measures what it is intended to measure. Thus,

Data Analysis and Findings

Laumann's analysis endeavored to establish whether individuals preferred to interact with persons of similar status or with persons of higher status. Since he obtained parallel findings when he measured respondent status by means of occupational position and by self-identified social class, only one set of results (self-identified social class) is reported here. To simplify the presentation further, the focus will be on upper-class, middle-class, and working-class respondents.

a scale must fulfill a concept's operational requirements. In assessing validity, social scientists search for evidence of a correspondence between scale scores and conceptual meaning. Since there is no way of demonstrating a correspondence between an empirical measurement and a concept, conclusions are based on inference. Four types of evidence are used to infer a scale's validity.

Face Validity This is the least satisfactory but most commonly used procedure in social science. In the case of face validity, a scale is accepted as valid if it looks or sounds valid to the researcher. Thus, professional judgment alone is used as a basis for face validity.

Predictive Validity Since scales frequently are constructed to predict outcomes, a scale is considered valid if it in fact successfully predicts. Thus, the validity of a racial prejudice scale may be determined by assessing its ability to predict racially discriminative behavior.

Content Validity If a scale is composed of a sample of items, then comparing the items in the scale with items which *could* have been used permits assessing the scale's content validity. This approach requires specifying the pool of all items so that a comparison can be undertaken.

Construct Validity Social scientists use "construct" to refer to a hypothetical variable (e.g., name given to some unobserved phenomenon thought to exist). An authoritarian personality, a cohesive group, and a democratic society are social constructs. There are a number of procedures available for determining the construct validity of a scale. If two groups known to be different are administered a scale, the scale should produce different scores. For instance, the construct validity of a racial prejudice scale could be assessed by administering the scale to the Ku Klux Klan and to an interracial fraternity. Different scores should result. Another procedure is to use a scale along with other measurement procedures to assess the interrelationships of multiple measurements.

Of the 327 respondents who provided usable responses, 242 identified themselves as belonging to one of these three class positions. The distribution follows:

Self-Identified Social Class	*Number of Respondents*
Upper class	25
Middle class	105
Working class	112
Total	242

7.3 STEPS IN CONSTRUCTING A LIKERT-BASED SCALE

1. On the basis of face validity, compile a list of items related to the phenomenon to be measured.

2. Eliminate extreme items. In other words, *the items should not form an ordinal scale.* Every item should be approximately equal to every other. (The analogue is a true-false test composed of items of equal difficulty.)

3. Select a continuum of responses *which form an ordinal scale.* The five most common response categories are strongly agree, somewhat agree, undecided, somewhat disagree, strongly disagree.

4. State some items positively and others negatively. This reduces the tendency of respondents to select choices without reading the statement. (The analogue is a true-false test composed of some statements which are true and others which are false.)

5. From the pool of items, select the best for inclusion in the questionnaire. (Usually twenty to thirty items is optimal.)

6. Collect the data.

7. Tabulate the results by
   (a) assigning a numerical value to each response category. Usually, a value of 1 is assigned the first ordinal position of response categories, a value of 2 to the second ordinal position, and so forth;
   (b) summing the response choices of a respondent, using the assigned weights, and the result is an overall respondent score;
   (c) ranking the respondents according to the obtained score.

8. Assess the reliability of the items. This is necessary since the items were selected on the basis of face validity, and some items may be invalid. (The analogue is a test which examines material not assigned by the instructor. These items do not belong in the test; the instructor made a mistake.) The following procedure is one of several recommended for assessing the usefulness of an item.

If an item is useful, it should discriminate between high scorers and low scorers. (Like a good test item, students earning an A should get it right while students earning an F should get it wrong.) Therefore, compare the responses of the high scorers (usually the top 25% scorers) with the responses of the low scorers (usually the bottom 25% scorers).

The following (item/sample) illustrates how the comparison procedure works for a sample of 200 respondents. The hypothetical item is under examination for its possible use in a scale of community dissatisfaction.

Item: How pleased are you with public safety in the community?

	VERY PLEASED	SOMEWHAT PLEASED	NEITHER PLEASED NOR DISPLEASED	SOMEWHAT DISPLEASED	VERY DISPLEASED
Weights	(1)	(2)	(3)	(4)	(5)
High scorers ($N = 50$)					
Frequency distribution	0	3	5	12	30
Low scorers ($N = 50$)					
Frequency distribution	20	15	11	4	0

Calculations

HIGH SCORERS

Weight		Frequency		Total
(1)	×	0	=	0
(2)	×	3	=	6
(3)	×	5	=	15
(4)	×	12	=	48
(5)	×	30	=	150
		Total	=	219

Mean = 219/50 = 4.39

LOW SCORERS

Weight		Frequency		Total
(1)	×	20	=	20
(2)	×	15	=	30
(3)	×	11	=	33
(4)	×	4	=	16
(5)	×	0	=	0
		Total	=	99

Mean = 99/50 = 1.98

Difference (discriminatory power) = 4.38
−1.98
2.40

These calculations show that both high and low scorers on the average have different views of this item. In fact, they differ by 2.4 units. As a rule, if the difference between high and low scorers is equal to or greater than the unit distance between adjoining positions, an item is sufficiently reliable for inclusion in the scale. Of course, the larger the difference between high and low scorers on an item the more reliable the item. If the difference is less than one unit, the item is considered unreliable.

If items are discarded, it is necessary to repeat the entire process. That is, a new total score must be calculated for each respondent, using only the retained items. The respondents must again be ordered, and the items reassessed for their reliability. (The analogue involves rescoring a test which was changed when some test items were eliminated. Student scores can be expected to change when some test items are eliminated.)

By repeating this process as many times as necessary, researchers may eventually achieve a scale which will rank respondents reliably.

These respondents were analyzed as separate groups. To obtain Occupational Social Distance scores for each group, Laumann calculated a mean score for each occupation by summing the responses and dividing by the number of respondents. For example, for the occupation of physician, the scores for upper-class respondents were totaled and divided by 25. Similarly, the scores for middle-class respondents were totaled and divided by 105, and those for working-class respondents were totaled and divided by 112. The result was three separate mean Occupational Social Distance scores for physicians: a score for upper-class, middle-class, and working-class respondents. In like manner, Laumann obtained three scores for the remaining sixteen occupations. The results are presented in Table 7-1.

Table 7-1. Mean Occupational Social Distance Scores by Self-Selected Social Class for Seventeen Occupations.[a]

	RESPONDENT'S CLASS POSITION (SELF-REPORTED)		
OCCUPATIONS	Upper Class	Middle Class	Working Class
Sample sizes	25	105	112
Physician	14.9	15.9	17.0
College professor	15.2	18.2	18.9
Top executive	16.6	17.6	18.7
Electrical engineer	17.8	17.7	17.9
High school teacher	16.8	18.5	18.6
Banker	17.6	18.9	20.0
Owner-manager	19.2	19.6	20.1
Bank teller	21.5	20.3	20.5
Factory foreman	21.0	21.2	21.5
Carpenter	21.2	20.2	20.7
Garage mechanic	23.2	21.9	21.2
Salesclerk	23.5	23.0	22.3
Machine operator	23.8	22.5	21.6
Truck driver	23.9	22.8	22.1
Unskilled construction worker	26.1	25.7	24.7
Janitor	26.6	25.6	25.0
Street sweeper	27.8	27.4	26.3

SOURCE: Laumann, "Subjective Social Distance," p. 31, Table 1.
[a]Data for this table were reconstructed from information in the original article. The rank and relationships have been preserved, but the numbers are only approximations.

Table 7-1 indicates therefore that social distance scores decrease as occupational status increases. This observation holds for each class of respondents. For upper-class respondents, the social distance score for street sweepers is 27.8, for carpenters 21.2, and for physicians 14.9. For middle-class respondents, the score for street sweepers is 27.4, for carpenters

Figure 7-1. Mean Social Distance Scores for Seventeen Occupations by Three Social Categories: Upper Class, Middle Class, and Working Class.

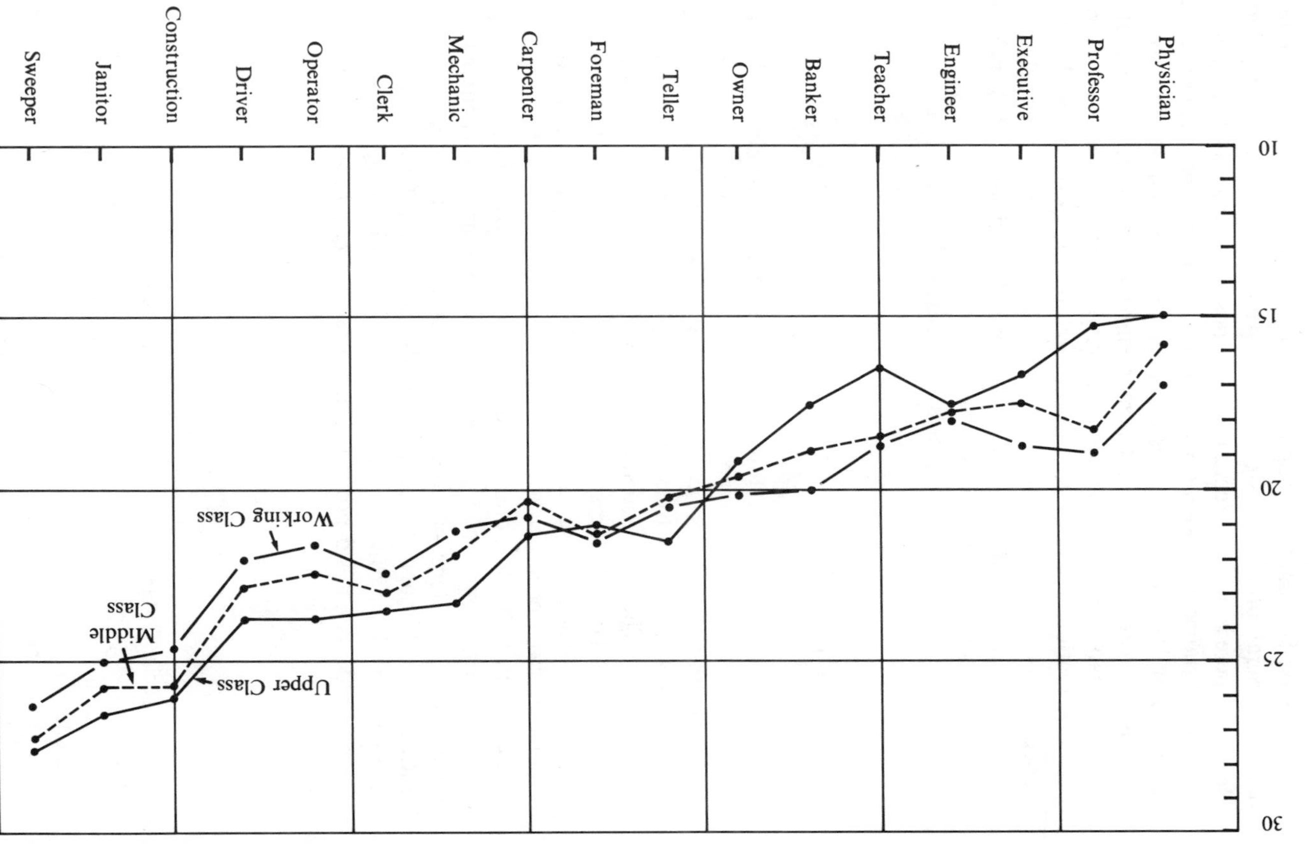

SOURCE: Table 7-1

20.2, and for physicians 15.9. For those of the working class, the respective scores are 26.3, 20.7, and 17.0.

The similarity in rankings supports the higher status hypothesis: individuals in general prefer to interact with persons of higher social status. However, there is some evidence that class position influences the "amount" of social distance individuals wish to maintain between themselves and others. For instance, the scores of upper-class respondents indicate that there is a greater distance between members of this group and street sweepers than between working-class respondents and street sweepers. This observation holds at the upper end of the scale as well. Thus, working-class respondents prefer more distance between themselves and physicians than do upper-class respondents and physicians. This phenomenon operates throughout the scale.

The pattern of these relationships is plotted in Figure 7-1.

SUMMARY

Laumann used a Likert technique to construct an ordinal scale in an attempt to examine two hypotheses. These were, first, that individuals prefer to interact with persons of similar social status and, second, in contradistinction, that individuals prefer to interact with persons of higher social status. The data tended to support the hypothesis that most people prefer to interact with persons of higher social status. However, there was some evidence that social position influenced the magnitude of social distance between occupations.

The Likert technique offers several advantages over face-validity procedures of scale construction. Perhaps most important was the capacity to eliminate those items which did not discriminate between positions on a continuum. Although this contrivance did not establish the validity of the scale (since validity can be determined only by comparing the scale with external evidence), it did provide a measure of internal consistency.

KEY IDEAS AND CONCEPTS

Bogardus Social Distance Scale
construct validity
content validity
continuum
discriminatory power
extreme item
face validity
internal consistency
Likert technique
mean score
predictive validity
reliability
scale
social distance
stability
subjective class measure
summated ratings
validity

ISSUES AND PROBLEMS

1. At a general level, define the concepts reliability and validity.
2. Identify the strengths and weaknesses of face validity.
3. Discuss the notion of construct validity in relation to the idea of measuring unobserved phenomena.
4. Discuss the logic underlying the split-half approach to measuring a scale's reliability.
5. Educators frequently use purchasable standardized tests for measuring pupil IQ. Social scientists frequently develop their scales of measurement from the data which have been collected. In one case a scale is applied for purposes of measuring. In the other a scale is developed for purposes of measuring. Discuss the differing characteristics of these two approaches.
6. In developing a scale using Likert techniques, it has been recommended that extreme items be eliminated from consideration. Discuss the advantages and disadvantages of this strategy.
7. Discuss the factors relevant to determining the level of discriminatory power a researcher might set for selecting or rejecting items for a Likert scale.
8. Create a pool of items which could be used for developing a Likert-based scale of political activity. Arrange to administer this scale to approximately twenty people (perhaps other students in your class) and attempt to develop a Likert scale. (Since there are ethical issues in collecting and using social data, you may wish to review the concluding chapter on ethics in this text.)

RECOMMENDED READINGS

Edwards, Allen L.
1957 *Techniques of Attitude Scale Construction.* New York: Appleton-Century-Crofts.

Provides a reasoned overview of the major techniques available for constructing scales.

Laumann, Edward O.
1966 *Prestige and Association in an Urban Community.* Indianapolis: Bobbs-Merrill.

Extends the research reported in this chapter in a number of directions, and provides detailed discussion of the scaling procedures used.

Schuessler, Karl
1971 Chapter 7, "Attitude Measurement," in *Analyzing Social Data: A Statistical Orientation.* Boston: Houghton Mifflin.

Addresses the issue of why social scientists use a variety of techniques for constructing scales and assesses alternative strengths and weaknesses. Sections of this chapter require a modest background in statistics.

Upshaw, Harry S.
1968 "Attitude Measurement," in Hubert M. Blalock and Ann B. Blalock (eds.), *Methodology in Social Research.* New York: McGraw-Hill.

Provides a broad overview of scaling techniques and their applicability. Sections of this article require a modest background in statistics.

8

ORDINAL SCALING USING A GUTTMAN TECHNIQUE: MEASURING POLITICAL ALIENATION

GENERAL ISSUE

Scaling procedures often compel researchers to discard valuable data. For example, information about an individual's response to specific items is discarded when his or her replies are totaled in order to arrive at a single scale score. Since different response patterns may yield the same score, information concerning individual patterns may be lost. This process is similar to summing the correct responses on a true-false test. Two persons may have the same number of correct answers while varying in the substance of their responses to specific questions.

In 1941, Louis Guttman proposed a scaling procedure which yielded a single scale score and simultaneously reflected the pattern of responses responsible for the score.* His scaling procedure has generated a great deal of controversy.

The main reasons for this disputation lie in the fact that the procedures involved in Guttman scaling differ in many ways from other procedures of scaling. First, Guttman scaling requires and assumes unidimensionality for the property being scaled. That is, the items used for the scale must tap one and only one property. For example, in scaling racial attitudes,

* Louis Guttman, "The Quantification of a Class of Attributes: A Theory and Method of Scale Construction," in P. Horst et al., *The Prediction of Personal Adjustment* (New York: Social Science Research Council, 1941), pp. 319–348.

Guttman requires that the items relate only to attitudes toward race and not to attitudes toward social class or other phenomena. Second, Guttman scaling decrees that items be ordinal. This requirement differs from Likert scaling, for example, where the responses, rather than the items, are ordinal. Third, the Guttman method permits researchers to change a respondent's score if the data indicate that he or she was misclassified.

Despite these issues, many social scientists use the Guttman approach. As with all such procedures, Guttman scaling should be used only when circumstances warrant its application and the advantages exceed the disadvantages. In this chapter, a study of the relationship between voting and alienation demonstrates the usefulness of Guttman's method.

THEORETICAL PROBLEM

In democratic societies, citizens influence government policy most directly when they elect public officials. In America, however, not all citizens exercise their right to vote. Some fail to register, and others, although registered, neglect to go to the polls. Social scientists have directed a great deal of research toward identifying the social, economic, demographic, and attitudinal factors which distinguish voters from nonvoters.

Among their observations is the finding that nonvoters frequently are alienated from the political system. Social scientists therefore have concluded that, as the level of alienation increases, the probability of participating in the political system decreases. That is, the alienated generally eschew politics. This conclusion is qualified by the additional observation that alienated citizens often *do* vote in local elections, which they believe hold more vested interest. In other words, alienation appears to be associated with nonvoting primarily at the national level. At that level the relationship is *negative* (alienated citizens *do not* vote) while at the local level it is *positive* (alienated citizens *do* vote).

Among the explanations offered to account for differential voting patterns is one that focuses on structural differences between national and local political institutions. According to this reasoning, the character and structure of the national political system inhibits the participation of alienated citizens. In national elections, citizens do not vote on specific government policy or programs; rather they choose government representatives from a small number of charismatic individuals. Aside from reacting to broad policy, many voters find it impossible to determine a candidate's position on specific issues. Consequently, since the national political structure provides little opportunity for the direct expression of negative attitudes on specific issues but requires trust in representatives, the alienated have few options to manifest their sentiments. Primarily, they express their alienation by not participating in national elections, in effect abstaining.

The structure for voting at the local level is different. Here, political life frequently involves specific issues, such as building a highway bypass, rezoning a neighborhood, fluoridating water, or constructing a new school. In contrast to national, local politics provides visible targets for citizens' decision making. As a result, according to this argument, the alienated express their sentiments about issues and candidates by voting in community referendums and elections.

Although this explanation fits the data, it contains several assumptions for which empirical evidence is lacking. Even allowing for structural differences between national and local political institutions, there is no evidence that voters perceive these differences, or that these contribute to nonparticipation at the national level and participation at the local. In fact, the voting rate of the unalienated is relatively high at both levels. The alienated, on the other hand, presumably respond to these differences by not participating nationally while still participating locally. Kenneth Eckhardt and Gerry Hendershot focused on these disparities when they studied alienation and voting in a midwestern setting.*

Research Setting

In May 1966, a twice-defeated school tax levy once more came before the voters in a small, midwestern community. The mobilization of citizens for and against the tax provided Eckhardt and Hendershot with an opportunity to study the relationship between alienation and political strength.

In five election precincts, Eckhardt and Hendershot drew a random sample of registered males from lists provided by the local Board of Elections. They then mailed questionnaires to 357 potential voters one week prior to the May referendum. Approximately one-half of the questionnaires (167) were returned. Although the original sample of potential voters was random within each precinct, the precincts were purposively selected in order to represent both community socioeconomic areas and past voting

Table 8-1. Precinct Majority Vote by Previous School Tax Referendums.

PRECINCT	PRECINCT MAJORITY VOTE IN NOVEMBER 1965	PRECINCT MAJORITY VOTE IN DECEMBER 1965
A	For	For
B	For	For
C	Against	For
D	Against	For
E	Against	Against

* Kenneth W. Eckhardt and Gerry Hendershot, "Transformation of Alienation into Public Opinion," *Sociological Quarterly*, 8(1967):459–467.

patterns. Table 8-1 reports the voting patterns of these precincts on the previously defeated school tax levy.

Scaling Alienation

Eckhardt and Hendershot used the responses to four questionnaire items to measure alienation. They were:

In this community, some organizations and individuals have more to say about what gets done than others.

(a) Basically Agree______ (b) Basically Disagree______

The problem with this town is that an average citizen like me has little chance of influencing what gets done around here.

(a) Basically Agree______ (b) Basically Disagree______

No matter how you vote or what you want, people in public office generally do what they want anyway.

(a) Basically Agree______ (b) Basically Disagree______

For the most part, I disagree with what public officials and other important people want to do in this community.

(a) Basically Agree______ (b) Basically Disagree______

In terms of face validity, these items seemed to tap four aspects of political alienation. The first item dealt with the respondent's *perception of the power structure*, the second with his *perception of his ability to influence decisions*, the third with his *perception of the power of officeholders*, and the fourth with his *judgment of community goals*.

In Eckhardt and Hendershot's view, alienation could be viewed as a hypothetical continuum or ladder on which individuals could be arranged so that one position reflected more alienation than another. They believed that the magnitude of alienation would increase as four conditions were met. First, individuals must perceive that a power structure exists. If they do so, they are on the first rung of a ladder of alienation. Second, individuals must feel they have little influence in the power structure. Persons who suspect that a power structure exists and that they have little influence are on the second rung of the ladder. They are more alienated than those who believe in a power structure but believe that they exercise some influence.

Third, individuals must perceive that the politically powerful are able to exercise their will independently of the will of others. Persons who believe that a power structure exists, that they have little influence, and that those in power exercise their own will are on the third rung. Finally, individuals must disagree with the decisions of those in power. Those who believe that a power structure exists, that they have little influence, that the politically powerful implement their own goals, and that they (the voters) disagree with these goals of the powerful are on the fourth rung. They are the most alienated.

Using this as their definition of alienation, Eckhardt and Hendershot devised the four questions which then appeared in their questionnaire. According to their understanding of alienation, they expected to find the following pattern of responses for individuals in their study.

As is clear in Figure 8-1, the items are arranged in an ordinal pattern from least alienated to most alienated. Positions on the scale are designated by both the number and pattern of "yes" responses. Persons with a response pattern of Type I, who had a scale score of 0, did not endorse any of the items and were the least alienated. Persons with a response pattern of Type II, with a scale score of 1, endorsed only the first item but none of the others. Those with a response pattern of Type III, with a scale score of 2, endorsed both the first and second items but did not endorse any others. Those having a response pattern of Type IV, and with a scale score of 3, endorsed the first, second, and third items but not the fourth.

Figure 8-1. Logical Pattern of Responses.

	PATTERN TYPE	PERCEIVES A POWER STRUCTURE	PERCEIVES LITTLE INFLUENCE	PERCEIVES POWER IS USED	DISAGREES WITH GOALS	SCALE SCORE
Least Alienated	I	No (0)	No (0)	No (0)	No (0)	0
	II	Yes (1)	No (0)	No (0)	No (0)	1
	III	Yes (1)	Yes (1)	No (0)	No (0)	2
Most Alienated	IV	Yes (1)	Yes (1)	Yes (1)	No (0)	3
	V	Yes (1)	Yes (1)	Yes (1)	Yes (1)	4

Finally, persons with a response pattern of Type V, and who had a scale score of 4, endorsed all four items and were the most alienated.

Of course, this is only a logical pattern consistent with Eckhardt and Hendershot's conception of alienation. When they examined the questionnaires they found that not all respondents fit the logical patterns described above. Still, a majority of respondents *did* fit the patterns as described. In fact, of 668 responses (4 responses for each of 167 respondents), 628 or 94 percent fell into one of the 5 patterns. Thus, 94 percent of the individual responses could have been predicted on the basis of a single score ranging from 0 to 4. This prediction, in the form of a decimal (.94), is termed the *coefficient of reproducibility*.

DATA ANALYSIS

For convenience of presentation, Eckhardt and Hendershot divided respondents into two groups of approximately equal size. Patterns I and II were combined into a "least alienated" category ($N = 87$), and patterns III, IV, and V were combined into a "most alienated" category ($N = 80$).

Eckhardt and Hendershot began their analysis by investigating the relationship of social status to political alienation. They observed that alienation is associated with social status. People of lower socioeconomic status were likely to be most alienated. This finding holds whether socioeconomic status is measured by occupation or by educational attainment (see Table 8-2). On this basis, the data support the interpretation

Table 8-2. Political Alienation as Related to Position in the Community Social Structure.

POSITION	PERCENTAGE		TOTAL	
	Most Alienated	Least Alienated	%	*N*
Occupation				
Managerial	39	61	100	56
Professional	41	59	100	44
Skilled blue and white collar	63	37	100	30
Semi- and unskilled	79	21	100	19
Retired	72	28	100	18
Education				
College graduate	36	64	100	70
Some college	61	39	100	33
High school graduate	58	42	100	38
Less than high school graduate	76	24	100	21

SOURCE: Eckhardt and Hendershot, "Transformation of Alienation," p. 462, Table 1.

that people who lack economic power also tend to feel estranged from political power. Since lower socioeconomic status people are, in fact, likely to lack political power, the data suggest that the alienated accurately perceive the unequal distribution of power.

Eckhardt and Hendershot then studied the relationship of alienation to political participation. As indicated in Table 8-3, they found that alienation had little impact on voter interest in local issues. However, they did find that it had a significant impact on the direction of interest and its expression at the polls. First, alienated persons did not differ from the unalienated in terms of frequency of discussing the school tax levy with their neighbors. Forty-three percent of the voters in both categories said they

Table 8-3. Political Interest and Behavior Toward the School Tax Levy as Related to Political Alienation.

CHARACTERISTIC	PERCENTAGE WITH CHARACTERISTIC	
	Most Alienated ($N = 87$)	Least Alienated ($N = 80$)
Discussed issue with neighbor		
A great deal	43	43
A little, or none	57	57
	100	100
Followed issue in newspapers		
A great deal	64	66
A little, or none	36	34
	100	100
Voted in November election	(82)	(91)
Voted for	50	82
Voted against	50	50
	100	100
Voted in December election	(67)	(87)
Voted for	54	84
Voted against	46	16
	100	100
Intended to vote in May (excludes undecided)		
For	72	89
Against	28	11
	100	100

SOURCE: Eckhardt and Hendershot, "Transformation of Alienation," p. 464, Table 3.

discussed the issues a great deal. There also was little difference in the percentage of people who were following the issue in the newspapers.

Second, in all three referenda, the unalienated supported the school tax overwhelmingly (82, 84, and 89 percent). The alienated were split on the issue (in November there were 50 percent for and 50 percent against; in December there were 54 percent for and 46 percent against; and in May there were 72 percent for and 28 percent against).

Third, the alienated and unalienated turned out in equally large proportions to vote in the November referendum (91 percent of the latter and 82 percent of the former). It appeared that the alienated were weakening in their confrontation with the power structure. While 82 percent voted in the November referendum, only 67 percent voted in December. Furthermore, the fact that public officials placed the tax issue before the voters in November, again in December, and finally in May testified to their power as well as to their intention to eventually pass the tax. Indeed, the school tax levy did pass in May.

To assess another dimension of perceived power, Eckhardt and Hendershot asked voters to predict the outcome of the May referendum. They expected that the alienated would overestimate their strength. The actual percentages of most alienated and least alienated incorrectly predicting the referendum outcome appear in Table 8-4.

Table 8-4. Distribution of Predictions in Percentages for the Forthcoming School Tax Referendum.

	PERCENT CORRECTLY PREDICTING OUTCOME	PERCENT INCORRECTLY PREDICTING OUTCOME	TOTAL	
			%	*N*
Most alienated	56	44	100	87
Least alienated	74	26	100	80

SOURCE: Eckhardt and Hendershot, "Transformation of Alienation," p. 465, Table 4.

The data indicate that the most alienated voters were less likely to correctly predict the referendum outcome than were least alienated voters. This finding further supports the argument that the least alienated participate in local politics because they believe that they are powerful.

SUMMARY

Using Guttman scaling procedures, Eckhardt and Hendershot were able to construct a logical scale of political alienation which empirically ranked respondents into five scale patterns. Because the scale achieved a *coefficient of reproducibility* of .94, they had some confidence that the items reliably scaled alienation. Although they assessed the scale primarily in terms of face validity, they could not overlook the fact that the majority of the alienated on this scale were persons of low socioeconomic status. This suggests the scale identified respondents who had characteristics similar to those classified as alienated in other studies.

In general, Eckhardt and Hendershot found support for the argument that the alienated participated in local politics because they perceive themselves to be powerful and because they have visible targets at which they can take aim.

Technical Insert III

Guttmann Scaling Procedures

Unlike the scaling procedures previously discussed, Guttman scaling involves ordering both respondents and items. Its purpose is to develop a scale which permits the ranking of respondents and the recovery of item responses responsible for the scale score.

Using the hypothetical example of developing an attitude scale about homosexuality, the procedures of Guttman scaling appear below.

1. Using face validity, it is necessary first to compile a list of statements expressing attitudes toward homosexuality. The statements should be ranked from least tolerant to most tolerant. Then those statements which duplicate each other should be eliminated. From the remaining list, a reasonable number of the best statements (usually ten to fifteen) should be selected.
2. Some of the statements should be worded positively and others negatively. Therefore, agreeing with the positive statements indicates a liberal or tolerant attitude while disagreeing with the negative statements suggests an illiberal or intolerant attitude. (Usually two response choices, such as *agree* or *disagree,* are provided. However, it is possible to use Guttman scaling procedures if more than two choices are provided though the procedures become more complicated.)
3. It is now necessary to collect the data. For this example, data have been collected from twelve persons who each responded to four statements. As a matter of research practice, usually more than four statements are involved, and the number of respondents is much larger. In this example, the statements are each worded in a positive direction so that agreement expresses a liberal or tolerant position.
4. The value of 1 should be assigned to a response which agrees with the statement and a value of 0 to a response which disagrees with the statement.

   A *respondent's score* is calculated by summing his responses to the four items. The range of scores in this example will be from 0 to 4; 0 indicates the respondent disagreed with each statement, and 4 indicates the respondent agreed with each statement.

   A *statement's score* is calculated by summing the individual responses to the statement. In this example, the score can range from 0 to 12. A score of 0 indicates that all respondents disagreed with the statement; a score of 12 indicates that all respondents agreed with the statement.

   All statements are eliminated that were given either the minimum or maximum score. In this case, all statements with either a score of 0 or 12 are eliminated. These statements are eliminated because they do not contribute to the ranking of respondents. (An analogy might be a true-false question which everyone answers either correctly or incorrectly. The question does not discriminate between learners and nonlearners, so the question cannot contribute to the ranking of individuals.)

Figure III-1 illustrates how respondent scores and statement scores are calculated.

Figure III-1

		1 = AGREE		0 = DISAGREE		
Respondent	Statement A	Statement B	Statement C	Statement D		Respondent Score
1	1	1	1	1	=	4
2	0	0	1	0	=	1
3	1	1	1	1	=	4
4	0	0	0	0	=	0
5	1	1	0	1	=	3
6	0	0	0	1	=	1
7	1	1	0	1	=	3
8	0	0	0	1	=	1
9	1	1	0	1	=	3
10	1	0	0	1	=	2
11	0	0	0	1	=	1
12	1	0	0	1	=	2
Statement Score	7	5	3	10		

5. Using the statement score, the modal (most frequent) response for each statement is determined. This response is the best predictor for each statement. That is, it would provide the fewest errors in guessing an individual's response if a researcher had no other information about that individual's response. This can be seen in Figure III-2.

Figure III-2

Statement	Score	Most Frequent Response	Pattern
A	7	agree	1
B	5	disagree	0
C	3	disagree	0
D	10	agree	1

Figure III-3 shows that the best prediction pattern for all respondents is agree, disagree, disagree, agree, that is, 1001. This pattern would permit seven correct predictions of responses to statements A and B, nine correct predictions for statement C, and ten correct predictions for statement D.

Figure III-3

Statement	Most Frequent Response	Most Frequent Response	Predict	Correct Predictions	Incorrect Predictions	Total Predictions
A	agree	1	1	7	5	12
B	disagree	0	0	7	5	12
C	disagree	0	0	9	3	12
D	agree	1	1	10	2	12
Total				33	15	48

6. Determine the proportion of correct predictions.

$$\frac{\text{Number of correct predictions}}{\text{Total predictions}} = \frac{33}{48} = .687 \text{ or } 68.7\%$$

This value is the *Marginal Coefficient of Reproducibility*. It represents the proportion of responses which can be correctly predicted, using the most frequent response to each statement.

7. The next step in the procedure is to rank both the respondents and the statements. The information presented in Figure III-4 is the same information as provided in Figure III-1, but it has been rearranged to fit the ranking rule.

Figure III-4

Respondent	Statement D	Statement A	Statement B	Statement C		Respondent Score
1	1	1	1	1	=	4
3	1	1	1	1	=	4
5	1	1	1	0	=	3
7	1	1	1	0	=	3
9	1	1	1	0	=	3
10	1	1	0	0	=	2
12	1	1	0	0	=	2
6	1	0	0	0	=	1
8	1	0	0	0	=	1
11	1	0	0	0	=	1
2	0	0	0	1	=	1
4	0	0	0	0	=	0
Statement Score	10	7	5	3		

By examining the pattern of responses associated with each scale score type, it is possible to select the best predictive pattern.

The best pattern for respondents with score 4 is 1111 No errors
The best pattern for respondents with score 3 is 1110 No errors

The best pattern for respondents with score 2 is 1100 No errors
The best pattern for respondents with score 1 is 1000 Two errors
(Respondent 2 has a 0001 pattern. Therefore, responses for Statements D and C are incorrectly predicted).
The best pattern for respondents with score 0 is 0000 No errors

By using scale scores to predict responses, only two errors result from 48 predictions. The proportion of correct predictions is calculated below.

$$\text{Coefficient of Reproducibility} = \frac{\text{Correct predictions}}{\text{Total predictions}} = \frac{46}{48}$$

$$= .958 \text{ or } 95.8\%$$

Thus, while the marginal coefficient of reproducibility was .687 (68.7%), the coefficient of reproducibility resulting from ordering both respondents and statements was .958 (95.8%). Consequently, there has been a meaningful gain in the proportion of correct predictions using scale scores as the basis for prediction (.958 − .687 = .271).

8. Figure III-4 demonstrates that the statements are ordered. All respondents, with the exception of respondent 2, who agreed with statement C, also agreed with statements B, A, and D. All respondents who disagreed with statement C but agreed with statement B also agreed with statements A and D. All respondents who disagreed with statement B but agreed with statement A also agreed with statement D. All respondents with the exception of respondent 2, who disagreed with statement D, also agreed with statements A, B, and C.
9. If the procedures of analysis stopped here, there might be less controversy over Guttman scaling. Unfortunately, the matter is more complex. The complexity arises over what to do about respondent 2. He was classified with other respondents who had a score of one, and this produced two incorrect predictions. Perhaps his response to statement C was a mistake. Perhaps he really meant to disagree with statement C. If this is the case, he has been misclassified and moving him to scale type 0 is the best decision. If he is reclassified, there is only 1 incorrect prediction. His pattern is 0001, and placing him in the 0 category predicts a 0000 pattern for only 1 incorrect prediction. But should he be reclassified? If yes, the coefficient of reproducibility improves. Whether the respondents should be reclassified is a major point of controversy in Gutmann scaling.

$$\frac{\text{Correct predictions}}{\text{Total predictions}} = \frac{47}{48} = .979 \text{ or } 97.9\%$$

Since a Guttman scale is acceptable only if the *Coefficient of Reproducibility* is .90 or better, moving respondents who have errors improves the coefficient.

Some methodologists recommend reclassifying error patterns until the minimum number of incorrect predictions is achieved. This means that many scales which did not originally achieve coefficients of .900 or better will now exceed that value. There is much controversy over whether reclassification distorts data, and over how much reclassifying should be allowed. Consequently, the flexibility of classifying respondents is an important issue.

Furthermore, if the scale results in a large number of respondents in the one primary scale pattern, the coefficient will be high, but the scale may not have arrayed the respondents along a continuum. In other words, the distribution will be skewed. Consequently, the distribution of respondents is another important issue.

There are other problems but these are too detailed to explore here. Guttman scaling, like other scaling procedures, must be used cautiously. If a suitable ordering of respondents cannot be achieved using Guttman procedures, an alternative approach should be used. Scaling procedures should be used only if they fit the conditions of measurement needed for the research problem.

KEY IDEAS AND CONCEPTS

coefficient of reproducibility
empirical pattern
Guttman technique
hypothetical continuum
logical pattern
marginal coefficient of reproducibility
negative relationship
positive relationship
proportion
respondent's score
statement's score

ISSUES AND PROBLEMS

1. Discuss the essential differences between a Likert-based scale and a Guttman-based scale. Discuss their similarities.
2. In developing a pool of items to be used in eventually creating a Guttman-based scale, is it essential to have developed a logical pattern of responses in advance? Why or why not?
3. A Guttman-based scale like a Likert-based one is said to emerge from the data. What problems are generated if an acceptable Guttman scale emerges from the data but conflicts with a logical pattern that one had developed in advance? What resolutions do you suggest for these problems?
4. If an acceptable Guttman-based scale fails to emerge from the data, what additional procedures might a researcher attempt?
5. Discuss the idea of the marginal coefficient of reproducibility. What is its lowest possible value?
6. Discuss the idea of the coefficient of reproducibility. What is its highest possible value?
7. Do researchers seek to obtain marginal coefficients of reproducibility and coefficients of reproducibility which are as distant from each other as possible or as close to each other as possible. Why?
8. In attempting to develop a Guttman-based scale of political activity, a researcher used the following four items. By examining the items and the response patterns obtained from twelve respondents, determine if the researcher was successful. In this exercise, calculate a marginal coefficient of reproducibility and a coefficient of reproducibility and produce the best Guttman-based scale possible.

(*Hint*: to accomplish this it will be necessary to rearrange items and respondents and perhaps rescore some patterns.)

Listed below are some political activities. Some people engage in these activities and other people do not. Please indicate whether you do or do not engage in them.

Item	Engage	Do Not Engage
1. Attend political rallies specifically for purposes of supporting a political candidate.	______	______
2. Raise money for a specific candidate by door-to-door soliciting or some other such technique.	______	______
3. Display support for a specific candidate by wearing a button, displaying a bumper sticker, or some other such technique.	______	______
4. Contribute money directly to the support of a specific candidate.	______	______

RESPONSES + = engage − = do not engage

RESPONDENTS	ITEM 1	ITEM 2	ITEM 3	ITEM 4
1	−	+	+	+
2	+	+	+	+
3	+	−	+	+
4	−	+	+	+
5	+	−	−	−
6	+	+	+	−
7	+	−	+	+
8	−	−	+	+
9	−	−	−	−
10	+	−	−	−
11	−	−	+	+
12	+	−	+	+

RECOMMENDED READINGS

Borgatta, Edgar F.
1955 "An Error Ratio for Scalogram Analysis," *Public Opinion Quarterly*, 19:96–100.

Discusses an alternative technique for assessing the reliability of a Guttman scale.

Dotson, Louis E., and Gene F. Summers
1970 "Elaboration of Guttman Scaling Techniques," pp. 203–213 in Gene F. Summers (ed.), *Attitude Measurement*. Chicago: Rand McNally.

Edwards, Allen L.
1957 *Techniques of Attitude Scale Construction.* New York: Appleton-Century-Crofts.

Reviews in detail the procedures of Guttman scaling in Chapter 7, "Scalogram Analysis," pp. 172–200.

Schuessler, Karl
1971 *Analyzing Social Data: A Statistical Orientation.* Boston: Houghton Mifflin.

Reviews in detail the procedures of Guttman scaling in Chapter 7, "Attitude Measurement," pp. 326–331.

PART FOUR

Exploring Relationships Among Variables

9

MEASURING RELATIONSHIPS WITH YULE'S *Q*: THE RELATIONSHIP BETWEEN SOCIOECONOMIC CHARACTERISTICS AND DRUNKEN DRIVING CONVICTIONS

GENERAL ISSUE

In analyzing data, social scientists search for relationships between variables. Often this search is guided by formal hypotheses specifying expected relationships. Perhaps equally often, social scientists scrutinize their data in hope of discovering an unanticipated relationship. In conducting this analysis, they attempt to establish and describe the causes of social phenomena.

The concept of cause refers to the notion that a change in one variable produces a change in another. Although philosophers have demonstrated the logical impossibility of proving the existence of a force called cause, this has not prevented scientists from developing theories which employ causal propositions. The latter go beyond the idea of a mere relationship between variables, since a relationship means only that two variables co-occur or that a change in one variable is followed by a change in the other. A causal relationship, however, implies that a change in one variable produces a change in another.

Three conditions must be met before scientists will infer that a causal relationship exists. First, there must be evidence that a relationship of some kind exists between two variables. Second, there must be evidence that a change in the first variable preceded a change in the second. Third, there must be evidence that a third variable did not cause the changes observed in the first two.

It is generally recognized that experimental designs provide the best logical and empirical evidence for inferring a causal relationship. (The subject of experimental designs will be taken up later in this text.) Nonexperimental designs, however, provide evidence that two variables are or are not related. Indeed, nonexperimental designs occasionally can provide evidence as to whether a third variable was responsible for changes observed in the two others.

This chapter introduces the general logic of nonexperimental designs. It focuses on the procedures involved in controlling a third variable while examining the relationship between two variables. It also introduces a statistical procedure known as Yule's Q, one of several mathematical procedures available for summarizing the strength of a relationship between two variables.

THEORETICAL PROBLEM

An examination of the conviction statistics for driving while intoxicated (DWI) reveals that persons with low socioeconomic characteristics are represented in numbers disproportionate to their frequency in society. Two theoretical explanations have been advanced to account for this finding.

The Impartial Law Enforcement Theory

This theory holds that persons with low socioeconomic characteristics drink and drive more frequently than others. As a result, persons with these characteristics are arrested and convicted more frequently for the offense of DWI. Consequently, since these persons commit the offense more frequently than others, they are represented disproportionately in conviction statistics. This theory implies that an impartial law enforcement system exists in which arrests and convictions are in proportion to the frequency with which the offense is committed.

The Discriminatory Law Enforcement Theory

This theory holds that the police and courts systematically discriminate against persons with low socioeconomic characteristics. Thus, although there is no true relationship between socioeconomic characteristics and behavior resulting from drinking and then driving, persons having low socioeconomic characteristics are more likely to be arrested by the police and convicted by the courts. Consequently, this theory holds that systematic discrimination by the law enforcement system explains the disproportionate representation of persons with low socioeconomic characteristics in DWI conviction statistics.

Harvey Marshall and Ross Purdy undertook research to determine the credibility of these two theories.* Their research employed the logic of a nonexperimental design; they used an analysis involving *cross-sectional* data. Marshall and Purdy sought evidence that there was no true relationship between socioeconomic characteristics and conviction for driving while intoxicated. If they could obtain no such evidence, then, by implication, the theory of discriminatory law enforcement could be supported.

The reason for approaching the problem in this manner is that theories never can be proven true; they can only be proven false. This is due to the fact that some unexamined theory might eventually better explain the data than the theory at hand. Consequently, failure to disprove the theory at hand makes that theory credible, but does not prove that the theory is correct.

DATA AND THE FORM OF THE NULL HYPOTHESIS

Although national data regarding the relationship between socioeconomic characteristics and conviction for DWI would permit the best assessment of the null hypothesis, limited funds compelled Marshall and Purdy to make a more limited test. For this reason, they focused on intoxicated drivers in Los Angeles County. Consequently, the results of their study are limited to this political jurisdiction.

In order to assess the relationship between socioeconomic characteristics and conviction for DWI, Marshall and Purdy needed data on intoxicated drivers. They sampled intoxicated drivers from two sources: those arrested by the police and convicted by the courts (a convicted sample) and those who might have been, but were not, convicted (an unconvicted sample).

The Convicted Sample

Although there are many traffic courts in Los Angeles County, four process a majority (60 percent) of all cases involving drinking and driving. Marshall and Purdy believed that a random sample of the cases processed by these four courts would be reasonably representative of all cases processed in Los Angeles County. To obtain the necessary data on socioeconomic characteristics, they sent questionnaires to a randomly selected sample of convicted drivers. This procedure produced a total of 863 completed questionnaires.

* Harvey Marshall and Ross Purdy, "Hidden Deviance and the Labelling Approach: The Case for Drinking and Driving," *Social Problems*, 19(1972):541–553.

9.1 USING THE NULL HYPOTHESIS TO PROVE A THEORY FALSE

In science, a theory never can be proven true. When a theory is inconsistent with available data, scientists will consider it to be proven false. However, scientists must be cautious when confronted with a theory that is consistent with available data.

The fact that a theory is consistent with the existing data does not make that theory true. The only thing that is established in this case is that currently available data do not contradict the theory. Researchers can have no assurance that data found in the future will not contradict the current theory. Nor can they be sure that a theory with more power or scope will not emerge at a later date.

The null hypothesis lies at the center of the attempt to disprove a proposed theory when samples are involved. A null hypothesis is a statement that contradicts the proposed theory. If this contradictory statement fits the data, it provides the basis for rejecting the proposed theory. If the contradictory statement does not fit the data, then all that can be said is that momentarily the proposed theory has survived, to be tested another time. In other words, the null hypothesis has been rejected and the theory has been retained.

The use of the null hypothesis is basically conservative, because the standards for rejecting it are quite stringent. These standards developed in conjunction with statistical theory regarding the assessment of data based upon random samples. Although the subject of sampling and associated tests of significance are discussed later in the text, the logic of the null hypothesis is discussed here.

If the null hypothesis can be rejected, then the proposed theory will be tentatively accepted. If the proposed theory is actually false—although accepted temporarily as true—then an error in decision has been made. The error of accepting a false theory is known as a Type I error.

If, on the other hand, the null hypothesis is not rejected, then the proposed theory must be rejected. If the proposed theory proves actually true, then, again, an error in decision has been made. The error of rejecting a true theory is known as a Type II error.

The implications of Type I and Type II errors are serious. If one commits a Type I error, and accepts a false theory, scientists will waste their time researching false leads. If one commits a Type II error, and rejects a true theory, the growth of scientific knowledge is delayed. Scientists generally view both errors as serious. However, they see Type I errors as more damaging to science than Type II errors. Consequently, they set up decision-making procedures so that Type I errors are less likely to be committed than Type II errors.

Although the null hypothesis is one that simply contradicts the research hypothesis, null hypotheses in social science usually state there is no relationship between variables. This is because most social science theories posit a relationship between variables. Consequently, the null form states that there is no relationship.

The Unconvicted Sample

Following a similar procedure, Marshall and Purdy sought socioeconomic data about drivers who might have been, but were not, convicted of a traffic offense involving intoxication. In order to accomplish this, they selected five geographically scattered Los Angeles County Department of Motor Vehicles (DMV) offices. They did so because in California all persons seeking to renew their licenses or obtain a license for the first time must make application to the DMV. Through this selection, they hoped to obtain a sample of unconvicted intoxicated drivers which would be representative of the entire county. One thousand three hundred and twenty of the questionnaires administered to applicants were returned to Marshall and Purdy, and 545 questionnaires contained information indicating that respondents drove automobiles after consuming alcohol.

The combined data base for this study consisted therefore of 1,408 drinking drivers: 863 individuals convicted for driving while intoxicated and 545 unconvicted individuals who admitted to drinking prior to driving an automobile.

OPERATIONAL DEFINITIONS

Drinking and Driving

The courts defined intoxication by the percent of alcohol in the blood. Since this measure of intoxication was available only for the court sample, Marshall and Purdy developed an alternative measure of intoxication applicable to all respondents. Respondents were asked: "How often do you usually drive after drinking at least two drinks of hard liquor or three beers?" Response categories ranged from "never" through "once or twice a year" to "daily." Respondents who indicated "never" were excluded from the analysis. All other respondents were regarded as being potentially convictable of a traffic offense. While two drinks of hard liquor or three beers is probably insufficient to sustain a charge of legal drunkenness, it is probably sufficient to sustain a charge of reckless driving. Thus, the 1,408 respondents in the study met the minimum condition of potential conviction for a traffic offense related to drinking. Quite clearly, the court sample went beyond this minimum condition of intoxication. Some of the DMV sample probably also went beyond this condition, although the exact number is unknown.

As a further means of measuring drinking and driving, Marshall and Purdy asked respondents two additional questions: "How many drinks can you handle and still drive well?" and "How often have you driven in the last twelve months after having consumed more than this amount?" They used these questions to establish a measure of serious offense behavior. Respondents who indicated they "never" drove in this condition were placed in a category entitled "least serious," while all other respondents were placed in a category entitled "most serious."

Conceptually, therefore, the sample consisted of 1,408 respondents either convicted or potentially convictable of a driving offense related to drinking. The sample was subdivided into two categories: least serious and most serious offenders.

Socioeconomic Status

Marshall and Purdy measured socioeconomic status in three ways: according to level of education, annual income, and race or ethnic background. Using questionnaire data, respondents who indicated they had not completed high school were placed in a low-education group, while all other respondents were placed in a high-education category. With respect to income, respondents who reported their annual income as $9,999 or above were placed in a high-income category while all other respondents were placed in a low one. With respect to race and ethnicity, respondents were dichotomized into two groups: white and nonwhite. Mexican-Americans and blacks were part of the nonwhite category; other respondents, with the exception of Indians and Orientals, were considered white. Because there were so few Indians and Orientals in the sample, Marshall and Purdy excluded them from the study.

Although the two investigators exercised reasonable caution in drawing both the court and DMV samples, there is the possibility that the samples are not representative of the larger Los Angeles County population. This is not to say that the sample is unrepresentative, only that the possibility exists. This possibility is substantial, for the court sample was drawn from only four of the courts processing traffic offenders. The DMV sample was drawn from among all persons renewing or applying for new licenses in only five of the local DMV offices. Insofar as the four courts and five DMV offices served distinct subgroups of the total Los Angeles County population, the sample is biased. However, if one can assume that there are no differences between the population served by these courts and DMV offices and the population served by the remaining ones, the samples are likely to be representative. (The topic of sampling is taken up in Chapters 11 through 13.)

Perhaps more serious is the use of questionnaires and self-reported data for measuring drinking and driving. California residents seeking to renew their licenses or to obtain a license for the first time may have been reluctant to report their drinking behavior accurately. Similarly, persons recently convicted of a DWI offense also may have reported their drinking behavior inaccurately. Since respondents would be more likely to underestimate rather than overestimate their drinking and driving behavior, the bias in this study may not be an important consideration. If the analysis shows that there *is* a relationship between socioeconomic status and illegal drinking and driving behavior, then the true relationship is likely to be stronger than that observed.

ANALYSIS

Phase I of the analysis sought to determine if a relationship existed between socioeconomic status and conviction for driving while intoxicated. Using three separate measures of socioeconomic status (education, income, and race), Marshall and Purdy constructed three two-by-two contingency tables: one table for each of the variables. Tables 9-1, 9-2, and 9-3 display the data.

Each of the accompanying tables provides three types of information: the frequency distribution of respondents according to the two variables being considered, the percentage distribution of conviction status according to the independent variable, and a summary measure of association. The measures of association are known as *zero-order measures* since they have no variables introduced as controls. If a control variable is employed, the measures of association are referred to as *partials*. Each table reveals a relationship between the independent variable and the dependent variable. Table 9-1 indicates that 42 percent of the respondents with a high educational level were convicted of a drinking/driving offense, but 72 percent of the respondents with a low educational level were similarly convicted. The strength of the relationship, as measured by Yule's Q, is $-.57$. Table 9-2 indicates that 44 percent of the respondents with a high-income level were convicted of a drinking/driving offense, while 72 percent of the respondents with a low income level were similarly convicted. The strength of the relationship, as measured by Yule's Q, is $-.53$. Table 9-3 indicates that 32 percent of the white respondents were convicted of drinking while driving, while 84 percent of the nonwhite respondents were similarly convicted. The strength of the relationship, as measured by Yule's Q, is $-.83$.

9.2 RELATIONSHIPS BETWEEN VARIABLES

One of two ideas may apply to the notion of a relationship between variables: the idea of covariation and the idea of joint occurrence.

I. *Covariation* A covarying relationship between two variables exists when a change in the value of one accompanies change in the value of the other. The direction of the relationship may be either positive or negative.

A *positive relationship* exists when the changes of each variable are in the same direction. That is, a positive relationship exists when an increase in the value of one variable is accompanied by an increase in the value of the second. Such a relationship also exists when a decrease in the value of one variable occurs concurrently with a decrease in the value of the second.

A *negative relationship* exists when the change in the value of one variable occurs along with a change in the opposite direction in the value of the second.

(continued)

(continued)

Covariation is applied to variables which are capable of increasing and decreasing their values (e.g., interval variables). Figure A graphically portrays a positive relationship, while Figure B portrays a negative one.

II. *Joint Occurrence* A joint occurrence between two variables exists when the presence of one variable is accompanied by the presence of another.

Figure A. Positive relationship.

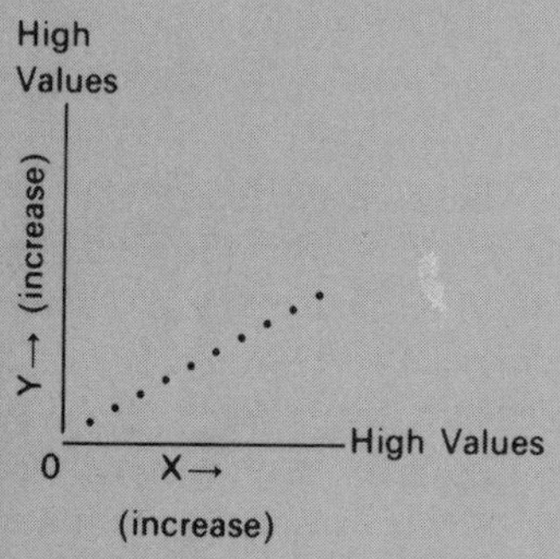

Figure B. Negative relationship.

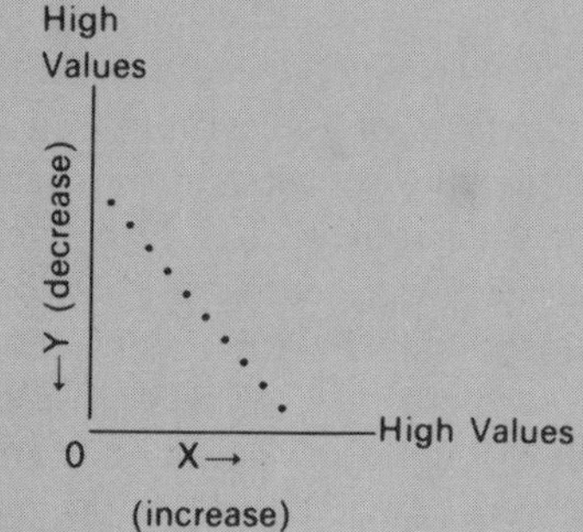

If one variable occurs, the other also occurs. The idea of joint occurrence is applied usually to nominal variables. It may be applied also to ordinal, interval, or ratio variables when these are separated into two or more categories (e.g., classifying income—a ratio variable—into two categories, high and low income). These occurrences are of two types: two-way association and one-way association. The direction of the relationship may be positive or negative, depending upon the type of problem.

A Perfect Two-Way Relationship A perfect two-way relationship exists when the presence of one variable always accompanies the presence of the second, and the absence of one occurs along with the absence of the other. Table A presents a perfect two-way relationship between variables *X* and *Y*.

Table A. Perfect Two-Way Relationship.

	VARIABLE *Y* PRESENT	VARIABLE *Y* ABSENT	TOTAL CASES
Variable *X* present	50	0	50
Variable *X* absent	0	50	50
Total	50	50	100

It is clear from Table A that whenever variable X is present, variable Y is present; whenever variable Y is absent, variable X is also absent. This table represents a perfect two-way relationship. A knowledge of one variable being present or absent permits perfect prediction of the other variable being present or absent.

Of course, in real life perfect relationships seldom occur. Typically, there are many apparent exceptions. This may result from measurement error or the presence of additional variables which have an impact on the relationship. Since perfect relationships are seldom found, we need a measure which will reflect the strength of the relationship when it is less than perfect. This task will be taken up shortly.

A Perfect One-Way Relationship A perfect one-way relationship exists when knowledge of the status of one variable permits perfect prediction of the second variable, but knowledge of the second variable does not permit prediction of the first. For instance, innoculation against measles may permit the one-way prediction that an innoculated person will not get the measles, but knowing that a person did not get the measles does not permit prediction that the person was innoculated. Table B presents a perfect one-way relationship between variables X and Y.

Since in real life, perfect one-way relationships seldom occur, a measure which will reflect the strength of the relationship when one-way relationships are less than perfect is necessary. This issue will be taken up shortly.

Table B. Perfect One-Way Relationship.

Innoculations	MEASLES		
	Variable Y Absent	Variable Y Present	Total Cases
Variable X present	50	0	50
Variable X absent	25	25	50
Total	75	25	100

Direction of the Relationship When the relationship between two nominal variables is under consideration, the idea of direction conveys little meaning. For instance, if variable X is sex, then one category is male while the other category is female. If we obtain a positive relationship between variable X and a second variable (Y), it does not mean that as X (sex) increases, Y increases. Some procedures for measuring the relationship between variables automatically yield a sign (positive or negative), but the sign of the relationship may have little meaning.

If, on the other hand, the variables being examined are of the ordinal, interval, or ratio type, the direction of the relationship has meaning. The meaning depends upon the character of the variables under examination. For instance, if the X variable is age, and Y is income, a positive relationship means that, as age increases, income increases.

These data suggest that the theory of impartial law enforcement should be rejected, and the discriminatory law enforcement theory should be accepted. Before drawing this conclusion, however, the influence of other variables must be considered.

Table 9-1. Education and Conviction Status Among Potential Convictable Persons.

EDUCATIONAL LEVEL	CONVICTION STATUS Convicted	Not Convicted	TOTAL
High	208 (42%)	292 (58%)	500 (100%)
Low	655 (72%)	253 (28%)	908 (100%)
Total	863	545	1408

Measure of Association: $Q = -.57$

Table 9-2. Income and Conviction Status Among Potential Convictable Persons.

INCOME LEVEL	CONVICTION STATUS Convicted	Not Convicted	TOTAL
High	238 (44%)	300 (56%)	538 (100%)
Low	625 (72%)	245 (28%)	870 (100%)
Total	863	545	1408

Measure of Association: $Q = -.53$

Table 9-3. Race and Conviction Status Among Potential Convictable Persons.

RACE	CONVICTION STATUS Convicted	Not Convicted	TOTAL
White	200 (32%)	418 (68%)	618 (100%)
Nonwhite	663 (84%)	127 (16%)	790 (100%)
Total	863	545	1408

Measure of Association: $Q = -.83$

(The data in the tables have been reconstructed from data presented by Marshall and Purdy, "Hidden Deviance and the Labelling Approach," so they are approximations of the original findings.)

9.3 A STRATEGY FOR MEASURING ASSOCIATION: YULE'S Q

The general strategy for measuring a relationship between two variables is to *compare an expected distribution if there were no relationship with an observed distribution obtained from the data.*

For instance, assume that there is no "expected" relationship between sex status and the likelihood of voting. If there are 50 males and 50 females (the independent variable), and 50 persons who vote and 50 persons who do not vote (dependent variable), what is the expected distribution in Table A?

Table A. Expected Distribution for No Relationship Between Sex and Voting Status.

	VOTING STATUS		
SEX	Voted	Did Not Vote	TOTAL
Male			50 (row 1, marginal)
Female			50 (row 2, marginal)
Total	50 (column 1 marginal)	50 (column 2 marginal)	100

Table B presents the expected distribution in cases where there is no relationship between sex status and voting status. The absence of a relationship in this case means that 25 of the 50 males voted and 25 of the 50 females voted.

Table B. Distribution for No Relationship Between Sex and Voting Status.

	VOTING STATUS		
SEX	Voted	Did Not Vote	TOTAL
Male	25	25	50
Female	25	25	50
Total	50	50	100

It is possible to intuitively arrive at the expected distribution presented in Table B. However, it is more difficult to provide the distribution for no relationship between sexual status and the likelihood of voting, for the row and column marginals of Table C.

In this instance there are unequal row and column marginals (i.e., column totals of 80 and 320, and row totals of 100 and 300), and the correct answer is not intuitive. The solution is to recognize that the internal cells must have the same proportion as the columns and rows for a condition of no relationship to exist. Since one-fourth of the

(continued)

Table C. Expected Distribution for No Relationship Between Sexual Status and Voting.

	VOTING STATUS		
SEX	Voted	Did Not Vote	TOTAL
Male	(*a*)	(*b*)	100 (row 1, marginal)
Female	(*c*)	(*d*)	300 (row 2, marginal)
	80 (column 1 marginal)	320 (column 2 marginal)	400

sample is male, one-fourth of those persons who voted should be male. Thus, 20 males should have voted ($\frac{1}{4}$ times 80) if there is no relationship between sexual status and the likelihood of voting (cell (*a*)).

It is possible to complete the remaining internal cells in one of two ways. Once one cell in a four-cell table is calculated, the remaining cells can be determined by subtraction. For example, since 20 males voted, 80 males must not have voted ($100 - 20 = 80$ in cell (*b*)). Since 20 males voted, 60 females must have voted in order to produce a total of 80 voters ($80 - 20 = 60$ in cell (*c*)). Since 60 females voted, 240 females must not have voted ($300 - 60 = 240$ in cell (*d*)). This procedure illustrates that a 2×2 table contains some latitude in determining the value of 1 cell, but once the value of that cell has been established, the values of the remaining 3 cells are fixed.

The other procedure for completing the internal cell distribution is to continue employing the technique used for determining the distribution of the first cell. For instance, since one-fourth of the sample is male, and 320 persons did not vote, then one-fourth of the 320 persons who did not vote should be male ($\frac{1}{4}$ times $320 = 80$ in cell (*b*)). This logic also applies to the remaining cells.

Comparing the Expected and the Observed Distributions There are many strategies for comparing expected and observed distributions. Each strategy has certain advantages. The strategy followed here is based on the procedure developed by the English statistician G. Udney Yule. Yule observed that when no relationship exists between two variables, the cross-products of the internal diagonal cells will be equal ($ad = bc$). Using this knowledge, he developed a measure of association which he named Q in honor of the nineteenth-century statistician Quetelet. His procedure is outlined below.

Table D

a	*b*
c	*d*

$$Q = \frac{ad - bc}{ad + bc}$$

(continued)

Since $ad = bc$ when there is no relationship between two variables, the numerator in the above equation becomes zero and Q becomes zero. The calculation of Q for Tables B and C are calculated below.

Table B-1

25 (*a*)	25 (*b*)
25 (*c*)	25 (*d*)

$$Q = \frac{ad - bc}{ad + bc}$$

$$= \frac{25(25) - 25(25)}{25(25) + 25(25)}$$

$$= \frac{625 - 625}{625 + 625} = \frac{0}{1250} = 0$$

Table C-1

20 (*a*)	80 (*b*)
60 (*c*)	240 (*d*)

$$Q = \frac{ad - bc}{ad + bc}$$

$$= \frac{20(240) - 80(60)}{20(240) + 80(60)}$$

$$\frac{4800 - 4800}{4800 + 4800} = \frac{0}{9600} = 0$$

Yule also determined that a perfect relationship between two variables will yield a value of 1.0 according to this procedure. Tables E and F illustrate this. Note how well one could predict the dependent variable with knowledge of the independent variable in both tables, and the slight limitation on prediction in Table F.

Table E

50	0
0	50

$$Q = \frac{50(50) - 0(0)}{50(50) + 0(0)}$$

$$= \frac{2500}{2500}$$

$$Q = 1.0$$

Table F

80	20
0	280

$$Q = \frac{80(280) - 20(0)}{80(280) + 20(0)}$$

$$= \frac{22{,}400}{22{,}400}$$

$$Q = 1.0$$

These tables also illustrate a peculiarity of Yule's Q. That is, a value of 1.0 exists for a perfect two-way relationship (Table E) and a perfect one-way relationship (Table F).

As a result, Yule's Q does not distinguish between one-way and two-way associations. This is neither a strength nor a weakness but simply a constraint on interpretation. Other statistical measures behave in different ways. It is possible to select a measure which does distinguish between one-way and two-way associations between variables.

Although an empirical relationship exists between socioeconomic characteristics and conviction status, it is possible that a third variable might explain this finding. Phase II of the analysis explored this possibility by asking whether persons with low education, low income, and a minority background were simply more serious violators of the law. If so, official statistics might merely reflect this fact. If these differences in "seriousness" explain the relationship, then the theory of impartial law enforcement cannot be rejected after all.

Evaluating this alternative explanation involves the following logic. If the notion of "seriousness" explains the relationship, then when one controls for seriousness, the original relationship should disappear (go to zero). Tables 9-4 and 9-5 display the relationship between educational status and conviction status for two levels of "seriousness." The measures of Q provided in these tables are referred to as partials since one or more variables are being controlled.

Table 9-4. Educational Level and Conviction Status for the Most Serious Offenders.

EDUCATIONAL LEVEL	CONVICTION STATUS		TOTAL
	Convicted	Not Convicted	
High	149 (75%)	51 (25%)	200 (100%)
Low	314 (77%)	94 (23%)	408 (100%)
Total	463	145	608
	$Q = -.07$		

Table 9-5. Educational Level and Conviction Status for the Least Serious Offenders.

EDUCATIONAL LEVEL	CONVICTION STATUS		TOTAL
	Convicted	Not Convicted	
High	80 (27%)	220 (73%)	300 (100%)
Low	320 (64%)	180 (36%)	500 (100%)
Total	400	400	800
	$Q = -.66$		

Table 9-4 contains data only for the most serious offenders. It indicates that there is a weak relationship ($Q = .-07$) between educational level and conviction status for serious offenders. Consequently, the theory of the impartial law enforcement cannot be rejected for these persons.

Table 9-5, containing data on the least serious offenders, indicates that there is a moderately strong relationship ($Q = -.66$) between education level and conviction status. Consequently, the theory of impartial law enforcement can be rejected for the least serious offenders. Law enforcement agencies appear in this study to be using discretion in less serious cases to the advantage of the more highly educated. Therefore, they are considered discriminatory.

Similar findings occur for the relationship between income level and conviction (Tables 9-6 and 9-7). However, the relationship between racial/ethnic background and conviction status remains high for both conditions of seriousness (Tables 9-8 and 9-9).

The data present a very interesting picture of relationships as summarized in Table 9-10.

Table 9-6. Income Level and Conviction Status for the Most Serious Offenders.

INCOME LEVEL	CONVICTION STATUS Convicted	Not Convicted	TOTAL
High	202 (77%)	61 (23%)	263 (100%)
Low	261 (76%)	84 (24%)	345 (100%)
Total	463	145	608

$Q = -.03$

Table 9-7. Income Level and Conviction Status for the Least Serious Offenders.

INCOME LEVEL	CONVICTION STATUS Convicted	Not Convicted	TOTAL
High	85 (31%)	190 (69%)	275 (100%)
Low	315 (60%)	210 (40%)	525 (100%)
Total	400	400	800

$Q = -.54$

Table 9-8. Racial Background and Conviction Status for the Most Serious Offenders.

RACIAL BACKGROUND	CONVICTION STATUS Convicted	Not Convicted	TOTAL
White	140 (47%)	160 (53%)	300 (100%)
Non-White	260 (84%)	48 (16%)	308 (100%)
Total	400	208	608

$Q = -.72$

Table 9-9. Racial Background and Conviction Status for the Least Serious Offenders.

RACIAL BACKGROUND	CONVICTION STATUS Convicted	Not Convicted	TOTAL
White	136 (43%)	182 (57%)	318 (100%)
Non-White	424 (88%)	58 (12%)	482 (100%)
Total	560	240	800

$Q = -.87$

Table 9-10. Zero Order and Partial *Q*'s (Controlling for Seriousness) Between the Independent Variable and Convictions for Driving and Drinking.

INDEPENDENT VARIABLES	ZERO-ORDER *Q*'s	PARTIAL *Q*'s Seriousness Most	Least
Education	−.57	−.07	−.66
Income	−.53	−.03	−.54
Race	−.83	−.72	−.87

SOURCE: Marshall and Purdy, "Hidden Deviance and the Labelling Approach," p. 548, Table 1.

INTERPRETATION

These data can be interpreted as follows:

1. With respect to education and income, the null hypothesis for the most serious offenders is accepted. Socioeconomic status is not related to conviction for DWI ($Q = -.07$ and $-.03$). The implication is that "justice is blind" when violations are serious. In this respect, the law enforcement process is impartial with regard to education and income.

2. With respect to education and income, the null hypothesis for least serious offenders is rejected. Socioeconomic status is related to convictions for driving while intoxicated in the least serious cases ($Q = -.66$ and $-.54$). The implication for these is that the law enforcement process discriminates against persons with low-education and low-income levels.

3. With respect to racial status, the null hypothesis is rejected for the most serious and the least serious offenders. There is a strong relationship between racial status and conviction for DWI regardless of the seriousness of the offense ($Q = -.72$ and $-.87$). The implication is that the law enforcement process systematically discriminates against minority-group members.

SUMMARY

Marshall and Purdy analyzed self-reported drinking and driving behavior for a sample of Los Angeles driver's license applicants and California convictions for DWI. They sought to determine the relationships, if any, between socioeconomic characteristics and law enforcement. Using Yule's Q as a statistical measure of association, they found a negative relationship between the independent variables (education, income, race) and the dependent variable (conviction status). Thus, at the zero-order level of association, it appeared that the law enforcement system uniformly discriminated against persons of low social status.

However, when Marshall and Purdy introduced seriousness of the offense as a control variable, they obtained different results. For persons classified as most serious offenders, education and income made no difference in conviction status. Race, however, continued to show a relationship to conviction. For persons classified as least serious offenders, education, income, and race all continued to show a relationship to conviction.

The partial Q's suggest that a complex law enforcement system is operating. When the offense is considered nonserious, socioeconomic variables influence its operation. When the offense is considered serious, only the variable of race appears to influence the likelihood of conviction.

KEY IDEAS AND CONCEPTS

association
causal proposition
cause
column marginal
contingency table
control
covariation
cross-product
cross section
dependent variable
diagonal
disproportion
expected distribution
independent variable
joint occurrence
measure of association
null hypothesis
observed distribution
operational definition
perfect one-way relationship
perfect two-way relationship
proportion
rejection of null hypothesis
relationship
row marginal
self-report
Type I error
Type II error
Yule's *Q*

ISSUES AND PROBLEMS

1. State the conditions necessary for inferring cause. Distinguish between a causal relationship and a mere relationship.
2. Discuss why it is impossible to establish the empirical existence of cause.
3. Discuss the logic of the null hypothesis in theory testing. List the implications of the Type I error. List the implications of a Type II error.
4. Using the data provided in Table 2-1, perform the following:
   a. Using the independent variable descent, classify societies into matrilineal and nonmatrilineal. Using the dependent variable sexual permissiveness, classify societies into permissive and nonpermissive. Using Yule's *Q* as a measure of association, calculate the strength of the relationship between descent and sexual permissiveness. How strong do you consider the relationship?
   b. Using the row and column marginals developed above, calculate the distribution of societies for each cell assuming no relationship between descent and sexual permissiveness. Calculate Yule's *Q*.
   c. Using the row and column marginals developed above, provide the distribution for a perfect two-way relationship between descent and sexual permissiveness. Calculate Yule's *Q*.
   d. Using the same marginals, provide a distribution meeting the requirements for a perfect one-way relationship between descent and sexual permissiveness. Calculate Yule's *Q*.
   e. Using the data provided in the table for question 4a, multiply row 1 by 2 and recalculate Yule's *Q*. Why didn't the value of Yule's *Q* change?
5. Often in searching for a relationship between two variables, it is necessary to control for a third. Discuss the logic underlying the idea of controlling for a third variable.

RECOMMENDED READINGS

Downey, Kenneth J.
1975 *Elementary Social Statistics.* New York: Random House.

A highly readable introduction to the field of statistics. The discussion of contingency, Yule's Q, and related matters in Chapter 11 are well worth pursuing.

Mueller, John H., Karl F. Schuessler, and Herbert L. Costner
1970 *Statistical Reasoning in Sociology* (2d ed.). Boston: Houghton Mifflin.

A highly readable introduction to the field of statistics. The idea of statistical association, discussed in Chapter 9, and the establishment of Yule's Q as a special case of gamma, discussed in Chapter 10, are well worth pursuing.

Weiss, Robert S.
1968 *Statistics in Social Research: An Introduction.* New York: Wiley.

A highly readable introduction to the field of statistics. The idea of association, discussed in Chapter 9, and the development of measures of association appropriate to nominal, ordinal, and metric data, discussed in Chapters 10 and 11, are well worth pursuing.

10

USING RELATIONSHIPS TO ASSESS COMPETING MODELS: THE RELATIONSHIP OF REFERENCE GROUPS, ATTITUDES, AND BEHAVIOR

GENERAL ISSUE

In social science, one frequently encounters two or more theories which seem to explain an observed set of empirical relationships equally well. All theories, however, have the power of generating implications which extend beyond the initially formulated propositions. An examination of these implications may reveal empirical data contradictory to expectations. When this occurs, there are grounds for rejecting a proposed theory.

It may also be possible to reject some of the alternate theories if systematic examination of evidence fails to support their theoretical implications. This strategy, in conjunction with an extension of the logic of third-variable analysis, is explored in this chapter.

THEORETICAL PROBLEM

"Do as I say and not as I do" is an expression which draws attention to an important sociological problem, to wit, the relationship between attitudes and behavior. Previous research has provided only inconsistent evidence about this relationship. Under some circumstances, attitudes are excellent predictors of behavior: knowledge of a person's attitudes toward an object serves as a reliable basis for predicting his behavior with regard to the same object. Under other circumstances, however, there appears to be no relationship between attitudes and behavior. Predictions based upon knowledge of attitudes in these circumstances are as likely to be incorrect as correct. Those factors which account for this varying relationship provide a source of continuing interest for sociologists.

This chapter seeks to unravel the relationship between attitudes and behavior through the inclusion of a third variable, reference groups. Earlier research established that there is an association among these three variables. This chapter assesses opposing theoretical models that include all three variables, as a means of increasing knowledge about the relationship between attitudes and behavior.

James Fendrich, in a study of racial attitudes and behaviors, advanced four alternative theoretical models to specify the relationships between reference groups, attitudes, and behavior.* Since theories can be examined logically or empirically, the procedure he used first clarified the logic of the four models, and then examined the empirical evidence to determine which model best fit the data.

Model I

The first model suggests that reference group support (*RGS*) determines attitude (*A*) and behavior (*B*). According to this model, any observed relationships between attitude and behavior can be explained in terms of the association between *RGS* and *A*, and between *RGS* and *B*. This means that attitudes alone are not good predictors of behavior. In fact, the relationship between attitude and behavior is spurious. This model is represented as follows:

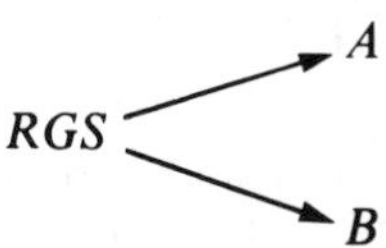

The arrows connecting *RGS* to *A* and *RGS* to *B* describe the inferred causal relationships: *RGS* causes both *A* and *B*. The absence of an arrow from *A* to *B* signifies that there is no causal relationship between attitude and behavior. The implication of Model I is that *if* RGS *were eliminated, any previously observed empirical relationship between* A *and* B *would disappear.* Therefore the null hypothesis states the contradictory case, namely, that there is a relationship between attitudes and behavior if reference group support is controlled. If the null hypothesis is rejected, then it is possible that Model I correctly describes the relationships between *RGS*, *A*, and *B*. However, since other explanations may also fit, Model I is only tentatively accepted.

* James M. Fendrich, "Perceived Reference Group Support: Racial Attitudes and Overt Behavior," *American Sociological Review*, 32(1967):960–970.

Model II

The second model suggests that reference groups, attitudes, and behaviors are interrelated in a sequential manner. Reference groups determine attitudes, and attitudes in turn determine behaviors. This model can be represented as follows:

$$RGS \longrightarrow A \longrightarrow B$$

In this model, attitude is conceived of as an "intervening variable" between reference group and behavior. The implication of Model II is that *if attitudes were eliminated, any empirical relationship previously observed between* RGS *and* B *would disappear.* Therefore, the null hypothesis challenges the model by stating that there is a relationship between *RGS* and *B* when *A* is controlled. Again, the model is acceptable only if the null hypothesis is rejected.

Model III

The third model suggests that reference group and attitude each independently determine behavior. Therefore, there is no relationship between reference groups and attitude; instead, each independently causes behavior. This model can be drawn as follows:

In this model, reference groups and attitude are independent of each other, but they separately influence behavior. The implication of Model III is that *if behavior were eliminated, any empirical relationship observed between* RGS *and* A *would disappear.* Therefore, Fendrich's null hypothesis states the contradiction: there is a relationship between *RGS* and *A* if *B* is controlled. Again, the model is acceptable only if the null hypothesis is rejected.

Model IV

The fourth model suggests that reference groups determine both attitudes and behavior. It also states that attitudes independently influence behavior. This model implies that a force other than the reference group determines attitudes. It also suggests that the influence of reference groups is both direct and indirect. It is direct in that they directly influence behavior; it is indirect in that some of the influence of reference groups goes through attitudes before having an impact on behavior. This model is as follows:

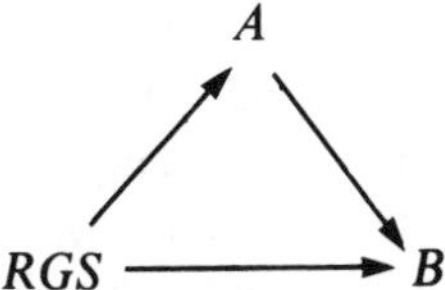

The implications of this model are twofold. (1) *If attitudes were eliminated, any previously observed empirical relationship between* RGS *and* B *would be reduced but not eliminated.* (2) *If reference groups were eliminated, any previously observed empirical relationship between* A *and* B *would be reduced but not eliminated.* Therefore, there are four null hypotheses to be considered. Two of them contradict the first statement and two contradict the second. The null hypotheses contradicting the first statement are (1) if *A* is controlled, the relationship between *RGS* and *B* is not reduced, and (2) if *A* is controlled, the relationship between *RGS* and *B* is eliminated. Similarly, the null hypotheses contradicting the second statement are (1) if *RGS* is controlled, the relationship between *A* and *B* is not reduced, and (2) if *RGS* is controlled, the relationship between *A* and *B* is eliminated. Accepting any one of these four null hypotheses results in the rejection of Model IV.

Having moved to this point, the task becomes one of empirically assessing the four models to determine which null hypotheses are not valid. If the null hypotheses for one of the models can be *rejected*, then that model can be termed tentatively *acceptable.*

METHODOLOGY

Sample

Dr. Fendrich gathered data to measure reference groups, attitudes, and behavior from students enrolled in an upper division social psychology course at a Big Ten university. Three screening criteria were used to select students: (1) they had to be U.S. citizens, (2) they had to reside on campus or in the adjacent community, and (3) they had to be full-time students. The purpose of these criteria was to eliminate freshmen and other students who, for various reasons, would be less of an integral part of the university community and who, therefore, might influence the research in unknown ways. These procedures resulted in a loss of 10 respondents from a total of 199, with a resultant *N* of 189 respondents. Fendrich categorized each student's response according to the nature of reference group support, attitude, and behavior. He used the following scaling techniques, developing three scales to measure *RGS*, *A*, and *B*.

Reference Group Support Scale

Fendrich devised a reference group support scale to measure the degree to which reference groups were seen as willing to participate in interracial activities. He viewed each individual in the sample as having five possible reference groups: (1) closest friends of the same sex, (2) closest friends of the opposite sex, (3) parents, (4) roommates (or husband or wife), and (5) older persons whom they might respect.

He asked respondents nine questions about the expected interracial behavior of each of the five groups. There were three possible answers for each question: yes, maybe, and no. Two examples of the nine questions are as follows:

1. Would the following people you know agree to go to coffee or lunch with a mixed racial group to talk about interracial problems?
   (a) Yes (b) Maybe (c) No
2. Would the following people you know agree to protest against segregated housing in their hometown?
   (a) Yes (b) Maybe (c) No

This procedure resulted in forty-five bits of information about an individual's reference groups (i.e., nine questions each asking about five groups equals forty-five pieces of information). Fendrich gave yes answers a score of 1 while he gave maybe and no 0. Possible scores ranged from 0 to 45. The split-half reliability of this reference group's support scale was .96.

Attitude Scale

Fendrich also developed a thirty-two item Likert scale to measure racial attitudes. The items had a seven-point response scale: (1) strongly agree, (2) agree, (3) agree in part, (4) neither agree nor disagree, (5) disagree in part, (6) disagree, and (7) strongly disagree. The thirty-two items covered a variety of campus experiences such as dating, athletics, and student government. Thirteen items stated a favorable attitude toward black students, while nineteen items stated an unfavorable attitude. Below are some examples of the thirty-two items.

1. Negro students all look alike.
2. I wouldn't want Negroes in positions of responsible student leadership on campus.
3. Negroes on campus want too much.
4. I would feel extremely uncomfortable dancing with a Negro student.
5. I would prefer sharing living quarters with any white rather than with a Negro student.

The split-half reliability of the Likert scale was .89.

Behavior Scale

Fendrich used a Guttman approach to develop a scale ranging from stated willingness to engage in limited behavior on up to commitment to continuing activity. First, students answering the questionnaire were asked whether they were willing to attend small group discussions scheduled for the near future with members of the campus chapter of the NAACP. During the five-day period following the administration of the questionnaire, Fendrich contacted students to determine whether they would attend one of six scheduled meetings. They were asked to indicate which meeting they would attend. This was followed up by a direct invitation from a member of the NAACP. Then came the small group discussion itself. During its course students were asked whether they would sign up for future civil rights activities. The results were rated on a five-point scale.

1 = Agreeing in general to participate in small group discussions.
2 = Agreeing to attend a definite meeting by circling the time and the day the meeting was to be held.
3 = Accepting the invitation of the NAACP representative to attend small group discussions to improve race relations on campus.
4 = Participating in small group discussions.
5 = Signing up for on-going civil rights activities.

The application of scalogram procedures to these five items resulted in a coefficient of reproducibility of .99.

		ITEM 1	ITEM 2	ITEM 3	ITEM 4	ITEM 5
(Most liberal)	Type I	+	+	+	+	+
	Type II	+	+	+	+	−
	Type III	+	+	+	−	−
	Type IV	+	+	−	−	−
	Type V	+	−	−	−	−
(Least liberal)	Type VI	−	−	−	−	−

(+ indicates behavior described by the item was performed)

$$CR = \frac{\text{Total correct predictions}}{\text{Total respondents} \times \text{Total items}} = .99$$

CLASSIFYING RESPONDENTS

Fendrich decided to place respondents into two categories for each variable. That is, each respondent was classified as being in one of two categories as a result of the nature of his reference group support. Each respondent was also classified in one of two categories based upon his attitudes, and in one of two categories based upon his behavior. The factors considered in this classification process are as follows:

Classifying by Reference Group Support

As is frequently the case with social science research, there was no absolute measurement of reference group support. Furthermore, there was no way to ascertain an absolute zero point for such support or establish the upper boundary of the *RGS* scale. Consequently, the best strategy available was to rank-order respondents, beginning with those who received the highest reference group support for interracial activity and going down to those who received the lowest such support for the same activity. Having rank-ordered the respondents, Fendrich decided to split the respondents into two groups: those who received strong reference group support and those who received weak support. The dividing point was the *median* score, that above which were 50 percent of the scores and below which lay the remaining 50 percent. He felt that this dividing point would be least likely to bias the data.

Classifying by Attitudes

In similar fashion, Fendrich decided to split the respondents by attitudes into two groups: those with the most favorable attitudes and those with the least favorable. Again, the cutting point was the median.

Classifying by Behavior

Unfortunately, the distribution of respondents' behaviors did not permit dividing at the median because most respondents failed to make any interracial commitments or behaviors. As a result, Fendrich found it impossible

Table 10-1. Frequency and Percentage Distribution of Respondents for Variables: Reference Group Support, Attitudes, and Behavior.

VARIABLE	*N*	%
Reference group support		
Strong	94	49.7
Weak	95	51.3
Total	189	100.0
Attitudes		
Most favorable	96	50.7
Least favorable	93	49.3
Total	189	100.0
Behavior		
Most liberal	34	18.0
Least liberal	155	82.0
Total	189	100.0

to arrive at a cutting point which distributed the respondents into two equal categories. He therefore classified respondents in scale types I, II, and III as demonstrating the most liberal interracial behavior, while respondents in scale types IV, V, and VI had the least liberal interracial behavior.

Table 10-1 provides the frequency and percentage distribution of respondents for each dichotomized variable.

ANALYSIS

The first step in the analysis was to establish the relationships between each of the variables. This was accomplished by cross-tabulating each variable with the other and employing Yule's Q to measure the relationship. Tables 10-2A, B, and C present the results.

It is clear from these data that there were empirical relationships of moderate strength among all possible pairings of the three variables. The problem next confronting the analysis was to determine which of the four previously discussed theoretical models "best fit" the data.

Table 10-2A. Relationship Between Reference Group Support and Racial Attitudes.

REFERENCE GROUP SUPPORT	ATTITUDES	
	Favorable	Unfavorable
Strong	64	30
Weak	32	63
	$N = 189$	$Q = .62$

(A moderately strong relationship between *RGS* and *A*)

Table 10-2B. Relationship Between Reference Group Support and Behavior.

REFERENCE GROUP SUPPORT	BEHAVIOR	
	Most Liberal	Least Liberal
Strong	28	66
Weak	6	89
	$N = 189$	$Q = .72$

(A moderately strong relationship between *RGS* and *B*)

Table 10-2C. Relationship Between Attitudes and Behavior.

	BEHAVIOR	
ATTITUDES	Most Liberal	Least Liberal
Favorable	28	68
Unfavorable	6	87
	$N = 189$	$Q = .71$

(A moderately strong relationship between *A* and *B*)

SOURCE (Tables 10-2A, B, C): Fendrich, "Perceived Reference Group Support," p. 965, Tables 1a, 1b, and 1c.

Examining Model I

Model I $RGS \genfrac{}{}{0pt}{}{\nearrow A}{\searrow B}$ suggested that *RGS* might determine *A* and *B* but that there was no relationship between *A* and *B*. If this model fit the data, then when *RGS* was controlled the observed relationship between *A* and *B* ($Q = .71$) should disappear. Table 10-3 portrays the relationships between *A* (Attitude) and *B* (Behavior) when controlling for *RGS* (Reference Group Support). Table 10-3 indicates that the relationship between *A* and *B* varies considerably from ($Q = .70$) when *RGS* is strong to ($Q = .35$) when *RGS* is weak. However, the *average* Q does not drop to zero; it is merely reduced from the original value of .71 to .52. (In this case, the average value of Q represents that value obtained when controlling for *RGS*.) It should be recalled that the null hypothesis for Model I stated that there would be a relationship between *A* and *B* when controlling for *RGS*. Since there *is* a relationship (mean $Q = .52$), the null hypothesis cannot be rejected. Consequently, Model I has to be rejected.

Table 10-3. Relationship Between Behavior and Attitudes When Controlling for Reference Group Support.

RGS STRONG			*RGS* WEAK		
	Behavior			*Behavior*	
Attitudes	*Most Liberal*	*Least Liberal*	Attitudes	*Most Liberal*	*Least Liberal*
Favorable	25	39	Favorable	3	29
Unfavorable	3	27	Unfavorable	3	60
	$Q = .70$	$N = 94$		$Q = .35$	$N = 95$

$$\text{Average } Q = (.497).70 + (.503).35 = .522$$

SOURCE: Fendrich, "Perceived Reference Group Support," p. 967, Table 2a.

10.1 AVERAGING *Q* VALUES

Statisticians recommend a number of different procedures for averaging *Q* values. Since there does not seem to be one procedure which has a clear advantage over others, the one used here was chosen for its simplicity.

Data from Tables 10-2 and 10-3 are used to illustrate the method. The relationship between attitudes and behavior, as measured by *Q*, was .71. This *Q* value was based on 189 cases (see Table 10-2). When reference group support was strong, the *Q* value between attitudes and behavior was .70 (see Table 10-3). This *Q* value was based on 94 of the 189 cases, and is weighted accordingly. That is, since 49.7 percent (94/189 × 100) of the cases were used to calculate this *Q*, then 49.7 percent of the average *Q* should be based on them.

Similarly, when reference group support was weak, the *Q* value between attitudes and behavior was .35 (Table 10-3). This value was based on 95 of the 189 cases and weighted accordingly. That is, since 50.3 percent (95/189 × 100) of the cases were used to calculate *Q*, then 50.3 percent of the average *Q* should be used on them.

Therefore, the average *Q* is

$$\begin{array}{r} .497 \times .70 = .346 \\ .503 \times .35 = .176 \\ \hline .522 \end{array}$$

In other words, the average *Q* of .522 is a *weighted average*. Weighted averages are used where some of the components to be averaged should have more influence than others. Thus, in this method of averaging *Q*'s, it is assumed that the *Q*'s based on a larger number of cases should have more influence on the average than *Q*'s based on fewer cases.

Examining Model II

Model II suggests that *RGS* influences *A* and *A* in turn influences *B* ($RGS \rightarrow A \rightarrow B$). If this model fits the data, then, when *A* is controlled, the observed relationship between *RGS* and *B* ($Q = .72$) should disappear. Table 10-4 portrays the relationships between reference group support and behavior when controlling for attitude. Table 10-4 indicates that the relationship between *RGS* and *B* varies considerably when *A* is favorable ($Q = .72$) and when it is unfavorable ($Q = .38$). However, the average *Q* does not go to zero, but is merely reduced from the original value of .72 (Table 10-2B) down to .55. The null hypothesis for Model II stated that there would be a relationship between *RGS* and *B* when controlling for *A*. Since there *is* such a relationship, the null hypothesis cannot be rejected. Consequently, Model II cannot be accepted.

Table 10-4. Relationship Between Reference Group Support and Behavior When Controlling for Attitudes.

ATTITUDES FAVORABLE			ATTITUDES UNFAVORABLE		
	Behavior			Behavior	
Reference Group Support	*Most Liberal*	*Least Liberal*	Reference Group Support	*Most Liberal*	*Least Liberal*
Strong	25	39	Strong	3	27
Weak	3	29	Weak	3	60
	$Q = .72$	$N = 96$		$Q = .38$	$N = 93$

$$\text{Average } Q = (.508).72 + (.492).38 = .554$$

SOURCE: Fendrich, "Perceived Reference Group Support," p. 967, Table 2b.

Examining Model III

This model suggests that *RGS* and *A* independently influence *B*, and that *RGS* and *A* have no association except through their relationship to $B\left(\begin{smallmatrix} RGS \searrow \\ \quad B \\ A \nearrow \end{smallmatrix}\right)$. If this model fits the data, then controlling for *B* should cause the relationship between *RGS* and *A* to go to zero. The data from Table 10-5 provide a test of this prediction.

Table 10-5 indicates that the relationship between *RGS* and *A* varies considerably when *B* is most liberal ($Q = .79$) and when *B* is least liberal ($Q = .50$). The null hypothesis, however, stated that the relationship between *RGS* and *A* would not disappear when *B* was controlled. The data revealed a continuously strong relationship ($Q = .55$) which was consistent with the null hypothesis rather than the model. Consequently, Fendrich could not reject the null hypothesis and he could not accept Model III.

Table 10-5. Relationship Between Reference Group Support and Attitudes When Controlling for Behavior.

BEHAVIOR MOST LIBERAL			BEHAVIOR LEAST LIBERAL		
Reference Group Support	Attitudes		Reference Group Support	Attitudes	
	Favorable	*Unfavorable*		*Favorable*	*Unfavorable*
Strong	25	3	Strong	39	27
Weak	3	3	Weak	29	60
	$Q = .79$	$N = 34$		$Q = .50$	$N = 155$

$$\text{Average } Q = (.179).79 + (.820).50 = .551$$

SOURCE: Fendrich, "Perceived Reference Group Support," p. 967, Table 2c.

Examining Model IV

Finally, Model IV suggests that *RGS* directly influences *B* and also that *RGS* influences *B* through *A* $\left(RGS \nearrow A \searrow B;\ RGS \longrightarrow B \right)$. The data for assessing Model IV are contained in Tables 10-3, 4, and 5. Fendrich examined four specific null hypotheses for testing this model. The first stated that, if *A* is controlled, the relationship between *RGS* and *B* is not reduced. In fact, the data indicated that the uncontrolled relationship of .72 (Table 10-2B) is reduced by controlling for *A* to .55 (Table 10-4). Thus, the first null hypothesis had to be rejected, and the model now faced its second challenge.

The second null hypothesis, like the first, explored this model's consequences of controlling for *A*. It stated that if *A* were controlled, the relationship between *RGS* and *B* would be eliminated. The data presented above for the first hypothesis already eliminated this hypothesis because the controlled relationship was .55.

The third null hypothesis stated that if *RGS* were controlled, the relationship between *A* and *B* would not be reduced. The actual data, however, indicate that the uncontrolled relationship of .71 (Table 10-2C) is reduced by controlling for *RGS* to .52 (Table 10-3). Clearly, the null hypothesis can be rejected.

The fourth null hypothesis, like the third, explored this model's consequences of controlling for *RGS*. It stated that if *RGS* were controlled, the relationship between *A* and *B* would be eliminated. The data presented in an effort to reject the third null hypothesis also eliminated this one, because the controlled relationship was .52 rather than approximating zero.

In sum, Fendrich had to reject Models I, II, and III because their null hypotheses were not rejected. Model IV, reproduced below, was not contradicted and, for the moment, is considered acceptable.

Model IV

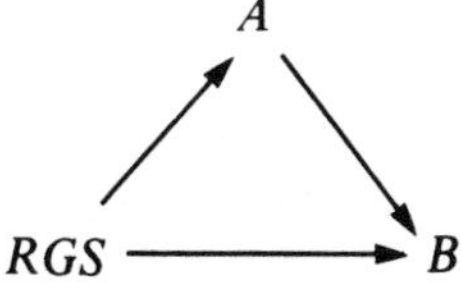

SUMMARY

In examining empirical data Fendrich used Yule's Q to evaluate four theoretical models. Based on the results obtained, he concluded that Models I, II, and III ought to be rejected. He accepted Model IV tentatively. Does this mean that Model IV is "true"? Of course not.

It only means that it satisfies the data better than any of the other three. However, other models, still to be created, may fit the data even better. Since these others could not be examined, Fendrich only provisionally settled for Model IV.

KEY IDEAS AND CONCEPTS

dichotomous variable
direct causal effect
independent causal effect
indirect causal effect
intervening variable
Guttman scale
Likert scale
moderately strong relationship
median
split-half reliability
spuriousness
strong relationship
theoretical model
weighted average

ISSUES AND PROBLEMS

1. Define the concept of spuriousness. Provide an example of two variables which are theoretically unrelated to each other and yet where each is related to a third variable. Using the diagram for Model I provided in the chapter, diagram your example.
2. Provide an example in which two variables are related through a third variable as illustrated by Model II. Define and discuss the idea of an intervening variable.
3. Provide an example in which two unrelated variables influence the behavior of a third, as is the case with Model III.
4. State the null hypotheses for each of the examples you provided in questions 1, 2, and 3. Discuss the implications of rejecting the null hypotheses in each case.
5. Discuss the logic of controlling for a third variable. Set up hypothetical tables for testing the models generated in questions 1, 2, and 3. Discuss the idea of an average weighted Q.

RECOMMENDED READINGS

Hirschi, Travis, and Hanan C. Selvin
1967 *Delinquency Research: An Appraisal of Analytic Methods.* New York: Free Press.

Discusses issues of hypothesis and theory testing in the context of problems of measurement and causal analysis. A scholarly discussion worth reading.

Rosenberg, Morris
1968 *The Logic of Survey Analysis.* New York: Basic Books.

Discusses the strategy of analysis for examining possible variable relationships in model form. A scholarly discussion worth reading.

PART FIVE

Sampling and Sampling Designs

11

SIMPLE RANDOM SAMPLING: CORRELATES OF SUCCESS AMONG AMERICAN SOCIOLOGISTS

GENERAL ISSUE

Government, the business community, and scientists frequently rely on information obtained from a sample to arrive at generalizations about the characteristics of a population. The study of a sample, in lieu of a whole population, has several advantages deriving from the fact that the former is only a portion of the latter. Since a sample *is* smaller, the time and cost involved in data collection often can be greatly reduced. Additionally, if the population is large, widely scattered, or changing rapidly, the study of a sample may produce more accurate information because of fewer errors in data collection. Furthermore, if data collection procedures alter or destroy the population, as would be the case, say, in determining the longevity of lightbulbs, the study of a sample is necessary.

Section I of this chapter explores the usefulness of sampling procedures in arriving at generalizations about a population. Section II examines the problem of drawing inferences about a population from relationships observed in a sample. Specifically, these procedures are examined in the context of research investigating the impact of social background characteristics on a career in sociology.

11.1 ALTERNATIVE SAMPLING PROCEDURES AND THE TABLE OF RANDOM NUMBERS

The object of most sampling procedures is to produce a sample which is representative of the population, but there are no known procedures for guaranteeing that these will produce a sample that is representative. Consequently, there is always some risk in generalizing research results obtained from a sample to the rest of the population.

Two options are available for reducing this risk. The first is to use random sampling procedures in selecting the sample. The second is to use nonrandom sampling procedures in making the selection. Neither of these two procedures, however, guarantees that the sample is representative of the population from which it is drawn. The use of random sampling procedures, however, is supported by statistical theory. This theory permits statements of confidence and precision in generalizing sample results to the population. The theory is more fully explained in the first Technical Insert found at the end of this section, starting on page 165.

Simple Random Sampling and the Table of Random Numbers. Simple random sampling requires that each member of the population has an equal chance of being included in the sample. To meet this requirement, it is first necessary to precisely define the population so as to include all members and exclude all nonmembers. Then, it is necessary to obtain a complete list of all members of the population. This list is necessary for drawing the sample.

Scientists frequently prefer the use of a table of random numbers over other procedures in drawing the sample because of its ease of application and absence of bias. Each member of the population is assigned a number. If numbers then are drawn randomly, each member of the population has an equal chance of being included. To facilitate the selection of numbers, statisticians have generated a list of numbers

THEORETICAL PROBLEM

On the one hand, science consists of a set of procedures for exploring and deriving theoretical explanations about empirical observations. On the other, it has vocational dimensions, for it offers careers in academia, government, and various industries. Social scientists frequently seek to describe and analyze the characteristics of scientists, their behavior, and their values in an effort to understand how these influence the development of scientific theory and method.

The Influence of Background Characteristics on a Career in Sociology

In the early days of American sociology, many persons attracted to the discipline came from rural families which had strong religious orientations. Observers of this phase of sociology have suggested that this was an appro-

randomly arranged (see page 382 ff.). Beginning anywhere in the list (it makes no difference when the list is random), record those numbers which correspond to numbers preassigned members of the population. Whenever there is a match between numbers, the member with that number is included. Numbers which do not match are ignored. If a number matches a previously selected one, two options are available. (1) Numbers which are duplicated can be ignored. This is called *simple random sampling without replacement.* (2) Numbers which are duplicated can also mean that a member of the population should be counted more than once, i.e., information obtained about that member is treated as if there was more than one member with those characteristics in the sample. This is called *simple random sampling with replacement.* The list of numbers which has been referred to is commonly called a table of random numbers.

Nonrandom Sampling. There are several nonrandom sampling procedures. If a researcher deliberately selects those cases which are judged to be typical of the population, he is using *judgment sampling procedures.* If a researcher requests volunteers from a population, he is using *volunteer sampling procedures.* If he selects those cases which are convenient, he is using *accessibility sampling procedures.* Finally, if he defines the characteristics of the sample he desires, and then fills a quota for each type, he is using *quota sampling procedures.*

Each of these nonrandom sampling procedures involves a researcher's decision and therefore permits human bias in selecting the sample. In judgment sampling, there may be an error in defining and selecting typical cases. In volunteer sampling, volunteers may differ in relevant ways from nonvolunteers. In accessibility sampling, cases which are convenient may differ in relevant ways from cases which are not. Finally, in quota sampling, there may be error in defining desired cases and in selecting those cases which qualify. As a result of these biases, scientists generally avoid the use of nonrandom sampling.

priate background for a successful career in a discipline which was strongly reformist. As sociology matured, it shed its interest in reform and developed more detached theory and research methodology. Several contemporary observers have suggested that background factors different than those of the earlier period may now contribute to a successful career in sociology.

To investigate this general hypothesis, Elizabeth M. Havens undertook *secondary research* on the background characteristics of sociologists.* (Secondary research is research using data that was originally collected for other purposes.) She expected to find differences in the backgrounds of the more successful and less successful members of the profession.

* Elizabeth M. Havens, "Correlates of Professional Success in American Sociology," *Sociology and Social Research,* 56(1972):301–319. These data were collected originally by Norval D. Glenn and David Weiner.

SECTION I. SIMPLE RANDOM SAMPLING

THE POPULATION AND THE SAMPLE

Lacking a list of all American sociologists, Havens redefined the population of interest to consist of sociologists listed as members in the directory of the American Sociological Association (ASA). Since she wished to avoid confounding the contribution of background variables with the contribution of sex as a factor in influencing success, Havens further redefined the population to consist only of male members of the ASA.* The original simple random sample was drawn from the list of approximately 3,600 sociologists registered with the ASA in 1967. A table of random numbers was used.

Data Collection

Havens mailed a questionnaire, which incorporated items to measure background variables, to the last-known address of 760 randomly selected male sociologists. Several weeks after the original mailing, a follow-up letter was sent to all nonrespondents. Of the original sample, 428 respondents (56 percent) eventually completed and returned questionnaires. The loss of 332 (44 percent) of the sample constituted a severe data loss. Some had moved and no forwarding address was available. Others may have died, been out of the country, or simply refused to participate.

If there were relevant systematic differences between those who returned the questionnaire and those who did not, the sample would be biased. Thus, although the sample was drawn randomly, Havens would find it impossible to generalize the results obtained from the sample to the population of sociologists. (Of course, if the amount and direction of bias were known, it would be possible to adjust the sample findings to take this into account.) On the other hand, if there are no systematic differences between these two groups regarding the variables under investigation, the sample would be diminished in size but still remain random. Havens assumed that there were no meaningful differences between respondents and nonrespondents.†

* Students and overseas members of the ASA were also excluded from consideration.

† When research conditions permit, it is desirable to evaluate the assumption that respondents and nonrespondents do not differ on relevant variables. This can be accomplished by (1) comparing respondent data with known information about the population, (2) pursuing a random subsample of nonrespondents for comparison with respondents, or (3) comparing late respondents with those who returned questionnaires earlier. While each of these procedures inevitably requires inferences and assumptions about the similarity of respondents and nonrespondents, they do provide evidence for decision making.

11.2 THE IMPORTANCE OF POPULATION CHARACTERISTICS AND SAMPLE SIZE

As a general rule, a large sample is most likely to be representative of a population. However, like most rules, this one has to be qualified.

1. The size of the sample required depends primarily upon the *characteristics* of the population. If the population is homogeneous, a sample of one member of the population will suffice. If the population is heterogeneous, a large sample size is required. (A single drop of blood suffices for laboratory analysis of a person's health, but a large number of citizens must be sampled to assess a president's popularity.)
2. The size required also depends upon the *precision* of the results desired. If the researchers wish to closely estimate the true values of the population from sample statistics, then a large sample may be necessary. If researchers are satisfied with a large error in their estimates, then a small one may be adequate.
3. Finally, the size also depends upon the level of *confidence* a researcher desires for his estimates. If researchers desire high levels of confidence, they must use a large sample; if a lower level is acceptable, they will use a smaller one.

Two factors, not closely related to the statistical considerations mentioned above, also influence sample size.

The first factor is the *amount of analysis* to be performed on the sample. Researchers who wish to analyze subgroupings of the original sample, for example, black college-educated females between the ages of twenty-one and thirty-five, may find that the original sample contained few persons with these characteristics. Consequently, a larger sample may have been required to produce a sufficient number of persons in desired subgroups. Researchers anticipating this problem should draw a large sample initially, or use an alternative sampling procedure.

The second factor is the *administrative cost* of data collection. Resources available to a research project may dictate a smaller sample than is otherwise desired.

Variables and Data Analysis

Four of the background variables investigated by Havens are reported here: family socioeconomic status, religious preference during adolescence, political orientation during adolescence, and the quality of graduate training in sociology. These background variables were operationalized through items employed in the questionnaire.

Family socioeconomic status (SES) was determined using the Duncan Socioeconomic Scale, one of the scales often used to combine a number of criteria for calculating an SES score.* Using the father's occupation and education, an SES score was computed for each respondent. Religious preference was determined by asking respondents to state their religious preference during adolescence. Political orientation was determined by asking respondents if they held very liberal, somewhat liberal, somewhat conservative, or very conservative political views during adolescence. The quality of graduate training was determined by asking respondents to name the institution in which they received their highest degree in sociology. Using a previously published list which classified institutions according to their quality of graduate instruction, each respondent was coded according to the institution attended.†

To measure professional success, Havens utilized the institution of employment. Those sociologists working at prestige universities were defined as more successful than those sociologists working at less prestigious ones. The list employed for classifying the quality of graduate training was also utilized for classifying professional success. Table 11-1 reports the statistics obtained for the sample.

Table 11-1. Religious Preference, Political Orientation, Family Socioeconomic Status, and Prestige of Graduate Training for the Sample of 428 Sociologists.

VARIABLE	PERCENT OR MEAN SCORE	*N*
Religious preference		
Present	74.4%	318
Absent	25.6%	110
		(428)
Political orientation		
Very liberal	14.5%	62
Other	85.5%	366
		(428)
Socioeconomic status score	47.0	428
Graduate background		
Prestige institution	49.1%	210
Other	50.9%	218
		(428)

SOURCE: Havens, "Correlates of Professional Success," Tables 1 through 4.

* For a description of this scale, see Otis D. Duncan, "A Socioeconomic Index for All Occupations," and "Properties and Characteristics of the Socioeconomic Index," in Albert J. Reiss, Jr., *Occupations and Social Status* (New York: Free Press, 1961), pp. 109–161.

† Allan M. Cartter, *An Assessment of Quality in Graduate Education.* Washington, D.C.: American Council on Education, 1966.

The statistics reported in Table 11-1 apply to the distribution of variables for the sample. Thus, 74.4 percent of the sample reported having a religious preference during adolescence, 14.5 percent reported holding a very liberal political orientation during adolescence, and 49.1 percent reported earning their highest degree from a prestige institution. The mean socioeconomic score for all respondents was 47.0. This was determined by summing the individual socioeconomic scores and dividing by the size of the sample ($N = 428$).

11.3 AVERAGE MEASURES

Measures obtained from populations are commonly termed *parameters*. Measures obtained from samples are commonly termed *statistics*. Three measures for obtaining average values are mean, median, and mode.

The *mean* is that average value which is obtained by summing the separate values and dividing by the number of values summed. The *median* is that average which divides a set of values in half, with 50 percent of the values larger than the median and 50 percent smaller. The *mode* is that value which occurs most frequently.

What estimates should one make about the distribution of these variables in the population? The best estimate of population values is that drawn from the statistics obtained in the sample. Consequently, the same distribution would be used to describe the population.

Although this information is useful, it is possible to make more refined statements. Since the sample was random, statistical sampling theory can be used to specify levels of confidence and precision with respect to the true values in the population. Table 11-2 reports this range of values for the 95 percent and 99 percent confidence levels.

Table 11-2 makes it clear that, as the width of the interval likely to contain the population value increases, the level of confidence increases. For instance, there is 95 percent confidence that the sociologists in the population who held a religious preference during adolescence is somewhere between 70.2 and 78.6 percent. Whereas there is 99 percent confidence that the sociologists who held a religious preference during adolescence is somewhere between 68.1 and 79.5 percent. (Most students are probably 99 percent confident that they can guess the age of their professor within 10 years, but only 95 percent confident that they can guess the age correctly within 5 years.) Thus, precision of estimates falls as the level of confidence climbs. The basis for these statistical estimates lies in a random sampling theory and the normal curve, discussed in Technical Insert IV (see pages 165–176).

Table 11-2. Range of Values for Two Levels of Confidence Within Which the True Population Values Are Likely to Fall.

VARIABLE	STATISTIC SAMPLE	FOR 95% CONFIDENCE THE TRUE POPULATION VALUE IS LIKELY TO BE WITHIN:	FOR 99% CONFIDENCE THE TRUE POPULATION VALUE IS LIKELY TO BE WITHIN:
Religious preference			
Present	74.4%	70.2% and 78.6%	68.1% and 80.6%
Absent	25.6%	21.4% and 29.8%	19.3% and 31.9%
Political orientation			
Very liberal	14.5%	11.1% and 17.9%	9.4% and 19.6%
Other	85.5%	82.1% and 88.9%	80.4% and 90.6%
Socioeconomic status			
Score	47.0	44.9 and 49.1	43.9 and 50.0
Graduate background			
Prestige institution	49.1%	44.3% and 53.9%	41.9% and 56.3%
Other	50.9%	46.1% and 55.7%	43.7% and 58.1%

Technical Insert IV

The Normal Curve and Random Sampling

Mathematics and the Rectangle. Mathematics is occasionally useful for describing the empirical world. For instance, according to the principles of geometry, the area of a rectangle is calculated by multiplying length times width. Where rectangular spaces occur this geometric principle can be applied. If a plot of land is 12 feet long and 10 feet wide, its area is calculated by multiplying length (12′) by width (10′). This area of 120 square feet then could be said to equal 100 percent of the total area. If the plot of land were divided in the middle, then, by definition, each half would contain 50 percent of the total area. (Further divisions would produce smaller percentages.) These principles are illustrated in Figures IV-1 and IV-2.

Figure IV-1

100% 10 ft

12 ft

$A = L \times W$

$A = 12 \times 10$

$A = 120$ sq ft

Figure IV-2

50% 10 ft   50% 10 ft

6 ft   6 ft

$A = L \times W$	$A = L \times W$
$A = 6 \times 10$	$A = 6 \times 10$
$A = 60$ sq ft	$A = 60$ sq ft

Mathematics and the Normal Curve. Using other principles, statisticians calculate the area under a curve. One curve which is of particular interest to researchers who use samples is known as the normal curve. Like a rectangle, such a normal curve is a mathematical form. It is a bell-shaped curve in which the mean, median, and mode coincide at the peak. A normal curve appears in Figure IV-3.

Figure IV-3. The normal curve.

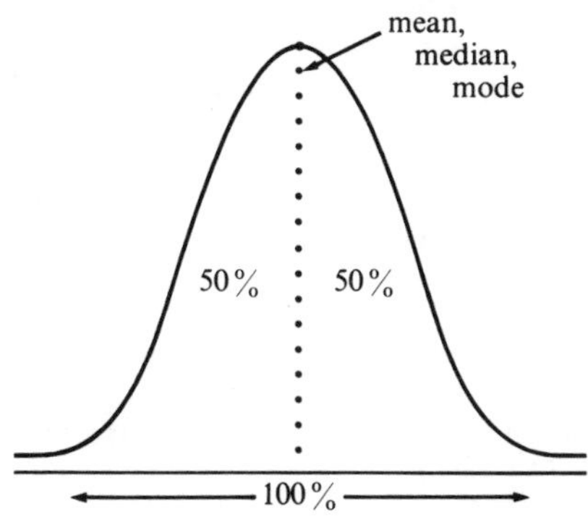

The normal curve has two additional properties that are useful. First, it is symmetrical: one half of the curve is the mirror image of the other half. Second, the area of each of these symmetrical halves can be divided into smaller sections. This is done by taking the center as the zero point, and dividing the axis into internal widths known as standard deviates. Figure IV-4 displays a normal curve with +1, +2, and +3 standard deviates to the right of the center, and −1, −2, and −3 standard deviates to the left.

It is known that 34.13 percent of the total area under the curve falls between the center and the +1 standard deviate. Since the normal curve is symmetrical, 34.13 percent of the area also falls between the center and the −1 standard deviate. An additional 13.59 percent of the total area lies in the area between 1 standard deviate and 2 standard deviates, and 2.15 percent of the total area lies between 2 and 3 standard deviates. A normal curve divided in this way is shown in Figure IV-4.

Figure IV-4. Areas under the normal curve.

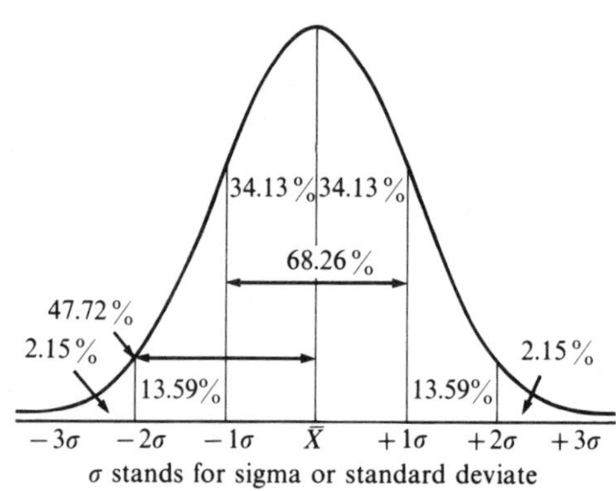

Since the normal curve is symmetrical, it is evident that the following also holds.

The area between +1 and −1 standard deviates =
(2) × (34.13%) or 68.26%

The area between +2 and −2 standard deviates =
(2) × (34.13% + 13.59%) or 95.44%

The area between +3 and −3 standard deviates =
(2) × (34.13% + 13.59 + 2.15%) or 99.74%

Since there are many areas under the curve which may be of interest, statisticians have produced a table which permits quick determination of the area between two points. Because the normal curve is symmetrical, the table describes only one-half of the curve. Multiplying by 2 provides the total area. Table IV-1 provides the areas under the curve in proportions that can be converted to percents simply by multiplying by 100.

Using Table IV-1, determine the area under the curve for the following problems:

1. The area between the mean and 1.0 standard deviates.
   Answer: (34.13%)
2. The area between the mean and 1.9 standard deviates.
   Answer: (47.13%)

Table IV-1. Proportions of Area Under the Normal Curve.

(A) z (STANDARD DEVIATION UNITS)	(B) AREA BETWEEN MEAN AND z	(C) AREA BEYOND z	(A) z (STANDARD DEVIATION UNITS)	(B) AREA BETWEEN MEAN AND z	(C) AREA BEYOND z
0.00	.0000	.5000	0.45	.1736	.3264
0.01	.0040	.4960	0.46	.1772	.3228
0.02	.0080	.4920	0.47	.1808	.3192
0.03	.0120	.4880	0.48	.1844	.3156
0.04	.0160	.4840	0.49	.1879	.3121
0.05	.0199	.4801	0.50	.1915	.3085
0.06	.0239	.4761	0.51	.1950	.3050
0.07	.0279	.4721	0.52	.1985	.3015
0.08	.0319	.4681	0.53	.2019	.2981
0.09	.0359	.4641	0.54	.2054	.2946
0.10	.0393	.4602	0.55	.2088	.2912
0.11	.0438	.4562	0.56	.2123	.2877
0.12	.0478	.4522	0.57	.2157	.2843
0.13	.0517	.4483	0.58	.2190	.2810
0.14	.0557	.4443	0.59	.2224	.2776
0.15	.0596	.4404	0.60	.2257	.2743
0.16	.0636	.4364	0.61	.2291	.2709
0.17	.0675	.4325	0.62	.2324	.2676
0.18	.0714	.4286	0.63	.2357	.2643
0.19	.0753	.4247	0.64	.2389	.2611
0.20	.0793	.4207	0.65	.2422	.2578
0.21	.0832	.4168	0.66	.2454	.2546
0.22	.0871	.4129	0.67	.2486	.2514
0.23	.0910	.4090	0.68	.2517	.2483
0.24	.0948	.4052	0.69	.2549	.2451
0.25	.0987	.4013	0.70	.2580	.2420
0.26	.1026	.3974	0.71	.2611	.2389
0.27	.1064	.3936	0.72	.2642	.2358
0.28	.1103	.3897	0.73	.2673	.2327
0.29	.1141	.3859	0.74	.2704	.2296
0.30	.1179	.3821	0.75	.2734	.2266
0.31	.1217	.3783	0.76	.2764	.2236
0.32	.1255	.3745	0.77	.2794	.2206
0.33	.1293	.3707	0.78	.2823	.2177
0.34	.1331	.3669	0.79	.2852	.2148
0.35	.1368	.3632	0.80	.2881	.2119
0.36	.1406	.3594	0.81	.2910	.2090
0.37	.1443	.3557	0.82	.2939	.2061
0.38	.1480	.3520	0.83	.2967	.2033
0.39	.1517	.3483	0.84	.2995	.2005
0.40	.1554	.3446	0.85	.3023	.1977
0.41	.1591	.3409	0.86	.3051	.1949
0.42	.1628	.3372	0.87	.3078	.1922
0.43	.1664	.3336	0.88	.3106	.1894
0.44	.1700	.3300	0.89	.3133	.1867

Table IV-1 ***(Continued)***

(A) z (STANDARD DEVIATION UNITS)	(B) AREA BETWEEN MEAN AND z	(C) AREA BEYOND z	(A) z (STANDARD DEVIATION UNITS)	(B) AREA BETWEEN MEAN AND z	(C) AREA BEYOND z
0.90	.3159	.1841	1.35	.4115	.0885
0.91	.3186	.1814	1.36	.4131	.0869
0.92	.3212	.1788	1.37	.4147	.0853
0.93	.3238	.1762	1.38	.4162	.0838
0.94	.3264	.1736	1.39	.4177	.0823
0.95	.3289	.1711	1.40	.4192	.0808
0.96	.3315	.1685	1.41	.4207	.0793
0.97	.3340	.1660	1.42	.4222	.0778
0.98	.3365	.1635	1.43	.4236	.0764
0.99	.3389	.1611	1.44	.4251	.0749
1.00	.3413	.1587	1.45	.4265	.0735
1.01	.3438	.1562	1.46	.4279	.0721
1.02	.3461	.1539	1.47	.4292	.0708
1.03	.3485	.1515	1.48	.4306	.0694
1.04	.3508	.1492	1.49	.4319	.0681
1.05	.3531	.1469	1.50	.4332	.0668
1.06	.3554	.1446	1.51	.4345	.0655
1.07	.3577	.1423	1.52	.4357	.0643
1.08	.3599	.1401	1.53	.4370	.0630
1.09	.3621	.1379	1.54	.4382	.0618
1.10	.3643	.1357	1.55	.4394	.0606
1.11	.3665	.1335	1.56	.4406	.0594
1.12	.3686	.1314	1.57	.4418	.0582
1.13	.3708	.1292	1.58	.4429	.0571
1.14	.3729	.1271	1.59	.4441	.0559
1.15	.3749	.1251	1.60	.4452	.0548
1.16	.3770	.1230	1.61	.4463	.0537
1.17	.3790	.1210	1.62	.4474	.0526
1.18	.3810	.1190	1.63	.4484	.0516
1.19	.3830	.1170	1.64	.4495	.0505
1.20	.3849	.1151	1.65	.4505	.0495
1.21	.3869	.1131	1.66	.4515	.0485
1.22	.3888	.1112	1.67	.4525	.0475
1.23	.3907	.1093	1.68	.4535	.0465
1.24	.3925	.1075	1.69	.4545	.0455
1.25	.3944	.1056	1.70	.4554	.0446
1.26	.3962	.1038	1.71	.4564	.0436
1.27	.3980	.1020	1.72	.4573	.0427
1.28	.3997	.1003	1.73	.4582	.0418
1.29	.4015	.0985	1.74	.4591	.0409
1.30	.4032	.0968	1.75	.4599	.0401
1.31	.4049	.0951	1.76	.4608	.0392
1.32	.4066	.0934	1.77	.4616	.0384
1.33	.4082	.0918	1.78	.4625	.0375
1.34	.4099	.0901	1.79	.4633	.0367

Table IV-1 ***(Continued)***

(A) z (STANDARD DEVIATION UNITS)	(B) AREA BETWEEN MEAN AND z	(C) AREA BEYOND z
1.80	.4641	.0359
1.81	.4649	.0351
1.82	.4656	.0344
1.83	.4664	.0336
1.84	.4671	.0329
1.85	.4678	.0322
1.86	.4686	.0314
1.87	.4693	.0307
1.88	.4699	.0301
1.89	.4706	.0294
1.90	.4713	.0287
1.91	.4719	.0281
1.92	.4726	.0274
1.93	.4732	.0268
1.94	.4738	.0262
1.95	.4744	.0256
1.96	.4750	.0250
1.97	.4756	.0244
1.98	.4761	.0239
1.99	.4767	.0233
2.00	.4772	.0228
2.01	.4778	.0222
2.02	.4783	.0217
2.03	.4788	.0212
2.04	.4793	.0207
2.05	.4798	.0202
2.06	.4803	.0197
2.07	.4808	.0192
2.08	.4812	.0188
2.09	.4817	.0183
2.10	.4821	.0179
2.11	.4826	.0174
2.12	.4830	.0170
2.13	.4834	.0166
2.14	.4838	.0162
2.15	.4842	.0158
2.16	.4846	.0154
2.17	.4850	.0150
2.18	.4854	.0146
2.19	.4857	.0143
2.20	.4861	.0139
2.21	.4864	.0136
2.22	.4868	.0132
2.23	.4871	.0129
2.24	.4875	.0125

(A) z (STANDARD DEVIATION UNITS)	(B) AREA BETWEEN MEAN AND z	(C) AREA BEYOND z
2.25	.4878	.0122
2.26	.4881	.0119
2.27	.4884	.0116
2.28	.4887	.0113
2.29	.4890	.0110
2.30	.4893	.0107
2.31	.4896	.0104
2.32	.4898	.0102
2.33	.4901	.0099
2.34	.4904	.0096
2.35	.4906	.0094
2.36	.4909	.0091
2.37	.4911	.0089
2.38	.4913	.0087
2.39	.4916	.0084
2.40	.4918	.0082
2.41	.4920	.0080
2.42	.4922	.0078
2.43	.4925	.0075
2.44	.4927	.0073
2.45	.4929	.0071
2.46	.4931	.0069
2.47	.4932	.0068
2.48	.4934	.0066
2.49	.4936	.0064
2.50	.4938	.0062
2.51	.4940	.0060
2.52	.4941	.0059
2.53	.4943	.0057
2.54	.4945	.0055
2.55	.4946	.0054
2.56	.4948	.0052
2.57	.4949	.0051
2.58	.4951	.0049
2.59	.4952	.0048
2.60	.4953	.0047
2.61	.4955	.0045
2.62	.4956	.0044
2.63	.4957	.0043
2.64	.4959	.0041
2.65	.4960	.0040
2.66	.4961	.0039
2.67	.4962	.0038
2.68	.4963	.0037
2.69	.4964	.0036

Table IV-1 ***(Continued)***

(A) z (STANDARD DEVIATION UNITS)	(B) AREA BETWEEN MEAN AND z	(C) AREA BEYOND z	(A) z (STANDARD DEVIATION UNITS)	(B) AREA BETWEEN MEAN AND z	(C) AREA BEYOND z
2.70	.4965	.0035	3.05	.4989	.0011
2.71	.4966	.0034	3.06	.4989	.0011
2.72	.4967	.0033	3.07	.4989	.0011
2.73	.4968	.0032	3.08	.4990	.0010
2.74	.4969	.0031	3.09	.4990	.0010
2.75	.4970	.0030	3.10	.4990	.0010
2.76	.4971	.0029	3.11	.4991	.0009
2.77	.4972	.0028	3.12	.4991	.0009
2.78	.4973	.0027	3.13	.4991	.0009
2.79	.4974	.0026	3.14	.4992	.0008
2.80	.4974	.0026	3.15	.4992	.0008
2.81	.4975	.0025	3.16	.4992	.0008
2.82	.4976	.0024	3.17	.4992	.0008
2.83	.4977	.0023	3.18	.4993	.0007
2.84	.4977	.0023	3.19	.4993	.0007
2.85	.4978	.0022	3.20	.4993	.0007
2.86	.4979	.0021	3.21	.4993	.0007
2.87	.4979	.0021	3.22	.4994	.0006
2.88	.4980	.0020	3.23	.4994	.0006
2.89	.4981	.0019	3.24	.4994	.0006
2.90	.4981	.0019	3.25	.4994	.0006
2.91	.4982	.0018	3.30	.4995	.0005
2.92	.4982	.0018	3.35	.4996	.0004
2.93	.4983	.0017	3.40	.4997	.0003
2.94	.4984	.0016	3.45	.4997	.0003
2.95	.4984	.0016	3.50	.4998	.0002
2.96	.4985	.0015	3.60	.4998	.0002
2.97	.4985	.0015	3.70	.4999	.0001
2.98	.4986	.0014	3.80	.4999	.0001
2.99	.4986	.0014	3.90	.49995	.00005
3.00	.4987	.0013	4.00	.49997	.00003
3.01	.4987	.0013			
3.02	.4987	.0013			
3.03	.4988	.0012			
3.04	.4988	.0012			

SOURCE: Richard P. Runyon and Audrey Haber, *Fundamentals of Behavioral Statistics* (Reading, Mass.: Addison-Wesley, 1967), pp. 290–291.

3. The area between 0.5 and 1.0 standard deviates.
   Answer: (34.13% − 19.15% = 14.98%)
4. The area between −0.5 and +1.0 standard deviates.
   Answer: (19.15% + 34.13% = 53.28%)

Recall that the normal curve is only a mathematical form. *It is useful for describing empirical distributions only if they have the shape of a normal curve.* Fortunately, many empirical distributions do approximate the shape of a normal curve. When this occurs, the properties of such a curve are useful for describing the distribution. Test scores, for instance, frequently are distributed in the shape of a normal curve.

Test Scores and the Normal Curve. The scores for a hypothetical test are reported below. The normal curve will be used to describe the distribution of these scores.

TEST SCORE	FREQUENCY OF STUDENTS OBTAINING THIS SCORE	TEST SCORES WEIGHTED BY NUMBER OF STUDENTS OBTAINING THEM	
		Score × Frequency	
100	0	100 × 0 =	0
98	0	98 × 0 =	0
96	1	96 × 1 =	96
94	2	94 × 2 =	188
92	3	⋮	276
90	4	⋮	360
88	5	⋮	440
86	6	⋮	516
84	10	⋮	840
82	11	⋮	902
80	12	⋮	960
78	12	⋮	936
76	11	⋮	836
74	10	⋮	740
72	6	⋮	432
70	5	⋮	350
68	4	⋮	272
66	3	⋮	198
64	2	⋮	128
62	1	⋮	62
60	0	⋮	0
58	0	⋮	0
Total	108		8532

$$\text{Mean}(\overline{X}) = \frac{8532}{108} = 79.0$$

A total of 108 students took the test with 1 student receiving a test score of 96, 2 receiving a test score of 94, and so on. The mean score on the test is found by summing all the scores and dividing by the number of scores. Therefore, the mean equals 8532 ÷ 108 equals 79.0. Converting this distribution into a frequency polygon for representation results in Figure IV-5. Superimposed on Figure IV-5 is a normal curve. Hence the empirical distribution of scores approximates the shape of a normal curve.

One major step remains before the normal curve can be used. Test scores must be transformed into standard deviate scores. Procedures for calculating standard deviation of the test score distribution are reflected in Table IV-2, where column A contains all test scores and column B contains the mean of test scores. Column C, where the mean is subtracted from each score, indicates

Figure IV-5.

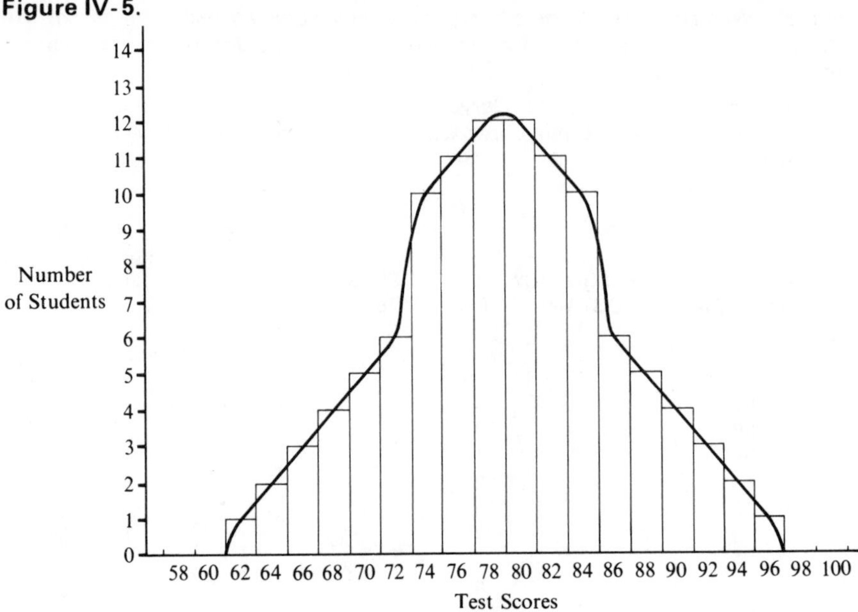

Table IV-2. Calculating the Standard Deviation.

TEST SCORE	MEAN	DIFFERENCE (A) − (B)	DIFFERENCE SQUARED		DIFFERENCE SQUARED TIMES FREQUENCY
(A)	(B)	(C)	(D)		(E)
96	79.0	17.0	289.0	×	1 = 289.0
94	79.0	15.0	225.0	×	2 = 450.0
92	79.0	13.0	169.0	×	3 = 507.0
90	79.0	11.0	121.0	×	4 = 484.0
88	79.0	9.0	81.0	×	5 = 405.0
86	79.0	7.0	49.0	×	6 = 294.0
84	79.0	5.0	25.0	×	10 = 250.0
82	79.0	3.0	9.0	×	11 = 99.0
80	79.0	1.0	1.0	×	12 = 12.0
78	79.0	−1.0	1.0	×	12 = 12.0
76	79.0	−3.0	9.0	×	11 = 99.0
74	79.0	−5.0	25.0	×	10 = 250.0
72	79.0	−7.0	49.0	×	6 = 294.0
70	79.0	−9.0	81.0	×	5 = 405.0
68	79.0	−11.0	121.0	×	4 = 484.0
66	79.0	−13.0	169.0	×	3 = 507.0
64	79.0	−15.0	225.0	×	2 = 450.0
62	79.0	−17.0	289.0	×	1 = 289.0
		Sum 00.0			108 5580.0

$$\text{Variance } (\sigma^2) = \frac{\text{sum of squared distances from the mean}}{\text{number of cases}} = \frac{5580}{108} = 51.667$$

$$\text{Standard deviation } (\sigma) = \text{square root of the variance} = \sqrt{51.667} = 7.188$$

σ = sigma or standard deviation.
σ^2 = sigma squared or variance.

the distance of each score from the mean. Note that all distances to the left of the mean in Figure IV-5 are positive, all to the right are negative, and the positive scores equal the negative because the distribution of scores is symmetrical. Summing the scores in column C would produce a score of zero.

Negative scores are eliminated according to the rules of algebra when the difference scores are squared as in column D. Then, in column E, these squared difference scores are weighted by the frequency with which they actually occurred. The sum of this column (5580) is a measure of the total squared deviation of all 108 individual scores from the mean. One measure of how far, on the average, these squared deviation scores depart from the mean is known as the *variance*. It is calculated by dividing the total of squared deviations (5580) by the number of cases (108) to indicate the average of squared distances from the mean in the actual test (5580 ÷ 108 = 51.667). On the average, then, the squared distance from the mean is 51.667.

A second measure, known as the ***standard deviation***, is the square root of the variance ($\sqrt{51.667} = 7.188$). It is obtained by first subtracting the mean from every test score, then squaring the difference between the mean and the test score, summing the squares, dividing by the number of cases, and finally taking the square root.

The standard deviation, as explained earlier, specifies the area (or percentage of cases) under the curve for a normal distribution. In this test, with a standard deviation of 7.188 and a mean of 79.0, Table IV-1 can be used to indicate that 34.13 percent of all scores fall between the mean at 79.0 and the first standard deviate at 86.188 (79.0 + 7.188). An additional 34.13 percent of scores falls between 79.0 and 71.812 (79.0 − 7.188).

This method of calculation becomes cumbersome, however, when one needs to use portions of standard deviations or when one desires test scores to fall within an already specified portion of the curve. Therefore, Table IV-3 is used to calculate the standard deviates for the range of test scores. The formula is $(X - \bar{X})/\sigma$, or raw score minus the mean divided by the standard deviation.

Table IV-3. Converting Test Scores to Standard Deviates.

TEST SCORE	DISTANCE FROM MEAN	STANDARD DEVIATES
(A)	(B)	(C)
96	17.0	17.0 ÷ 7.188 = 2.37
94	15.0	15.0 ÷ 7.188 = 2.09
92	13.0	13.0 ÷ 7.188 = 1.81
90	11.0	11.0 ÷ 7.188 = 1.53
88	9.0	9.0 ÷ 7.188 = 1.25
86	7.0	7.0 ÷ 7.188 = .97
84	5.0	5.0 ÷ 7.188 = .70
82	3.0	3.0 ÷ 7.188 = .42
80	1.0	1.0 ÷ 7.188 = .14
78	−1.0	−1.0 ÷ 7.188 = −.14
76	−3.0	−3.0 ÷ 7.188 = −.42
74	−5.0	−5.0 ÷ 7.188 = −.70
72	−7.0	−7.0 ÷ 7.188 = −.97
70	−9.0	−9.0 ÷ 7.188 = −1.25
68	−11.0	−11.0 ÷ 7.188 = −1.53
66	−13.0	−13.0 ÷ 7.188 = −1.81
64	−5.0	−15.0 ÷ 7.188 = −2.09
62	−17.0	−17.0 ÷ 7.188 = −2.37

Table IV-3 reports the distance between the mean and any particular test score measured in standard deviate units. Thus, a test score of 94 is 2.09 standard deviates from the mean, while a test score of 92 is 1.81 from the mean, and so on. Using Tables IV-1 and IV-3, it is now possible to establish the proportion of students earning particular test scores.

1. What percent of students earned a test score above 79.0?
   Answer: 50 percent of the students are above the mean in this example.
2. What percent of students earned a test score between 84 and the mean (79.0)?
   Answer: The distance is .70 standard deviates. According to Table IV-1, 25.8 percent of the scores are between the mean and .71 standard deviates.
3. What percent of students earned a test score between 86 and 79.0?
   Answer: According to Table IV-1, 33.4 percent of the scores are between the mean and .97 standard deviates.

Using Normal Curves to Infer Population Values from Sample Statistics
The normal curve has uses beyond describing a population. As suggested, it can be used to make inferences about population values when all that is known are sample statistics. Imagine a population from which repeated *random* samples of a fixed size are drawn. As might be expected, the means of these samples will tend to cluster around the mean of the population. The mean of the sample means, in fact, will equal the mean of the population.

Figure IV-6. Distribution of sample means around the population mean.

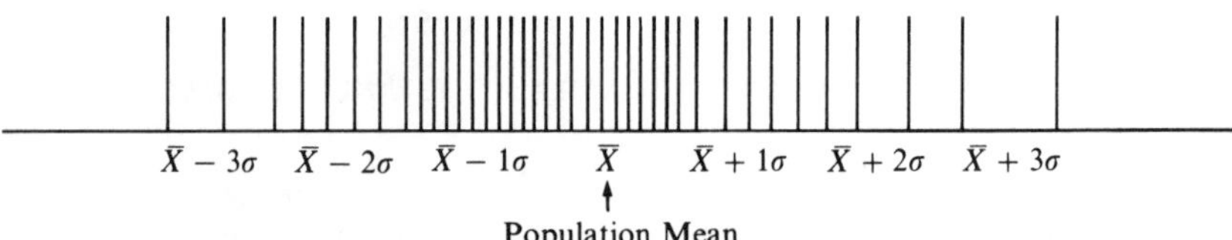

The *central limit theorem* adds further to our knowledge of the sample. It states that these sample means will have a normal distribution if the population has a normal distribution.

However, the population does not always need to have a normal distribution. According to the *law of large numbers*, the distribution of sample means will approximate a normal curve when the sample size is greater than 30. This holds true even when the population does not have a normal distribution.

The distribution of sample means around a population mean is illustrated by the vertical lines in Figure IV-6. Each line represents one sample mean. As can be observed, most sample means are rather close to the population mean, but a few are quite distant. The same phenomenon is presented as a normal curve in Figure IV-7, where each dot represents a sample mean. Using this normal distribution, the likelihood of selecting a sample whose mean is distant from the population mean (i.e., the likelihood that a sample mean will be a poor estimate of the population mean) can be calculated.

Figure IV-7. Distribution of sample means around a population mean.

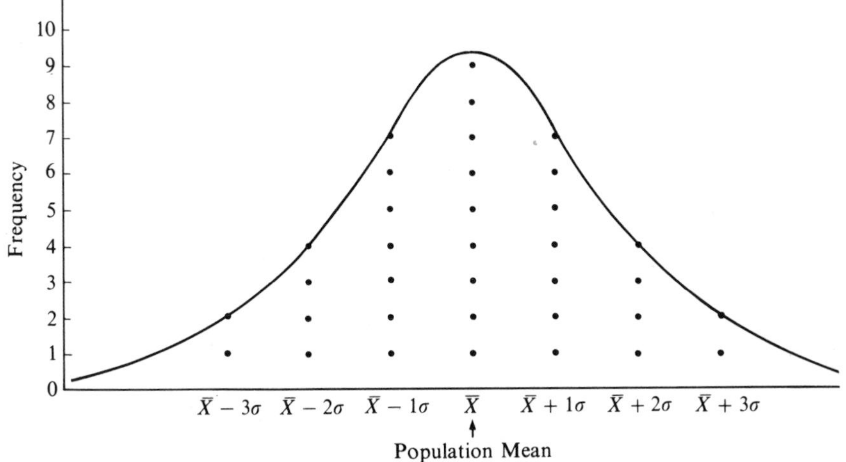

According to sampling theory if repeated samples of a fixed size greater than 30 are drawn randomly, then (1) the mean of the sample means will equal the mean of the population, (2) the distribution of the sample means will be normal, and (3) the standard deviation of the sample means (known as the *standard error)* will equal the standard deviation of the sample divided by the square root of the sample size minus 1.

$$\text{Standard Error} = \text{SE} = \frac{\sigma}{\sqrt{N-1}}$$

(For proportions, the formula is $\text{SE} = \sqrt{(pq)/(N-1)}$ where p represents one population proportion and q represents the remainder.)

Propositions (1) and (2) of sampling theory have been explained, but a brief illustration of the calculation of the standard error may be helpful for understanding proposition (3). Assume that a random sample of 101 students at a university has a mean grade point average of 3.0 and a standard deviation of .20. The standard error of the sample means would then be

$$\text{SE} = \frac{.20}{\sqrt{101-1}} = \frac{.20}{10} = .02$$

If the grade point average for the entire student body was actually 3.02 (the true population value), then the sample mean of 3.0 would have been well within the range of sample means chosen 95.46 percent of the time. A sample mean of 3.06 would be barely among those chosen 95.46 percent of the time, while a sample mean of 2.97 would be quite unlikely. These scores are illustrated in Figure IV-8.

Figure IV-8. Hypothetical distribution of sample means around the population mean.

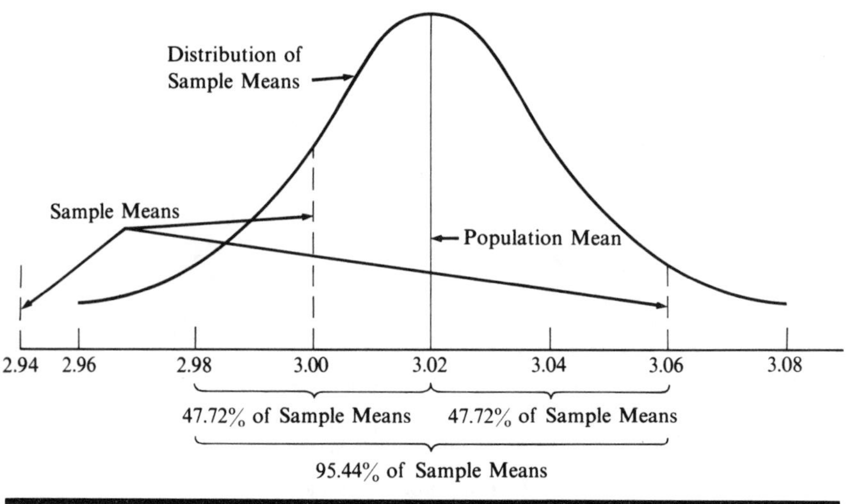

SECTION II. GENERALIZING RELATIONSHIP IN THE SAMPLE TO THE POPULATION: THE USE OF CHI-SQUARE.

The analysis thus far has been concerned with making inferences about unknown population values from known sample statistics. Now the analysis turns to the inferences about general population relationships when all that is known are relationships obtained for a particular sample. To accomplish this, the remainder of the chapter focuses on chi-square as a test of significance. For the aforementioned random sample of sociologists, the relationships between the dependent variable of professional success and the independent variables of adolescent religious preference, political preference, family's socioeconomic status, and graduate training are presented in Tables 11-3, 11-4, 11-5, and 11-6.

Yule's Q was used to measure the strength of the relationships between variables in the sample. Sociologists who reported no religious preference during adolescence were more likely to be employed at high-prestige institutions than sociologists who reported a religious preference (26 v. 12 percent, $Q = .443$). The value of chi-square (10.69) indicates that the chance of drawing a sample with this distribution from a population in which the variables are unrelated is less than one in a thousand. Although sociologists who reported a very liberal preference during adolescence were more likely to be employed at high-prestige institutions (16

Tables 11-3–11-6. Summary Tables of Strength and Probability of Relationships Among Variables.

Table 11-3

RELIGIOUS PREFERENCE	PROFESSIONAL SUCCESS Yes %	N	No %	N	%	N
Absent	26	(22)	74	(64)	100	(86)
Present	12	(40)	88	(302)	100	(342)
Total	14	(62)	86	(366)	100	(428)

$Q = .443$; $\chi^2 = 10.690$; $P < .001$

Table 11-4

POLITICAL PREFERENCE	PROFESSIONAL SUCCESS Yes %	N	No %	N	%	N
Very liberal	16	(30)	84	(153)	100	(183)
Other	7	(32)	93	(213)	100	(245)
Total	14	(62)	86	(366)	100	(428)

$Q = .130$; $\chi^2 = .943$; $P > .05$

Table 11-5

SOCIOECONOMIC STATUS	PROFESSIONAL SUCCESS Yes %	N	No %	N	%	N
Above mean	16	(36)	84	(186)	100	(222)
Below mean	13	(26)	87	(180)	100	(206)
Total	14	(62)	86	(366)	100	(428)

$Q = .145$; $\chi^2 = .2906$; $P > .05$

Table 11-6

GRADUATE TRAINING	PROFESSIONAL SUCCESS Yes %	N	No %	N	%	N
High-prestige	21	(49)	79	(181)	100	(230)
Other	7	(13)	93	(185)	100	(198)
Total	14	(62)	86	(366)	100	(428)

$Q = .587$; $\chi^2 = 18.659$; $P < .001$

v. 7 percent), the measured relationship was weak ($Q = .130$) and the value of chi-square indicated that the chance of drawing a sample with this distribution from a population in which the variables were unrelated was greater than five times in a hundred.

Similar findings were obtained for the relationship between socioeconomic status and employment at high-prestige institutions. Sixteen percent of the sociologists reporting SES scores above the mean and 13 percent of the sociologists reporting scores below the mean were employed at high-prestige institutions. The relationship was weak ($Q = .145$) and the chi-square value indicated that the chance of drawing a sample with this distribution from a population in which the variables are unrelated is greater than five times in a hundred. With respect to graduate training, sociologists who had obtained advanced degrees at high-prestige institutions were more likely to be employed at high prestige institutions than sociologists educated elsewhere (21 v. 7 percent). Yule's Q provided a measure of relationship at .587 and the value of chi-square indicated that the chance of drawing a sample with this distribution from a population in which the variables are unrelated is less than one in a thousand.

The relationships reported in these tables apply solely to the sample of sociologists studied. This sample was but one of many random samples that could have been drawn, some of them perhaps indicating quite different relationships. More importantly, the actual relationships among these variables in the population are still unknown. Whether the relationships observed in the sample represented a chance finding or reflected the actual relationships in the population is a problem which needs to be resolved.

To approach the problem, it is necessary to determine the probability that the observed relationship did not occur by chance. That is, it is necessary to determine whether this sample could have been drawn from a population with no relationships between the variables. Chi-square (χ^2) (explained in Technical Insert V, beginning on page 180) can be used to measure the likelihood that a sample in which two variables are related was drawn from a population in which the two variables are unrelated.

Table 11-3 indicates that $\chi^2 = 10.69$; therefore, the probability is less than .01 that this sample came from a population in which there was no relationship between religious preference and current prestige. Stated somewhat differently, the chance of drawing this sample from a population where religious preference and professional success are unrelated is less than one in a hundred. Similarly, Table 11-6 indicates that the chances are less than .001 (one in a thousand) that the sample has been drawn from a population where high-prestige graduate training is unrelated to professional status. On the other hand, Tables 11-4 and 11-5 indicate that the sample quite possibly could have been drawn from a population where political preference and socioeconomic status were unrelated to professional success.

SUMMARY

This chapter began with the problem of studying the relationships between background characteristics and professional success in sociology. A random sample of sociologists was drawn, and the properties of the normal curve in conjunction with sample statistics were used to make inferences about the values of variables in the population. Later, the chi-square test was used to make inferences about the relationships between variables in the population. It was indicated that such a sample was most likely to be drawn from a population where professional success was related to the absence of religious preferences and the existence of high-prestige graduate training.

Technical Insert V

The Use of Chi-Square

Using the Chi-Square Test for Inferring the Probability of a Relationship Between Variables in the Population. A sample, by definition, is only a portion of a population. Consequently, observations obtained from a sample may not be representative of the observations which would have been obtained if the entire population had been studied. The chi-square test reports the probability that relationships observed in a random sample are representative of those which would have been observed if the entire population had been studied.

This test follows a logic similar to assessing the null hypothesis. Chi-square first establishes the hypothetical distribution of variables for a population in which there is no relationship between variables. Then, the observed distribution is compared with the hypothetical distribution. If the difference between the observed and the hypothetical distribution is large, the likelihood is small that the sample was drawn from an actual population with a distribution similar to the hypothetical one. Consequently, it can be inferred that the sample observations did not occur by a chance drawing of a particular sample but occurred because the sample was representative.

Statisticians refer to this likelihood as the *significance level.* A significance level of .01, for instance, indicates that the chances are one in a hundred that a sample with an observed relationship between variables was drawn from a population with no relationship between variables. A significance level of .05 indicates that the chances are five in a hundred that a sample with an observed relationship between variables was drawn from a population with no relationship between variables.

The calculation of chi-square for the observed relationship between religious preference and professional success in the sample is illustrated in Table V-1.

Table V-1

OBSERVED DISTRIBUTION FOR THE SAMPLE

	Professional Success		
Religious Preference	*Yes*	*No*	*Total*
Absent	22	64	86
Present	40	302	342
Total	62	366	428

Table V-2

HYPOTHETICAL OR EXPECTED DISTRIBUTION FOR THE SAMPLE

	Professional Success		
Religious Preference	*Yes*	*No*	*Total*
Absent	12.46	73.54	86
Present	49.54	292.46	342
Total	62	366	428

Table V-1 reports the observed distribution in the sample, while Table V-2 gives the hypothetical or expected distribution for a sample in which there was no relationship between variables in the population. The procedures for calculating Table V-2 are straightforward.

Eighty-six of 428 respondents reported no religious preference during adolescence. This represents 20 percent of the total sample. Consequently, 20 percent of those respondents who are professionally successful (62 respondents) should also report no religious preference *if this sample is representative of a population in which there is no relationship between no religious preference and professional success.* Similarly, 20 percent of those respondents who are not professionally successful (366 respondents) should also report no religious preference. In like manner, 80 percent of all respondents reported a religious preference during adolescence. Therefore, a like percentage (80 percent) of the professionally successful respondents (62) should report a religious preference if this sample is representative of a population in which there is no relationship between religious preference and professional success. This logic also applies to the remaining category of respondents—those not professionally successful. Eighty percent of this group should also report a religious preference if the sample is representative of a population in which there is no relationship between these variables.

These calculations yield the distribution reported in Table V-2.

$(86/428) \times 62 = 12.46$ (cell a)
$(86/428) \times 366 = 73.54$ (cell b)
$(342/428) \times 62 = 49.54$ (cell c)
$(342/428) \times 366 = 292.46$ (cell d)

The formula for calculating chi-square involves a comparison of the expected (hypothetical) distribution with the observed (sample) distribution. Such calculations are presented in Table V-3. First, the expected frequencies are subtracted from the observed frequencies for each cell. Then each of the differences is squared to remove the negative sign. Each squared difference is then divided by the corresponding expected frequency. Finally, these values are summed. These calculations are summarized in the formula:*

$$\chi^2 = \Sigma \frac{(O_f - E_f)^2}{E_f}$$

Table V-3. Calculation of Chi-Square.

CELL	OBSERVED FREQUENCY (O_f)	EXPECTED FREQUENCY (E_f)	OBSERVED − EXPECTED ($O_f - E_f$)	SQUARED $(O_f - E_f)^2$	SQUARED DIVIDED BY EXPECTED $\frac{(O_f - E_f)^2}{E_f}$
a	22	12.46	9.54	91.01	7.3043
b	64	73.54	−9.54	91.01	1.2375
c	40	49.54	−9.54	91.01	1.8371
d	302	292.46	9.54	91.01	.3111
				Total chi-square value	10.690

* Under certain conditions (e.g., when sample size is small) a formula incorporating an adjustment in calculations is required. This adjustment, called a *correction for continuity,* is discussed in most statistics texts. For instance, consult Hubert M. Blalock, Jr., *Social Statistics,* 2d ed. (New York: McGraw-Hill, 1972), pp. 285–287.

An examination of the logic of calculating chi-square reveals that, as the difference between the observed and expected frequencies increases, the value of chi-square increases. The larger the total difference, the greater the probability that the observed distribution was *not* drawn from a population similar to the hypothetical one created for a population with no relationship between variables. Statisticians have provided tables for measuring precisely this probability. The relevant portion of a table for this problem is produced below.

Table V-4. Chi-Square and Probability Values for a 2 × 2 Table.

Chi-square value	.455	1.054	1.642	2.706	3.841	5.412	6.635	10.827
Probability value	.50	.30	.20	.10	.05	.02	.01	.001

According to the table, the probability of obtaining a chi-square value as large as 10.690 is less than .01 (one in a hundred) and greater than .001 (one in a thousand). This interpretation follows from the fact that 10.690 is larger than 6.635 and smaller than 10.827. Consequently, the odds that this sample was drawn from a population in which there is no relationship between religious preference and professional success is less than one in a hundred. Therefore the relationship is accepted as significant, that is, unlikely to have occurred as a result of selecting a sample from a population in which the variables are unrelated.

A final few words about the use of chi-square values are needed. Contingency tables vary as to the number and rows for each variable. Some contingency tables have two rows and two columns, others have two rows and three columns, and so on. Each type of contingency table has a specific chi-square table associated with it. To simplify matters, statisticians have arranged contingency tables and the associated chi-square distribution by the *number of degrees of freedom* in the contingency table. The degrees of freedom are the number of cells which can be filled independently of the other cell values.

In a two-by-two table (two columns and two rows), one cell is independent of the other cells. Once the frequency for one cell is determined, the remaining frequencies can be determined by a process of subtracting the internal cell values from the marginal totals. Thus, a two-by-two table has one degree of freedom. In a two-by-three table (two rows and three columns), there are two degrees of freedom. Once the frequency of two cells has been determined, the remaining frequencies can be determined by subtracting the internal cell values from the marginal totals. A general rule for contingency tables is that degrees of freedom are equal to the product of the number of rows (r) minus one times the number of columns (c) minus one.

$$\text{Degrees of Freedom} = (r - 1)(c - 1)$$

Consequently, in using a chi-square test of significance, first calculate the chi-square value for the table, then calculate the degrees of freedom; finally, find the appropriate chi-square table and determine the probability of obtaining the observed distribution by chance. A chi-square table and its explanation are presented in Appendix 3 (see pages 382–383).

KEY IDEAS AND CONCEPTS

accessibility sampling
biased sample
confidence
degrees of freedom
expected frequency
judgment sampling
nonrandom sampling
normal curve
observed frequency
population
population characteristics
precision
quota sampling
random sampling
sample size
secondary research
significance level
standard deviates
standard deviation
standard error
table of random numbers
variance
volunteer sampling

ISSUES AND PROBLEMS

1. Specify the conditions necessary for drawing a random sample. List the advantages of a random sample over a nonrandom type.
2. In Havens' study of American sociologists, she obtained a 56 percent response rate. Describe the characteristics of those sociologists most likely to respond to her questionnaire. Describe the characteristics of those sociologists least likely to respond. List the ways in which these characteristics might influence the results of the study.
3. Frequently, samples are drawn from population lists.
   a. Evaluate the accuracy of a campus phone directory for drawing a simple random sample of faculty.
   b. Specify any possible differences between a theoretical definition of a faculty member and the definition used for inclusion in the campus phone directory.
   c. List the reasons the results of a sample drawn from the campus phone directory might differ from the results of a study of the total population of faculty members.
4. Define the concept of sample. Define the concept of population. Specify the circumstances when college seniors at your university would constitute a population. When they would constitute a sample. Explain why any aggregate may be considered a population for purposes of a particular study.
5. Reproduced in Table A are Census Bureau data for sixty-nine blocks in the Milwaukee urban area. For purposes of this example, these blocks are defined as a population. (The data are adapted from Appendix 1 of Chapter 4.)
   a. Using the Table of Random Numbers in Appendix 3 and beginning in row 00085, draw a simple random sample of 21 blocks.
   b. Calculate the mean percent of persons sixty-two years and over in these blocks.
   c. For all blocks, the mean of persons sixty-two years and over is 9.9 percent. Provide a theoretical explanation why the obtained sample mean differs from the population mean. Explain why repeated random samples of 21 blocks would yield a distribution of sample means which would have the appearance of a normal curve.

Table A. Characteristics of Persons by Blocks: Milwaukee Coun Wisconsin, 1970.

BLOCKS WITHIN CENSUS TRACTS	PERCENT OF BLOCK	
	Negro	62 Years and Over
104		
101	95	11
102	98	9
103	98	4
104	99	6
105	93	7
106	85	5
107	97	7
201	46	9
202	..	..
203	96	7
204	89	16
205	100	9
206	98	11
207	97	5
301	94	14
302	74	17
303	88	24
304	98	6
305	98	9
307	100	15
105		
101	88	8
102	78	20
103	89	10
104	77	23
105	92	6
106	87	14
107	80	10
201	91	9
202	75	..
203	100	..
204	95	15
205	98	4
206	95	13
207	99	7
208	98	11

BLOCKS WITHIN CENSUS TRACTS	PERCENT OF BLOCK	
	Negro	62 Ye and O
106		
101	47	14
103	82	3
104	95	6
105	89	6
106	78	8
107	53	9
108	21	13
201	44	10
202	84	5
203	69	2
204	86	5
205	69	3
206	46	8
207	46	1
208	80	8
209	93	5
107		
101	1	14
102	6	15
103	3	9
104	..	16
105	4	11
106	28	8
201	34	13
202	33	10
203	26	8
204	10	17
205	5	10
206	..	12
301	..	40
305	..	4
306	9	17
307	37	14
308	15	9
309	26	9

6. Societies with high birth rates tend to have small proportions of their population in the aged categories. Since the birth rate for blacks is higher than that for whites, it might be hypothesized that those city blocks which are occupied primarily by blacks will also have smaller proportions of their populations sixty-two years of age or older. Using Table B, organize your data to assess this hypothesis.

Table B. Cross-classification of Block Racial Composition by Block Age Composition.

	BLOCK AGE COMPOSITION	
BLOCK RACIAL COMPOSITION	Less than 10% of the block 62 years of age or older	10% or more of the block 62 years of age or older
Black composition less 50%		
Black composition 50% or higher		

a. Calculate Yule's Q.
b. Calculate chi-square.
c. What is the probability that this sample of twenty-one blocks was drawn from a population of blocks in which there is a relationship between racial composition and age composition at the block level?

RECOMMENDED READINGS

Conway, Freda
1967 *Sampling: An Introduction for Social Scientists.* London: Allen & Unwin.

A brief and thorough overview of most aspects of simple random sampling.

Lazerwitz, Bernard
1968 "Sampling Theory and Procedures," pp. 278–328 in Hubert M. Blalock, Jr., and Ann B. Blalock (eds.), *Methodology in Social Research.* New York: McGraw-Hill.

A basic and brief quantitative overview of sampling.

Moroney, M. J.
1956 *Facts from Figures.* Baltimore: Penguin Books.

Lucidly written introductions to sampling, normal distributions, and other statistical issues.

Mueller, John H., Karl F. Schuessler, and Herbert L. Costner
1970 *Statistical Reasoning in Sociology.* Boston: Houghton Mifflin.

Provides a clear introduction to normal distribution (Chapter 6), sampling (Chapter 12), and confidence intervals (Chapter 13).

Stephens, William N.
1968 *Hypotheses and Evidence.* New York: Crowell.

An excellent discussion of the issues involved in moving from observations and measurements to generalizations and conclusions.

Warwick, Donald P., and Charles A. Lininger
1975 *The Sample Survey: Theory and Practice.* New York: McGraw-Hill.

A good review of the various aspects of survey sampling. Includes an excellent chapter on sampling.

12

STRATIFIED RANDOM SAMPLING: CATHOLIC EDUCATION AND THE FERTILITY OF COLLEGE WOMEN

GENERAL ISSUE

Among the available procedures for drawing a sample, simple random sampling is the most straightforward. Its primary advantage is in its ease of application, since it requires only that the population be precisely defined and that a complete list of the population be available. However, its disadvantages are twofold. First, the researcher may find it impossible to obtain an accurate list of the population. Second, simple random sampling generally requires a larger sample than alternative procedures and therefore is less efficient.

In this chapter, a related procedure, *stratified random sampling*, will be considered. Although it also requires a precise definition and a complete list of the population, it requires a smaller sample than simple random sampling for the same level of precision and confidence. Additionally, stratified random sampling guarantees that population subgroups will be represented. Its major disadvantage is that it requires more knowledge about the population *prior* to drawing the sample than does simple random sampling. This knowledge is required in order to create homogeneous strata from which random samples will be drawn.

The methodological focus of this chapter is on the procedures of stratified random sampling, while the theoretical focus is on the impact of education and religion on college women in America.

Schooling and Fertility

By using data obtained from a survey of currently married women under forty-five years of age, the 1970 National Fertility Study was able to report a negative relationship between years of formal schooling and fertility.* As in previous years, this study indicated that as the number of years of formal education increases, the desired and actual number of births for married women decreases. Table 12-1 reports the observed relationship between education and fertility for 1970.

Table 12-1. Estimated Children by Educational Level for Married Women Under 45 Years of Age.

EDUCATIONAL LEVEL	MOST LIKELY NUMBER OF BIRTHS PER WOMAN	PERCENT OF BIRTHS 1960–1970 UNWANTED[a]	PERCENT OF BIRTHS 1960–1970 UNPLANNED[a]	ESTIMATED BIRTHS PER WOMEN WITHOUT UNWANTED BIRTHS
College, 4 yrs+	2.5	7	32	2.4
College, 1–3 yrs	2.8	11	39	2.6
High School, 4 yrs	2.8	14	44	2.6
High School 1–3 yrs	3.4	20	48	2.9
Less than 1 yr H.S.	3.9	31	56	3.0
Average	3.0	15	44	2.7

[a] Unplanned births included unwanted births.

An examination of Table 12-1 reveals that the relationship between education and fertility is consistent for all categories. As education increases, the most likely number of births, the percent of unwanted births, and the estimated number of births minus unplanned births all decrease.

These observations suggest a causal relationship between years of formal education and desired, planned, and actual fertility. Some theorists believe that educational institutions foster the development of values which compete with the values of home, family, and children. Educational institutions are said to exercise a powerful influence in altering and shaping such basic values as fertility. This argument will be referred to as the *institutional effect hypothesis.*

* Cited in *The American Almanac for 1974: The Statistical Abstract of the U.S.* (New York: Grosset & Dunlap, 1974), Table 74, p. 55. *Original source*: U.S. Commission on Population Growth and the American Future, *Population and the American Future* (Washington, D.C.: Government Printing Office, 1970).

Other theorists explain the relationship between education and fertility differently. In their view, basic values generally are unaffected by formal schooling. These theorists believe that basic values are established in the family, and that formal schooling is unlikely to have any significant impact. To explain the observed relationship between education and fertility, they believe that women who value education also value a low level of fertility, while women who do not value education value a high level of fertility. As a result, there is thought to be a correlation between years of education and fertility, but not a causal relationship. This correlation results from the fact that women who do not value fertility tend to obtain more education than do women who value it. This argument will be referred to as the *recruitment effect hypothesis*.

When religion is considered, the relationship between formal education and fertility becomes even more complex. While Catholic, Jewish, and Protestant women educated in nonreligious institutions tend to have low levels of fertility, Catholic women educated at Catholic institutions tend to have high levels of fertility for the same years of education. This has led some theorists to believe that the educational experience in Catholic schools fosters, sustains, and promotes high fertility in contrast to the educational experience in non-Catholic schools. Counterbalancing this institutional interpretation is the argument that Catholic schools tend to recruit women who already value fertility. Consequently, those women with lower fertility values attend non-Catholic schools.

Research conducted by Charles Westoff and Raymond Potvin sought to explore the merits of these two interpretations with respect to the fertility values of college women in religious and nonreligious institutions.* The recruitment and institutional effect hypotheses were formulated as follows:

1. Freshman women at Catholic institutions will desire more children than freshman women at non-Catholic institutions. (This would result from the recruitment of women with different fertility values.)
2. Senior women at Catholic institutions will desire more children than senior women at non-Catholic institutions even when the entering level of fertility is controlled. (This would result from the institutional effect of education.)

THE POPULATION AND STRATIFIED RANDOM SAMPLING

The population to be studied was defined as freshman and senior women in four-year institutions of higher learning throughout the continental United States. Since a list of all freshman and senior women in four-year

* Charles F. Westoff and Raymond H. Potvin, "Higher Education, Religion and Women's Family-Size Orientations," *American Sociological Review*, 31(1966):489–496; *College Women and Fertility Values* (Princeton: Princeton Univ. Press, 1967).

institutions was unavailable, Westoff and Potvin engaged in a two-stage sampling process: first, they selected a sample of institutions, and then they selected the students.

Drawing a Sample of Institutions

Prior to selecting the sample of institutions, the population of institutions was *purified*. Various types were excluded from the population of interest because the research focused only on four-year institutions of higher learning with specific characteristics. Thus, junior college, theological and religious schools, professional and art schools, colleges with enrollments under 300, institutions for men only, technical and semiprofessional schools, and black colleges were excluded. A total of 683 schools that can be best described as four-year universities, liberal arts colleges, and teachers colleges with full-time undergraduate female enrollments of at least 300 students remained for inclusion in the study.

Although a purified list of all four-year institutions was available, simple random sampling as a procedure for selecting institutions was rejected. The nature of the population made such sampling of institutions costly and inefficient.

First, the population of institutions was heterogeneous. Such heterogeneity meant that a relatively large sample would be required if institutions with varying characteristics (e.g., Catholic and non-Catholic, coeducational and female only, large and small) were to be represented in the sample.

Second, even a large sample size (short of the entire universe) would not have guaranteed that each type would be represented in sufficient number for analysis. This is true because each institution, regardless of its unique characteristics or theoretical importance, if selected by simple random sampling processes, would have an equal chance for inclusion in the sample. Thus, the more common types of four-year institution (e.g., small colleges) would be more likely to be selected than less common types, (e.g., Catholic colleges for women only).

Because of these considerations, a stratified random sampling procedure was utilized to select institutions. First, four-year institutions were divided into three groups on strata: Catholic schools, Protestant schools, and nonsectarian schools. Second, each of the three groups was divided into two strata: coeducational and women-only institutions. Six distinct lists of schools now existed. Next, each of the six groups was divided into four strata by region of the country: Northeast, North Central, South, and West. The result was twenty-four distinct institutional lists grouped by (1) type of institutional control, (2) sex composition, and (3) regions of the country. Table 12-2 reflects this distribution.

Finally, institutions were stratified by size. The twenty-four lists were divided into three categories of size: small, medium, and large enrollments. The operational definitions of small, medium, and large varied with size of

Table 12-2. Frequency Distribution of Educational Institutions by Three Strata: Control, Sex Composition, and Region.

FIRST STRATUM INSTITUTIONAL CONTROL	SECOND STRATUM SEX COMPOSITION	THIRD STRATUM REGION			
		Northeast	North Central	South	West
Catholic	Coed	1	2	3	4
	Female	5	6	7	8
Denomination	Coed	9	10	11	12
	Female	13	14	15	16
State	Coed	17	18	19	20
	Female	21	22	23	24

enrollments of institutions in each of the twenty-four strata.* Since some strata could not be subdivided into the three categories indicated, the actual result was 48 lists of institutions out of a possible maximum of 72 lists (3 × 24), differentiated by institutional control, sex composition, region of the country, and size.

The final step was to determine the number of institutions from each stratum to be included in the sample. This decision was influenced by

Table 12-3. Type and Number of Institutions in the Sample.

INSTITUTIONAL CONTROL	*N*	%	%
Catholic			
Coeducational	8	17.7	(53.3)
Female only	16	35.6	
Protestant			
Coeducational	3	6.7	(46.7)
Nonsectarian			
Coeducational	15	33.3	
Female only	3	6.7	
	45	100.0	100.0

SOURCE: Westoff and Potvin, "Higher Education," p. 11, Table 1.

* Nonsectarian coeducational institutions were divided into (1) schools with fewer than 1,000 women (but at least 300), (2) schools with between 1,000 and 3,000 women, and (3) schools with more than 3,000 women. On other strata, such as the Catholic coeducational institutions and nonsectarian colleges, only one cutting point was used: (1) schools with less than 1,000 women and (2) schools with 1,000 or more women. For Protestant coeducational schools, a cutting point of 700 was employed: (1) schools with less than 700 women and (2) schools with 700 or more women. Finally, the Catholic women's colleges were divided into three categories: (1) 1,000 women or over, (2) 600 to 999 women, and (3) 300 to 599 women. Protestant women's colleges had to be dropped from the study due to their small enrollments.

12.1 STRATIFIED RANDOM SAMPLING

The objective of random sampling is to produce an unbiased sample which is representative of the population and which permits statistical estimates of population values from sample statistics. When the population to be studied is heterogeneous, it is necessary to draw a relatively large sample in order to provide reasonable precision and confidence in estimating population values. When the population is relatively homogeneous, a small sample will yield reasonably precise estimates with confidence.

The main objective of stratification is to increase sampling efficiency while decreasing the cost of the research. This is accomplished by taking advantage of information about the homogeneity and heterogeneity of the population *prior* to drawing the sample. If the population can be stratified into distinct categories which are relatively homogeneous, then small samples can be drawn from each stratum. (The unusual situation of perfect stratification would permit a sample size of one from each stratum.)

Several conditions must be met in order to use stratified random sampling. First, like simple random sampling, a complete list of all units in the population must be available. Second, knowledge of the population is required in order to properly stratify it. Third, each unit in the population must be assigned to one and only one stratum.

Stratification is effective only if the created strata reduce the heterogeneity of the dependent variable. For instance, if a researcher is trying to estimate the extent of alienation in society, it would be meaningless to stratify the population by eye color even though this might be possible. (This statement assumes that eye color is unrelated to alienation.) Stratifying a population on any variable will not do; stratification must be accomplished with variables which make a difference in the distribution of the dependent variable. In the case of alienation, income might be a reasonable basis for stratification. *The objective of stratification is to produce strata which are internally homogeneous (the dependent variable has little variation) while retaining heterogeneity between strata (the dependent variable has large variation from stratum to stratum).*

Once the strata have been created, a simple random sample within each stratum can be drawn. At this point it is possible to use either proportionate or disproportionate sampling ratios to select cases from each stratum.

Proportionate Sampling. In proportionate sampling, strata are represented in the sample in the same proportion that they exist in the population. Table A reflects a 10 percent sample proportionately distributed across all strata. The sampling ratio for each stratum is 1 : 10. In this table, it is clear that proportionate sampling results in a sample whose composition on the stratified dimensions is identical to that of the population. A 10 percent sample has been selected in each stratum.

Table A. Proportionate Sampling.

STRATA	POPULATION N	POPULATION %	SAMPLE N	SAMPLE %	SAMPLING RATIO
College	2,000	20.0	200	20.0	1 : 10 (200 : 2000)
High school	5,000	50.0	500	50.0	1 : 10 (500 : 5000)
Elementary	3,000	30.0	300	30.0	1 : 10 (300 : 3000)
Total	10,000	100.0	1,000	100.0	1 : 10 (1,000 : 10,000)

Proportionate stratified random sampling has many advantages. Perhaps the major advantages are ease of implementation and calculation of the results. However, proportionate sampling may be inefficient in producing sample sizes which are either too small or unnecessarily large for a specific stratum. For instance, a sampling ratio of 1 : 10 produced a sample in which 50 percent of the students came from the high school stratum. This many high school students may be larger than needed. To resolve this problem, disproportionate stratified random sampling may be used.

Table B. Disproportionate Sampling.

STRATA	POPULATION N	POPULATION %	SAMPLE N	SAMPLE %	SAMPLING RATIO
College	2,000	20.0	333	33.3	1 : 6 (333 : 2000)
High school	5,000	50.0	334	33.4	1 : 15 (334 : 5000)
Elementary	3,000	30.0	333	33.3	1 : 9 (333 : 3000)
Total	10,000	100.0	1,000	100.0	1 : 10 (1,000 : 10,000)

Disproportionate Sampling. In disproportionate sampling, strata are represented in the sample in unequal proportions relative to their proportions in the population. Table B reflects a 10 percent total sample disproportionately distributed across all strata. However, the sampling ratio for each stratum is different. Here it can be seen that disproportionate sampling yields a sample different in composition from the population although the sample size remains the same (10 percent or 1,000). The college portion of the 1,000 students in the sample is 33.3 percent, which reflects a 16 percent sample of the 2,000 students in the college stratum (a sampling ratio of 1 : 6 = 16 percent). The high school portion of the sample is 33.4 percent, which reflects a 7 percent sample from the high school strata (a sampling ratio of 1 : 15), while the elementary portion of the sample is 33.3 percent, which reflects an 11 percent sample of the elementary strata (a sampling ratio of 1 : 9).

The advantages of disproportionate sampling are increased precision in estimating population value and improved adequacy of the size of each stratum sample for analysis. The disadvantage is the occasionally cumbersome mathematical calculations which are necessary. This presents no insurmountable problem as long as the researcher recalls that the strata have been differentially weighted and that the weights must be employed in the calculations.

administrative considerations and the number of students required for statistical analysis. The net result was to aim for a total probability sample of forty-eight institutions divided equally between Catholic and non-Catholic. Consequently, a simple random sample of institutions was drawn within each stratum. Three of the institutions selected for the study declined to cooperate. The final sample is described in Table 12-3.

Drawing a Sample of Students

The intended research design involved collecting data from all freshman and senior women in the forty-five institutions. To minimize response bias, data were to be collected through questionnaires administered in the classroom. By including all women, the researchers intended to eliminate student sampling error. By administering the questionnaire in the classroom, the researchers intended to obtain a high rate of response. These intentions were compromised in two ways.

First, it became impossible to study all women at all institutions. While it was possible to collect data from all freshman and senior women at all twenty-four Catholic institutions and at thirteen of the twenty-one non-Catholic schools, the number of women enrolled in the eight larger institutions made this method impractical. Consequently, at eight institutions it was necessary to draw a sample of freshman and senior women. Where sampling was undertaken, different sampling ratios were employed for selecting freshman and senior women.

The second compromise occurred in data collection. At the larger institutions it was impossible to administer the questionnaire in a central location. Consequently, questionnaires were mailed to students and returned by mail to a research address. At the remaining institutions, the questionnaires were administered either in the classroom or in an auditorium. Whether the questionnaires were directly administered or mailed, confidentiality of answers was stressed. The higher response rate for Catholic than non-Catholic schools, reflected in Table 12-4, may have resulted from the differences in data-collection procedures used in the smaller, more centralized Catholic schools compared to the larger and less centralized Protestant and secular institutions.

The response rate for each institution is based upon the enrollment figures for freshman and senior women supplied by its administration. In many cases these were only approximate, for exact figures were unavailable. The response rates were calculated by dividing the total freshman and senior female enrollment into the total number of returned questionnaires. As such, nonrespondents include persons absent on the dates of data collec-

Table 12-4. Distribution of Non-Catholic and Catholic Schools by Percent of Questionnaires Returned by First- and Fourth-Year Women.

RESPONSE RATE %	NON-CATHOLIC SCHOOLS				CATHOLIC SCHOOLS			
	First		Fourth		First		Fourth	
	N	%	*N*	%	*N*	%	*N*	%
90 and higher	4	19	2	10	5	21	4	17
80–89	3	14	4	19	9	38	8	33
70–79	4	19	2	10	4	17	5	21
60–69	4	19	4	19	—		1	4
50–59	3	14	7	33	1	4	1	4
40–49	2	10	2	10	1	4	2	8
30–39	—		—		1	4	3	13
20–29	1	5	—		3	13		
Total[a]	21	100	21	101	24	101	24	100

SOURCE: Westoff and Potvin, "Higher Education," p. 2, Table 2.
[a] Due to rounding not all percent column totals add to 100.

tion, students who were missed by the researchers, and students who refused to participate. Although a refined rate would have been desirable, more accurate figures were unavailable.

It should be noted that some of the completed returns were dropped from the analysis if the respondent possessed certain characteristics. Respondents who were nonwhite, foreign born, above twenty-five years of age, or had attended more than one college or university were excluded from the analysis. The imposition of race, nativity, and age restrictions homogenized the sample. The result was approximately 15,000 questionnaires available for analysis (an overall return rate of 72 percent).

ANALYSIS AND RESULTS

Table 12-5 cross-classifies religious preference and the number of children desired by freshman and senior women. Mean values are reported.

As expected, Catholic women desired the largest number of children, followed by Mormons, Protestants, Jews, and women with no religious preference. This pattern held for both freshman and senior women.

Table 12-6 reports the mean number of desired children for freshman and senior women by type of institution.

Table 12-5. Mean Number of Children Desired by Religious Preference for Freshman and Senior Women.

RELIGIOUS PREFERENCE	FRESHMAN		SENIOR	
	$\bar{X}$	N	$\bar{X}$	N
None	3.2	205	3.1	182
Jewish	3.4	514	3.2	319
Protestant	3.5	4286	3.4	1967
Mormon	4.6	229	4.8	154
Catholic	5.6	3249	5.3	1781

SOURCE: Westoff and Potvin, "Higher Education," p. 36, Table 7.

Table 12-6. Mean Number of Desired Children by Type of Institution for Freshman and Senior Women.

INSTITUTIONAL TYPE	FRESHMAN		SENIOR	
	$\bar{X}$	N	$\bar{X}$	N
Nonsectarian	3.5	4557	3.4	2406
Protestant	3.8	600	3.4	195
Catholic	5.5	3247	5.3	1781

SOURCE: Westoff and Potvin, "Higher Education," p. 2, Table 2.

On the average, women entering nonsectarian institutions desired the fewest number of children (3.5), while women entering Catholic institutions desired the largest number (5.5). Thus, there is some evidence that women entering Catholic institutions have higher fertility values than do women entering Protestant and nonsectarian institutions. It can be observed also that senior women at all three types of institutions desire fewer children than do freshman. Further, senior women at Catholic institutions desire more children than senior women at Protestant or nonsectarian ones.

Table 12-7 presents the interrelationships between religious preference, institutional type, and desired number of children. The data indicate that religiously affiliated institutions tended to attract students desiring the most children. Further, it can be observed that senior women in all institutions, with the exception of Mormons, desire fewer children than their freshman counterparts. If it is assumed that freshman women have fertility values similar to those held by senior women when they were freshmen, then formal education in all institutions may tend to reduce the number of children desired.

Table 12-7. Mean Number of Desired Children by Religious Preference for Each Institutional Type by Freshman and Senior Status.

INSTITUTION	RELIGIOUS PREFERENCE	FRESHMAN		SENIOR	
		$\overline{X}$	N	$\overline{X}$	N
Nonsectarian	None	3.2	205	3.1	182
	Jewish	3.4	514	3.2	319
	Protestant	3.5	3609	3.4	1751
	Mormon	4.6	229	4.8	154
	Catholic	4.4	793	4.1	485
Protestant	Protestant	3.8	600	3.4	195
Catholic	Protestant	3.7	77	3.3	21
	Catholic	5.5	3987	5.3	1781

SOURCE: Westoff and Potvin, "Higher Education," p. 2, Table 2.

Thus, the data provide the greatest support for the recruitment hypothesis in explaining differences in fertility values among women educated at different institutions. For instance, Catholic freshman women at Catholic institutions desired an average of 5.5 children while Catholics at nonsectarian institutions desired an average of 4.4. The data provided little support for the institutional hypothesis. Differences between freshman and senior women at all colleges were slight, but in all cases (with the exception of the small number of Mormons) seniors definitely desired fewer children. The fact that the freshman-senior variation was similar in Catholic and non-Catholic institutions suggests that the variation results from aging rather than educational experience.

SUMMARY AND QUALIFICATIONS

A stratified sample of colleges and universities was drawn, and the population or a sample of freshman and senior women at each institution was administered a fertility questionnaire. Catholic institutions tended to recruit women with higher fertility values than non-Catholic institutions. At each place, senior women held only slightly different fertility values than freshmen. It appears that education has little effect on college women's fertility values.

However, several important limitations regarding the research design must be considered. First, freshman and senior women may not be comparable groups. Changes in the larger society may have produced differences in fertility values unrelated to formal schooling. Only by assuming that senior women held the same fertility values as current freshmen when they, the seniors, were freshmen is it possible to infer the effect or absence of effect of education. (The procedure of substituting one group for another over time is referred to as a *synthetic cohort* technique.) In this instance, there was no evidence to indicate that the number of children desired by seniors when they were freshmen was different from the number desired by current freshmen. However, the possibility of real differences which may be established by future evidence must be considered.

A related limitation is the assumption that the mean number of children desired by the senior class approximates the mean number of children which will be desired by the freshman class when they become seniors. This may be questioned in that not all freshmen matriculate to their senior year. Students drop out of school for academic reasons, marriage, and numerous personal causes. Thus, seniors represent a naturally self-selected group. The important factor for this study is not simply the loss of students from freshman to senior year but whether those students who leave hold fertility values different from those who continue. If there is no difference in fertility values, the loss of students does not affect the distribution of the dependent variable. If there is a difference, the loss of students impairs the comparability of senior and freshman women. Since the effect of attrition was not examined, it remains a consideration with respect to the findings of this study.

A third and final limitation regarding the design is the failure to include a *control group* of noncollege women. A control group is not subjected to the independent variable, but is otherwise similar to the group being studied (see Chapter 21, page 311). The use of a control group would have established the effect of age, if any, independently of education on fertility values. In this study, the use of a control group would have been costly, since it would have been difficult to obtain a random sample of a group widely dispersed in society. Despite the practical difficulty of utilizing a control group, its absence in the design prohibits the untangling of age and education as distinct factors influencing fertility.

Technical Insert VI

Using Stratified Samples to Estimate Population Values

In the type of analysis presented in this chapter, stratified sampling was used to compare values for selected strata. Stratified samples can be used to describe the values of the entire population from which the sample was drawn. To do this, however, the relative weights of the strata must be taken into account. Table VI-1 contains the necessary information for estimating the average of the institutional means. Note that the 683 institutions, not the students they contain, are the units of analysis. Each institution in the study is thus given equal weight regardless of the number of students it contains.

Following Table VI-1 are explanations of each row, and a list of steps in estimating a population parameter from stratified samples.

Table VI-1. Population and Sample Data.

		CATHOLIC	NON-CATHOLIC	TOTAL
Row 1	Universe of institutions	137	546	683
Row 2	Proportion in each stratum	.20	.80	1.00
Row 3	Sample drawn from each stratum	24	21	
Row 4	Mean number of children desired (freshmen)	5.62	3.84	
Row 5	Standard deviation	.36	.29	

Row 1 reports that there were 137 Catholic colleges and 546 non-Catholic colleges in the universe, for a total of 683 colleges.

Row 2 reports that 20 percent of the 683 colleges were Catholic and 80 percent were non-Catholic. This is the weight that will be assigned to the strata.

Row 3 indicates that 24 colleges were randomly drawn from the Catholic strata and 21 colleges from the non-Catholic strata.

Row 4 gives the mean number of children desired by freshman women per institution as 5.62 for Catholic universities and 3.84 for non-Catholic.

Row 5 reports that the standard deviation (see page 173) for the 24 Catholic universities was .36 and for the 21 non-Catholic universities, .29.

STEPS IN ESTIMATING PARAMETERS FROM STRATIFIED SAMPLES

1. *Calculate the weighted mean of the strata.* Table VI-1 indicates that the mean value of Catholic institutions in the sample is 5.62 and that 20 percent of the population of institutions is Catholic. The sample mean of Catholic institutions (5.62) is therefore multiplied by .20 in order to obtain the contribution of Catholic institutions to the estimated mean of the population. Similarly, the sample mean of non-Catholic institutions (3.84) is multiplied by the

non-Catholic proportion of the population, in order to obtain the contribution of non-Catholic institutions. The sum of these contributions is the weighted mean of the institutional values:

$$
\begin{aligned}
\text{Weighted mean } \overline{X} &= (\text{weight})(\text{sample statistic}) \\
&\quad + (\text{weight})(\text{sample statistic}) \\
&= (.20)(5.62) + (.80)(3.84) \\
&= 4.196 \\
&= 4.2
\end{aligned}
$$

2. *Calculate the standard error for each stratum.* As explained earlier, the standard error refers to the chance distribution of sample means around the population mean. In this case, the standard error is calculated using the formula:

$$\text{Standard error} = \frac{\text{Standard deviation}}{\sqrt{N-1}}$$

Table VI-1 indicates that 24 Catholic schools were sampled from the population of Catholic schools, and the standard deviation of these 24 schools from their mean was .36. Therefore, the estimated standard error for the entire Catholic stratum is

$$\frac{.36}{\sqrt{24-1}} = .075$$

And the standard error for the non-Catholic stratum can be seen to be

$$\frac{.29}{\sqrt{21-1}} = .065$$

3. *Combine the standard errors for the various strata.* The goal here is to obtain a measure of the distribution of the sample means for the entire population. The statistical formula for combining standard errors of the strata is

$$
\begin{aligned}
\text{S.E.} = &\sqrt{(\text{weight squared})(\text{stratum standard error squared})} \\
&+ \sqrt{(\text{weight squared})(\text{stratum standard error squared})}
\end{aligned}
$$

Therefore, for this illustration, the standard error of the sampling distribution for the population is

$$
\begin{aligned}
\text{S.E.} &= \sqrt{(.20)^2(.075)^2} + \sqrt{(.80)^2(.065)^2} \\
&= .015 + .052 \\
&= .067
\end{aligned}
$$

These formulas can be extended to accommodate complex designs incorporating three or more strata.

4. *Estimate the population mean.* The best single estimate of the population mean is the mean of the sample. The weighted mean of the sample was calculated to be 4.196 in step 1 above. However, this figure is only an estimate of the population based on a single

sample. The sample could have been drawn from a population whose value was other than 4.196. Estimating the range of populations from which this sample would likely be drawn is a straightforward process.

A 95 percent confidence interval is equal to the estimated mean, plus and minus 1.96 standard deviations. In this example, the likelihood is less than 5 percent that this sample would be drawn from a population whose mean is less than 4.065[4.196 − 1.96(.067) = 4.065] or greater than 4.327[4.196 + 1.96(.067) = 4.327]. That is, the probability is less than .05 that a sample such as this would have been drawn from a population whose mean lies outside the range of 4.065 and 4.327. Therefore, there is 95 percent confidence that the true mean of the population is somewhere between 4.1 and 4.3.

KEY IDEAS AND CONCEPTS

confidence
disproportionate sampling
heterogeneity
homogeneity
institutional effect
precision
proportionate sampling
purified population
recruitment effect
response rate
standard deviation
standard error
stratified sampling
stratum
synthetic cohort
weighted mean
variance

ISSUES AND PROBLEMS

1. Specify the reasons why simple random sampling procedures are easier to implement than stratified sampling procedures.
2. List the advantages of stratified sampling over simple random sampling.
3. In creating strata, it is necessary to stratify on variables correlated with the dependent variable. Explain.
4. In this chapter, institutions of higher learning were stratified on a variety of dimensions. Discuss the contribution of each dimension below to the heterogeneity of the dependent variable.
   a. sex composition of the institution
   b. size of the institution
   c. regional location of the institution
5. Members of college faculties vary in their attitudes toward collective bargaining and unionization. In some cases, faculty have voted to unionize, in other cases they have not. Using a directory of college faculty, list the dimensions which could be used for stratifying. Discuss the merits of each dimension.
6. Discuss the merits of proportionate and disproportionate sampling procedures. Assess these approaches in the context of problem 5.

RECOMMENDED READINGS

Moser, C. A.

1958 *Survey Methods in Social Investigation.* New York: Macmillan.

Contains a clear introduction to stratified and other types of sampling (Chapter 6) in addition to other topics important to survey research.

Stephan, Frederick F., and Philip J. McCarthy

1958 *Sampling Opinions: An Analysis of Survey Procedure.* New York: Wiley.

Contains a good discussion of the uses and advantages of stratification (Chapter 20), as well as discussions of many other sampling topics.

Yates, Frank

1960 *Sampling Methods for Census and Surveys.* New York: Hafner.

A discussion of stratified sampling and of other aspects of surveys.

13

CLUSTER SAMPLING: RELIGIOUS AFFILIATION AND ECONOMIC SUCCESS

GENERAL ISSUE

As suggested, simple and stratified random sampling procedures are useful when a complete list of the population is available, and when the cost of data collection is reasonable. For large populations, however, a list is often unavailable, or the respondents are so scattered that the cost of data collection is prohibitive. One solution is to use cluster sampling.

Cluster sampling takes advantage of the geographical concentration of portions of the population and does not require a complete list of the population. Sampling hospital patients in the United States may be used to illustrate these points. First, a complete list of patients is not readily available, and second, even if it were, patients are scattered throughout the entire country. However, they *are* concentrated in hospitals, and a list of these could be compiled. If the mix of patients varied little from one hospital to another, then a sample of hospitals could be drawn and the information obtained from patients in these could be generalized to all patients. Statistically, in this illustration, hospitals are viewed as *clusters* of patients. Each cluster is heterogeneous, that is, each contains a *mix* of patients; but the clusters are homogeneous, that is, the clusters (hospitals) are similar to each other. Regrettably, hospitals do vary as to their mix of patients, and consequently, a more complex cluster design than that just illustrated would have to be used.

This chapter explores the justification for cluster sampling and specifically focuses on the theoretical problem of the impact of religious values on economic success.

THEORETICAL PROBLEM: ECONOMIC AND RELIGIOUS VALUES

Max Weber, the influential European sociologist of the early twentieth century, proposed that religious and economic values were interdependent. He developed the thesis that Western economic growth emerged partly as a by-product of the Protestant, and especially Calvinist, search for evidence of God's grace through economic success. His thesis is responsible for much of the research undertaken to determine if current economic differences between Protestants and Catholics can be accounted for by religious values.

Some theorists believe that American Protestants and Catholics share similar economic values, but that Catholics possess still other religious values which hinder their achievement and place them at a competitive disadvantage with Protestants. Other theorists believe that any religious values which once may have influenced the success or lack thereof of Catholics have long since disappeared. Consequently, these theorists believe that the causes of any economic difference between Protestants and Catholics lie in other factors.

The research reported here seeks to explore these alternative theories through an analysis of data obtained in a national probability sample of American Protestants and Catholics.* The methodological focus is on cluster sampling as a procedure for studying national populations.

Hypotheses

Two opposing hypotheses concerning occupational status flow from the theories of Weber and his critics:

1. The occupational achievement of Catholics will be lower than the occupational achievement of Protestants, even when nonreligious factors (e.g., ethnicity) are controlled. (This hypothesis is based on Weber's theory.)
2. The occupational achievement of Catholics will not differ from the occupational achievement of Protestants when nonreligious factors are controlled. (This hypothesis is based on the arguments of Weber's critics.)

* Elton F. Jackson, William S. Fox, and Harry J. Crockett, Jr., "Religion and Occupational Achievement," *American Sociological Review*, 35 (1970):48–63.

Research Design

Data for the analysis were collected during interviews conducted by a permanent staff of part-time interviewers employed by the University of Michigan's Survey Research Center. Unlike most of the research reported in previous chapters of this text, these data are national (forty-eight states plus the District of Columbia) rather than local. Therefore, a different set of economic and statistical considerations influenced the sampling design.

The Survey Research Center rejected the techniques of simple random sampling as well as simple stratified random sampling because of the impracticalities of these when used for a national sample. First, a complete list of all American citizens was unavailable; and second, the cost of locating, and then sending, interviewers to respondents dispersed throughout the continental United States was prohibitive. Consequently, the research followed a *multistage area cluster design.*

The three central features of this design are incorporated in its designation: multistage, area, and cluster. The word *multistage* indicates that sampling proceeds through several stages prior to drawing the final sample of respondents. The word *area* indicates that the primary sampling unit (psu) is a geographic area. (The final sample unit, the individual, is selected eventually from a series of samples of geographic areas.) The word *cluster* indicates a novel theoretical basis for constructing the primary sampling units.

In the University of Michigan version, the primary sampling unit was a county, a group of counties, or an SMSA (Standard Metropolitan Statistical Area). The primary sampling unit was viewed as a cluster, a concept based on the idea of heterogeneity. Moreover, the county is often an ideal heterogeneous unit. Within its political boundaries are cities and towns, suburban and rural areas, and a population mix similar to that of the larger society. If each county was identical to every other, only one would need to be studied in order to capture all the features of the larger society. Obviously this level of similarity among counties does not exist, so it is necessary to create strata which contain counties (or groups of counties) that are similar in their heterogeneity.

The University of Michigan's multistage area cluster design used in this research contained 66 strata. Thus, the approximately 3,000 U.S. counties and a small number of SMSA's were each assigned to one of 66 strata. *The strata were designed to be different from each other* (the principle of stratified sampling). *Within each stratum, however, the clusters were similar to one another with respect to the size of their largest city, their major industry, geographic region of the country, and population mix.*

After every county was placed in a stratum, the first stage in the sampling process was to draw a single cluster from each of the sixty-six strata. Each cluster, therefore, had a chance of appearing in the sample, and all strata were represented. The sample thus consisted of sixty-six clusters, each representing the stratum from which it was drawn.

These clusters were further divided into smaller components such as cities and towns and suburban and rural areas. A probability procedure was employed to select these secondary sampling units. This constituted the next stage of the sampling procedure.

The cities, towns, suburbs, and rural areas drawn in this second stage were then subdivided into smaller areal units. In this case, the units were either city blocks and/or rural geographical areas known as chunks. A probability sample of those blocks and chunks was drawn for this third stage of the sampling procedure.

For the fourth stage, a list of all dwelling units in the selected blocks

13.1 CLUSTER SAMPLING

Cluster sampling is based on the principle of heterogeneity, in contrast to stratified sampling which is based on the principle of homogeneity. Where the assignment of sample units is under the control of the researcher, the objective is to create clusters which are identical to each other. Each cluster would be composed of heterogeneous units which would be comparable to the heterogeneity of any other cluster. In most instances, researchers are compelled to utilize natural clusters, since they lack control over the assignment of units.

For example, assume that one had a truck of unsorted fruit, for example, apples, oranges, and pears. In *stratified sampling,* the objective would be to create strata (baskets) each composed only of apples, pears, or oranges. If researchers separated the fruit into three large baskets, then a simple random sample within each basket (stratum) would permit a description of units in each basket, and eventually a description of the population of unsorted fruit. In accordance with the principle of homogeneity, the contents within each basket are considered to be alike, while the contents between baskets are considered to be different.

If *cluster sampling* were applied to this problem, the objective would be to create baskets which were internally heterogeneous, i.e., each basket would contain apples, oranges, and pears. Assume that three baskets (clusters) were created. Each basket would be like every other; yet the contents of each would be heterogeneous. In drawing a sample, the researcher would randomly select one of the baskets. If it were not too large, all of its contents could be studied. If it were large, a sample of the contents could be drawn for study. In a sense, each cluster is a miniature representation of the universe; consequently, only one basket has to be studied in order to provide a basis for estimating the characteristics of the remaining baskets (clusters) and, by implication, the characteristics of the population.

As this description suggests, cluster sampling is complex. Generally, there are two sources of sample error: (1) that contributed by the sample of clusters from the population of clusters, and (2) that contributed by the sample of units within each cluster.

and chunks was compiled. Again a probability sampling procedure was employed, this time to draw the sample of dwelling units from which respondents would eventually be selected. Adjustments were made for previous imbalances so that every dwelling unit in the continental United States had the same overall probability of selection.

The final sampling stage involved the selection of eligible respondents. The interviews, conducted in the field, were directed toward adults living in the sample dwelling units. The analysis reported here, however, is restricted to a subsample of adults with desired characteristics. The final sample consisted of 766 white, male, American-born respondents, retired or employed full time, for whom occupational information was available for themselves and for their fathers, and who designated themselves as Protestant or Catholic.

DATA ANALYSIS

Problems of Invalid Interpretations

To avoid an invalid interpretation of the relationship between religion and economic achievement, variables which potentially affected economic achievement had to be controlled in the analysis. In this case, six were controlled: socioeconomic position of the family of origin, ethnicity, immigrant generation, age, size of the community during adolescence, and region of the country during adolescence. The potential importance of these variables is discussed below.

Socioeconomic Position. Since current economic achievement is partially a function of one's starting point in the economic hierarchy, it is necessary to control the effect of economic origin.

Ethnicity. American society contains elements of discrimination and prejudice. Since racial and ethnic background may influence individuals' lives in a manner beyond their control, controlling for ethnicity permits a more reliable and valid assessment of the impact of religious values.

Immigration Generation. Cultural background may influence the value orientations of individuals independently of their religion. First- or second-generation Americans are different from those whose ancestral roots extend back for several generations. Consequently, generation is one variable which should be controlled in order to eliminate its effect on economic achievement.

Age. Economic achievement is partially a function of age. Older persons have had a longer time in which to achieve success than younger ones.

Like the previous variables, therefore, age must be controlled in order to eliminate its effect.

Community. The structure and value influence of the community during the formative period of adolescence may affect an individual's orientation toward, and achievement of, success. To eliminate this effect, community during adolescence should be controlled in examining the relationship between religion and economic achievement.

Region. Regional economic and cultural characteristics during the adolescent formative period may similarly affect the achievement orientation and opportunity of individuals. Consequently, region as an additional variable should be controlled in the analysis.

Certain variables, however, should not be controlled. These include education, and region and community of current residence. Religious values may influence economic achievement partly by reducing (or increasing) the desire to obtain higher education or by influencing a move to a community or region of greater economic opportunity. Controlling for these would not assist in determining whether the effect of religion is of any consequence, because these variables may be part of the causal chain. Consequently, they should not be controlled in the analysis.

Operationalization of Concepts

Economic achievement was operationally measured by the occupational achievement of respondents. Responses as to the respondent's and his father's occupations were coded into seven categories: (1) professional, (2) business, (3) white collar (clerical, technical, and sales), (4) skilled manual, (5) semiskilled, (6) unskilled, and (7) farmer. Although there may have been considerable variation as to the prestige of occupations and economic achievement within these categories, it was assumed that the categories were approximately rank-ordered and formed an ordinal scale.

Religious affiliation was determined by the question: "What is your religious preference?" Although Protestant men differed considerably from one another as to their theology and occupational achievement, they were treated as one homogeneous group in the analysis. This precluded the problem of small sample sizes for each denomination and permitted a focus on the differences between Protestants and Catholics.

Since religious values presumably have their greatest impact during adolescence, it would have been desirable to measure respondents' religious preference during this time. Such an attempt was not undertaken in the survey. Consequently, current religious preference was employed as an indicator. This was not as problematic as it may appear. Although there may be a high rate of interdenominational mobility (i.e., altering one's religious preference), this is primarily true of Protestants. Thus, Episcopalians may become Lutherans, and Lutherans may embrace Methodism,

Table 13-1. Occupation of Respondents (White, Male, U.S.-Born) and Respondents' Fathers, by Religion.

RELIGION	OCCUPATION (IN PERCENTAGES)							TOTAL	N
	Professional	Business	White Collar	Skilled	Semi-Skilled	Unskilled	Farmer		
Panel A Respondent's Occupation									
Protestant	9.5	14.6	12.5	25.5	16.1	6.5	15.3	100%	(589)
Catholic	5.1	11.9	22.6	28.2	20.3	6.8	5.1	100%	(177)
Difference	4.4	2.7	10.1	2.7	4.2	.3	12.2		
Panel B Respondent's Occupation—Urban Occupations Only									
Protestant	11.2	17.2	14.8	30.1	19.0	7.6		100%	(499)
Catholic	5.4	12.5	23.8	29.8	21.4	7.1		100%	(168)
Difference	5.8	4.7	9.0	.3	2.4	.5			
Panel C Respondent's Father's Occupation									
Protestant	4.6	10.5	7.5	16.8	11.2	3.7	45.7	100%	(589)
Catholic	3.4	12.4	5.6	28.2	21.5	11.3	17.5	100%	(177)
Difference	1.2	1.9	1.9	11.4	10.3	7.6	28.2		
Panel D Respondent's Father's Occupation—Urban Occupations Only									
Protestant	8.4	19.4	13.8	30.9	20.6	6.9		100%	(320)
Catholic	4.1	15.1	6.8	34.2	26.0	13.7		100%	(146)
Difference	4.3	4.3	7.0	3.3	5.4	6.8			

SOURCE: Jackson, et al., "Religion and Occupational Achievement," p. 54, Table 1.

and so on. However, since the Protestant denominations were treated as a single group, interdenominational mobility became less of a concern.

Exploring the Data

Table 13-1 presents the occupational distributions of the aforementioned 766 Protestants and Catholics as well as those of their fathers. From the distribution in Panel A, it can be observed that Protestant respondents are more likely than Catholics to hold professional, business, and farming occupations. For instance, 9.5 percent of the Protestant respondents were professionals compared to 5.1 percent of the Catholics, whereas Catholics were in white-collar (i.e., clerical, technical, and sales) occupations more often than Protestants. Catholics appeared somewhat more likely to hold skilled manual and semiskilled jobs.

The distribution in Panel B also focuses on respondents' occupations, but is confined to urban occupations and thus excludes farmers. Compared to Panel A, Panel B indicates an even greater Protestant advantage in professional and business occupations, with the Protestant-Catholic difference in percent of professionals increasing from 4.4 to 5.8 percent.

Panels A and B reflect the respondents' current occupational positions but yield no information about occupational origins. Panels C and D reflect the occupational distribution of fathers. It is evident that differences in origins exist. Catholics (28.2 + 21.5 + 11.3 = 61 percent) are more likely than Protestants (16.8 + 11.2 + 3.7 = 31.7 percent) to have fathers with manual jobs, while Protestants are more likely to come from farming households. Panel D, which again is restricted to the distribution of urban occupations, indicates that Protestants have higher occupational origins than Catholics.

The next step in the analysis was to determine if these dissimilarities in origin accounted for the differences in current occupational distributions of Protestants and Catholics.

Table 13-2. Occupation of Respondents (White, Male, U.S.-Born) *Standardized* for Father's Occupation, by Religion (in Percentages).

RESPONDENT'S OCCUPATION	PROTESTANT	CATHOLIC	DIFFERENCE (PROTESTANT – CATHOLIC)
Professional	9.6	5.7	+3.9
Business	14.3	12.2	+2.1
White-collar	12.9	22.0	−9.1
Skilled manual	26.2	21.9	+4.3
Semiskilled	16.9	19.4	−2.5
Unskilled	6.4	7.6	−1.2
Farmer	13.7	11.4	+2.3

SOURCE: Jackson, et al., "Religion and Occupational Achievement," p. 55, Table 2.

Table 13-3. Occupation of Respondents (White, Male, U.S.-Born), Reared in Nonsouthern Region, Northwest European Ethnicity, by Religion.

	RESPONDENT'S OCCUPATION (IN PERCENTAGES)						
RELIGION	Profession or Business	White Collar	Skilled Manual	Semi- or Unskilled	Farmer	TOTAL	*N*
Panel A	Standardized for Father's Occupation						
Protestant	25.9	13.4	27.4	22.4	10.9	100%	(295)
Catholic	15.1	21.3	25.9	25.2	12.4	100%	(85)
Panel B	Standardized for Age and Father's Occupation[a]						
Protestant	26.6	13.7	26.7	22.0	11.2	100%	(294)[b]
Catholic	13.9	19.1	28.6	26.5	12.0	100%	(85)
Panel C	Standardized for Generation and Father's Occupation[a]						
Protestant	25.6	12.6	27.8	23.4	10.6	100%	(265)[b]
Catholic	15.5	21.8	25.1	26.6	11.0	100%	(81)
Panel D	Standardized for Community of Origin and Father's Occupation[a]						
Protestant	25.1	13.7	27.5	22.7	11.1	100%	(287)[b]
Catholic	15.9	21.0	26.4	25.8	11.1	100%	(82)

SOURCE: Jackson, et al., "Religion and Occupational Achievement," p. 58, Table 4.

[a] Direct standardization could not be used due to sample cell sizes. The technique utilized is described in Evelyn M. Kitagawa, "Standardized Comparisons in Population Research," *Demography* 1 (1965): 296–315.

[b] Differs from above total *N*'s due to missing data on control variable.

Using a technique developed by demographers to standardize two or more groups, the impact of the father's occupation was controlled by creating equivalent distributions of that occupation for Protestants and Catholics. The results are seen in Table 13-2.

In terms of nonmanual occupations, Protestants had the advantage in following professional and business occupations while Catholics were more likely to enter white-collar positions. With respect to manual occupations, Protestants were more likely to enter skilled manual and farming occupations, but Catholics were more likely to enter semiskilled and unskilled occupations. For most occupational categories, with the exception of white-collar, the percentage difference was slight. If the differences are considered as forming a pattern, however, there appears to be a slight occupational advantage for Protestants, even when origin as measured by the father's occupation is standardized.

The remainder of the analysis provided controls for age, generation, and community of origin. To simplify presentation and to provide a sufficient number of cases for analysis, some occupational groups were combined. The data were restricted to an analysis of respondents reared in a nonsouthern region and who were of northwest European ethnicity. The results are reported in Table 13-3.

Panel A of Table 13-3 indicates that, even when father's occupation is standardized, Protestants (25.9 percent) are more likely to hold professional or business occupations than Catholics (15.1 percent). The latter, on the other hand, are more likely to hold white-collar positions. With respect to manual occupations, there are negligible differences. Panels B, C, and D indicate that the introduction of controls for age, generation, and community of origin do not change this pattern. The similarity of these summary panels suggests that age, generation, and size of community of origin have little effect on the relationship between religion and achievement.*

DATA INFERENCE

The use of broad controls, occasional small sample size, and the use of indirect standardization procedures in part of the analysis must qualify any conclusions. However, analysis of the data suggests that some Protestant-Catholic differences in economic achievement do exist, and that these probably can be attributed to religious factors. The result, however, can be interpreted in three ways:

* Age divisions used in the analysis were 21–29 years, 30–39, 40–49, 50–65, and over 65. Community of origin was standardized in terms of the responses to the question: "Were you brought up mostly on a farm, in a town, in a small city, or in a large city?"

1. The observed differences in occupational achievement are religious in origin, but are not large enough to be theoretically important.
2. The observed differences are religious in origin and theoretically important, but are due to aspects of religion other than those generating economically relevant values. (For instance, Catholics come from larger families, and resources necessary for individual occupational attainment may be allocated to the support of the family.)
3. The observed differences in occupational achievement are religious in origin, theoretically important, and due to differences in economically relevant values.

The choice of the proper interpretation of the findings obtained in this study remains somewhat ambiguous.

SUMMARY

A multistage area cluster design was used to select a national sample of white, male, U.S.-born respondents. The data collected from this sample indicate that there are religious differences in occupational level, even when controlling for potentially confounding variables. However, the occupational differences cannot be attributed to religious values with certainty until further possible explanations (e.g., family size) are eliminated.

KEY IDEAS AND CONCEPTS

cluster
cluster sampling
heterogeneity
homogeneity
multistage sampling
national probability sample
standardization
stratum
variance

ISSUES AND PROBLEMS

1. Briefly specify the characteristics of
   a. simple random sampling
   b. stratified sampling
   c. cluster sampling
2. Explain why it is important that each cluster be internally heterogeneous but that the clusters considered as an aggregate be homogeneous.

3. In most communities, there exists a large number of apartment complexes. Each complex contains many separate buildings and each building contains many apartments. Develop a cluster sampling approach for a study of resident satisfaction. Specify the dimensions and decisions employed in each step of the study. Compare your approach with that of a colleague and discuss the merits of each. (Be detailed in your discussion.)
4. Table 13-A indicates that the tuberculosis rate varies considerably within and across cities. Design a multistage sampling approach which permits the drawing of six cities. Following the selection of six cities, design a sampling approach for eventually interviewing 200 respondents in each city. Specify and discuss the criteria employed at each stage of the sampling process.

Table 13-A. Death Rates for Tuberculosis,[a] by Poverty Status of Area of Residence and Race, for Nineteen U.S. Cities, 1969–1971 Average.

	POVERTY AREAS		NONPOVERTY AREAS	
	White TB Rate	Negro TB Rate	White TB Rate	Negro TB Rate
Atlanta	7.5	—	2.4	—
Baltimore	16.0	14.2	5.5	5.7
Buffalo	10.5	—	2.8	—
Chicago	19.3	9.4	3.4	4.0
Cincinnati	15.0	14.2	3.0	4.9
Cleveland	5.0	—	4.4	—
Dallas	8.9	4.1	1.1	2.0
Denver	6.5	3.6	2.4	2.3
Indianapolis	10.0	10.9	1.9	1.3
Los Angeles	9.4	5.1	2.9	3.2
Memphis	4.1	—	1.1	—
Minneapolis	5.0	—	1.7	—
New York City	5.2	12.6	2.5	6.0
Bronx County	4.1	8.4	2.3	2.6
Kings County	4.5	12.4	2.7	7.1
New York County	7.6	16.8	3.7	11.5
Queens County	8.2	9.1	1.9	4.6
Richmond County	—	—	2.3	6.3
Philadelphia	14.3	—	4.0	—
Pittsburgh	11.3	—	2.9	—
San Diego	4.9	1.1	1.6	—
San Francisco	12.9	3.0	2.5	1.3
Seattle	4.6	—	1.3	2.3
Washington, D.C.	20.9	—	3.9	—

SOURCE: Stephanie J. Ventura, *Selected Vital and Health Statistics in Poverty and Nonpoverty Areas of 19 Large Cities, United States, 1969–1971*. DHEW Publication No. (HRA)76-1904 (Washington, D.C.: Government Printing Office, 1975), p. 35.

[a] Rates per 100,000 population in specific group as of April 1, 1970.

RECOMMENDED READINGS

Cochran, William G.
1953 *Sampling Techniques.* New York: Wiley.

An advanced quantitative introduction to sampling.

Kish, Leslie
1965 *Survey Sampling.* New York: Wiley.

Discusses sampling at a high level of sophistication and quantification.

Yamane, Taro
1967 *Elementary Sampling Theory.* Englewood Cliffs, N.J.: Prentice-Hall.

An advanced quantitative introduction to sampling theory and techniques.

PART SIX

Issues in Questionnaire Data

14

RELIABILITY AND VALIDITY OF INTERVIEW DATA: THE PROBLEM OF ACQUIESCENCE IN DATA COLLECTION

GENERAL ISSUE

The empirical sciences depend upon data-collection procedures to obtain reliable and valid measurements. However, data-collection procedures *per se* may introduce measurement error. Such error ranges from the not-so-serious to the serious, from the known to the unknown, and from the random to the systematic. Responsible researchers seek to eliminate such error by selecting appropriate data collection procedures and, where error cannot be eliminated, endeavor to assess the magnitude of the error impact to avoid erroneous interpretations.

Examples of collection procedures which result in measurement error abound in the physical and social sciences. The simple act of measuring the temperature of a liquid by using a thermometer introduces error if the thermometer is of a different temperature than the liquid. Similarly, subjects of an experiment may consciously or subconsciously alter their behavior from their "normal" actions if they become aware of their participation in it. In like manner, individuals who are being observed in natural settings or who respond to questionnaires or interviews may be influenced by the data-collection procedures which the interviewer employs.

This chapter reexamines the reliability and validity of empirical data which have been interpreted as demonstrating that lower-class persons, more than their middle- and upper-class counterparts, are likely to be in a state of "normlessness." The substantive focus is on the use of Srole's

Anomia Scale; the methodological focus is on the influence of the content and situation of the interview on the verbal responses of lower-class respondents.

THE SROLE ANOMIA SCALE

The concept of anomie has played an important role in the development of sociological theory. Perhaps because of the subtlety, richness, and complexity of the state of normlessness to which this concept refers, it has resisted a universal definition. As frequently occurs, a theorist will offer a definition which differs somewhat from those employed by others and an empirical researcher will construct alternative measurement procedures.

Leo Srole, in the 1950s, sought to construct a scale which would measure *anomie*, defined as "an individual's generalized pervasive sense of self-to-others belongingness at one extreme compared with self-to-others distance and self-to-others alienation" at the other extreme.* The resulting scale, commonly referred to as Srole's Anomia Scale, has been utilized frequently for measuring the extent and distribution of *anomie* in American society.

Despite its frequent use, a number of social scientists have questioned both the validity and reliability of the scale. It has been suggested, for instance, that Srole's definition confuses the concepts of alienation and anomie, a distinction some theorists prefer to retain. Additionally, it has been charged that Srole's definition of anomie as a psychological state departs from the more traditional meaning of the phenomenon as a property of a social system, a theoretical meaning originally contributed by Emile Durkheim. Even if one grants the right of a theorist to create a definition which meets theoretical needs (providing it clarifies rather than confuses accepted meanings), some researchers have questioned the ability of the Srole Scale to measure anomie due to certain questionable measurement properties of the scale itself.

14.1 RELIABILITY AND VALIDITY

Briefly stated, the *reliability of measurement* refers to the ability of measurement procedures to produce stable measurements. The *validity of measurement* refers to the ability of measurement procedures to produce empirical data consistent with the theoretical meaning of the concept to be measured.

* Leo Srole, "Social Integration and Certain Corollaries: An Exploratory Study," *American Sociological Review*, 21 (1956):709–716.

The Srole Anomia Scale consists of five items designed so that agreement with the statement indicates anomie while disagreement with the items indicates its absence. More technically, it is an ordinal scale designed to locate respondents with respect to their relative state of anomie. The five-item scale is reproduced for examination.

Srole Anomia Scale

	Agreement	Disagreement
1. These days a person does not really know whom he can count on.	____	____
2. It's hardly fair to bring children into the world the way things look for the future.	____	____
3. In spite of what some people say, the lot of the average man is getting worse, not better.	____	____
4. Nowadays a person has to live much for today and let tomorrow take care of itself.	____	____
5. There's little use in writing to public officials because often they are not really interested in the lot of the average man.	____	____

SOURCE: Srole, "Social Integration," pp. 712–713.

The wording of the Srole Anomia Scale raises a number of interesting problems. First of all, there are possible problems with the choice of words in the individual statements. For instance, a comparison of items 3 and 5 shows that it is unclear whether these both refer to the situation of the respondent or to the situations of others. It may be that some respondents consistently identify the self with these situations, while others identify different persons with item 3 and the self with item 5. If both situations occur, unreliable measurements may be obtained. Two additional problems also concern us: the problem of *response set* and the problem of *acquiescence.*

The *response set* concept draws attention to the tendency of some respondents to consistently agree or disagree with a set of attitude or opinion statements. When statements are uniformly worded, some respondents will score "high" or "low" on a set of items merely as a result of their response set. Questionnaire format may also influence response set, for example, having the responses to a battery of items all neatly arranged along the left-hand column of a page. Since agreement with the Srole items reflects anomie, as previously defined, persons with an agreement response set tendency will score high on the scale. Failure to word some statements positively and other statements negatively may introduce measurement error which might have been reduced through use of a combination of positive and negative statements. However, the proper balance would be difficult to determine.

14.2 INTERVIEWING

Interviewing is a data-collection procedure involving verbal communication between the researcher and respondent either by telephone or in a face-to-face situation. While a number of differences exist between data collection by telephone and face-to-face interaction, there are a number of advantages and disadvantages common to personal contact. Of course, these advantages and disadvantages vary with the characteristics of the population to be interviewed, sponsorship of the research, content of the interview items, length of interview, and timing of the interview with the social condition of society and the personal circumstances of the interviewee.

Nonetheless, the general advantages of interviews include

1. A high response participation rate compared to self-administered questionnaire data-collection techniques, that is, those techniques relying on a distribution of questionnaires to individuals to be completed and returned at a later date.
2. An ability to collect data from persons incapable of completing a questionnaire without assistance, for example, young children and marginally literate or illiterate adults.
3. An ability to clarify questions or probe for additional information within the constraints of interview training.
4. An ability to verify or cross-check certain verbal responses with the observed conditions.

The general disadvantages of interviews include

1. The relatively high cost of interviewing respondents due to such factors as the travel expense of the interviewers, the time expended to physically locate a respondent whose address has changed or who may not be at home at the time of the initial interview (thereby requiring a call-back), and the salary costs of interviewers and field supervisors whose task it is to solve problems and maintain data-collection quality control.

The *acquiescence* concept draws attention to the social relationship created between a researcher and the participants in a research project. Research designs frequently locate the researcher in a social position "superior" to the participants. Often, research participants are being observed, experimented on, or interrogated by interview or questionnaire. Participants, therefore, may adopt an inferior position vis-à-vis the researcher and respond in verbal or behavioral ways which are thought least likely to displease him or her. The concept of acquiescence refers to this research phenomenon.

The behavioral patterns of response set and acquiescence have been researched primarily by psychologists interested in these phenomena as a personality variable. They also have been studied by sociologists, who have hypothesized that the two phenomena may be most pronounced among persons who occupy low social positions in society. Poor people

2. The possibility that the interviewer-interviewee relationship may produce reliability and validity measurement problems due to differences in social characteristics, such as, race, age, sex, ethnicity, perceived status differences, etc., and personality characteristics, that is, the degree to which the interviewer and interviewee develop a relationship of personal trust.
3. The possibility that interviewers may subtly change the intended meaning of questions through slight rewording or emphasis on some words in the items, through questions which probe the meaning of a response and may unintentionally threaten the respondent.

Rules of thumb for maximizing the advantages and minimizing the disadvantages of interviewing include

1. Matching interviewers with specific characteristics (e.g., race, sex, or ethnic background) to the characteristics of target populations.
2. Training interviewers to
   a. Adhere closely to a verbatim reading of the interview schedule as designed and to employ only those probes which convey a neutral response of the interviewer, such as: "You have just said that 'You frequently vote for Democratic candidates.' Could you clarify for me whether this means Democratic candidates for national, state, or local office?"
   b. Avoid expressions of approval, disapproval, or surprise at an interviewee's response, such as "Wow, you've just said 'Some Presidents deserved to be assassinated.' Do you feel that way because you think they are traitors to the Constitution?"
3. Using proper sampling techniques, such as cluster sampling for geographically distributed populations, updating addresses prior to entering the field, and selecting a time period during which the respondents are likely to be available.

and many blacks occupy such positions. Unfortunately, social scientists and professional staff who assist researchers in data-collection tasks have been (until recently) primarily whites of middle-class backgrounds, suggesting that these phenomena may have significantly influenced some types of data collection.

With this in mind, Leslie Carr hypothesized that measurement error resulting from the form, content, and past administration of the Srole Anomia Scale may have contributed to the empirical finding that more persons of low, rather than middle or high, social status tend to score anomic. To investigate this possibility, he undertook the research reported below.*

* Leslie Carr, "The Srole Items and Acquiescence," *American Sociological Review*, 36 (1971): 287–293.

DRAWING A SAMPLE SURVEY FOR INTERVIEWS

To study this problem, Carr drew a random sample of households from a list for the communities of Chapel Hill and Carrboro, North Carolina, compiled by the local Office of Economic Opportunity, which met a federal definition of the poor. Due to the refusal of 68 adult male and female heads of households to be interviewed, 332 respondents ultimately participated in the study. Since only 33 (10 percent) respondents were white, the sample was reduced to the 299 black respondents.

Research Design

To investigate the potential impact of social status, as measured by the race of the interviewer, white researchers were to interview 50 percent of the black interviewees. Black researchers were to interview the remaining 50 percent. However, an administrative error in the assignment of interviewers produced an unbalanced distribution. This distribution is reported in Table 14-1.

Table 14-1. Equivalent Black Groups by Education and Income.

RACE OF INTERVIEWER	RESPONDENTS WITH LESS THAN 12 YR EDUCATION AND INCOME LESS THAN $4,000		RESPONDENTS WITH AT LEAST 12 YR EDUCATION OR INCOME GREATER THAN $4,000	
	N	%	*N*	%
Black	94	62.3	136	91.9
White	57	37.7	12	8.1
Total	151	100.0	148	100.0

Table 14-1 reflects the administrative foul-up. White researchers interviewed only 12 (8 percent) of the black respondents with incomes greater than $4,000 and a minimum of 12 years education. Carr therefore concluded that comparisons involving the race of the interviewer were not meaningful for this subsample, and dropped all respondents ($N = 148$) with high incomes and education. Although the distribution of black and white interviewers for the remainder of the sample was also unbalanced, he concluded that useful comparisons for subsamples of this size could be undertaken.

To investigate the impact of the Srole Anomia Scale as a measurement instrument, Carr reworded the five items so that disagreement, rather than agreement, with the items would signify anomie. While this violates the principle that items should be stated in both positive and negative directions,

Carr concluded that resources did not permit the use of more than two scales in this study. Consequently, Carr employed both the Srole Scale and the Obverse Scale. For comparison, both scales are reproduced below.

Srole Anomia Scale	*A*	*D*	*Obverse Form Scale*	*A*	*D*
These days a person does not really know whom he can count on.	______	______	These days a person can know whom he can count on.	______	______
It's hardly fair to bring children into the world the way things look for the future.	______	______	This is a good time to bring children into the world the way things look for the future.	______	______
In spite of what some people say, the lot of the average man is getting worse, not better.	______	______	In spite of what some people say, the lot of the average man is getting better, not worse.	______	______
Nowadays a person has to live much for today and let tomorrow take care of itself.	______	______	Nowadays a person can't just live for today. You have to plan ahead for tomorrow.	______	______
There's little use in writing to public officials because often they are not really interested in the lot of the average man.	______	______	It is useful to write to public officials because often they are interested in the problems of the average man.	______	______

A = Agree D = Disagree

Carr hypothesized that if direction of wording did not influence responses, then the percent of respondents with anomic scores according to the Srole Scale should not differ from the percent of respondents scoring anomic according to the Obverse Scale.

Ideally, each respondent should have received both scales in the interview situation. Thus it would have been possible to compare a respondent's score on one scale with his score on the other. (The respondent serves as his own control.) Unfortunately, this design is not always possible. Researchers run the risk that respondents may remember their pattern of responses to one instrument (say the Srole Scale) and, in an effort to remain consistent with past answers, structure their responses to the second instrument. A useful compromise is to administer one instrument to 50 percent of the sample and an alternative equivalent instrument to the remaining 50 percent. As long as chance determines which respondents receive the Srole Anomia Scale and which receive the Obverse Scale, any differences beyond chance differences in the percent of respondents scoring anomic could be attributed to the influence of the form of the scale. Consequently, interviewers were instructed to administer the Srole Scale to the first respondent interviewed, the Obverse Scale to the second interviewed, the Srole Scale to the third, and so on. Assuming that no systematic differences existed between odd-numbered respondents and even-numbered ones this procedure would be effective.

DATA ANALYSIS

Table 14-2 presents the distribution of respondents according to their anomic scores as measured by the Srole Scale and the Obverse Scale.

Differences in the distribution of response patterns are quite clear. Of the respondents who responded to the Srole Scale, 69 percent scored highly anomic (agreeing with 4 or 5 of the items). However, only 7 percent of the respondents who replied to the Obverse Scale Form scored equally anomic. Evidently, wording of the two scales greatly influenced the pattern of responses received by interviewers for this sample. The Obverse Scale's failure to produce a distribution similar to the Srole Scale distribution casts doubt on the validity of the latter as a suitable measuring instrument. Of course, given the earlier discussion of the appropriateness of the theoretical definition, it is possible that the Obverse Scale is measuring "something other than anomie." Yet, it has been established for this research that merely changing the direction of the items produces responses unlikely to be the result of chance.

Table 14-2. Distribution of Respondents by Srole Anomia Scale and Obverse Form Scale.

NUMBER OF ITEMS		PERCENT OF RESPONDENTS AGREEING ON SROLE SCALE		PERCENT OF RESPONDENTS DISAGREEING ON OBVERSE SCALE	
		N	%	*N*	%
Low					
Anomic	0	0	0	16	24
.	1	3	4	18	27
.	2	6	7	14	21
.	3	17	20	14	21
High	4	24	29 } = 69	5	7 } = 7
Anomic	5	34	40	0	0
	Total	84	100	67	100

SOURCE: Carr, "Srole Items," p. 290, Table 1.

Table 14-3. Distribution of Respondents by Type of Scale and Race of Interviewer.

NUMBER OF ITEMS AGREED/DISAGREED WITH	PERCENT OF RESPONDENTS AGREEING ON SROLE SCALE			PERCENT OF RESPONDENTS DISAGREEING ON OBVERSE SCALE		
	White Interviewer	Black Interviewer	Difference	White Interviewer	Black Interviewer	Difference
	(A)	(B)	(C)	(D)	(E)	(F)
0	0	0	0	42	17	25
1	5	2	3	26	27	−1
2	3	11	−8	11	25	−14
3	13	26	−13	21	21	0
4	32	26	6	0	10	−10
5	47	35	12	0	0	0
	100	100		100	100	
	($N = 38$)	($N = 46$)		($N = 19$)	($N = 48$)	

SOURCE: Carr, "Srole Items," p. 290, Table 1.

Table 14-3 presents the distribution of responses to both the Srole Scale and the Obverse Scale by racial characteristic of the interviewer.

Within each scale administration, there are noticeable differences in the percentage of respondents agreeing or disagreeing with items. However, the differences are relatively small. In Column D one person equals 5 percent of the respondents, while in Column E one respondent equals 2 percent. Consequently, taking into account both the size of the samples and the absence of large systematic differences, there is reason to believe that the race of the interviewer had only a minor effect.

DISCUSSION

The response patterns to two scales similar in content but different in form produced unique distributions for each scale. The Srole Scale, which was "loaded" in the direction of agreement, produced response patterns indicating a high proportion of anomic respondents. The Obverse Scale, on the other hand, which was "loaded" in the direction of disagreement, produced patterns indicating a small anomic proportion. Therefore one may ask which scale produces the "most reliable and valid" measurement of anomie.

There are several answers to this question. Srole and others report that his scale is highly reliable. When used as a Guttman scale, the Srole Scale was given a coefficient of reproducibility equal to .90. The Obverse Scale has not been assessed for reliability; however, its reliability may also be high. The question of validity in this instance, however, is more important than that of reliability.

Previous research reports the existence of a social desirability phenomenon, that is, a desire of some respondents to report information most likely to project a positive self-image. Therefore, it is possible that a principle of self-depreciation for low-status persons operated with respect to the Srole items. Respondents who wanted to present the least-resistant, most-acquiescent and self-depreciating appearance may have agreed with items which were in fact most self-depreciating. This might well have been the case with low-income blacks. It would also account for the frequent number of respondents who scored as "anomic" in this study.

In the Obverse Scale, there exists cross-pressure between self-depreciation and the desire to merely agree with items. Consequently, respondents may feel pressure to agree with items regardless of content, while simultaneously also wishing to endorse those which project a self-depreciating image. This may account for the divergence between the frequencies obtained for the Srole Scale and the Obverse Scale. Thus, the scale scores may be an invalid indicator of anomie: rather, they may reflect the characteristics of the instrument, the respondents, and the norms of the research situation.

SUMMARY

Anomie has been found by previous research to be inversely related to a number of social phenomena including income and education. The present chapter explored whether this apparent relationship was the result of interviewer characteristics and measurement instruments that might produce reliable, but invalid, measures. It was discovered that the wording of questions was quite important. Indeed, a large percentage of respondents apparently agreed with items regardless of their content because of the latent social norms they perceived for the interview situation. Contrary to expectations, the race of the interviewer did not greatly influence responses.

Generalizations from this study should be made cautiously. The research was conducted on relatively small numbers of low-income, relatively uneducated blacks in two small, southern communities. Nonetheless, the research highlights important issues in seeking reliable and valid measures in interviewing and other data-collection procedures.

KEY IDEAS AND CONCEPTS

acquiescence
anomie
interview schedule
Obverse Form Scale
reliability
response set
self-depreciation
social desirability
Srole Anomia Scale
validity

ISSUES AND PROBLEMS

1. Describe the sociological features of an interview situation. Discuss how these may affect the reliability and validity of interview data.
2. Define acquiescence. Discuss the way in which it may affect validity. Discuss how it may affect reliability.
3. The appendix to this chapter contains a section of an interview schedule used in a nationwide study. *Part A.* Closely examine questions H10 through H16 of the schedule. Suggest problems of reliability or validity that may arise if
   a. the respondent were male and the interviewer female;
   b. the respondent were female and the interviewer male;
   c. the respondent and the interviewer were of the same sex;
   d. the respondent were lower class and the interviewer middle class.
   e. the respondent were upper class and the interviewer middle class.

   Part B. Closely examine questions H1 through H5 of the schedule. Using these, conduct a brief interview with three individuals.
   a. Discuss how traits of the interviewer and three respondents may have influenced the reliability and validity of the responses.
   b. Provide examples of how these questions may have been given different interpretations by the respondents.

4. In Chapter 9, self-reported information on drinking and driving was utilized to examine various models of law enforcement.
   a. Discuss how social class may have influenced the reliability and validity of self-reported behavior.
   b. Discuss how the setting in which the questionnaires were administered may have influenced the responses of lower-class persons; of middle-class persons.

RECOMMENDED READINGS

Lenski, Gerhard, and John C. Leggett
1960 "Caste, Class and Deference in the Research Interview," *American Journal of Sociology*, 65: 463–467.

A study of how social class and race may affect questionnaire responses.

Oppenheim, Abraham N.
1966 *Questionnaire Design and Attitude Measurement.* New York: Basic Books.

A text containing practical guides to question writing, attitude scaling, and projective techniques.

Richardson, S. A., B. S. Dohrenwend, and D. Klein
1965 *Interviewing: Its Forms and Functions.* New York: Basic Books.

Discusses interviewing techniques which may improve the validity of data.

Schuman, Howard
1966 "The Random Probe: A Technique for Evaluating the Validity of Closed Questions," *American Sociological Review*, 31: 218–222.

Proposes the use of follow-up probes to explore reliability and validity of respondent answers to forced choice questions.

APPENDIX TO CHAPTER 14

AN INTERVIEW SCHEDULE

In 1971, the Institute for Social Research at the University of Michigan undertook a study of the quality of life in America, using institute personnel to interview a random national sample of 2,000 people.* Section H of the interview schedule is reproduced below for your review. This section of the schedule seeks to measure various dimensions of interpersonal relationships. Of special interest are the use of closed-ended questions (where respondents must select a response from those available in the instrument), open-ended questions (where they are permitted to express responses in their own words), probes which seek clarification, and funneling procedures which ask some questions only of certain persons.

* Institute for Social Research, University of Michigan, "Quality of Life." Interview schedule used in Project 468110. (Institute for Social Research, Ann Arbor, Summer, 1971.)

SECTION H

H1. We have talked about some of the things you do and some of the things you have, now I have some other kinds of questions. First, what about your friendships: Would you say that you have a good many very good friends that you could count on if you had any sort of trouble, an average number, or not too many very good friends?

1. GOOD MANY | 3. AVERAGE NUMBER | 5. NOT TOO MANY

H2. How interested would you say you are in meeting new people and making new friends? Would you say you are *very* interested, *somewhat* interested, or *not very* interested?

1. VERY INTERESTED | 3. SOMEWHAT INTERESTED | 5. NOT VERY INTERESTED

H3. (HAND R CARD 3, WHITE) All things considered, how satisfied are you with your friendships—with the time you can spend with friends, the things you do together, the number of friends you have, as well as the particular people who are your friends? *Which number comes closest to how you feel?*

1 | 2 | 3 | 4 | 5 | 6 | 7

H4. All right, now let's talk about your family. First, are your father and mother both still living? (IF NO, PROBE TO CLARIFY WHETHER ONE IS STILL LIVING.)

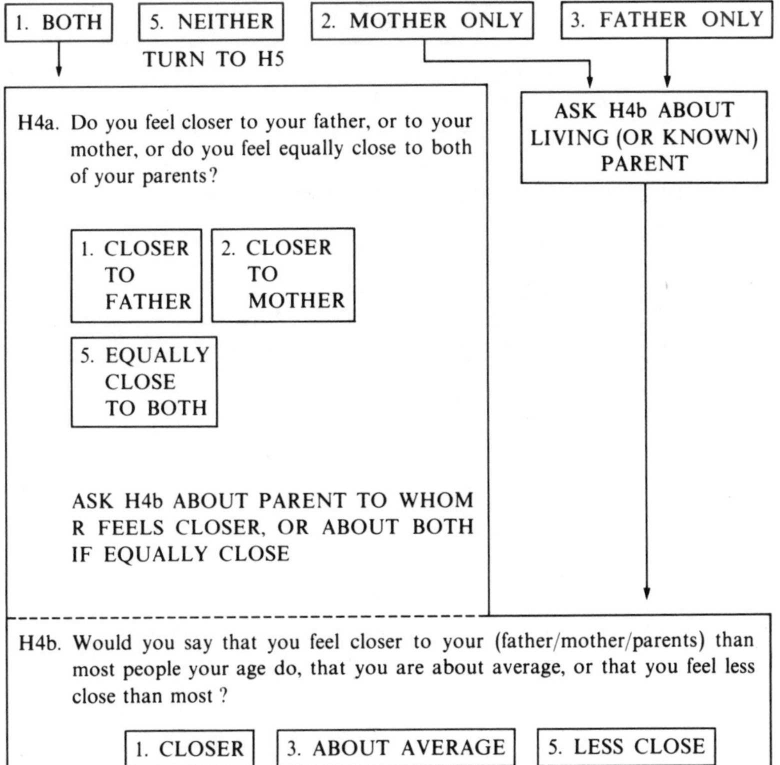

1. BOTH | 5. NEITHER | 2. MOTHER ONLY | 3. FATHER ONLY

5. NEITHER: TURN TO H5

2. MOTHER ONLY / 3. FATHER ONLY: ASK H4b ABOUT LIVING (OR KNOWN) PARENT

1. BOTH:

H4a. Do you feel closer to your father, or to your mother, or do you feel equally close to both of your parents?

1. CLOSER TO FATHER | 2. CLOSER TO MOTHER | 5. EQUALLY CLOSE TO BOTH

ASK H4b ABOUT PARENT TO WHOM R FEELS CLOSER, OR ABOUT BOTH IF EQUALLY CLOSE

H4b. Would you say that you feel closer to your (father/mother/parents) than most people your age do, that you are about average, or that you feel less close than most?

1. CLOSER | 3. ABOUT AVERAGE | 5. LESS CLOSE

ASK EVERYONE:

H5. Do you have any brothers or sisters living? (INCLUDE STEP BROTHERS AND SISTERS IF R WAS RAISED WITH THEM.)

1. YES | 5. NO —GO TO H6

H5a. How many of each do you have?

_________ BROTHERS _________ SISTERS

H5b. Would you say that you feel closer to your (SIBLINGS) than most people your age do, that you are about average, or that you feel less close than most? (IF FEELS CLOSER TO SOME THAN TO OTHERS, TRY TO GET AN OVERALL ANSWER.)

1. CLOSER | 3. ABOUT AVERAGE | 5. LESS CLOSE

H6. Are you married, widowed, divorced, separated, or have you never married?

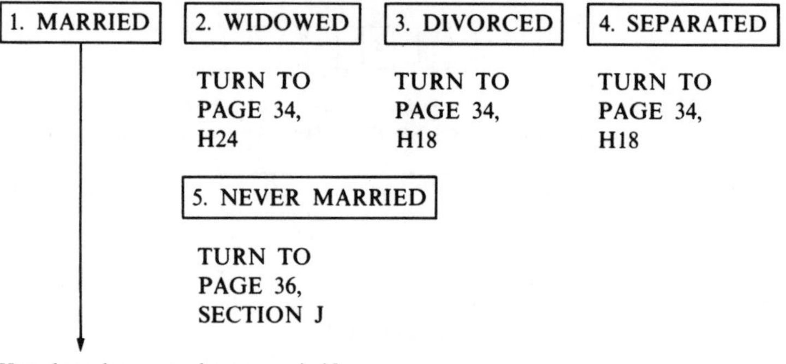

1. MARRIED | 2. WIDOWED | 3. DIVORCED | 4. SEPARATED

2. WIDOWED: TURN TO PAGE 34, H24

3. DIVORCED: TURN TO PAGE 34, H18

4. SEPARATED: TURN TO PAGE 34, H18

5. NEVER MARRIED: TURN TO PAGE 36, SECTION J

H7. How long have you been married? ____________________

H8. Is this your first marriage?

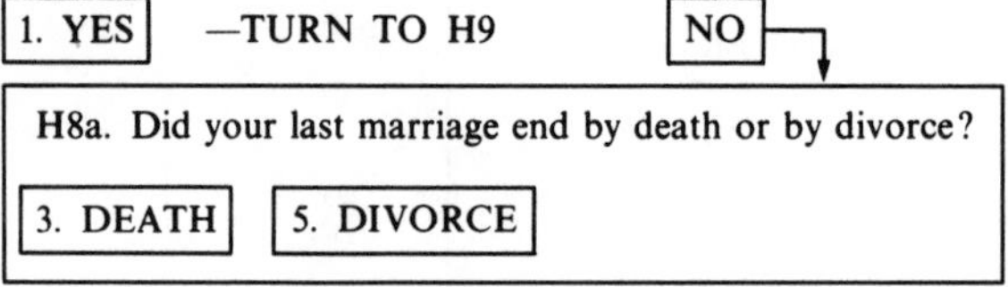

1. YES —TURN TO H9 | NO

H8a. Did your last marriage end by death or by divorce?

3. DEATH | 5. DIVORCE

H9. Is your (husband/wife) doing any work for money now?

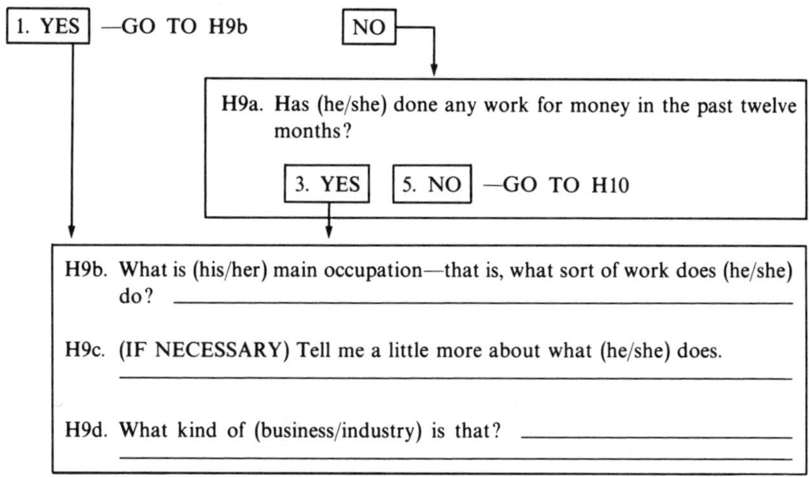

1. YES —GO TO H9b

NO

H9a. Has (he/she) done any work for money in the past twelve months?

3. YES

5. NO —GO TO H10

H9b. What is (his/her) main occupation—that is, what sort of work does (he/she) do? ______

H9c. (IF NECESSARY) Tell me a little more about what (he/she) does.

______

H9d. What kind of (business/industry) is that? ______

______

H10. (HAND R CARD 7, GRAY) How often do you disagree with your (husband/wife) about how much money to spend on various things—never, rarely, sometimes, often, or very often?

1. NEVER | 2. RARELY | 3. SOMETIMES | 4. OFTEN | 5. VERY OFTEN

H11. How well do you think your (husband/wife) understands you—your feelings, your likes and dislikes, and any problems you may have; do you think that (he/she) understands you very well, fairly well, not very well, or not well at all?

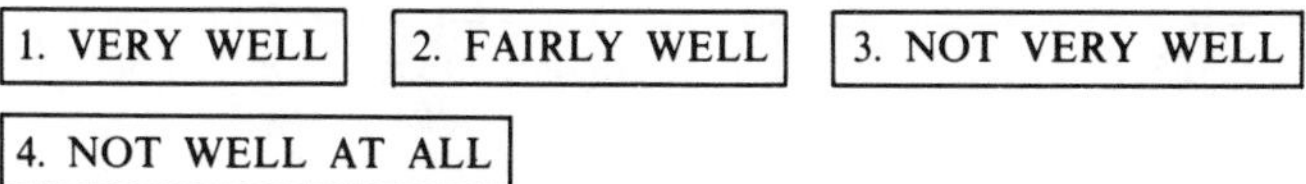

1. VERY WELL | 2. FAIRLY WELL | 3. NOT VERY WELL | 4. NOT WELL AT ALL

H12. And how well do you think *you* understand your (husband/wife)—very well, fairly well, not very well, or not well at all?

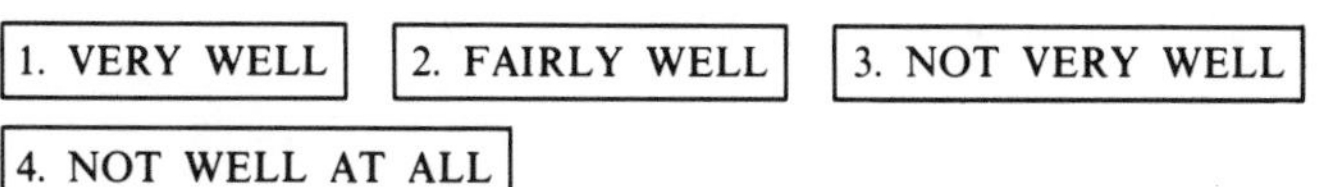

1. VERY WELL | 2. FAIRLY WELL | 3. NOT VERY WELL | 4. NOT WELL AT ALL

H13. How much companionship do you and your (husband/wife) have—how often do you do things together—all the time, very often, often, sometimes, or hardly ever?

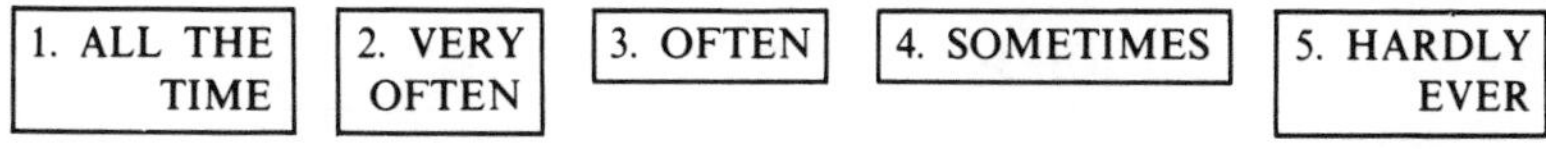

1. ALL THE TIME | 2. VERY OFTEN | 3. OFTEN | 4. SOMETIMES | 5. HARDLY EVER

PASTE PINK SHEET HERE

(HAND R THE PINK SHEET.) Here is another sheet, with three questions for you to answer. Just answer each one by putting an X in one of the boxes.

PINK SHEET

H14. HAVE YOU EVER WISHED YOU HAD MARRIED SOMEONE ELSE?

[1] YES, OFTEN [2] YES, SOMETIMES [3] YES, ONCE IN A WHILE

[4] YES, BUT HARDLY EVER [5] NO, NEVER

H15. HAS THE THOUGHT OF GETTING A DIVORCE EVER CROSSED YOUR MIND?

[1] YES, OFTEN [2] YES, SOMETIMES [3] YES, ONCE IN A WHILE

[4] YES, BUT HARDLY EVER [5] NO, NEVER

H16. ALL THINGS CONSIDERED, HOW SATISFIED ARE YOU WITH YOUR MARRIAGE? WHICH NUMBER COMES CLOSEST TO HOW SATISFIED OR DISSATISFIED YOU FEEL?

[1]—COMPLETELY SATISFIED [2] [3] [4]—NEUTRAL

[5] [6] [7]—COMPLETELY DISSATISFIED

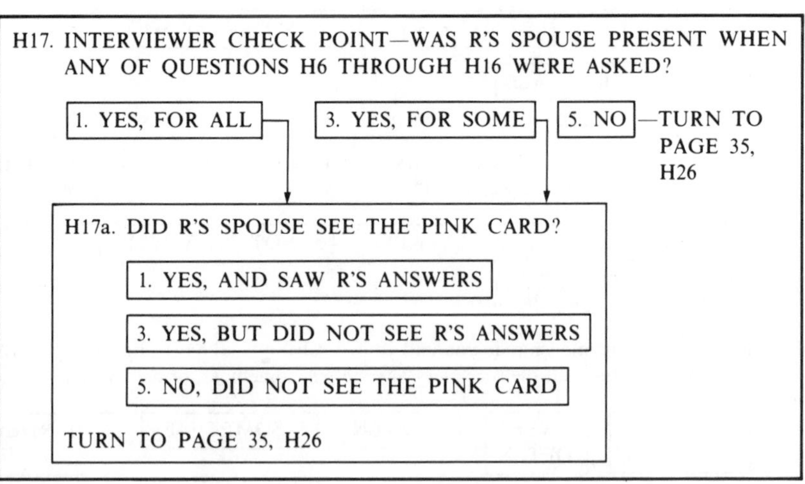

H17. INTERVIEWER CHECK POINT—WAS R'S SPOUSE PRESENT WHEN ANY OF QUESTIONS H6 THROUGH H16 WERE ASKED?

[1. YES, FOR ALL] [3. YES, FOR SOME] [5. NO]—TURN TO PAGE 35, H26

H17a. DID R'S SPOUSE SEE THE PINK CARD?

[1. YES, AND SAW R'S ANSWERS]

[3. YES, BUT DID NOT SEE R'S ANSWERS]

[5. NO, DID NOT SEE THE PINK CARD]

TURN TO PAGE 35, H26

IF R IS DIVORCED OR SEPARATED (ASK FOR MOST RECENT MARRIAGE):

H18. How long have you been (divorced/separated)? ____________

H19. How long were you married and living together? ____________

H20. (HAND R CARD 7, GRAY) Now I have some questions about your marriage before you were (divorced/separated). First, how often did you disagree with your (husband/wife) about how much money to spend on various things—never, rarely, sometimes, often, or very often?

1. NEVER | 2. RARELY | 3. SOMETIMES | 4. OFTEN | 5. VERY OFTEN

H21. How well do you think your (husband/wife) understood you—your feelings, your likes and dislikes, and any problems you may have had from time to time; do you think that (he/she) understood you very well, fairly well, not very well, or not well at all?

1. VERY WELL | 2. FAIRLY WELL | 3. NOT VERY WELL | 4. NOT WELL AT ALL

H22. And how well do you think *you* understood your (wife/husband)—very well, fairly well, not very well, or not well at all?

1. VERY WELL | 2. FAIRLY WELL | 3. NOT VERY WELL | 4. NOT WELL AT ALL

H23. How much companionship did you and your (husband/wife) have—how often did you do things together—all the time, very often, often, sometimes, or hardly ever?

1. ALL THE TIME | 2. VERY OFTEN | 3. OFTEN | 4. SOMETIMES | 5. HARDLY EVER

TURN TO H26

IF R IS WIDOWED:

H24. How long ago did your (husband/wife) die? ____________

H25. How long had you been married? ____________

H26.

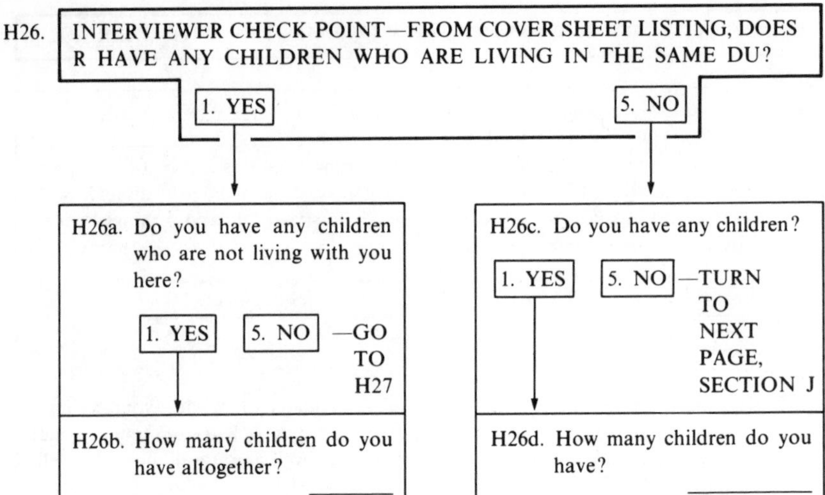

INTERVIEWER CHECK POINT—FROM COVER SHEET LISTING, DOES R HAVE ANY CHILDREN WHO ARE LIVING IN THE SAME DU?

1. YES 5. NO

H26a. Do you have any children who are not living with you here?

1. YES 5. NO —GO TO H27

H26b. How many children do you have altogether? ______

H26c. Do you have any children?

1. YES 5. NO —TURN TO NEXT PAGE, SECTION J

H26d. How many children do you have? ______

H27. Compared to most children would you say your children have given you *a lot* of problems, *quite a few* problems, *some* problems, *only a few* problems, or haven't they given you any problems at all?

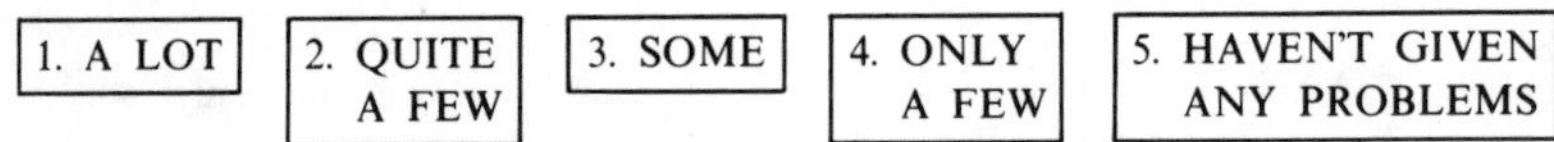

1. A LOT 2. QUITE A FEW 3. SOME 4. ONLY A FEW 5. HAVEN'T GIVEN ANY PROBLEMS

H28. Would you say that in your case, being a (father/mother) has *always* been enjoyable; that it has *nearly* always been enjoyable; that it has *usually* been enjoyable; that it has *sometimes* been enjoyable; or that being a (father/mother) has *hardly ever* been enjoyable?

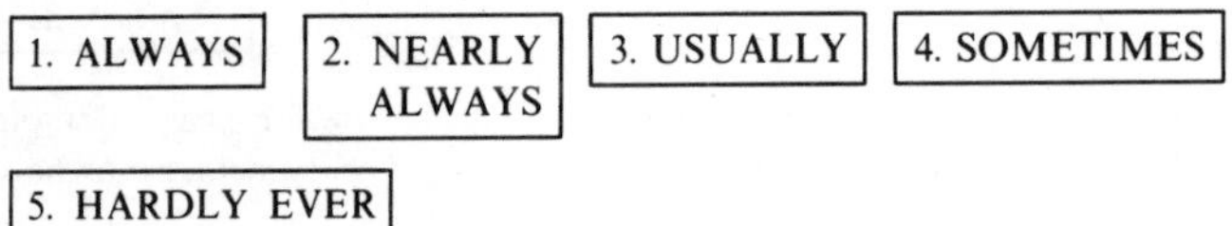

1. ALWAYS 2. NEARLY ALWAYS 3. USUALLY 4. SOMETIMES

5. HARDLY EVER

H29. Have you ever wished that you could be free from the responsibilities of being a (father/mother)?

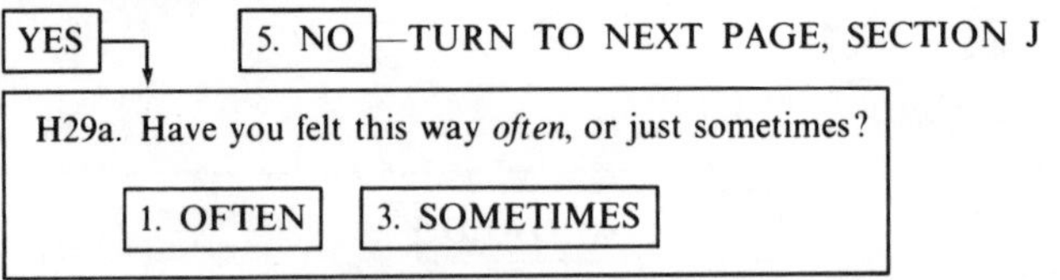

YES 5. NO —TURN TO NEXT PAGE, SECTION J

H29a. Have you felt this way *often*, or just sometimes?

1. OFTEN 3. SOMETIMES

15

SUBTLETIES IN INFERENCE FROM QUESTIONNAIRE DATA: PEERS, PARENTS, AND YOUTH CULTURE

GENERAL ISSUE

Philosophers of science frequently distinguish between the language of theory and that of research. The former is abstract. It consists of concepts and logical relationships among concepts. The language of research is more concrete. It employs techniques to produce measurements which are interpreted as indicators of concepts and relationships. For instance, although it is possible to imagine the existence of some phenomenon such as alienation, it is another matter to assume that research procedures produce an empirical measurement identical to the concept. Scientists believe there is an unbridgeable gap between the language of theory and that of research. That is, there is no logical or empirical test to prove that a measurement is equivalent to the theoretical concept of it. Efforts to solve this problem have resulted in two expediencies: the radical solution of *operationalism* and the less radical one of *operationalization.*

Operationalism emerged as a nineteenth-century scientific view which posited that concepts were neither more nor less than the measurements produced by research procedures. According to this view, a concept is identical with a measurement and vice versa. For instance, intelligence is neither more nor less than the score obtained on an intelligence test, social status neither more nor less than the score received on a social status scale, and alienation not more or less than the score received on an alienation scale. According to operationalism, the meaning of a concept is exhausted by the measurements obtained through research procedures. As far as theory is concerned, a difficulty with this position is that the meaning of a concept is tied to empirical measurement.

Concepts, therefore, have no independent integrity. To be more specific, imagine that three different intelligence tests were administered to an individual, and three different scores were obtained. Does each score represent a different intelligence? Unfortunately, operationalism says that it does. If concept equals measurement, then issues of reliability and validity cease to exist, for there are no independent standards for judgment. Operationalism as a solution has been rejected by most scientists because generalizations beyond specific measurements are excluded.

Operationalization as a solution recognizes the inherent gap between concept and measurement. Operationalists hold that concepts have an existence independent of empirical measurement. Consequently, while scientists make efforts to select and create acceptable empirical indicators of theoretical concepts, they simultaneously recognize that there is an unbridgeable gap between measurement and concept. It is only by convention (i.e., general agreement) that scientists finally accept a measurement as an indicator of a concept. Thus, it is only by convention that scientists accept an intelligence test score as an indicator of something theoretically conceived as intelligence. While this solution does not solve the problem, it does recognize it. Furthermore, it provides a foundation for scientific dialogue concerning the adequacy of empirical measurements as opposed to theoretical concepts.

Drawing theoretical inferences from empirical data consequently entails risk. Whether research procedures have adequately operationalized the meaning of a concept (i.e., whether such procedures are acceptable to other scientists) and whether the inferences drawn from empirical measurements to concepts are appropriate (i.e., whether they are acceptable to other scientists) are issues sparking continuous discussion.

The inference risk is especially pronounced when motives or attitudes are inferred from questionnaire or interview data. False inferences occur for two reasons: because changes in the responses to, or because changes in the questions included in, a given instrument may influence a respondent's interpretation and thereby alter his answer.

There are many reasonable ways to phrase a question and many reasonable contexts in which to ask it. As a result, phrasing of questions to produce reliable and valid data is difficult. An example of this problem follows.

The theoretical focus of this chapter is on the empirical existence of a youth culture. The methodological focus is upon the construction and interpretation of questionnaire data.

THEORETICAL PROBLEM

It is generally acknowledged that industrial societies such as the United States are in a continuous state of social change. Most adults possess skills which are implemented in places of work removed from adult-youth contacts and which will become outmoded. Consequently, it is not desirable for parents to seek to shape their children in their own images. Young people must be oriented toward the future and not the present or past.

Further, industrialized societies require specialization in labor skills, although this specialization may function in a unique way. Youth hence must be educated broadly in order to prepare for specialized positions in an unknown future. Adults, however, must narrowly specialize if they are to market their skills in the contemporary industrial economy. As a consequence of these and other factors, youth are age-segregated in schools; and the role of the parent in imparting occupational skills has correspondingly diminished.

According to some observers, segregation of youth has resulted in the emergence of an adolescent subculture. This subculture has norms and values sharply divergent from those of adult society. Other observers have questioned this inference. In their view, the emergence of an adolescent subculture with norms and values divergent from adult values is a myth. Rather, they suggest that adolescent culture reflects an extension and emphasis of adult values more than values in conflict with the larger society.

In sum, while the existence of large numbers of adolescents who are segregated in the educational institutions of industrial societies is unquestioned, the source, content, and meaning of the values which structure their life-style remains a source of debate. The assumptions which this argument attacks are that generational segregation has been promoted by the structure of industrial society and that the educational, age-graded, isolation of youth provided the foundation for the emergence of a distinct adolescent subculture.

THE COLEMAN STUDY

In the late 1950s, James S. Coleman undertook a major analysis of adolescent value systems in ten purposively selected secondary schools in northern Illinois.* His ultimate intention was to generalize research results to school systems and adolescent subcultures elsewhere in the United States. Coleman's research design involved several data-collection stages. These included:

* James S. Coleman, *The Adolescent Society* (New York: Free Press, 1961).

1. The selection of ten secondary schools judged to represent different adolescent value systems.
2. The administration of a questionnaire to all students in the fall of 1957, followed by the administration of a second questionnaire to all students in the spring of 1958.
3. The administration of questionnaires to all teachers and parents during 1957–1958.
4. Informal interviews with a sample of students in each of the ten schools during the spring of 1957 and the spring of 1958.
5. The recording of data (grades, IQ, etc.) from student files for all students in the spring of 1958.

15.1 QUESTIONNAIRE ADVANTAGES AND DISADVANTAGES

The use of questionnaires is a data-collection technique whereby a document containing either questions or statements is used to obtain information from a respondent who records answers thereon. As with interviews, questionnaires may involve face-to-face interaction (i.e., administering the questionnaires in a group setting such as a classroom) or may lack this aspect (i.e., administering the questionnaires by mail). The noticeable difference between questionnaires and interviews is that in the latter a researcher *asks* the question, while in questionnaires a respondent *reads* the question.

Questionnaires have advantages and disadvantages. Among the advantages are

1. They are less expensive than interviews whether they are administered in a group setting or self-administered by the respondent at home.
2. They reduce respondent-researcher interaction, thereby curbing any influence the researcher may personally exercise on the respondent.
3. They provide the respondent with a greater sense of privacy and anonymity than personal interviews.
4. They generally provide the respondent with more time for completing the instrument.

Some disadvantages of questionnaires are

1. Their response rates vary depending upon the method of administration. For example, questionnaires which are group administered generally have high completion rates although specific questions (e.g., of income or race) may be answered less frequently than others. Questionnaires delivered and returned by mail, however, may have response rates as low as 20 or 30 percent depending upon the research questions and the population being studied.
2. They pose special difficulties for illiterate and marginally literate respondents.
3. They allow little opportunity for respondents to seek clarification of questions or statements in the questionnaire.
4. They permit respondents to respond in any manner whatsoever to the questions asked.

Two items of empirical evidence cited by Coleman in support of the thesis of a distinct adolescent subculture are of interest here. Item 137 of the 1957 questionnaire, administered to all students in the ten schools, provides the first bit of evidence to support it:

Q. 137 Which one of these things would be hardest for you to take—your parents' disapproval, your teacher's disapproval, or breaking with your friend?
——— parents' disapproval
——— teacher's disapproval
——— breaking with friend

The distribution of responses to this question is reflected in Table 15-1.

Table 15-1. Responses to Question 137.

RESPONSE	MALE (PERCENT)	FEMALE (PERCENT)
Parents' disapproval	53.8	53.9
Teacher's disapproval	3.5	2.7
Breaking with friend	42.7	43.4
Total	100.0	100.0
N[a]	(3,621)	(3,894)

SOURCE: David C. Epperson, "A Reassessment of Indices of Parental Influence in *The Adolescent Society," American Sociological Review,* 37(1971): 94, Table 1.
[a] Excludes nonresponses.

Table 15-1 demonstrates that a significant number of adolescents found that breaking with a friend was harder to take than parental disapproval.

The second item of evidence supporting the adolescent subculture thesis emerged from the occupational plan of boys as compared with their fathers' occupations. To gather data on their fathers' occupations, question 58 of the autumn 1957 questionnaire asked

Q. 58 What is your father's occupation? What does he do? Be as specific as you can. (If he is dead, say what his occupation was.)

____

____

Later, Coleman asked about the occupational plans of the sons:

Q. 101. What kind of work do you plan to do when you finish your schooling?

____

____

He coded and tabulated responses to these two items to determine whether the intended occupation of the son was the same or different from the actual occupation of the father. The results are summarized in Table 15-2.

Table 15-2. Percentage of Boys Who Intended to Pursue Occupations the Same as or Different from Those of Father.

RESPONSE	SMALL-TOWN SCHOOLS %	SMALL-TOWN SCHOOLS *N*	CITY AND SUBURBAN SCHOOLS %	CITY AND SUBURBAN SCHOOLS *N*
Same	23.0	(163)	9.8	(213)
Different	77.0	(547)	90.2	(1,964)
Total classifiable	100.0	(710)	100.0	(2,177)
(Unable to classify)		(66)		(173)
No answer		(252)		(643)
Total in survey		(1,028)		(2,993)

As shown, 23 percent of the boys in small-town schools intended to pursue the occupations of their fathers, while only 9.8 percent of the boys in city and suburban schools had similar intentions. In both instances, only small percentages of boys intended to follow the occupations of their fathers. Coleman interpreted these data as resulting from peer group pressure for boys to pursue occupations different from those of their fathers.

The foregoing evidence suggests that the transition from adolescence to adulthood is accompanied by a shifting of loyalties and orientations away from parents and toward peers. Is this inference justified on the basis of the data—or did the construction of the question produce responses which have been misinterpreted by Coleman? Can these data be better explained through an alternative theoretical formulation?

A TWO-SCHOOL STUDY

A study with similar research intentions was conducted by Epperson in the early 1960s.* Part of Epperson's reason for undertaking it was to reassess the adequacy of Coleman's indexes of parent and peer influence.

In investigating the relative concern of adolescents for the approval of adults and peers, Epperson noted that Coleman had equated the *disapproval* of parents or teachers with the *breaking* with one's friend. The emotional equivalence of these two concepts for adolescents is problematical. Experiencing parental and teacher disapproval are probably events adolescents frequently experience, whereas breaking with a friend is likely to be a less frequent, more emotionally upsetting experience. Consequently, the alternatives posed by Coleman may have contributed to the relatively large

* David C. Epperson, "A Reassessment of Indices of Parental Influence in *The Adolescent Society*," *American Sociological Review*, 36(1971):93–96.

percentage of adolescents who reported that "breaking with a friend" would be harder to take than "parents' disapproval."

To determine the impact of the way the question was worded, the following query was constructed:

> Which one of these things would make you the most unhappy?
> 1. If my parents did not like what I did.
> 2. If my (favorite) teacher did not like what I did.
> 3. If my best friend did not like what I did.

The results obtained through this question for a sample of elementary and high school students are presented in Table 15-3, along with Coleman's findings. The data in Table 15-3 reflect a sharp discrepancy in the responses to Epperson's revised question as compared to the responses obtained by Coleman. There may be two explanations for these differences.

Table 15-3. Concern Expressed Over Evaluation by Reference Groups (in Percentages).[a]

	REVISED QUESTION		COLEMAN'S QUESTION
REFERENCE GROUP	Elementary	High School	Ten High Schools
Parent	74.4	80.5	53.9
Teacher	9.1	2.5	3.1
Friend	16.4	17.0	43.1
Total	99.9	100.0	100.1

SOURCE: Epperson, "A Reassessment," p. 94, Table 1, and p. 95, Table 2.
[a] For clarity of presentation, responses for males and females have been combined. There were no important differences between the two groups.

First, it is possible that the two samples of students are indeed different. Coleman's data in this case may be more representative, because his question was administered to ten high schools ($N = 7{,}515$ responses on this item), while the revised question was administered at only one elementary school ($N = 614$) and one high school ($N = 159$). Still, it is improbable that such large differences would have been obtained solely as a result of sampling.

Second, it is possible that neither Coleman's nor the revised question is an appropriate empirical indicator of the emergence or nonemergence of a distinct adolescent culture. Coleman's measurement procedures may be faulty in equating disapproval with breaking while the revised measurements may be faulty due to the generality of the question. Unhappiness as a measure of parent-peer cross-pressures may not be appropriate to the problem.

Thus, the proper inferences as to the meaning of the data examined so far remain problematic. Two additional bits of information remain to be examined. The first is already contained in Table 15-3. Contrary to expectations, the table provides little evidence that elementary students (grades 3 through 6) were less likely to choose peers over adults than were high school students (grades 10 to 12). However, if an adolescent subculture emerges in the teen years, there should be evidence of differences in the distribution of responses between elementary and high school students. No such differences were found.

The second item of information regarding a distinctive subculture focuses on the intent of males to pursue the occupations of their fathers. In the Coleman study, males were asked two distinct questions. The first inquired as to the occupation of their fathers, while the second asked what kind of work they planned to do when they finished high school. In order for a son's choice to be classified as the "same" as his father's, the two occupations mentioned had to be identical. In the revised question, Epperson asked: "When you grow up, would you like to do the same kind of work that your father does?" Thus, sons were not asked whether the occupation would be identical but whether they "would like to do the same kind of work." The possible responses were (1) yes, (2) maybe, (3) I don't think so, and (4) no. The data for sons in secondary school are presented in Table 15-4.

Table 15-4. Occupational Preferences of Sons in Secondary School: Epperson's and Coleman's Data (in Percentages).

RESPONSE	EPPERSON'S QUESTION			COLEMAN'S QUESTION
Yes	3.6	31.0	(same)	9.8
Maybe	27.4			
I don't think so	15.5	69.0	(different)	90.2
No	53.5			
Total	100.0			100.0

SOURCE: Epperson, "A Reassessment," p. 96, Tables 3 and 4.

Differences in the response options of the two questions unfortunately preclude direct equivalence of the findings. In the revised version, however, it was disclosed that a large percentage of boys did not intend to pursue occupations similar to those of their fathers. Nevertheless, they constituted a meaningfully smaller percentage (53.5 percent) than indicated by the figures obtained by Coleman (90.2 percent). If the responses of "I don't think so" and "No" on the revised question were combined as an index of "different occupation," the distributions would become somewhat closer (69.0 v. 90.2 percent). Conversely, combining "Yes" and "Maybe" re-

15.2 QUESTIONNAIRE RULES-OF-THUMB

As with interviews, a number of rules-of-thumb have been developed for questionnaires. Some of the most important of them are listed below.

1. Questions should be clear, simple, and concise. Long questions should be avoided. Each question should be limited to a single issue.
2. The vocabulary employed must be appropriate to the backgrounds of respondents. If respondents have a technical background in a field related to the questionnaire, then technical language should be used. If not, it should be avoided. In any case, the words used should have the same meanings for all respondents.
3. Questions ought not "lead" respondents by giving indirect hints as to your preferred responses. The following questions, for instance, each imply a different preference on the part of the researcher.
   a. *Do you think that policemen should have the right to strike just as other Americans have?*
   b. *Do you think that policemen should be permitted to strike despite the fact that there may be loss of property and perhaps even of lives?*
4. The layout and print of a questionnaire should be easy to follow. The sequence of questions, similarly, should be such that it will make sense to the respondent.
5. Questions should be sequenced so that the respondent is motivated to continue and answer all questions. Therefore, easily answered, nonsensitive questions usually open a questionnaire, while the most sensitive ones are reserved for later sections.
6. Questions should protect the ego of the respondent. For instance, a question on voting behavior might imply that the respondent has failed in his or her public responsibility unless softened in the following manner.
   Many people were not able to vote in the last election because of illness, prior obligations, and other important reasons. Were you able to vote in the last election?
7. Decide whether you need an open-ended or forced-choice question in a particular situation. If you choose the former, the question should be carefully worded so that it has the same meaning for all respondents and elicits responses that are comparable.
8. If you choose a forced-choice question, response alternatives must be appropriate to the question, cover the entire range of choices a respondent would be likely to use, and be stated so that they avoid confusing duplication.
9. The questionnaire document, once created, should be pretested. Respondents similar to those who will receive the questionnaire should be asked to fill it out and encouraged to express any problems or concerns that arise while completing it.

Further rules-of-thumb on questionnaire construction, as well as suggestions for increasing the percentages of returns, can be found in Delbert C. Miller, *Handbook of Research Design and Social Measurement*, 2d ed. (New York: McKay, 1970), pages 76–83.

sponses seems to indicate that, according to the revised question, more sons would like to do work similar to that of their fathers than was the case with the Coleman study (31.0 and 9.8 percent respectively).

DATA INFERENCE

In both studies, a large percentage of boys indicated that they planned to choose occupations different from those of their fathers. Coleman contends that this can be interpreted as an indication of adolescent male estrangement from the adult culture. However, the data also appear to support alternative interpretations. First, students may plan an occupation different from their fathers' because they have internalized aspirations of upward social mobility from their parents. They therefore would be likely to prefer occupations of higher status than those of their fathers. An alternative interpretation may be that changes in the occupational structure make it difficult or impossible for sons to follow in the occupational footsteps of their fathers. Consequently, they will have chosen alternative occupations. Both of these inferences appear reasonable based upon the data examined.

SUMMARY

Slight changes in the form and wording of questions may produce measurements different from those intended by the researcher. Consequently, false interpretations may result if researchers fail to give careful consideration to phrasing. The meaning of a question cannot be taken for granted. Inferring from a theoretical concept to an operational procedure for measurement, and from a measurement to a theoretical concept is a complex and hazardous process. Concepts and measurements interact in complex ways and mandate extreme caution in inferring conclusions.

In this chapter, one researcher's questionnaire data and resultant interpretations concerning the possible existence and nature of an adolescent subculture raised issues in the mind of a second investigator and prompted the collection of new data. The latter consisted of responses to revised questions for operationalizing the concept of an adolescent subculture. The data were interpreted to indicate that peer approval may not be as important as previously supposed, that adolescent values might not differ from preadolescent ones, and that indications other than that of a subculture could account for the observation that occupational preferences of sons differ from the actual pursuits of their fathers. As a result of re-examining the inferences based upon the questionnaire data, initially hypothesized causes and characteristics of an adolescent subculture were consequently questioned.

KEY IDEAS AND CONCEPTS

concept
convention
empirical indicators
operationalism
operationalization
purposive sample
questionnaire
reliability
theoretical inference
validity

ISSUES AND PROBLEMS

1. Specify the philosophical and theoretical problem to which operationalism and operationalization are addressed. Discuss the crucial differences between these two approaches.
2. List the advantages of questionnaires over interviews. List the advantages of the latter over the former. List the disadvantages of each.
3. In 1954, the following question was asked of a national probability sample of Americans and a smaller sample of community leaders.

   > If J. Edgar Hoover were to say that the FBI has most of the American Communists under its eye, would you feel pretty sure it was true, or wouldn't you?

   The data from this question were as follows:

Table 15-A

	PERCENTAGE ANSWERING	
	Among Community Leaders	In National Cross-Section
Would feel pretty sure	87	64
Would not	11	27
Don't know	2	9
	100	100

SOURCE: Samuel A. Stouffer, *Communism, Conformity, and Civil Liberties* (Gloucester, Mass.: Peter Smith, 1963), p. 229 (originally published in 1955).

Specify the logic employed in drawing each of the following inferences:

a. Community leaders generally had more faith in the capabilities of governmental agencies such as the FBI.
b. Such leaders were less willing to disagree with the statements of public officials.
c. The leaders were less willing to disagree with interviewers. Discuss the information required for narrowing the possible inferences.

4. In a study of male high school students, a researcher asked respondents about their college aspirations. He then classified students by the dominant characteristic of the schools they attended. The results are summarized in the following table.

Table 15-B. Percentage of Boys Aspiring to Go to College.

	TYPE OF SCHOOL		
FATHER'S OCCUPATION	Upper White Collar	Lower White Collar	Industrial
1. Professional	93	77	64
2. White Collar	79	59	46
3. Manual	59	44	33

SOURCE: Alan B. Wilson, "Residential Segregation of Social Classes and Aspirations of High School Boys," *American Sociological Review,* 24(1959): 836–845.

a. Reading across row 1 could lead to the inference that professional boys at "industrial" schools were less likely to aspire to college. On the other hand, row 1 could indicate that there is a great deal of peer pressure in industrial schools not to *say* that one wishes to go on to college. Explain the latter argument.
b. Explain how peer pressures may have caused some of the differences between response rates in row 3.

RECOMMENDED READINGS

Coleman, James S.
1961 *The Adolescent Society.* New York: Free Press.

Uses questionnaire data for a large number of schools to innovatively draw inferences about the social structures of the schools.

Kammeyer, Kenneth C. W., and Julius A. Roth
1971 "Coding Responses to Open-Ended Questions," pp. 60–78 in Herbert L. Costner (ed.), *Sociological Methodology 1971.* San Francisco: Jossey-Bass.

Discusses and illustrates problems of coding open-ended questions.

Schuman, Howard, and Otis Dudley Duncan
1974 "Questions About Attitude Survey Questions," pp. 232–251 in Herbert L. Costner (ed.), *Sociological Methodology, 1973–1974.* San Francisco: Jossey-Bass.

Emphasizes the importance and impact of changes in question wording and the hazard of forced choice questions in surveys.

PART SEVEN

Field Designs

16

A VARIATION IN INTERVIEWS: CALL GIRLS AS INFORMANTS

GENERAL ISSUE

As mentioned much earlier, exploratory and descriptive research are devoted to the discovery and presentation of new information. This information, in turn, contributes to the development of theory. Theory then yields hypotheses which may be assessed through hypothesis-testing research.

There are fewer rules of procedure to guide exploratory research than there are to guide hypothesis-testing research. The former, by definition, amounts to an adventure into the unfamiliar, and it results frequently in unanticipated findings. However, its flexibility of procedure often produces skepticism among scientists about the reliability and validity of findings. Quite frequently, such research is guided only by general objectives, vaguely stated hypotheses, and a degree of haphazardness in data-collection procedures. According to some observers, these aspects of exploratory research are weaknesses. For others, however, they are strengths because of the prospects of generating new information.

The potential value of this information appears to be twofold. First, the information may provide useful insights into previously uninvestigated phenomenon. Second, when confirmed, it may assist in modifying or developing theory and establishing a basis for hypothesis-testing research.

Evaluating exploratory research requires subtle judgment, since the usual standards of research procedure are difficult to apply. Consequently, scientists must decide whether information resulting from nonrigorous procedures of investigation contributes meaningfully to scientific knowledge.

This chapter examines the occupational career of females engaged in a particular form of deviancy, the call girl. The substantive focus is on the nature of this occupation, its organization, and how new members are recruited and socialized. The methodological focus is on the use of *snowball sampling* techniques which require persons initially sampled to suggest other persons for inclusion in the study and the use of interviewees as informants in exploratory research.

THEORETICAL PROBLEM

Psychological theory has played a major role in developing research devoted to the study of social deviance. Consequently, there are many studies which focus on the real and imagined anxieties, tensions, frustrations, self-images, and psychological traits of deviants. In recent years, however, sociological theory has been used to guide research on such deviance. The literature emerging from sociology emphasizes the social organization of deviance, the processes by which individuals are moved to it, and the social control processes implemented by those in power.

Specific forms of deviancy, such as call girl prostitution, may exhibit characteristics of a career. A career can be thought of as a sequence of social roles that typically is followed by people in occupational (and other) settings. In the case of call girl prostitution, these roles define call girls' relationships to other prostitutes, customers, and persons in the referral system. As a first step, women interested in being call girls must affiliate themselves with the occupation. This step is referred to as recruitment. The study of recruitment as it applies to call girls was the first research objective of a study undertaken by James H. Bryan.*

Unlike street prostitutes, call girls use referral networks to acquire customers, conduct most arrangements by phone, establish a clientele, and meet customers on a prearranged basis. Each of these activities requires specialized skills, values, and attitudes. Bryan's second research objective was to study the socialization process through which the girls acquire these skills, values, and attitudes.

SAMPLING CALL GIRLS

Random sampling procedures generally require a list of all persons in the population to be studied. For many populations—and this is true of call girls—such a list is simply not available. Bryan began his study of call

* James H. Bryan, "Apprenticeships in Prostitution," *Social Problems*, 12(1965):287–297.

girls through one contact who was a patient at a mental hospital in Los Angeles. Each girl was contacted and requested to identify other known call girls in the vicinity. Those who cooperated were in turn requested to identify other call girls. The process was repeated until thirty-three girls were identified. The initial sample consequently grew from one to thirty-three call girls.

16.1 SNOWBALL TECHNIQUES

Snowball techniques are most useful when there is a need to identify a previously unknown population. Linking members of a population to each other, either directly or indirectly, is a reasonable procedure for identifying all members of that population. For instance, the small population of persons influential in community affairs are frequently known to each other but are unknown to outsiders. Consequently, many studies begin with an initial identification of a few community influentials who are then asked, among other things, to nominate other influential persons. The process continues until there is reason to believe that all influentials have been identified.

Snowball techniques, however, are less convincing when used to identify a sample. In addition to the general requirement that members of the population either be known or linked directly or indirectly to each other, snowball sampling techniques require that the sequence of referral identifications be unbiased. That is, snowball sampling requires that the sample eventually selected be similar to those persons who would have been sampled if the snowball process had been allowed to continue. If this requirement is not met, the sample selected will not be representative. Unfortunately, it is difficult to establish whether this criterion has been satisfied in most studies using snowball sampling techniques.

The probability that a snowball sample is representative cannot be established statistically. The inability to establish this probability does not imply that the sample is necessarily biased. However, its representativeness must be judged by the logical reasonableness that the sample is representative of the population rather than through statistical technique. The evidence for judging this probability varies with the amount of knowledge possessed about that part of the population which was not studied.

DATA COLLECTION THROUGH INTERVIEWS

Lack of knowledge about call girls and the deviant nature of their prostitution required flexibility in data-collection procedures. First, the interviews took place in many different locations. Several girls preferred to be interviewed at their residences; others preferred their places of work. A few preferred the interviewer's office, and one preferred a public park. The practice of interviewing call girls in locations where they felt most comfortable may have increased the level of trust in the interviewer and produced candid information that otherwise might not have been available. On the other hand, variations in interview locations may have introduced factors which biased the data.

Second, the precise wording of the questions used in the interview varied from girl to girl. Unstructured interviews were required since it was impossible to design all research questions in advance. Information volunteered by one girl served as a basis for questions in the next interview. As a result, open-ended questions followed by probes were employed. This resulted in a free-flowing conversational interview which varied from respondent to respondent.

Third, the interviews focused on the information each girl could provide about the social organization of call girl prostitution as well as her own personal experiences, attitudes, and behavior. In this manner, girls were serving as informants. Since the only requirement of an informant was that she be knowledgeable about call girl prostitution, the nonrandom selection of the sample was not seen as a serious methodological weakness. It is necessary, however, that informants be willing and able to provide reliable and valid information.

16.2 INFORMANTS

Members of secret organizations, former prisoners of war, and other persons with unique experiences are able to provide valuable information to social scientists. As informants, such individuals permit the collection of data which otherwise would be either prohibitively time-consuming or impossible to obtain. The data usually relate to phenomena other than personal characteristics, experiences, or values.

Information from one informant may be checked and cross-checked with that provided by others in order to eliminate personal bias and provide a holistic picture of the phenomenon under investigation. In addition, informant information is cross-checked with any additional data available to the researcher. Such data may range from written records to expert opinion. These procedures are undertaken to provide evidence of the reliability and validity of informant data.

Informant interviewing, as well as snowball sampling, are two procedures which should be employed cautiously and whenever possible in conjunction with additional data-collection techniques.

Finally, in order to facilitate comparison of unstructured interviews, it was necessary to record the data verbatim. This was accomplished by using a tape recorder in thirty-one of the thirty-three interviews where permission was granted. The remaining two interviews required extensive note-taking. Taping provides the most accurate and complete record of an interview and small cassette recorders often are ignored by individuals after the early minutes of an interview.

It should be noted, however, that tapes are as unwieldy in data analysis as they are complete in data collection. Attempts to retrieve specific information from audio tapes is a tedious experience, especially when it involves listening to numerous unstructured interviews and then spending countless hours searching for specific information. For this reason, as in this study, interviews are often transcribed as a prelude to data analysis. It is more convenient to scan typed material than recall the location of specific information on a tape.

ANALYSIS AND FINDINGS

The burden of interpreting and assigning importance to information rests heavily on the individual ability of the researcher. In the absence of quantitative data, researchers must make independent judgments regarding the significance of various items of information. As a result, the private nature of data analysis makes it extremely difficult for researchers unfamiliar with the phenomenon under study to judge the adequacy of collection and analysis.

The Processes of Recruitment

All but one of the women reported that immediately prior to becoming a call girl they had contact with someone already involved in the field. About half of those interviewed said their initial contact was with a currently working call girl, while most of the rest had initial contact with a pimp. One respondent had her initial contact with customers of other girls. The importance of contacts is illustrated by the following response:

> I think I might have started a year sooner had I had a connection. You seem to make one contact or another . . . if its another girl or a pimp or just someone who will set you up and get you a client. . . . You can't just, say, get an apartment and get a phone in and everything and say, "Well I'm gonna start business now. . . ."

In some cases, the novice had had a long-time friendship with the experienced call girl who was her initial contact. Most contacts with call girls, however, were based on recent acquaintances, that is, the novice had known the experienced girl for less than a year. Those relationships do not appear to have been very close, since the novice spent little time with the experienced girl and shared little personal information with her. Most initial contacts with pimps, however, were as lovers, although occasionally it was purely a business relationship. The business relationship existed even in the case of lovers, with the male acting as manager of the girl's career for the benefit of them both.

In sum, recruitment patterns into call girl prostitution were loosely organized, diverse, and varied in emotional content.

The Processes of Socialization

When initial contact by the novice was with an experienced call girl, the latter herself supervised and conducted the training of the novice. When initial contact was with a pimp, he sometimes referred the novice to an experienced girl and conducted the training under his direct supervision. In all, twenty-four of the thirty-three interviewees were trained by experienced call girls.

The training consisted of an average of two to three months (sometimes as long as eight months) of "on-the-job" training in the apartment of the trainer. The trainer typically eavesdropped on the novice and subsequently offered advice and received one-half of the novice's fees as payment. This payment was not primarily for the teaching of sexual skills, which obviously could be learned on the streets. It was paid, first of all, for the establishment of a clientele. The customers acquired during training continued to be the novice's customers, and they provided her with additional referrals. The loss of customers caused few problems for the trainer because the demand for call girls' services exceeded the supply.

The second reason for having an experienced call girl as trainer was to teach social skills and occupational values. The interpersonal skills that a prospective call girl needs include phone solicitation techniques, means of getting payment before rendering services, methods for dealing with problem customers, skillful use of alcohol and drugs, and the all-important techniques of hygiene and cleanliness. The fundamental occupational value of training was to maximize one's gains and minimize one's efforts. Customers ("tricks") were considered by the value system to be basically corrupt and given to exploitation; they were therefore considered fair targets for exploitation in return. One call girl explained that she was taught to value

> never being nice or pleasant to a trick unless you are doing it for the money. . . . It was explained to me over a period of about six months. I learned that you were doing it to make money for yourself so that you could have nice things and security. . . .

Values that were taught, however, were often violated. While there was an effort to encourage girls not to experience orgasm, for instance, a number of informants indicated that this socialization was only partly effective. Similarly, values supporting fairness to one's pimp and to other girls were emphasized, though they were practiced in varying degrees. Some training

16.3 IN-DEPTH INTERVIEWING TECHNIQUES

The study of respondent acquiescence in Chapter 14 indicated that the wording of questions influences responses, because respondents may feel pressured to agree with questions, regardless of their content. While answering questions, the respondents are interacting with the interviewer. In short, interviewing is social interaction; the respondent bases answers partly on the content of the questions and partly on perceptions of the needs, desires, and intentions of the interviewer.

Below are four selected techniques for making interviewer-respondent interaction serve research goals.

1. The interviewer should use subtle encouragement, and silence, as helpful techniques. Respondents should be given the necessary time to stop and think, and be provided with encouragement through the use of neutral interested facial expressions and supportive phrases such as "I see" and "uh huh." Of course, the interviewer must be sensitive also to the fact that excessive silence can be an embarrassment. However, excessive silence is usually not a problem with novice interviewers who tend to move the interview along briskly because of their own nervousness.
2. The interviewer must use a carefully selected vocabulary. Not only must the chosen words be clearly understood by the respondent, but they must also (a) avoid causing biased answers because of their emotional content, and (b) establish a desired role relationship between the interviewer and the respondent. Emotionally loaded words can suggest an interviewer's preference, to which the respondent may adjust. The use of a technical vocabulary may intimidate the respondent and inhibit honest answers, while using the language of the group (when its meanings and nuances are clear to the interviewer) can facilitate communication and reduce social distance.
3. The interviewer must remain sensitive to how the sequence of questions can influence the content of answers. As with questionnaires, opening questions should be simple and unthreatening. More sensitive questions (i.e., on income or sexual behavior) usually are left to the end of the interview, when rapport and trust are high and when the purposes of the research are clearer than in the beginning.
4. Whenever possible, the interviewer should have an informal post-interview conversation with the respondent for four reasons. First, such a conversation will help the respondent feel satisfied with his or her performance and can provide clearer information about the research goals. Second, this conversation may aid in detecting possible inhibiting elements of the interview situation and in obtaining information which was not initially offered. Third, it will assist the interviewer in obtaining reinterviews and in preventing negative information from reaching other potential respondents. Fourth, it also will aid social scientists in retaining access to research populations.

periods ended abruptly, for example, when the novice stole her trainer's book of customers' names and phone numbers.

During the training period, the substantial financial rewards of the occupation became apparent to the novice and strengthened her commitment. Despite her lack of skills and experience, a novice is new on the "market" and is thus desirable and frequently successful. The end of her training period may come about quickly, as mentioned, and usually has little relation to mastering interpersonal skills or internalizing a value system. Rather, the training period ends when the novice seems to have enough customers to start on her own career. Thus, teaching of skills and values is really a relatively minor part of the training period for call girls.

SUMMARY

The basic elements of this chapter were general research objectives, snowball sampling techniques, the use of informants, and open-ended interviews in exploratory research. The flexibility of these elements permitted the collection of information which otherwise might have been impossible to obtain.

The advantages of these procedures in exploratory research must be balanced with the disadvantages, as demonstrated, of convincing other social scientists that the findings are reliable and valid. The need of science for research designs which produce new information as well as those which permit more rigorous hypothesis testing suggests that both categories are important.

KEY IDEAS AND CONCEPTS

descriptive research
exploratory research
hypothesis-testing research
in-depth interviewing
informants
interviewer-respondent interaction
open-ended interviews
post-interview conversation
rapport
snowball sampling
unstructured interviews

ISSUES AND PROBLEMS

1. Describe the research circumstances under which descriptive and exploratory studies are most useful. Describe the methodological strengths and weaknesses of such studies in comparison to hypothesis-testing types.

2. Describe possible methodological problems associated with Bryan's study of call girls along the following three dimensions.
   a. his choice of the initial informant;
   b. his use of the snowball technique;
   c. the usefulness of the findings for generalizing to the population of call girls.
3. In all communities some persons are more influential than others. Some of these influential persons, such as the mayor and the Chamber of Commerce president, are readily visible. Other influentials, such as a newspaper editor or a corporation president, may be less so.

   Describe a technique for using informants and snowball sampling for identifying the influentials in a small community of 15,000. Discuss methodological problems associated with choosing initial informants and the use of these to locate additional informants.
4. In what sense is the snowball technique appropriate for identifying a population? In what sense is it a technique for selecting a sample?
5. This chapter illustrates an exploratory study based almost entirely upon informant data. Often, however, investigators use informants in order to prepare for eventual hypothesis-testing research.

   Informants, for example, might be helpful in preparing for a hypothesis-testing study comparing the life-styles of jazz musicians and concert musicians. Describe specific ways informants might assist researchers in (a) drawing samples of both types of respondents; (b) developing an interview schedule for data collection; and (c) establishing rapport.

RECOMMENDED READINGS

Aiken, Michael, and Paul E. Mott

1970 *The Structure of Community Power.* New York: Random House.

A discussion of the advantages and disadvantages of snowball techniques for the study of power in communities (pp. 228–284).

Dean, John P., and William Foote Whyte

1958 "How Do You Know If the Informant Is Telling the Truth?" *Human Organization*, 17 (2) 34–38.

Emphasizes that the information provided by the informant is a filtered and modified perception containing what the respondent is willing to communicate in a particular interview situation. In this context, discusses the uses and strategies of informant interviewing.

Gordon, Raymond L.

1969 *Interviewing: Strategy, Techniques and Tactics.* Homewood, Ill.: Dorsey.

Explains strategies and tactics that aid in conducting research that uses interviews. A wealth of practical tips for persons who will be interviewing or will be training interviewers.

Hunter, Floyd

1953 *Community Power Structure.* Chapel Hill: Univ. of North Carolina Press.

A study of forty influentials in Atlanta using a snowball technique.

17

PARTICIPANT OBSERVATION IN A FIELD DESIGN: THE SOCIAL MEANING OF NUDITY IN NUDIST CAMPS

GENERAL ISSUE

Many topics and problems of scientific interest can neither be studied in the laboratory through experimental procedures nor in the field through survey research procedures. Researching such topics and problems generally involves a selection and combination of procedures which result in what is broadly classified as a *field design*. Field designs often are based on direct observation, informal interviewing, researcher-subject interaction in a natural setting, and an eclectic gathering of additional data deemed relevant to the research. Consequently, such designs are characterized by their open-endedness as to data-collection procedures and flexibility as to research objectives.

The present chapter extends the ground for field designs established in the exploratory research outlined in the last chapter as conducted on call girls. The major methodological focus is on the use of direct observation as a data-collection technique in field research. The major theoretical focus is on the interdependence of social norms as studied in nudist camps.

THEORETICAL PROBLEM

The public is generally fearful that deviation from a specific norm will lead to deviation from others. This fear, expressed as a scientific hypothesis, suggests that norms are interdependent, and that a domino effect is set into motion when certain ones are violated. A contrasting view is that norms vary as to their degree of interdependence. Thus, only under certain conditions will a domino effect be set into motion by violation of specific norms. Under different conditions, violation of one norm does not necessarily lead to deviation from others. Furthermore, it has been suggested that groups may establish social control mechanisms which permit violation of some norms but not others.

THE STUDY OF SEXUAL MODESTY IN NUDIST CAMPS

Martin S. Weinberg undertook research to investigate the interrelationship of norms regulating one area of social behavior, sexual modesty in nudist camps.* Theoretically, his research focused on whether the abandoning of specific norms of modesty tended to undermine closely related sexual norms.

Immodesty is interpreted frequently as an invitation to sexual interaction. Open display of the body, use of prurient language, listening with interest to such language, and suggestive looks or gestures are thought to be related actions. Departure from norms governing such actions generally is interpreted by society as signifying a willingness for sexual activity. In nudist camps, however, norms governing the display of the body are reversed. Consequently, such camps provide an excellent setting for investigations into the interrelationship of restraining social norms.

Two broadly stated opposing hypotheses are implied by Weinberg's research:

1. Since social norms about display of the body are weak in nudist camps, they will also have relatively weak norms governing language and gestures. Nudist camps will also be expected to have weak norms regulating sexual actions, since nudity will tend to communicate sexual availability and encourage carnal behavior.
2. Contrarily, since norms about the display of the body *are* weak there, nudist camps will have relatively strong norms governing language and gestures in order to compensate for the violation of norms of bodily display. The camps also will have strong norms regulating sexual actions.

Field Research Design

To assess the general hypotheses, Weinberg employed a two-stage research design. The first stage, field observation, consisted of direct observations of the language and behavior of nudists. Gaining access to groups that are

* Martin S. Weinberg, "Sexual Modesty, Social Meanings, and the Nudist Camp," *Social Problems*, 12 (1965): 311–318.

17.1 PARTICIPANT OBSERVATION

A data-collection technique called *participant observation* is employed when it seems the most appropriate means of understanding behavior, power structures, or attitudes within a group. Not surprisingly, such observation involves studying a group while partaking in its activities. However, this is not as simple as it may appear, because achieving research goals creates a tension between the behavior expected of a participant and that expected of an observer.

Participation requires that the researcher have personal and even intense interaction with the subjects. It involves sharing the everyday lives of subjects. It also requires that this interaction occur over an extended period of time. And, it necessitates that interaction occur in the subject's "world," rather than in a laboratory. In this way, the researcher is in a position to observe and comprehend the relevant aspects of the group.

Observational needs, however, set severe constraints on researchers' ability to participate, requiring that they not influence the phenomena being observed. Similarly, they must not be so personally and intensely involved that their participation interferes with their ability to observe.

sensitive about their relations to the public often is a problem. Communicating scientific interest and the rationale for research, however, sometimes provides access which otherwise might be denied. In this instance, Weinberg contacted three nudist camps near the Chicago metropolitan area, and they agreed to participate in his study.

The first stage of the research was exploratory in the sense that scientific concepts and hypotheses were in a formative stage and subject to refinement and change. Since the initial use of formal questionnaires or interviews might impair, rather than facilitate, the collection of data, Weinberg undertook direct field observations of the language and behavior of nudists by attending the camp during the summer.

When one undertakes field research as a participant observer, one must resolve the problem of whether to reveal one's identity as a social scientist. Weinberg did so. He found no evidence that the nudists' awareness of him as a scientific observer influenced their behavior. This openness relieved Weinberg of some of the personal and ethical dilemmas he would have experienced had he concealed his mission. His open identity also permitted him to participate in more detailed (frank) conversations with nudists and to add a second dimension to his research design.

During the course of participant observation, nudists attending the camp were asked to fill out name and address cards for more formal interviews to be conducted later. Rapport with participants was high, and few refused to grant a later interview. The later interviewing, done at the homes of 101 nudists living within 100 miles of Chicago, provided informa-

For these reasons, participation should be done with great reserve and then only to the extent necessitated by the research.

Participant observers can be differentiated from ordinary group members by the limitations on their participation and by their commitment to observation. They are also different from group members because they have

1. selected the observation site for its representativeness and theoretical interest;
2. committed significant amounts of time to making observations and recording them;
3. maintained career goals, friendships, and personal orientations outside the subjects' world;
4. acquired conceptual and methodological tools to aid in their observations and interpretations;
5. maintained the option of supplementing observations with interviews, governmental statistics, and other sources;
6. organized their observations so that the results may be communicated to social scientists and other nongroup members.

tion for cross-checking and supplementing Weinberg's inferences against the perceptions and experiences of the camp attendees themselves. These interviews were successful in gathering data which, if collected at camp, might have either disrupted activities or been influenced by social norms.

Interviews had a dual purpose. First, respondents provided data on their social backgrounds, personal characteristics, and beliefs. Second, they served as informants, disclosing facts about other nudist camps they had attended. Thus, by treating nudists as both respondents and informants, data were collected on twenty nudist camps in which the various respondents had had personal experience.

DISCUSSION

The Social Definition of Nudity

Observations and interviews suggested that nudists generally share these beliefs:

1. Nudism and sexuality are unrelated.
2. There is nothing shameful about exposing the human body.
3. Abandoning of clothes leads to feelings of freedom and natural pleasure.

4. Nude activities, especially full body exposure to the sun, lead to feelings of physical, mental, and spiritual well-being.

The first element of this definition most directly concerns the interrelationship of norms. It states that nudism—at nudist camps—does not promote sexuality. Observational and interview data indicated a number of ways in which the social organization of the camps influenced the development of behavioral norms which sustained this initial conception of nudity.

Behavior and Norms in Nudist Camps

There were rather strict norms for sexual modesty at nudist camps. Verbal immodesty was uncommon; there were few dirty jokes or sexually oriented discussions. In addition, there were taboos against body contact, nude dancing, and consumption of alcohol. This latter was due to the fact that drinking could possibly cause the nudists to relax other camp norms. The taking of photographs was forbidden, as was the accentuation or covering parts of the body in a manner that might be interpreted as arousing sexual interest. Women, especially, seemed unimpressed by the nudity of male camp members. The exchange below, with Weinberg's questions italicized in parentheses, illustrates the wide scope of these taboos.

(*Have you ever observed or heard about anyone staring at someone's body while at camp?*) I've heard stories—particularly about men who stare. Since I heard these stories, I tried not to, and even done (*sic*) away with my sunglasses after someone said, half-joking, that I hide behind sunglasses to stare. Toward the end of the summer I stopped wearing sunglasses. And you know what, it was a child who told me this.

Similarly, camp members were intolerant of those who suggested, by their attitudes or actions, that nudity was a form of sexuality. In response to a question about verbal immodesty, the following statements are representative:

One would expect to see less of that at camp than at other places. (*Why's that?*) Because you expect that members are screened in their attitude for nudism—and this isn't one who prefers sexual jokes.

They probably don't belong there. They're there to see what they can find to observe. (*What do you mean?*) Well, their mind isn't on being a nudist, but to see so-and-so nude.

Responses were similar with regard to the accentuation of parts of the body. One female nudist made the following statement about women who sit in an "unladylike" manner:

It's no more nice to do than when you are dressed. I would assume they have a purpose. (*What's that?*) Maybe to draw someone's attention sexually. I'd think it's bad behavior and it's one thing that shouldn't be done, especially in a nudist camp. (*Why's that?*) Because it could lead to trouble or some misfortune. (*Could you tell me some more about that?*) It could bring up some trouble or disturbance among those who noticed it. It would not be appreciated by "true nudists."

17.2 INTERVIEWING STRATEGIES

Interviewing strategies can be located on a continuum from "standardized" to "nondirective." *Standardized interviewing* involves asking the same questions in the same order and with the same wording of all respondents. Questions may be either "fixed-alternative" (e.g., Which of these things would be hardest for you to take . . . parents' disapproval, teacher's disapproval, breaking with friend) or "open-ended" (e.g., What is your father's occupation?). In either case, standardized interviewing is useful when groups of respondents are to be compared (e.g., rural youth v. urban youth) and when the phenomenon being measured is relatively clear-cut. Standardized interviews are most useful where theory and past research are well developed and where a large number of interviews is considered necessary.

Nondirective interviewing, at the other end of the continuum, places the initiative in the hands of the respondent. The respondent is asked to discuss a topic with a minimum of direction. For instance, the following was the first question asked in an interview study of university students: "What are some of the things you feel fairly happy about these days?" This type of question is most useful in determining highly subjective attitudes and behaviors, and in studying phenomena where existing theory and data are meager guides to research. Nondirective, open-ended questions, because of their time-consuming character, most frequently are administered to small numbers of respondents.

The strategy used in this chapter is intermediate between the standardized and nondirective approaches. Sometimes known as *focused interviewing*, it permits the researcher to focus on a clearly defined experience or situation, while leaving enough flexibility for respondents to provide unexpected responses and for researchers to follow unanticipated leads. This type of interview tends to be most useful when the study of attitudes or perceptions is intense, and when flexibility is desired because research is of an exploratory nature.

Note that the dialogues reproduced in this chapter have featured focused questions, followed by nondirective probes, such as "Why's that?" and "Could you tell me more about that?" Directive probes which ask "Do you mean . . .?" are rarely useful because the respondent may tend to acquiesce in what he perceives the interviewer wants. Similarly, in standardized interviewing, structured questions are usually not reworded by interviewers because the revised question may have subtle differences from the original. In most cases, when they ask for clarification, interviewers will read the question *verbatim* a second time.

17.3 RELIABILITY AND VALIDITY OF OBSERVATIONAL METHODOLOGIES

Reliability and validity problems confront all data collection methodologies. Observational techniques reduce some of these difficulties because the activity is being recorded by the researcher as it happens, rather than being reported by a respondent whose memory may have faded or who lacks interpretational concepts. Additionally, bias may be reduced because the researcher is less emotionally involved than the respondent.

For several reasons, observational techniques are vulnerable to the problems of unreliability and invalidity. The most important of these are

1. *Choice of research settings.* Lack of access to some research settings, or the use of a very small number of observational locations, increases the chance that selected settings are not representative.
2. *Sampling within research settings.* Since the observer usually observes only a fraction of the total activity, choices of time and activity to observe can provide unrepresentative data.
3. *Observer-caused effects.* Since the observer is necessarily a part of the environment being observed, his presence may have the unintended and unobvious consequence of changing the behaviors being studied.
4. *Failures of interpretation.* Observers may misinterpret activities being studied because they have personal biases or lack appropriate concepts for classifying and recording information.

Normative definitions contrary to existing norms are often established slowly. Some of the women in Weinberg's study reported that they expected everyone to look at them when they undressed. One woman reported:

> I got so mad because my husband wanted me to undress in front of other men that I just pulled my clothes right off thinking everyone would look at me.

She was amazed and disappointed when no one did.

Single persons and those whose motives are suspect are either discouraged from joining by being charged higher fees, or they are refused permission to join. When persons who have been admitted behave inappropriately, camp attitudes toward them are quite harsh. One respondent, when asked about individuals who break the norms prohibiting bodily contact, had the following reaction:

Some of the many tactics that have proven successful for reducing problems of reliability and validity are

1. *Recording raw data as soon and completely as possible.* Taking notes of and even tape recording conversations are often less disruptive than might be expected. When the topic being discussed is not sensitive for the respondent, these techniques may actually encourage more complete answers because the respondent realizes that he is being taken seriously. When concurrent note-taking is not possible, notes should be created as soon as possible while memories are still clear.
2. *Writing up and indexing notes as soon as possible.* An indexing system with appropriate categories should be used (and revised when necessary) so that observations can be located when the researcher is sorting out data for final reports.
3. *Breaking some observations into units which minimize emotion or judgment.* For instance, for each observed situation where two nudists walked past one another, did they look aside, make eye contact, or observe one another's bodies?
4. *Limiting emotional involvement in the situation being observed.* Friendships and personal commitments should be avoided to reduce potential bias. Observers often experience problems in "going native."
5. *Creating cross-checks on the data.* For instance, a second observer may independently observe the same phenomena. Also, multiple methodologies such as use of observation and informants can be used to study a single problem; or a search can be made for inconsistencies in observational data collected by a single researcher.

They are in the wrong place. (*How's that?*) That's not part of nudism. (*Could you tell me some more about that?*) I think they are there for some sort of thrill. They are certainly not there to enjoy the sun.

SUMMARY

In the case of norms of sexual modesty, the data indicate that some are independent of other apparently related ones. The nudist camps studied had strong norms regulating language, looks, and body contact, apparently to compensate for the suspension of norms of bodily display. They also had strong norms regulating sexual actions. Thus, other norms appear to have replaced those regulating clothing in the controlling of sexual interest. There was found to be no "domino effect" in which the breakdown of some norms caused the breakdown of others. The nudists appeared to have successfully compartmentalized their norms.

These inferences were based on data collected through a field design including two stages: the direct observation of behavior in a natural setting and interviews conducted at a later time. The flexibility of the design permitted the conduct of research which otherwise would have been impaired.

Problems of reliability and validity of observational data were discussed in the context of the study.

KEY IDEAS AND CONCEPTS

field design
focused interview
informant
multiple data-collection methodology
nondirective interview
participant observation
participant observer's role
probe
reliability
respondent
standardized interview
two-stage research design
validity

ISSUES AND PROBLEMS

1. Describe the advantages of data collection using participant observation versus the advantages of collection using questionnaires. Describe the disadvantages of each.
2. The data reported in this chapter were collected through participant observation in a sample of three nudist camps in the Chicago area. List some dimensions on which these three nudist camps might be unrepresentative of the population of American nudist camps. Specify the strategies used by the author to overcome the possibility of nonrepresentativeness and to therefore generalize to the population of nudist camps as a whole.
3. Melville Dalton conducted a study of four American firms. For reasons quoted below, Dalton chose not to reveal his identity as a participant observer to his co-workers.

> Because I expediently used any method that did not endanger the firm or personnel, my core efforts can be discussed under formal interviewing, work diaries, participant-observation, and socializing. I did little formal interviewing because of the obvious problems of explaining what I was doing, and the inadequacy of the approach for getting at unofficial activities. . . . I recorded events, biographical information, gossip, and initial hypotheses in loose-leaf notebooks. . . . [As a participant-observer] I was a member of staff groups which gave me—even required—great freedom of movement and wide contacts without raising questions. . . . Out-plant socializing enabled me to study activities at the Magnesia Yacht Club, which involved the community and leaders from many firms; to develop closer relations with the managers during their periods of relaxation. . . .
>
> Melville Dalton, *Men Who Manage* (New York: Wiley, 1959), pp. 277–281.

Discuss the advantages and disadvantages of Dalton's research strategy in terms of:

a. secrecy
b. multiple data sources
c. informal information gathering
d. ethics of secrecy

4. Design research using participant observation for a group where you are or were a member (ski club, Weight Watchers, a political party, etc.).
   a. Give the name of the group. If the name is not generally recognized, briefly describe the group's goals and functioning.
   b. Describe two categories of data that you might collect as a participant observer in this group.
   c. Discuss two possible problems with the validity of your observations as a participant observer.
   d. Discuss two possible problems of generalizing from your findings to other similar groups.
   e. Choose a group which is clearly deviant, and complete items (a) through (d) for that group. (You need not have belonged to this group.)
   f. Discuss two conflicts you might experience in your roles as a member-participant and as a participant-observer in the deviant group.
5. The following is from a participant-observation study conducted for seven months in the West End, an Italian neighborhood in Boston. Herbert Gans, the author, observed that

> while men are freely aggressive, both sexually and verbally, with a "bad" girl, they must control themselves with an inaccessible "good" girl. Among unmarried people, for example, when a "good" girl enters an all-male group, profanity and sexual talk are immediately halted, and the men seem momentarily paralyzed before they can shift conversational gears.
>
> What the men fear is their own ability at self-control. This attitude, strongest among young, unmarried people, often carries over into adulthood. The traditional Italian belief—that sexual intercourse is unavoidable when a man and a woman are by themselves—is maintained intact among second-generation West Enders. . . .
>
> Herbert J. Gans, *The Urban Villagers* (New York: Free Press, 1962), p. 49.

   a. How were Gans's observations limited by the fact that he is a male? What other personal traits might have also influenced his findings?
   b. Social scientists frequently infer motives from the behaviors they observe. What potential methodological problems are illustrated by Gans's inference that men fear "their own ability at self-control"?
   c. Select two of Gans's findings. Describe how data-collection techniques other than participant observation could have been used to support these findings.

RECOMMENDED READINGS

Becker, Howard S., and Blanche Geer
1957 "Participant Observation and Interviewing: A Comparison," *Human Organization*, 16(3):28–32.

Argues that participant observation provides researchers with data and experiences unavailable in interview settings.

Erikson, Kai T.
1967 "A Comment on Disguised Observation in Sociology," *Social Problems*, 14(Spring):366–373.

Argues that it is unethical for researchers to conceal their identities as social scientists when doing participant-observation research.

Filstead, William J. (ed.)
1970 *Qualitative Methodology: Firsthand Involvement with the Social World.* Chicago: Markham.

A sound collection of readings focused on the field worker's role, the collection and analysis of data, and problems of reliability and validity.

Whyte, William Foote
1955 *Street Corner Society: The Social Structure of an Italian Slum.* 2d ed. Chicago: Univ. of Chicago Press.

A classic participant-observation study of a poor Italian neighborhood, originally published in 1943. Contains a thorough appendix describing the research experiences of the author.

18

STRUCTURED OBSERVATIONS IN A FIELD DESIGN: THE BEHAVIOR OF CITIZENS DURING ENCOUNTERS WITH THE POLICE

GENERAL ISSUE

Field designs permit the use of structured and unstructured observations. Unlike unstructured observations, in which the categories for recording information emerge during the research, structured ones are based on a coding scheme developed prior to the collection of data. When researchers know in advance the forms of behavior they will observe and the categories they will use to code, they can establish detailed plans for recording information before they enter the field. Given these circumstances, structured observations can provide systematic, reliable data for describing the observed behavior and for testing causal hypotheses.

This chapter extends the basis for field designs established in the exploratory research on call girls and the descriptive and interpretative research done in nudist camps. The major methodological focus is on the use of *direct structured observations* as a data-collection technique in field research, while the major theoretical focus is on those social norms which govern police-citizen encounters.

THEORETICAL PROBLEM

Many social interactions occur amid conditions where it is difficult for society to enforce conformity to norms. For instance, physicians' behavior when they are with their patients is governed by professional ethics, but only on rare occasions is physician-patient behavior observed by those who have the power to enforce professional norms. Departures from these norms may therefore go unobserved and unsanctioned.

Police-citizen interaction, the subject of this chapter, represents another example of behavior which usually occurs beyond the scrutiny of the general public. Legal norms prescribe that a policeman's decision to arrest should be based on the availability of evidence and the seriousness of the offense. Since all policemen exercise discretionary power, social norms prescribe that the officer should ignore a citizen's race or social status when he is making an arrest. He should also overlook the social demeanor of a citizen, since it is not illegal to be impolite.

However, the accusations of some minority groups, some newspaper accounts, and some citizen testimony lend credibility to the argument that police are not always neutral in these matters. It must be admitted that these sources of data are themselves subject to bias. The accusations of minority groups may or may not have political ramifications. Newspaper reports frequently rely on secondhand data and may be written in a sensational manner. Self-reported experiences by citizens may only be giving expression to self-interest. As a result of these possible biases, the validity of those accounts which suggest that race, status, and behavior influence policemen's decisions on arrest are open to question. Thus, direct observation of police-citizen encounters appears to offer a useful technique for collecting data on this problem.

FIELD DESIGN

In June 1970, a research team at the University of Minnesota began a fifteen-month study.* It focused on three midwestern cities; one was a city of greater than 500,000 people, and the other two were suburbs of it. Its purpose was to investigate police in all three locations. More specifically, the project aimed to collect data about the role of citizen demeanor wherever police decided to arrest.

DATA-COLLECTION PROCEDURES: PREPARATION

Training Observers

The research team's first task was to recruit and train seven sociology graduate students so that they could effectively observe police-citizen encounters. For the first three months of the project, these observers spent

* Data reported in this chapter are based primarily upon Richard J. Lundman, "Routine Police Arrest Practices: A Commonweal Perspective," *Social Problems*, 22 (1974):127–141, and Richard J. Lundman and James C. Fox, "Maintaining Research Access in a Commonweal Bureaucracy." Paper prepared for Annual Meeting of the American Society of Criminology, Chicago, Ill., Nov. 1974.

approximately six hours a day learning techniques developed by the senior staff for observing and recording information.

As observers, the graduate students tended to see and record those elements of social interaction they personally believed important. Consequently, the training sessions emphasized the importance of a common frame of reference in that each observer would notice and record the same or similar information. To accomplish this objective, the team taught the observers how to use a common coding scheme.

To develop consistency in the use of the code and to gain some experience, observers watched and coded training films containing simulated police-citizen encounters. In order to gain further coding experience, they also watched television quiz shows, dramas, and police programs. At the conclusion of each session, observers checked and cross-checked their information. They discussed coding differences in an attempt to develop a common frame of reference.

At the termination of the three-month training period, observers were seeing and recording similar information. On the average, there was an 80 percent consistency among coders. Although there was disagreement as to 20 percent of the information observers gathered, they felt that the reliability level was high for this type of research.

Developing the Code

The coding scheme developed for recording direct observations proved complex and contained numerous components. The ability of the codes to adequately record the qualitative data being observed was crucial. Therefore, the team made a concerted effort to develop a series of codes which would work during both the collection and analysis phases of the research.

One of the coding dimensions the research team employed to measure social demeanor in police-citizen encounters consisted of a five-category, ordinal classification of behavior ranging from very polite to very impolite (see the accompanying list). These categories, developed during a seminar held in 1969, were based primarily on the writing of Erving Goffman. Goffman's categories were later replaced by three others (polite, civil, and impolite) because of difficulties in recognizing whether a specific behavior was very polite, somewhat polite, somewhat impolite, or very impolite. For purposes of analysis, civil behavior was later placed in the category of being polite. Hence the condensing of categories reduced earlier problems of inconsistency.

Category	*Definition*
1. Very polite	Speech or communicative behavior which is an attempt at subservience or flattery
2. Somewhat polite	More than usual cooperation, respect or courtesy in speech or behavior

3. Civil	Speech or behavior which is non-hostile and similar in manner and form to polite, middle-class interaction
4. Somewhat impolite	Speech and behavior which is non-aggressive, but non-compliant and which has high emotional loading
5. Very impolite	Speech or behavior which is characterized by name-calling, ridiculing, and personal vituperation

The second set of categories for measuring behavior (see the following list) was the result of observations by three members of the research team who, during the fall of 1968, were passengers in police cars. These categories were designed to code behaviors which occurred occasionally in police-citizen encounters. It was expected that some of the items would form a Guttman scale, but this did not prove to be the case.

1. Indication of solidarity, sympathy, or empathy
2. Humoring
3. Friendly humor, laughter
4. Voice raised above normal conversational level
5. Hostile and angry tone of voice
6. Verbal threat to normal freedom (e.g., "If you don't stop I'll have to arrest you.")
7. Verbal threat of physical attack
8. Territorial restraint (e.g., putting someone in the back seat of a squad car)
9. Physical restraint
10. Response to physical attack
11. Initiation of physical attack
12. Weapon (not a gun) ready for use
13. Weapon (not a gun) used
14. Gun drawn
15. Gun used

All coding categories were pretested in the field at the end of the training period. Minor revisions were made at that time.

DATA COLLECTION: IMPLEMENTATION

Gaining and Maintaining Research Access

Gaining access to the research setting was the first step in collecting data. Permission for observers to ride in patrol cars was obtained from adminis-

18.1 STRUCTURED OBSERVATION

At times, structured observation is necessary because of the complexity of the large number of observations to be recorded. However, as illustrated by the data of Table A below, structured observations also can be useful for recording simple observations when these are small in number.

Table A. Wearing of Protective Clothing by Doctors and Nursing Personnel in a TB Hospital.

	TIMES ENTERING ROOM	PERCENTAGES WEARING		
		Cap	Gown	Mask
Doctor	47	5	0	5
Professional Nurses	100	24	18	14
Aides	142	94	80	72
Students	97	100	100	100

Data for Table A were collected by Julius Roth, who was interested in the practices surrounding contagion control in a TB hospital. Roth hypothesized that the frequency with which protective clothing was worn would be negatively related to a person's position in the stratificational hierarchy.

To test this hypothesis, Roth used a simple tally sheet to record the wearing of caps, gowns, and masks by various levels of personnel in the hospital hierarchy. These records were made on ten different days (plus additional days for doctors and nurses because their numbers were smaller). To obtain a cross-section of personnel, observations were taken in three different wards with different sets of personnel, and on three work shifts in the hospital. The observational categories used were clear and reliable.

The findings in Table A suggest that the hypothesis was correct: Those whose occupations were higher in the stratification system wore protective clothing less frequently than those whose occupations were lower.

SOURCE: Adapted from Julius Roth, "Ritual and Magic in the Control of Contagion," *American Sociological Review,* 22(1957):310–314.

trators in charge of the police departments. Police chiefs in each of the three communities agreed to send explanatory memos describing the research to all precinct captains, and to sign picture identification cards for the observers. Furthermore, the research team sent representatives to all precinct roll calls in order to explain research objectives. Thus, official permission was obtained and communicated to police officers at the precinct level.

These efforts to explain the research were not completely successful. Despite attempts at explanation, observers were sometimes defined by the police as citizens who were permitted to ride in carefully chosen police cars as part of a public relations program. Since the research design called for randomly selecting police cars rather than purposive selection by the police, the observers in these instances withdrew gracefully from cars to which they were assigned. All such problems of gaining random access to cars were then resolved by the director of the research project.

Two major problems of maintaining access were also encountered. First, the project had only tenuous legitimacy in the eyes of the police. Therefore, observers tried to explain the general nature of the research, without disclosing its specific variables. Furthermore, observers would passively agree when officers made skeptical or hostile statements about the research. As a result of these tactics, observers came to be tolerated, but they were never enthusiastically welcomed.

A second problem of maintaining access was due to the difficulty of defining the field role of the observers. In the initial stages, the observers were treated as interested citizens, and observation periods began with tours of the precinct, lectures on police work, increased patrols, and apologies for lack of calls. To reduce these problems, observers attempted to emphasize the scientific nature of the project. This tactic was also unsuccessful. Ultimately, they emphasized that they were just doing a job. Policemen then no longer felt the need to make the observers' shifts more exciting or interesting. It is not known if police behavior was affected in less apparent ways.

Observing Police-Citizen Encounters

Observations occurred throughout the twelve months of data collection. Observers continued to appear at precinct stations to ride in randomly selected patrol cars. Random selection permitted statistical assessment of the representativeness of the data they ultimately collected.

Throughout their eight-hour shifts in police cars, observers attempted to minimize the impact of their presence. This was particularly difficult because they rode with police during such circumstances as antiwar protests, a police raid on a faculty member's home, and other university-related events. At the end of each shift, observers brought their coded data to research headquarters and were questioned about their experiences.

Recording Police-Citizen Interaction

While police-citizen interactions were in progress, observers coded the behavior of all participants. They used a small adding-machine-like keyboard with twelve buttons to code their observations. Each button imparted a unique signal to a tape cassette. This newly developed equipment, known as MIDCARS, could rapidly record observations, and the tapes could be placed on the computer without the need for manual translations. The equipment was also intended to minimize any disruptions caused by recording observations in other ways. Of course, identical data could have been entered on a worksheet similar to that of Figure 18-1 but would not have worked as efficiently.

18.2 A WORKSHEET FOR RECORDING OBSERVATIONS

Typically, structured observational data are recorded directly onto a worksheet using a numerical code. Thus, 1 may stand for male and 2 for female. Some number, such as 0, may be used by field supervisors to indicate that the observer forgot to code a given characteristic. Still other numbers may be used to indicate indecision on the part of the observer or the irrelevancy of the variable to be coded. Numbers are used in order to facilitate key-punching and eventual computer analysis of the data. In the research reported here, the social characteristics of persons in the police encounter situation were coded on the worksheet displayed as Figure 18-1.

DATA ANALYSIS

The 1,978 police-citizen interactions coded by the observers ranged from minor incidents to felonies—with public norms, arrest decisions, and police-citizen interactions varying greatly among the types of offenses. To assess the impact of social demeanor on outcomes of police-citizen encounters, data for one type of offense was examined by Richard J. Lundman. He selected public drunkenness (not involving a felony or a moving traffic violation) for the following two reasons:

1. There were more cases of public drunkenness than any other offense. This yielded a large number of cases for analysis.
2. Public drunkenness permits extensive discretion by police in deciding offense outcome. The courts and jails are crowded with drunken offenders and exert pressure to keep police arrests to a minimum. If social characteristics influence police action, they are likely to do so in this circumstance.

Public drunkenness accounted for 195 (approximately 10 percent) of the police-citizen encounters observed. However, only 60 (31 percent) of these contacts ended in arrest. Thus, the police were lenient in their dealings with drunken citizens. The question raised by the hypotheses, and addressed in Table 18-1, is whether this leniency is more prevalent when citizens are impolite than when they are polite.

Figure 18-1. Demographic Data Sheet Used for Each Police-Citizen Interaction.

Written Description of Interaction:

ROLE		SEX ? = 0 M = 1 F = 2	ETHNIC oth = 0 bla = 1 red = 2 whi = 3 for = 4	SES ? = 0 up = 1 mid = 2 work = 3 decl = 4	AGE ? = 0 chi = 1 ado = 2 Y.A = 3 Adu = 4 sen = 5	DK No = 0 alcoh = 1 drugs = 2 maybe = 3 comm. incoh = 4	WEAPONS none = 0 gun = 1 sharp = 2 other = 3	IDENT. ? = 0 conv = 1 mod = 2 hip = 3 oth = 4
Officers	A							
	B							
	C							
Bystanders	A							
	B							
	C							
	D							
Participants	A							
	B							
	C							
	D							

Violators	A							
	B							
	C							
	D							
Victims	A							
	B							
	C							
	D							
Complainant	A							
	B							
	C							
	D							

Outcome Code No.

Observer No.

Police No.

Table 18-1. Arrests for Polite and Impolite Drunkenness Offenders.

	POLICE DECISION		
OFFENDER BEHAVIOR	Arrest	Not Arrest	TOTAL
Polite	34	98	132
Impolite	28	35	63
			195

$Q = .40$ $\chi^2 = 6.923$ $p < .01$

SOURCE: Lundman, "Routine Police Arrest Practices," p. 135, Table 2.

Table 18-1 displays the data collected on politeness and arrest. With a chi-square (χ^2) of 6.923 and a probability less than .01, the data indicate a relationship between politeness and arrest which would occur less than one time in a hundred because of sampling error. Quick calculations show that only 26 percent (34/132) of polite offenders were arrested—while 44 percent (28/63) of impolite offenders were arrested.

These data can be used to test the null hypothesis that police arrest rates are not related to the social behavior of the person arrested. The data above are clearly inconsistent with the null hypothesis. Thus, there is evidence for rejecting the null hypothesis. Police *did* tend to favor polite offenders.

SUMMARY

This chapter has defined the term direct structured observation and illustrated how it can be used. In this instance, a research team including seven graduate student observers undertook a study of the police forces in three midwestern cities. One aspect of their research was to test the null hypothesis that a citizen's demeanor has little effect on police arrest-decisions. To do this, they focused on the norm which implies that impoliteness is not a criminal offense. They learned that police depart from this norm when their actions are not highly visible. In this study, the police arrested citizens who were drunk and impolite more frequently than those who were drunk and polite. Thus, the quantitative analysis of observational data resulted in a clear rejection of the null hypothesis.

KEY IDEAS AND CONCEPTS

code reliability
code validity
coding scheme
research access
researcher role
structured observation
unstructured observation

ISSUES AND PROBLEMS

1. Explain why structured and unstructured observation techniques usually differ with respect to
   a. flexibility in coding data
   b. flexibility in modifying hypotheses during the course of the research
   c. the collection of quantitative and qualitative data
   d. research goals (i.e., descriptive versus hypothesis-testing objectives)
2. People in different positions often observe and interpret a social phenomenon differently. Policemen and graduate student researchers, for instance, may interpret an event differently because they possess dissimilar attitudes and occupy disparate roles. In this chapter, the graduate student observers used the code categories in the list on p. 274 to record the behaviors of citizens. Policemen might have interpreted the same behaviors in different ways.

   Select two code categories from the list on p. 274 where police and graduate student observers could interpret a behavioral act differently. Illustrate your choices with examples.
3. It can be hypothesized that a teacher's likelihood of calling on a student varies with the student's classroom behavior and personal appearance.
   a. Construct a code sheet to record the behaviors and appearances of students seeking to be called upon.
   b. Attempt to use this code sheet in one class.
   c. Describe the limitations of the code. Describe its strengths.
   d. Revise the code, based on your experience, and use it in two courses.
   e. Evaluate the problems of your revised code sheet.
   f. Could further revisions eliminate the problems of such structured categories? Explain your answer.
4. Albert Wessen studied the relationships among workers in hospitals.* As part of his study, he wished to know the extent to which people talked exclusively to people holding a similar or identical occupation. Wessen believed there was relatively little communication among the members of the different occupational groups. He used the following procedure to measure communication between members of the different occupational groups:

   > Personnel on two units—one semi-private and one "charity" ward—were observed over a period of thirty hours (scattered through various parts of the day and over a period of several days). Each time two individuals were seen in conversation, it was noted who was speaking to whom. If there were more than two individuals in the conversation, the members of the group were divided into pairs. Thus, if two nurses and one doctor talked together, it was assumed that three conversations were taking place: one between the two nurses and two between a doctor and a nurse. Each conversation observed was designated as a single unit except that if it was observed to last more than three minutes, a second unit was scored—and so on every three minutes.

* Albert F. Wessen, "Hospital Ideology and Communication Between Ward Personnel" in E. Gartly Jaco, *Patients, Physicians and Illness.* 2d ed. (New York: Free Press, 1972) p. 319.

Wessen's results were as follows:

Table 18-A. Communication of Hospital Workers with Members of Their Own Occupations and with Members of Other Occupations.

	OCCUPATIONS (IN PERCENTAGES)		
	Doctors	Nurses	Others
Interaction with own group	74	62	62
Interaction with other groups	26	38	38
Total	100	100	100
N[a]	(228)	(562)	(441)

SOURCE: Wessen, p. 320.
[a] Total number of conversations observed involving members of the group

a. What percent of physician conversations were held with other physicians? What percent with nonphysicians?
b. Wessen's data-collection techniques did not allow him to study the content of the conversations, for example, to distinguish social conversations from job-related ones. Describe two techniques he might have used to collect such data. Evaluate the strengths and weaknesses of each technique.
c. Wessen used multiple data-collection techniques. One of his data sources was a questionnaire administered to doctors, nurses, and others working in the hospital. His questionnaire indicated that the attitudes of occupational groups differed from one another in a number of important job-related issues. He concluded that differences in beliefs resulted from the fact that the groups did not have sufficient communication with each other to arrive at similar ones. Name one other explanation of differences in attitudes. How might data on the content of intergroup communication have supported Wessen's conclusion? How might such data have failed to support his conclusion?

RECOMMENDED READINGS

Bales, Robert F.
1950 *Interaction Process Analysis: A Method for the Study of Small Groups.* Reading, Mass.: Addison-Wesley.

One of the most widely cited coding systems for recording interaction, usually based on coding of sentences. There are twelve coding categories, having titles such as "shows agreement," "shows tension," and "gives opinion."

Cancian, Francesca M.
1964 "Interaction Patterns in Zinacanteco Families," *American Sociological Review*, 29(Aug.):540–550.

Structured observations in Mayan families to record interactions among family members. For each pair of interacting persons the coding scheme could record affection, dominance, and rate of interaction.

Habenstein, Robert W.
1970 *Pathways to Data: Field Methods for Studying Ongoing Social Organizations.* Chicago: Aldine-Atherton.

Discussions by experienced researchers of field research in businesses, hospitals, legislatures, and other organizational settings.

Reiss, Albert J., Jr.
1971 "Systematic Observation of Natural Social Phenomena," pp. 3–33 in Herbert Costner (ed.), *Sociological Methodology 1971.* San Francisco: Jossey-Bass.

Explains problem selection, sampling, instruments, recording, access, reliability, rapport, and other aspects of structured observations in field research.

PART EIGHT

Unobtrusive Designs

19

THE UNOBTRUSIVE MEASURE OF A DEPENDENT VARIABLE: INNOVATION AND FRIENDSHIP PATTERNS OF PHYSICIANS

GENERAL ISSUE

The very procedures of data collection and measurement have the potential to alter the phenomena being studied. This potential is greatest in studies where researchers are directly or indirectly interacting with people. Thus, studies employing questionnaires, interviews, or participant observation techniques are especially susceptible.

Conversely, data-collection and measurement procedures which circumvent direct or indirect interaction with subjects are most likely to reduce or eliminate this undesired effect. In general, procedures which skirt such interaction use information unintentionally generated as a by-product of everyday behavior. Such unintentional information, referred to in the literature as *unobtrusive data*, falls into three main categories: physical traces, concealed observations, and written records.*

Physical Traces

Physical traces include the wearing down of, or the addition to, physical objects as a result of their use. Changes in physical objects therefore may serve as indices of the social phenomenon being studied. Examples

* Eugene J. Webb, Donald T. Campbell, Richard D. Schwartz, and Lee Sechrist, *Unobtrusive Measures: Non-Reactive Research in the Social Sciences* (Chicago: Rand McNally, 1966).

include garbage deposited in a city dump, which could provide a clue to consumption patterns, or wear and tear on books in a public library, which might furnish clues to people's reading tastes.

Concealed Observations

Concealed observations refer to observations recorded without the knowledge of the subjects being observed. Examples include observing children at play in a park and people betting at a racetrack.

Written Records

Written records include personal documentation and information recorded by such bureaucracies as government, industry, and schools. Examples also include the letters and diaries of immigrants, which hold clues to the assimilation process, and marriage and birth records, which can provide insight into the frequency of premarital pregnancy.

The collection and use of unobtrusive as well as obtrusive data raise both ethical and scientific questions. Since unobtrusive data are obtained without the consent of those being studied, questions of ethics and legality must be carefully considered beforehand. For scientific reasons, unobtrusive data must be examined carefully for reliability and validity.

Occasionally, such data may be sufficient in themselves. More frequently, however, they are used in conjunction with other types of information. The research reported here combines the use of written records and data from interviews.

THEORETICAL PROBLEM: INNOVATIONS AND THEIR ADOPTION

Social scientists have long been interested both in the conditions giving rise to innovation and the processes through which it diffuses to society. Although the general conditions and processes are well understood, there is much to be learned about the influence of specific variables.

New ideas or products are not adopted simply because they occur. Indeed, before any innovation can be adopted, knowledge of its existence and positive opinions concerning its worth must be spread by its creators to the population of possible users. The adoption of birth control techniques, for instance, can be traced over time across geographical areas as people learned of them by word of mouth and from formal communication networks. Analogous diffusions occur when voters make decisions about political candidates and consumers evaluate new products. In each case, persons must be informed about and convinced of the worth of an innovation before they adopt it.

The adoption and spread of medical innovations in the health community are of special interest to students of diffusion. Two factors make the study of these innovations especially valuable for the development of diffusion theory. First, professional norms predispose the health community to adopt medical innovations. Second, medical innovations occur frequently, and, consequently, the health community is confronted with the need to select from an overabundance of competing innovations.

This chapter reports on the diffusion processes generated by the adoption and spread of a new drug in the medical community. The methodological focus is on the use of *unobtrusive measures* for measuring diffusion in conjunction with the use of a survey interview.

Research Design

The general objective of the research reported here was to obtain information on the social processes which occurred between the initial trials of a new drug by a few physicians and its final use by the medical community.* Before the team of social scientists from Columbia University's Bureau of Applied Social Research embarked upon a full field study, however, they conducted a pilot study in a small New England community which had only thirty physicians. This pilot study helped develop and refine the research methodology eventually used in the full study.

19.1 PRETESTS AND PILOT STUDIES

Pretests and pilot studies are responses to the recognition that any research, no matter how well conceived, may encounter unforeseen problems.

Pretests have narrow goals and are generally restricted to an assessment of data-collection procedures. They are most frequently employed in studies involving the use of interviews or questionnaires. In a sense, the instruments are tried out to determine if they will produce the correct information. Problems of question bias, clarity, and ambiguity can be detected and corrected prior to the full collection of data. Pretests are also helpful in determining the usefulness of coding schemes in observational studies and the appropriateness of experimental designs.

Pilot studies are miniature rehearsals of large-scale research projects involving significant commitments of time, money, and personnel. They are particularly useful in highly structured research projects which would be difficult to change in the course of the study. Mistakes or weaknesses in research design, data-collection procedures, and measurement instruments would be costly and perhaps uncorrectable in large projects requiring standardized data. In this circumstance, a pilot study which permits an assessment and modification of design, collection, and measurement instruments is invaluable.

* James S. Coleman, Elihu Katz, and Herbert Menzel, *Medical Innovation: A Diffusion Study* (Indianapolis: Bobbs-Merrill, 1966).

Based upon the experience gained during the pilot study, the team modified the research design and sought data from physicians located in several cities. In order to reduce the cost of research and to eliminate possible regional differences in medical practice, the researchers restricted their search to cities located in the northeastern quarter of the United States. They sought neighboring cities which differed from one another in hospital facilities and population, but which were not under the influence of a single, large medical center. Three different sets of cities met these criteria. One set, containing four cities, was arbitrarily chosen as the research site.

Although the project involved collecting diverse information in order to assess several hypotheses, only one will be discussed here. The specific hypothesis is that friendship is an important intervening variable influencing the rate of diffusion of medical innovations in medical communities. The innovation under consideration was a new drug identified for research purposes only as "gammanym."

Measurement Instruments

Two instruments were necessary for measuring the variables under consideration. One was required to estimate the social integration (i.e., friendship) of a physician with other physicians. The second was needed to measure the diffusion of the medical innovation, the drug gammanym.

To assess social integration, the research team developed an interview schedule for use in the collection of data from physicians. Each physician interviewed was asked three sociometric questions: (1) To whom did he most often turn for advice and information? (2) During the course of an ordinary week, with whom did he most often discuss his cases? (3) Who were the friends, among his colleagues, whom he saw most often socially? The names of three doctors were requested in response to each of these questions. This made it possible to trace the interconnections among physicians. Social integration for each physician, as operationalized by friendship patterns, was determined by the number of nominations each received from colleagues. It should be noted that these questions, which so often are used merely to measure the values or the attitudes of those being interviewed, were here employed to measure the structure of relationships.

Those who prescribed the drug gammanym for their patients soon after it first became available were defined to be more innovative than those who prescribed it at a later date or who had not prescribed it by the conclusion of the study. A number of approaches for measuring a physician's innovativeness were considered and rejected. Each of these involved having physicians report their own behavior. For instance, one approach would have encouraged physicians to report when they first began prescribing gammanym. However, the research team realized that physicians would have been unlikely to recall accurately when they first began prescribing it.

Also possible was a series of interviews or mail-back postcards which required doctors to record their use of the drug. The very act of repeated measurements had the potential of stimulating use of the drug. Another alternative, that of asking physicians whether or not they were innovators, was rejected because it raised the problem of accurate self-perception.

For these reasons, the research team sought an unobtrusive measure of physicians' behavior. An ideal one appeared to be the prescription records maintained by those pharmacies serving this group of physicians. The team believed that such records would accurately indicate the data and frequency of specific prescriptions of the drug, but, at the same time, would have no unintended effects upon behavior.

Sampling Physicians and Pharmacy Records

The four communities selected for study contained 356 physicians in private practice. To obtain a sample, physicians were divided into four categories: general practitioners, internists, pediatricians, and others. The first three groups constituted those most likely to prescribe gammanym for their patients. Consequently, the team attempted to interview the entire 148 physicians who fell into these three groups. They successfully interviewed 125, or 85 percent, of these during the 6 weeks of data collection. This response rate was unusually high, given the busy schedules of physicians and the general difficulty of obtaining interviews with persons of high professional status.

The fourth group consisted of 208 physicians. Of these, 103 had been referred by the 125 physicians initially interviewed. The team interviewed a total of 228 physicians and calculated social integration scores for each.

In the four cities there were eighty-four pharmacies serving the medical community. Cooperation in searching prescription records was obtained from sixty-four of them. Although twenty pharmacies refused to cooperate, the research team concluded that only two of these twenty were likely to have a substantial trade in the drug being studied. Thus, the team decided that not having access to the prescription records of these two would not introduce significant error. The research therefore proceeded without their cooperation.

The research team attempted to record each physician's use of the drug gammanym from its introduction in the community to a point some sixteen months later. Because of the large number of prescriptions filled by these pharmacies during the sixteen-month period, the research team recorded all prescriptions written on a sample of days during each month. Three consecutive sample days of prescriptions were recorded for each month of the sixteen-month period for each of the sixty-four pharmacies. To cover a workweek, a Monday, Tuesday, Wednesday period was sampled one month, and a Thursday, Friday, Saturday period was sampled the next.

DATA ANALYSIS

The new drug being studied was quickly tried by many physicians. Table 19-1 indicates that, by the end of the first six months of the drug's availability, 48 percent of the general practitioners, internists, and pediatricians had prescribed it. Of course, 52 percent of the group had not yet prescribed it. In terms of the research project, the interesting question was whether these two groups differed as to their social integration into the community of physicians.

Table 19-1. Frequency and Percent of Physicians Prescribing Gammanym at Least Once.

MONTHS AFTER DRUG AVAILABILITY	NUMBER AND PERCENT OF PHYSICIANS PRESCRIBING DRUG DURING TWO-MONTH PERIOD		CUMULATIVE PERCENT PRESCRIBING DRUG
	(N)	(%)	(%)
1–2	19	15	15
3–4	19	15	30
5–6	23	18	48
7–8	21	17	65
9–10	6	5	70
11–12	6	5	75
13–14	9	7	82
15–16	4	3	85
	107[a]	85	

SOURCE: Coleman, et al., "Medical Innovation," p. 26, Figure 1.

[a] This total excludes the eighteen physicians who did not prescribe the drug gammanym during the sixteen-month period according to pharmacy records.

Based on the nominations provided by the 228 interviewed physicians, the team constructed a sociogram of social integration. This sociogram for one city is portrayed in Figure 19-1. There an arrow from one doctor to another indicates that the first nominated the second in his response to one or more of the three questions in the interview schedule. Thus, physician 24 in the lower left corner of Figure 19-1 nominated physicians 04, 07, and 19. Physician 04 reciprocated by nominating physician 24. In addition, it can be observed that physician 08 nominated physician 24.

Table 19-2 tests the effect of friendship on drug diffusion. In this table, physicians are grouped as isolates, those who received no friendship choices; integrated, those who were chosen one or two times; and well-integrated, those who were chosen three or more times.

This table indicates that the group of physicians which was best integrated socially was also the group which tried the new drug earliest. For

Figure 19-1. Friendship Network in City D. Includes interviewed physicians, plus the three others named by them as friends (slashed circles).

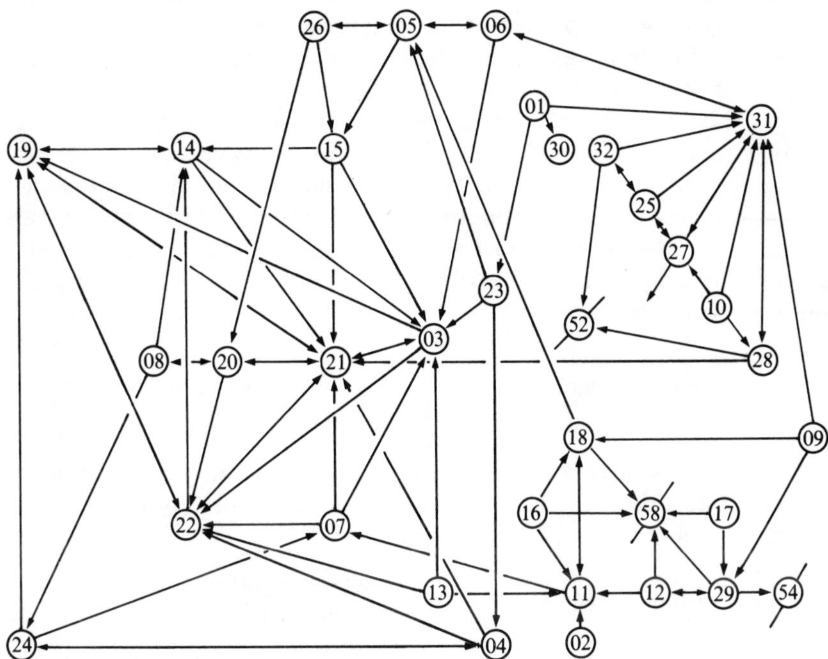

SOURCE: Coleman, et al., "Medical Innovation," p. 78, Figure 18.

Table 19-2. Cumulative Percents of Isolated, Integrated, and Well-Integrated Physicians Trying New Drug at Least Once.

AT END OF MONTH	ISOLATED	INTEGRATED	WELL-INTEGRATED
2	8	20	15
4	19	36	36
6	31	51	70
8	42	66	91
10	46	70	94
12	65	71	94
14	76	76	94
16	83	82	96
	(N = 36)	(N = 56)	(N = 33)

SOURCE: Coleman, et al., "Medical Innovation," p. 26, Figure 1.

instance, six months after the drug became available, twice the percentage of well-integrated physicians had tried the drug as had isolates (70 v. 31 percent). The physicians designated as being somewhat integrated were in an intermediate position (51 percent). Moreover, at the end of the sixteen-month period, only 4 percent of the well-integrated doctors had not tried the drug. Eighteen percent of the somewhat integrated physicians and 17 percent of the isolates did not try gammanyn.

How should these data be interpreted? Do they show that, in this case study, social integration influenced the diffusion process? Responses to one of the questions in the interview schedule indicated that half of these physicians enjoyed talking about their work on social occasions. Consequently, those who were most socially integrated may have learned of gammanyn and prescribed it earlier than the others. The causal model in this case would be

Social integration into the medical community → Innovativeness in drug use

However, two alternative models also are consistent with the data presented. First, there is the possibility that being an innovative doctor makes one more attractive to colleagues:

Innovativeness → Social integration into the medical community

Second, there is the strong possibility that doctors who are most competent professionally are also likely to be innovative. This, in turn, seems to lead to their having a large circle of friends. The variables in this model are as follows:

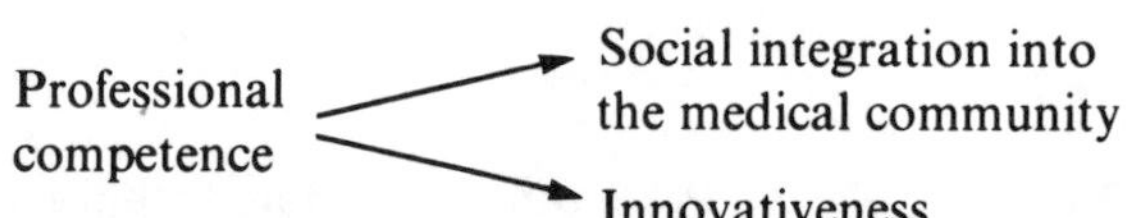

Thus, while friendship is implicated in the diffusion process, the causal relationship among variables remains unclear. The researchers addressed this idea and concluded that there was some evidence to support the first model.

SUMMARY

To investigate the social processes of diffusion, a research team studied physicians in three communities. They traced the diffusion process by examining prescription records of sixty-four pharmacies. Social integration, as measured by friendship patterns, appeared to be the primary variable explaining whether local physicians were early or later adopters of the new drug gammanym.

The research design incorporated several novel features. First, the research team utilized a pilot study. This study revealed several weaknesses in the original design which the team corrected before committing resources to the full field study. Second, the research team avoided certain reliability and validity measurement problems by using an unobtrusive measure of diffusion, drug prescriptions. Third, the team presented a novel use of sample survey techniques by constructing a measure of social relationships (a structural variable) from interview data.

KEY IDEAS AND CONCEPTS

concealed observation
model
physical traces
pilot study
pretest
sociogram
unobtrusive measures
written records

ISSUES AND PROBLEMS

1. Define "unobtrusive measures." Under what circumstances are they likely to be most useful to a researcher? Under what circumstances are they likely to be least useful?
2. List two benefits that might come from pretesting a questionnaire.
3. Many drugs are introduced each year in the United States. Explain how findings from the pilot study might have influenced researchers in selecting the specific drug reported in this chapter.
4. Pharmacy records are not normally open to public scrutiny. Explain how the pilot study for the research reported in this chapter might have aided in gaining access to such records.
5. Suggest how a researcher might unobtrusively collect data on
   a. the amount of alcohol consumed in a "dry" town (e.g., through physical traces);
   b. the effects of a recession on the reading habits in a community (e.g., through written records);
   c. popularity of competing political candidates who come to town on separate days to deliver speeches (e.g., through concealed observations).
6. Evaluate the validity and reliability of each of the unobtrusive techniques described in question 5.
7. The following table reports the length of marriages that ended in divorce for selected years.
   a. Draw a conclusion from the data in Table 19-A.
   b. State two different hypotheses which might explain the reported changes between 1950 and 1960.

c. Attitudes are often inferred from behaviors that are unobtrusively measured. For instance, one could infer from these data that the attitudes toward divorce did not change very much between 1960 and 1969. Can these written records provide unambiguous data about attitudes toward divorce? Explain your answer.

Table 19-A. Median Duration of Marriages Ending in Divorce During Selected Years.

YEAR	MEDIAN DURATION
1950	5.3 years
1960	7.1 years
1969	6.9 years

SOURCE: U.S. Bureau of the Census, *Statistical Abstract of the U.S.* 94th ed. (Washington, D.C.: Government Printing Office, 1973), Table 90.

RECOMMENDED READINGS

Blau, Peter M.
1955 *The Dynamics of Bureaucracy.* Chicago: Univ. of Chicago Press.

Used productivity records maintained by a bureaucracy as unobtrusive data. Also illustrates multiple data collection techniques using structured observations of interaction among personnel, and interviewing in respondents' homes.

Burch, Philip H., Jr.
1972 *The Managerial Revolution Reassessed: Family Control in America's Largest Corporations.* Lexington, Mass.: Heath.

An example of unobtrusive measurement using great quantities of readily available financial data to determine whether control of large corporations has shifted from owners to managers.

Menzel, Herbert, James S. Coleman, and Elihu Katz
1959 "Dimensions of Being 'Modern' in Medical Practice," *Journal of Chronic Diseases*, 9:20–40.

A further example of the combined use of interview responses and prescription records to address the question of ways in which early gammanym users may have been more innovative.

Webb, Eugene J., Donald T. Campbell, Richard D. Schwartz, and Lee Sechrist
1966 *Unobtrusive Measures: Non-Reactive Research in the Social Sciences.* Chicago: Rand McNally.

Describes and advocates the use of a wide range of imaginative, unobtrusive measures. Many require low levels of time and money to produce substantial amounts of data.

20

CONTENT ANALYSIS AS AN UNOBTRUSIVE DATA-ANALYSIS PROCEDURE: ADVERTISEMENTS FOR A MARRIAGE PARTNER BY AN IMMIGRANT GROUP

GENERAL ISSUE

Unobtrusive data serve many research purposes. These range from direct measurement of the frequency or duration of an event to indirect measurement of subjective phenomena such as motives, attitudes, or values. Whether the procedures involve direct or indirect measurement, the analysis of recorded information falls within the broad rubric of *content analysis*.

All types of recorded information are potential sources of unobtrusive data. Personal documents such as letters and diaries, and public materials such as newspapers and agency reports, are especially valuable. These materials may be historical or contemporary and, when appropriately analyzed, may provide rich sources of information about individuals or groups which is not otherwise available.

This chapter introduces some of the procedures and techniques employed in content analysis. Their application is to an analysis of the spouse-wanted classified advertisements which appeared in a New York newspaper in an earlier era.

Love, Marriage, and Spouse Selection

Americans typically think of love as a prelude to marriage. They generally believe persons who are in love should marry, and married persons no

20.1 CONTENT ANALYSIS

Content analysis involves coding, tabulating, and analyzing existing data. The intent of analysis may be either quantitative or qualitative. That is, the analysis may be directed toward determining the time, frequency, or duration of an event, or it may be directed toward more subjective information such as motives, attitudes, or values. Certain studies require a combination of quantitative and qualitative analyses.

Once the research problem and hypotheses have been specified, the development of appropriate codes is required. Sometimes the codes are based on the appearance of specific words, while in others they are related to broader concepts. Codes should be so constructed that the categories closely approximate the meaning contained in the original communication. This reduces the likelihood of erroneous interpretations at the data-analysis stage. The choice of code categories is perhaps the most important decision undertaken in content analysis.

Coding categories may take many forms. For instance, one may tabulate

1. *The number of occurrences of a symbol* (e.g., the frequency with which occupation was mentioned in a marriage advertisement).
2. *The prominence of a symbol* (e.g., whether occupation was mentioned before or after other characteristics).

longer in love should divorce. In this view, economic and social considerations play an insignificant role in spouse selection. Indeed, it is considered either poor taste or wicked to consider social position or wealth as primary factors in the selection of a marriage partner.

In many societies, however, marriage is a means for establishing a relationship between family units. Family reputation, wealth, political power, and social rank thus figure prominently in selecting a spouse. Even within American society, there appears to be discreet consideration of these factors by persons contemplating marriage. Their importance, however, may vary with a group's position in society.

Social scientist Emil Bend examined the importance of socioeconomic and personality characteristics in marriage partner preferences of eastern European Jewish immigrants.* His research, utilizing the techniques of content analysis, is reported here.

* Emil Bend, "Marriage Offers in a Yiddish Newspaper," *American Journal of Sociology*, 58(1952):60–66. This paper was prepared when the author was a junior in college. He noted this in a private communication to emphasize that students can produce publishable research.

3. *The attitude toward a symbol* (e.g., whether an attitude expressed about an occupation was positive, neutral, or negative).
4. *The intensity of feelings about a symbol* (e.g., whether an occupation was mildly or strongly preferred).

Content analysis can provide a basis for inference. Three types of inference, for instance, may be drawn from content-analytic data:

1. *Trend inferences.* Such inferences relate to changes over time in the quantity, prominence, attitude, and intensity of feeling about a symbol (e.g., changes in the quantity and the nature of references to occupation between 1935 and 1950).
2. *Covariation inferences.* Such inferences are based on the joint occurrence in two or more symbols contained in the material being analyzed (e.g., how occupational characteristics are related to educational ones).
3. *Causal inferences.* Such inferences are based on perceived relationships between the environment and the use of a symbol (e.g., how changes in the economic conditions of a group influence the references to occupation).

RESEARCH DESIGN

During the latter part of the nineteenth century and the early decades of the twentieth, a large number of Jews migrated from Russia and other areas of eastern Europe to the United States. Yiddish was the language of Jews in eastern Europe, and a Yiddish-language newspaper, *The Day*, emerged to serve their needs. This paper, published in New York City, contained a classified spouse-wanted column. Such marriage advertisements were placed by individuals (not by marriage bureaus) seeking potential spouses. This form of spouse selection was considered quite acceptable and continued until at least the 1950s.

In their ads, persons seeking a spouse specified the characteristics of desired partners which were most important to them. Two excerpts from actual advertisements illustrate the types of characteristics frequently mentioned: "Parents seek physician for pretty daughter . . ." and "Intelligent young lady . . . seeks doctor or businessman." Bend sought to determine if the value preferences stated for spouses varied with time. Specifically, he entertained two hypotheses:

1. Socioeconomic characteristics will be more important in the period immediately following immigration than they will be at a later period.

2. Personal characteristics will be less important in the period immediately following immigration than they will be at a later period.

DATA COLLECTION

To test these and related hypotheses, Bend undertook a content analysis of the spouse-wanted columns appearing in *The Day*. He selected the years 1935 and 1950 as representative of the periods immediately following, and some time distant from, the era of immigration. To reduce the number of ads to be analyzed, he drew a random sample of fifty advertisements placed by males and fifty advertisements placed by females during the months of November and December for each of these years. An examination of these yielded ten mutually exclusive codes for tabulating the contents of each ad. This inductively developed coding scheme is presented in the list following.

Characteristic

1. Appearance (e.g., physical features, attractiveness, etc.)
2. Character (e.g., intelligence, temperament, personality, etc.)
3. Educational attainment
4. Wealth
5. Age
6. Occupation
7. Background (e.g., information pertaining to family, place of residence, etc.)
8. Marital state (e.g., previous marriage, children, etc.)
9. Business connections
10. Jewishness

Each advertisement was searched to determine whether the characteristics were present or absent. If present, they were given a sequence number indicating their location in the advertisement. Thus, the first characteristic mentioned, if present, was given a one, the second characteristic mentioned, a two, and so on. Only the first five characteristics mentioned in the ad were coded. Limiting data collection to the first five traits did not appear to appreciably distort the frequency of cited characteristics.

DATA ANALYSIS

For purposes of analysis, Bend assumed that the first characteristic mentioned in an advertisement was more important than the second which, in turn, was more important than the third, and so forth. Since he rated the characteristics on a scale of five to one, five points were given to the first-mentioned characteristic, four to the second, and so on. This arbitrary assignment of weights served his next objective, ranking in order of importance the characteristics for 1935 and 1950.

The scores calculated in this manner are shown in columns B, D, F, and H of Table 20-1. These data are then converted to ordinal scales in columns C, E, G, and I so that the relative importance of traits can be determined. A rank of 1 indicates that a trait received the highest score for husband (wife) preference in the specified year, a rank of 2 that it received the second highest score for that year, and so forth.

As hypothesized, socioeconomic considerations in spouse selection were quite important in the 1935 advertisements for husbands. The males' occupation (column B) indicates a score of 136, equal to the score for character and exceeding all other traits. The occupations most mentioned were either in the professions or in business. Background was socioeconomically important since it included Americanization (connoting successful adaptation to American economic realities), family characteristics, and place of residence (also suggesting financial success). It is clear that women seeking husbands through the newspaper were concerned with the socioeconomic status of a potential husband, particularly his occupation.

For men seeking wives in 1935, occupation was a less-important consideration, earning a score of only 24. Other SES related considerations—wealth (63), background (42), and business connections (40)—were important, reflecting the traditional financial roles of wives.

20.2 MOTIVATIONAL INFERENCES FROM SOCIAL SCIENCE DATA

It is a common practice for social scientists to infer motivations from the overt behaviors that they study. For instance, when this study clearly demonstrated that men seeking wives emphasized different socioeconomic characteristics than did women seeking husbands, the following could be inferred: men were not seeking financial security by pursuing women with good jobs because doing so might undermine the male's dominant position in the family. Rather, men were seeking financial security by pursuing women whose wealth and connections would enhance the males' own careers. This type of inference, while reasonable, should nevertheless be recognized as conjecture, and should be weighed accordingly.

What were advertisers seeking in spouses in the later period represented by the year 1950? Data in Table 20-1 indicate that personal traits received prominent attention in that year. For husbands and wives, character and age were most important. Nonetheless, women seeking husbands were concerned with socioeconomic factors as measured by wealth (49), occupation (46), and background (26). Men seeking wives were concerned with appearance (100), background (31), and occupation (17). In 1950, personal traits were considered most important by both prospective husbands and wives, but socioeconomic characteristics were meaningful too, particularly in the evaluation of potential husbands.

Table 20-1. Desired Traits for Spouses—1935 and 1950.

TRAIT	1935				1950			
	Traits Desired for Husbands		Traits Desired for Wives		Traits Desired for Husbands		Traits Desired for Wives	
	Score	*Rank*[a]	*Score*	*Rank*	*Score*	*Rank*	*Score*	*Rank*
(A)	(B)	(C)	(D)	(E)	(F)	(G)	(H)	(I)
Occupation	136	1.5	24	7	46	4	17	6
Character	136	1.5	124	1	141	1	142	1
Age	88	3	58	4	120	2	95	3
Background	29	4	42	5	26	6	31	5
Looks	15	5	83	2	32	5	100	2
Marital state	8	6	—	10	7	9	—	9
Business connections	2	7	40	6	—	10	—	9
Wealth	—	9	63	3	49	3	40	4
Formal education	—	9	2	8	18	7	—	9
Jewishness	—	9	2	9	12	8	6	7

SOURCE: Bend, "Marriage Offers," pp. 63–64, Tables 5–8.

[a] Tied positions received the same rank score.

DATA INFERENCES

The issue raised by the hypotheses was whether socioeconomic and personal characteristics differed in importance between 1935 and 1950. To evaluate this, Table 20-2 was constructed to indicate changes in rank. This was accomplished by subtracting rank in the later year from that in the earlier. For instance, the occupations of potential husbands held a rank of 1.5 in 1935 and 4.0 in 1950, so the difference is a change of −2.5. Occupation of potential husbands declined 2.5 ranks between 1935 and 1950.

Table 20-2. Changes in Ranking of Desired Trait of Spouses—Rank in 1935 Minus 1950 (1935 ranks are in parentheses).

TRAIT	TRAITS DESIRED FOR HUSBANDS		TRAITS DESIRED FOR WIVES	
Occupation[a]	(1.5)	−2.5	(7)	+1
Character	(1.5)	+.5	(1)	no change
Age	(3)	+1	(4)	+1
Background[a]	(4)	−2	(5)	no change
Appearance	(5)	no change	(2)	no change
Marital status	(6)	−3	(10)	+1
Business connections[a]	(7)	−3	(6)	−3
Wealth[a]	(8)	+6	(3)	−1
Formal education	(9)	+2	(8)	−1
Jewishness	(10)	+1	(9)	+2

[a] Reflecting SES (socioeconomic status).

A review of Table 20-2 leads to the following conclusions about differences between 1935 and 1950: For potential husbands, most socioeconomic characteristics were less important in 1950, as evidenced by the negative scores for occupation, background, and business connections. However, wealth did make a dramatic gain. Personal traits such as character, age, appearance, and marital status either were higher in 1950 or held their rank. The inference that can be drawn from these differences is that Jewish women seeking husbands through newspaper advertisements were generally less interested in the finances of potential spouses in 1950, and more interested in personal traits.

Men's preferences for wives were consistent with the foregoing, but produced less clear differences between the two years. Decreased emphasis was placed on wealth and business connections in 1950, suggesting that socioeconomic considerations were less important. However, occupation of potential wives was given a slightly higher rank in 1950, and background retained its rank. The personal traits of character, appearance, age, and Jewishness remained high or increased in emphasis. The inference that can be drawn from the data is that men seeking spouses through these advertisements in 1950 had less of an interest in socioeconomic factors and a greater interest in personal traits than had men in 1935.

The data thus suggest that emphasis on socioeconomic factors in spouse selection was higher in a representative early year than in a representative later one; and emphasis on personal traits was lower in the earlier year than the later. Does this indicate that marriage preferences are related to time elapsed following immigration? Not necessarily. As explained previously in this text, a theory never can be proven true. One can only show that the theory is consistent with available data, *and* that no other plausible explanations are equally consistent with them. In this case, there are at least two alternative plausible explanations of the data.

1. Social variables other than those being studied had changed, and had caused the observed differences. Marital values in this subculture may have undergone a temporary change, due to changes in the mass media, which deemphasized socioeconomic considerations and emphasized personal traits. Figure 20-1 portrays this possible temporary change in its simplest form. The data for 1935 and 1950 represent actual statistics, based on summing male and female scores for both socioeconomically related traits

Figure 20-1. Actual Total Preference Scores, 1935 and 1950; and Hypothetical Total Preference Scores, 1920 and 1965.

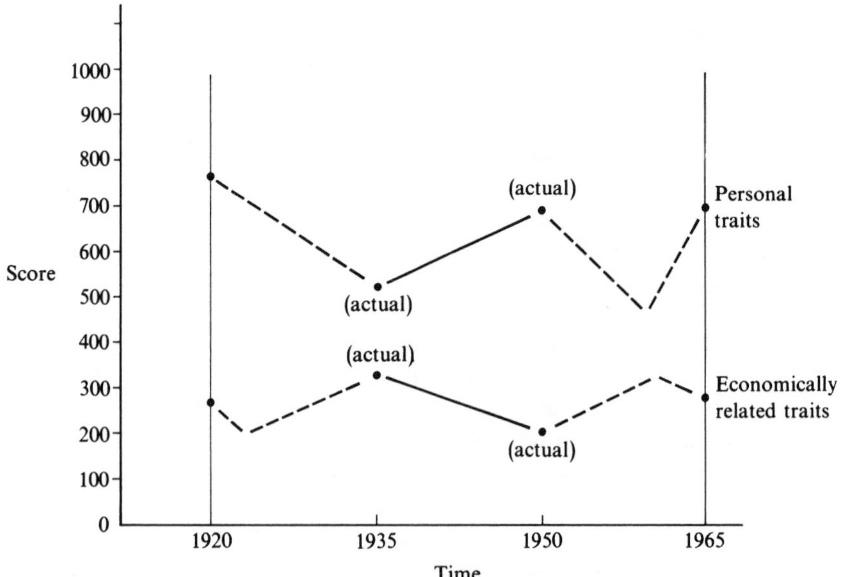

and personal ones.* The data for 1920 and 1965 are hypothetical and assume other forces altered the direction of change after 1950. In fact, the hypothetical data suggest the absence of any long-term trend. The content analysis presented in this chapter does not preclude this plausible alternative explanation.

2. The population being studied had changed, resulting in the observed differences. For instance, consider the following possibilities:

a. The newspaper (while retaining its name and basic nature) lost some readership groups and added others with different values.
b. The entire Yiddish-speaking population absorbed some dominant American values emphasizing personal traits during the 15 years between 1935 and 1950. Conversely, values of post-World War II immigrants differed from values of prewar immigrants.

Until these alternatives are explored and rejected, one can only state that marital values as reflected in advertisements were different in 1935 and 1950. These findings are consistent with an explanation that relates observed differences in values to known differences in elapsed time since immigration—but they are also consistent with other explanations which have yet to be tested.

SUMMARY

A content analysis was performed to collect data on criteria for spouse selection in two time periods. Ten coding categories were used to tabulate the relative frequency and importance of socioeconomic and personal traits. Results of the content analysis suggest that criteria had indeed changed, although different inferences can be drawn from the findings.

KEY IDEAS AND CONCEPTS

causal inference
coding scheme
content analysis
covariation inference
motivational inference
mutually exclusive categories
personal documents
qualitative data
quantitative data
trend inferences
unobtrusive data

* For instance, the 1935 score for economically related traits equals occupation (136 + 24) plus background (29 + 42) plus business connections (2 + 40) plus wealth (0 + 63), for a total score of 336.

ISSUES AND PROBLEMS

1. Describe the research circumstances when content analysis might be more useful than interviews, questionnaires, and observations.
2. Explain how a content analysis of suicide notes differs from careful reading of such materials. Develop codes for a content analysis of
   a. the stated reasons for the suicide;
   b. the suicide victim's attitudes toward persons mentioned in the note.
3. Complete a content analysis of one of the following:
   a. the social characteristics of the victims of violence in four television police shows;
   b. the issues discussed in twenty letters to the editor of your local newspaper.
   Discuss the strengths and weaknesses of your codes.
4. Table 20-A is based upon a content analysis of a leading German newspaper for the years of direct American involvement in World War II (1941–1945), and the years immediately preceding the war. The table contains an analysis of attitudes toward the United States expressed in editorials of that paper. For each year, the hostile and nonhostile references toward the United States are presented as percents of all references to it.

Table 20-A. Hostile and Nonhostile References as Percents of All References to the United States, in a Prestigious German Newspaper (*Volkischer Beobachter*), 1938–1945

YEAR	PERCENT OF REFERENCES THAT WERE Hostile	Nonhostile	TOTAL
1938	0	100	100
1939	0	100	100
1940	0	100	100
1941	60	40	100
1942	55	45	100
1943	83	17	100
1944	67	33	100
1945	83	17	100

SOURCE: Ithiel de Sola Pool, *The Prestige Press: A Comparative Study of Political Symbols* (Cambridge, Mass.: MIT Press 1970), p. 241.

   a. What percent of references to the United States were hostile in 1940? In 1941? What might the differences between these two years suggest about government influence on this newspaper?
   b. The data reported above indicate only whether attitudes were positive or negative. What coding categories might have been used to determine specific Nazi attitudes toward the United States during this period?
   c. Briefly discuss the advantages of content analysis to evaluate the attitudes of elites during a war.

RECOMMENDED READINGS

Budd, Richard W., Robert K. Thorp, and Lewis Donohew
1967 *Content Analysis of Communications.* New York: Macmillan.

Describes and illustrates content analysis with the help of numerous examples. Contains an annotated bibliography of 300 entries.

Carney, Thomas F.
1972 *Content Analysis: A Technique for Systematic Inference from Communications.* Winnipeg: Univ. of Manitoba Press.

A text with thorough discussion of many of the issues and techniques of content analysis.

Seider, Maynard S.
1974 "American Big Business Ideology: A Content Analysis of Executive Speeches," *American Sociological Review*, 39 (Dec.):802–815.

A content analysis that compares speeches by corporate executives in various industries. Speeches are coded by their emphasis on nationalism, profit-making, and so forth.

PART NINE

Experimental Designs

21

PRETEST-POSTTEST CONTROL-GROUP DESIGN: TEACHER EXPECTATIONS AND THE SELF-FULFILLING PROPHECY

GENERAL ISSUE

Most social scientists use a *correlation design* for collecting and analyzing data. Such designs are ideally suited for the study of phenomena under natural conditions since they do not require that variables be physically manipulated or controlled. When the objective is to establish causal relationships among variables, however, correlational designs have limitations. While these designs can expose relationships, they do not establish the temporal sequence of links among variables. Knowledge exterior to the design can provide this information, however. Experimental designs, on the other hand, by their structure incorporate the temporal sequence of variables.

In an *experimental design*, scientists both manipulate and control variables. Through these procedures, they are able to meet the three conditions necessary for inferring cause. First, an experimental design provides evidence that variables are related. That is, it confirms that a change in one variable is related to a change in another. Second, such a design establishes that a change in the dependent variable did not precede a change in the independent variable. This confirmation is necessary for inferring a causal relationship, because the idea of cause holds that an effect may not precede its cause. Consequently, a change in one variable, the dependent one, must not occur prior to a change in another, the independent one, if the first is to be said to cause the second. Third, an experimental design provides evidence that some unsuspected third variable did not cause the change observed in the other. In other words, an experimental design provides evidence that covariation in the two given variables is not the result of some common influence of a third.

This chapter introduces the principles governing experimental designs and explores in detail one type: the *pretest-posttest control-group design.*

THEORETICAL PROBLEM

Correlational designs have established that children of lower-class backgrounds tend to do less well in school than children of middle-class backgrounds. Social scientists have offered a number of theories to explain these differences, but choosing among the theories has been difficult, for cause-and-effect relationships have been difficult to establish.

In recent years, one theory has received extensive correlational support. This holds that the attitudes and values of the classroom teacher significantly influence student performance. In hypothesis form, it suggests that if a teacher expects good (bad) performance, the student will perform well (poorly). According to this theory, a teacher's expectations are a primary cause of high or low student performance.

The relationship between expectations and performance illustrates the more general theory of the *self-fulfilling prophecy*: phenomena will occur because they are expected to occur. Since most research testing the implications of the self-fulfilling prophecy have relied on correlational designs, it is not known whether the prophecy caused the outcome or whether the evidence already in existence caused the prophecy. For instance, at the beginning of the semester, a classroom teacher may identify a particular student as being a poor performer. He or she may indeed perform poorly throughout the semester. However, the teacher may have based his or her expectations on subtle clues gleaned from the student's past performance. Therefore, the teacher's "correct prophecy" may reflect sophisticated prediction rather than being a cause of the student's poor performance.

To more clearly establish a possible cause-and-effect relationship between teacher expectations and student performance, Robert Rosenthal and Lenore Jacobson undertook a pretest-posttest control-group experiment at a public elementary school identified only as Oak School.*

THE PRETEST-POSTTEST CONTROL-GROUP DESIGN

The general requirements of a pretest-posttest control-group design are as follows:

* Robert Rosenthal and Lenore Jacobson, *Pygmalion in the Classroom: Teacher Expectations and Pupils' Intellectual Development* (New York: Holt, Rinehart and Winston, 1968).

1. A pool of subjects is required. Some of the subjects (the experimental group) will be exposed to the independent variable, and some (the control group) will not be so exposed.
2. Those subjects assigned to the experimental group should be as similar as possible to those assigned to the control group.
3. Subjects should not know whether they are in the experimental or control group nor, if possible, should they know they are participating in an experiment.
4. A pretest measurement of the dependent variable should be obtained from the experimental and control subjects at the beginning of the experiment.
5. The experimental subjects, but not the controls, should receive the independent variable, sometimes referred to as the treatment or experimental variable.
6. At the end of the experiment, a posttest measurement of the dependent variable should be obtained for experimental and control subjects.
7. In order to determine if there are any differences on the dependent variable, the experimental and control groups should be compared.

The logic of this design appears in Table 21-1.

Table 21-1. Essential Logic of the Pretest-Posttest Experimental Design.

RANDOM ASSIGNMENT OF UNALERTED SUBJECTS TO EITHER:	PRETEST OBSERVATION	INTRODUCE EXPERIMENTAL VARIABLE	POSTTEST OBSERVATION
Experimental group (*R*)	0_1	*X*	0_2
Control group (*R*)	0_3		0_4

Random assignment (*R*) creates groups which differ only by chance on all relevant variables.

$0_2 - 0_1$ represents the difference in the experimental group due to the experimental variable and any uncontrolled variables which affected the group between the pretest and posttest observation.

$0_4 - 0_3$ represents the difference in the control group due to any uncontrolled variables which affected the group between the pretest and posttest observation.

Subtracting the difference obtained in the control group from the difference obtained in the experimental one yields the influence of the experimental variable.

21.1 ASSIGNING SUBJECTS TO EITHER THE EXPERIMENTAL OR CONTROL GROUP

In experimental research, there is always the possibility that differences in the dependent variable for the experimental and control groups are due to differences that existed before the experiment began. To preclude this possibility, scientists have developed a number of techniques for creating equivalent groups at the beginning of an experiment.

1. *Subject Matching.* Pairs of subjects are located who are identical on all relevant variables. One of the pair is assigned to the experimental group while the other is assigned to the control group. By itself, this procedure is difficult to follow. First, locating pairs of subjects which are identical is frequently administratively impossible. Second, researchers often lack a theory which permits them to identify all relevant variables. Without such a theory, there is no basis for matching subjects.

2. *Group Matching.* Two groups are created which are equivalent in terms of group averages for relevant variables. Consequently, the experimental and control groups may have the same average educational level, income, age, sex distribution, and so forth. This procedure, while administratively feasible, has two disadvantages. First, the relevant variables may be unknown. Second, group averages may conceal important individual differences or individual combinations of variables.

3. *Randomization.* Subjects are randomly assigned either to the experimental or control group. With a large number of subjects, chance makes it highly probable that two equivalent groups will be established. The advantages of this procedure are that (1) a theory of relevant variables is not required, and (2) human bias in assignment is eliminated.

Implementing the Design at Oak School

To implement the pretest-posttest control-group design, Rosenthal and Jacobson secured the cooperation of administrators and teachers at a public elementary school in a large western city. Although their research concerned the relationship between teacher expectations and student performance, the true purpose of the experiment was concealed. Administrators and teachers were told that the experiment involved a test to identify children who would show rapid intellectual growth. The major test to be used was identified as the "Harvard Test of Inflected Acquisition," whereas, in reality, it was a standardized, relatively nonverbal test of intelligence, Flanagan's (1960) Tests of General Ability (TOGA). Each teacher in the school received the following description of the experiment and the test:

STUDY OF INFLECTED ACQUISITION

All children show hills, plateaus, and valleys in their scholastic progress. The study being conducted at Harvard with the support of the National Science Foundation is interested in those children who show an unusual forward spurt of

> academic progress. These spurts can and do occur at any level of academic and intellectual functioning. When these spurts occur in children who have not been functioning too well academically, the result is familiarly referred to as "late blooming."
>
> As part of our study we are further validating a test which predicts the likelihood that a child will show an inflection point or "spurt" within the near future. This test, which will be administered in your school, will allow us to predict which youngsters are likely to show an academic spurt. The top 20 percent (approximately) of the scores on this test will probably be found at various levels of academic functioning.
>
> The development of the test for predicting inflections or "spurts" is not yet such that *every* one of the top 20 percent will show the spurt or "blooming" effect. But the top 20 percent of the children *will* show a more significant inflection or spurt in their learning within the next year or less than will the remaining 80 percent of the children.
>
> Because of the experimental nature of the tests, basic principles of test construction do not permit us to discuss the test or test scores either with the parents or the children themselves.
>
> Upon completion of this study, participating districts will be advised of the results. [p. 66]

In addition to describing the "purpose" of the test, Rosenthal and Jacobson told the teachers that testing would occur in May 1964, January 1965, and May 1965.

As planned, the test was administered in the spring of 1964 to all 650 children in grades kindergarten through five. This test provided a measure of IQ—the *dependent variable.* Sixth-graders were excluded from the first testing (*the pretest*) since they were going on to junior high school and would not be returning to Oak School the following year. The administration of Oak School assigned students to one of three classrooms depending on grade. These classrooms represented ability groupings termed either high, middle, and low or fast, medium, and slow tracks. Student assignment to one of these tracks was based upon a school-administered achievement test and teacher judgment of reading ability.

As a result of independent classrooms and tracking, Rosenthal and Jacobson created an *experimental* and *control group* within each class by randomly designating approximately 20 percent of the students in each class to the former and the remainder to the latter. They used a table of random numbers in assigning students. Teachers, on the other hand, were led to believe that the 20 percent of students identified in their class as potential "bloomers" or "spurters" were so designated as a result of their performance on the "Harvard Test of Inflected Acquisition." In this manner, the independent variable, teacher expectation, was introduced for the experimental students. Although the names of students who could be expected to show unusual academic gains were reported to their teachers, the teachers were cautioned not to discuss the "test findings" with either the students or their parents. In reality, then, the only difference between those students identified as potential "bloomers" or "spurters" (the experimental group) and the remaining students (the control group) was in the mind of the teacher.

The *posttest* measurement of IQ was obtained by testing all students again in May 1965, one year after the start of the experiment. By comparing pretest and posttest IQ measurements for the experimental and control groups, Rosenthal and Jacobson sought to determine if teacher expectations influenced test performance.

RESULTS

Since the experiment involved an experimental and a control group in eighteen classrooms representing three tracks within the school, separate analyses for each grade level were performed. Only the pooled results for each grade level are presented in Table 21-2.

Table 21-2. Pretest and Posttest Total IQ Scores of the Experimental and Control-Group Students for Each Grade Level.

GRADE AT POSTTEST		EXPERIMENTAL	CONTROL	
One	Posttest	117.7	100.2	
	Pretest	90.3	88.2	
	Difference	27.4	12.0	+15.4
Two	Posttest	109.4	107.6	
	Pretest	92.9	100.6	
	Difference	16.5	7.0	+9.5
Three	Posttest	105.4	113.6	
	Pretest	100.4	108.6	
	Difference	5.0	5.0	0.0
Four	Posttest	135.5	111.5	
	Pretest	129.9	109.3	
	Difference	5.6	2.2	+3.4
Five	Posttest	117.8	117.5	
	Pretest	100.4	100.0	
	Difference	17.4	17.5	−0.1
Six	Posttest	130.0	112.5	
	Pretest	120.9	101.8	
	Difference	10.0	10.7	−0.7
All Grades	Posttest	119.0	109.7	
	Pretest	106.8	101.3	
	Difference	12.2	8.4	+3.8

SOURCE: Rosenthal and Jacobson, "Pygmalion in the Classroom."

The results are rather remarkable. As a whole, for total IQ, students in the experimental group showed a larger gain than students in the control group—a gain of +3.8 points. This difference is beyond the realm of chance and suggests a causal relationship between teacher expectations and performance on Flanagan's IQ test. An examination of differences by grade level, however, suggests that the greatest differences in total IQ gain between the experimental and control students occurred in the early grades. This in turn indicates that teacher expectations may be most important for younger children. From these results, and similar analyses performed by Rosenthal and Jacobson, it would seem that children who are expected to grow intellectually will do so.

DISCUSSION

This study employed a pretest-posttest control-group design, thereby enhancing the credibility of a causal relationship between teacher expectations and student performance. As a result, a number of variables which ordinarily give rise to rival explanations were controlled or eliminated. The possible effects of these variables and the controls for them are discussed below.

1. *Selection Effect.* It is difficult to argue that IQ gain disparity resulted from initial differences possessed by the experimental and control-group subjects, since students were randomly assigned to either group.
2. *Maturation Effect.* Although some IQ gain could be expected, due to natural intellectual growth independent of teacher expectations, this normal growth would have occurred in both the experimental and control groups. Consequently, the differences in IQ gain could not be attributed to maturation.
3. *Instrumentation Effect.* Inasmuch as the same test was used for both the pretest and posttest measurements, it is not possible to claim that gain scores were the result of tests with varying degrees of difficulty. Even if this were so, the use of the same tests for both the experimental and control groups would have meant that both groups would have been influenced equally by the tests. Consequently, differences in gains could not have been due to a change in instruments.
4. *History Effect.* Occasionally, an unknown variable will influence subjects during the course of an experiment. If this happens, the results can be impaired. Although a history effect may have occurred across classrooms, such an effect cannot account for differences between experimental and control students within each classroom. Since a history effect, if any, influenced both groups of students, it could not account for differences in gains.

5. *Mortality Effect.* It is not unusual for subjects to withdraw from an experiment after it has begun. This happened in Oak School, but the percent of students lost was similar for experimental and control groups. Pretest measurements could be used to adjust any findings to take into account the differential loss of students.
6. *Pretest Effect.* Taking a test twice frequently results in improved performance because the individual has become familiar with the form of the test and its contents. If a pretest effect occurred among Oak School students, it occurred equally for both the experimental and control groups. Consequently, a pretest effect could not account for differences in gains for the two groups.
7. *Regression Effect.* On any particular day, some students will do especially well on a test because they have a good deal of luck. Others will do poorly for the opposite reason. If students who do well on a test are assigned to the control group and students who do poorly are assigned to the experimental one, then, the next time they are tested, the control group will go down and the experimental group up. This results from the fact that people with extra good luck one time will have average or bad luck the next time, and vice versa. Differences due to this phenomenon are termed a regression effect. Since students were randomly assigned to the experimental and control groups, independent of how well or poorly they did on the pretest, then differences in gain scores could not have caused a regression effect.
8. *Interaction Effect.* Two or more variables in combination may have a different effect than would each variable independently. Whatever interaction effect occurred in this experiment, it occurred equally for both the experimental and control groups and therefore could not explain the differences in gain scores.

The effects discussed above threaten the *internal validity* of an experiment, that is, they may be responsible for false interpretations of the results for the subjects studied. A pretest-posttest design guards against these threats and, if properly implemented, produces reliable and valid results. Several other threats exist, however, with respect to the *external validity* of an experiment, and these are listed below. External validity refers to the degree to which the results can be validly generalized to a larger population.

9. *Sampling Effect.* Although the students at Oak School were assigned randomly to either a control or experimental group, it is possible that the students there were unrepresentative of students elsewhere. Consequently, the study may be internally valid for the students studied, but its results may be limited to

this group. To ensure external validity, subjects participating in an experiment must be representative of a larger population.

10. *Reactivity Effect.* Subjects who are aware they are participating in an experiment may be influenced by that knowledge. In the case of the Oak School experiment, a reactivity effect was unlikely. Students were unaware of the experiment, and its true nature was concealed from administrators and teachers.
11. *Pretest-Experimental Variable Interaction Effect.* The combination of a pretest measurement and the presence of the experimental variable may produce effects different from the mere presence of the experimental variable. Thus, in a larger population, where a pretest cannot be administered, the results of applying only the experimental variable may be different from results obtained in an experimental situation which used a pretest measurement. Consequently, the results of an experiment may not be generalizable. In the Oak School experiment the pretest, in combination with the experimental variable, appears not to have had a distinguishable and unique effect.

KEY IDEAS AND CONCEPTS

control group
correlation
covariation
dependent variable
equivalent groups
experimental design
experimental group
experimental variable
external validity
group matching
history effect
independent variable
instrumentation effect
interaction effect
internal validity
maturation effect
mortality effect
posttest
pretest
pretest effect
pretest-independent variable effect
pretest-posttest design
random assignment
randomization
reactivity effect
regression effect
rival explanation
sampling effect
selection effect
standardized test
subject matching
treatment variable
variable interaction

ISSUES AND PROBLEMS

1. List the distinctive features of an experimental design.
2. Specify the major strengths of an experiment. Specify the major weaknesses.
3. List the advantages of an experimental design over a correlational design. List the advantages of a correlational design over an experimental design.

4. Discuss the strengths and weaknesses of various techniques for assigning subjects to experimental or control groups.
5. Distinguish between internal and external validity.
6. Social scientists and others are often concerned about the impact of an institutional experience on a person's self-esteem. Using a pretest-posttest control-group design, design an experiment to measure the effects of institutionalization on the self-esteem of juvenile offenders. Discuss the experiment's strengths and weaknesses with respect to the following effects: selection, maturation, instrumentation, history, mortality, pretest, regression, interaction, sampling, reactivity, and pretest-independent variable interaction.

RECOMMENDED READINGS

The Logic of Experimental Designs

Campbell, Donald T., and Julian C. Stanley
1963 *Experimental and Quasi-Experimental Designs for Research.* Chicago: Rand McNally.

A highly readable discussion of alternative designs in social research. Well worth pursuing.

Ross, John, and Perry Smith
1968 "Orthodox Experimental Designs," in Hubert M. Blalock and Ann B. Blalock (eds.), *Methodology in Social Research.* New York: McGraw-Hill.

A highly readable discussion of alternative designs in social research. Well worth pursuing.

Statistical Analysis and Experimental Designs

Edwards, Allen L.
1968 *Experimental Design in Psychological Research.* 3d ed. New York: Holt, Rinehart and Winston.

A highly readable introduction to the logic of experimental designs and the usefulness of various statistical procedures for analysis.

Wood, Gordon
1974 *Fundamentals of Psychological Research.* Boston: Little, Brown.

Integrates the logic of research, experimental designs, and statistical procedures in a highly readable manner.

22

POSTTEST CONTROL-GROUP DESIGN: THE EFFECT OF LEGAL STIGMA ON EMPLOYMENT OPPORTUNITY

GENERAL ISSUE

A pretest-posttest design, such as that described in the preceding chapter, often is too costly to be used in social research. At other times it must be avoided because of pretest effects. The latter constitute an important problem when the pretest measurement might inform subjects about the existence or nature of the experiment and influence their behaviors. A pretest-posttest design thus often poses great difficulties when the researcher chooses to use deceit. Given these circumstances of limited funds and reactivity, a posttest control-group design may be required.

This chapter introduces the principles of a posttest control-group design. This design was used to study how a criminal accusation affects employment opportunities.

THEORETICAL PROBLEM

Legally an individual is innocent until proven guilty. However, the burden of establishing one's innocence may extend far beyond the anxiety, effort, and cost of a trial. Mere accusation of wrongdoing may produce long-lasting and harmful consequences to persons charged with committing a crime. A damaged reputation, the loss of friends, and social ostracism frequently result. Even after an individual establishes his innocence in a court of law, the stigma of legal accusation may continue.

The realization of the discrepancy between a law which, in theory, presumes the innocence of an accused, and the actual social consequences of being accused is an interesting subject for investigation. In the research described here,* Richard D. Schwartz and Jerome H. Skolnick attempted to obtain information by using a posttest control-group design. They wanted to study the causal relationship of legal stigma to employment opportunities.

HYPOTHESES

The hypothesis underlying this research is that persons who have been accused of a crime, but proven innocent, will nevertheless have poorer employment opportunities than persons who were never so accused. The null hypothesis states that persons accused and found not guilty will have employment opportunities equal to those who were never accused. Therefore, if the hypothesis which suggests that having been wrongly accused leaves a lasting stigma is correct, then the null hypothesis will be rejected.

THE DESIGN

The general requirements of a posttest control-group design are as follows:

1. It is necessary to have a pool of subjects, some of whom can serve as experimental and some of whom can serve as control subjects.
2. Those subjects assigned to the experimental group should be as identical as possible to those assigned to the control group.
3. Subjects should not know if they are in the experimental or control group. Indeed, they should not even know they are participating in an experiment.
4. The experimental subjects should receive the experimental variable. The control subjects should not.
5. At the end of the experiment, there should be a posttest measurement of the dependent variable for both the experimental and control subjects.
6. The experimental and control groups should be compared to determine if there are any differences as to the dependent variable.

The logic of this design is presented in Table 22-1.

* Richard D. Schwartz and Jerome H. Skolnick, "Two Studies of Legal Stigma," *Social Problems*, 10 (1962):133–142.

Table 22-1. Essential Logic of the Posttest Control-Group Design.

RANDOM ASSIGNMENT OF NAIVE SUBJECTS TO EITHER:	PRETEST OBSERVATION	EXPERIMENTAL VARIABLE	POSTTEST OBSERVATION
Experimental group (*R*)	None	*X*	0_1
Control group (*R*)	None		0_2

Random assignment (*R*) creates groups which differ only by chance on all relevant variables.

$0_1 - 0_2$ represents the difference between the experimental group and the control group. This difference is due to the experimental variable.

Implementing the Design Among Employers

Since the consequences of legal stigma may vary with the severity and type of crime, Schwartz and Skolnick limited their research to the study of assault. As the independent variable, they selected the legal stigma associated with a record of assault. As the dependent variable, they selected employment opportunities. Circumstances made it possible to undertake the study in resort hotels in the Catskill Mountains.

As a first step, Schwartz and Skolnick compiled a list of all resort hotels (the population) in the Catskills. From this, they drew a random sample of one hundred hotels. Next, they assigned each hotel to one of four groups. One was designated the control group. To the remaining three groups they assigned one of three experimental conditions. They did this in order to permit variation in the strength of the independent (treatment) variable.

Schwartz and Skolnick manipulated the experimental variable (accusation) by creating four employment dossiers. With the exception of the treatment variable all dossiers were identical. In the first, the job applicant was described as being thirty-two years old, single, male, trained in mechanical trades, and previously employed as kitchen helper, maintenance worker, and handyman. No reference was made to any previous criminal involvement. The second dossier differed from the first in only one respect; it indicated that the applicant had been accused of the crime of assault but had been acquitted. Included was a letter from the trial judge affirming the applicant's innocence. The third dossier differed from the second only in that it did not include a letter from the trial judge. The fourth dossier described the applicant as having been accused, found guilty, and sentenced for the crime of assault. However, in describing personal and social characteristics, the fourth dossier was identical to the first three.

Schwartz and Skolnick were thus able to assemble dossiers which provided four levels of the experimental variable:

1. Experimental variable absent;
2. Experimental variable present and including acquittal and trial judge letter;

3. Experimental variable present and including acquittal but excluding trial judge letter;
4. Experimental variable present and including data on conviction and sentencing.

To implement the design and measure the dependent variable, a law student masquerading as an employment agent approached each hotel employer with one of the assigned dossiers. The employer was then asked if he could use the applicant described in the dossier. This deception provided realism and reduced the possibility of a *reactive effect.* (A reactive effect occurs if participants in an experiment modify their behavior simply as a result of knowing they are in an experiment.)

The responses of the hotel employers fell into two categories: those who expressed a willingness to consider the applicant in any way were termed *positive*; those who made no response or who explicitly refused to consider the candidate were denoted *negative.* The analysis was accomplished by comparing the frequency of positive and negative responses for the three experimental and one control groups.

The relationship between legal stigma and the consequences therefrom appears to be straightforward. As demonstrated in this experiment, the greater the stigma, the greater the chance that job opportunities were diminished.

Table 22-2. Effect of Legal Stigma on Job Opportunities.

GROUP	EXPERIMENTAL VARIABLE	POSITIVE: WOULD CONSIDER FOR EMPLOYMENT	NEGATIVE: WOULD NOT CONSIDER FOR EMPLOYMENT	TOTAL	
		%	%	%	*N*
Control group	Absent	36	64	100	25
Experimental group 1	Present, acquitted with letter	24	76	100	25
Experimental group 2	Present, acquitted without letter	12	88	100	25
Experimental group 3	Present, convicted, and sentenced	4	96	100	25
				Total	100

SOURCE: Schwartz and Skolnick, "Two Studies," p. 137, Table 1.

Nine of the twenty-five control-group employers (36 percent) would consider for future employment the job applicant having no arrest record. Since the experiment was conducted at a time when most hotels had probably filled their employment needs, this 36 percent figure serves as a reasonable estimate of general employment needs at hotels in the area. That is, with no stigma present, approximately one-third of the hotels in each group could have been expected to express interest in the job applicant. Because the hotels were assigned randomly to each group, the average need for labor should have been approximately equal across all four groups.

In comparing the experimental groups with the control one, the following can be observed. For (experimental) Group 1, positive responses were made by six (24 percent) of the hotels presented with a dossier in which the applicant had been acquitted and had a letter from the trial judge. This decreased to only three (12 percent) of Group 2 which received the dossier without the trial judge's letter. In Group 3, only one (4 percent) of the twenty-five hotel employers expressed employment interest in the applicant. Thus, job opportunities declined as the stigma became more pronounced. As can be seen, applicants who had a criminal record of assault had few prospects for employment.

These findings lend themselves to the inference that legal stigma continues to operate, according to the theory of justice, even after a convicted individual's debt to society has been paid. Further, the legal stigma of accusation has an impact beyond the official intention of the law. That is, actual practice violates the principle that persons found innocent of crimes should suffer no ill consequences from accusation. The findings instead point to the conclusion that the stigma of accusation has negative consequences for the innocent as well as the guilty.

DISCUSSION

The posttest design used in this study shares many of the advantages of the pretest-posttest one. These advantages, and several new ones, are summarized below.

1. *Selection Effect.* The random assignment of employers to the control group or to one of the experimental groups eliminated any selection effect.
2. *Maturation Effect.* Any changes in employment needs were unlikely. Employers were requested only to indicate their potential willingness to hire the applicant. Since data collection occurred over several months, however, some change in employment need may have occurred. Still, this effect was randomized over all four groups. In any event, maturation effects could have been controlled in the posttest control-group design if investigators simultaneously collected data from all employers.

3. *Instrumentation Effect.* The use of a common posttest measurement for all four groups eliminated any instrumentation effect.
4. *History Effect.* Changes in employer perception of applicant characteristics could not have occurred between exposure to the experimental variable and posttest measurement. This is because the measurement was taken in conjunction with independent-variable exposure. Thus, the possibility of a history effect was eliminated.
5. *Mortality Effect.* Since all employers were interviewed and no pretest measurement was taken, a mortality effect could not have occurred.
6. *Pretest Effect.* Since employers were not given a pretest, there could be no pretest effect.
7. *Regression Effect.* The random assignment of employers to one of the four groups eliminated the possibility of a regression effect.
8. *Interaction Effect.* Whatever interaction among variables occurred should be present in the control and experimental groups. Consequently, its effect was controlled.
9. *Sampling Effect.* Insofar as a random sample of resort hotels was concerned, the results are generalizable to the population of resort hotels in the Catskill Mountains. However, the results of the study cannot be generalized to hotels outside this region or to individuals with different personal and social characteristics accused of different types of crime.
10. *Reactivity Effect.* Since employers were deceived into believing they were considering a real job applicant, there was little possibility of a reactivity effect.
11. *Pretest-Experimental Variable Interaction Effect.* The elimination of a pretest eliminated the possibility of this effect.

Comparing these items of the posttest design with a pretest-posttest design discloses many similarities and a few differences. Two major differences, however, deserve comment. First, the posttest design avoids completely the *pretest effect* and the *pretest-experimental variable effect*, and is superior in this respect. Since the posttest design requires only a posttest measurement, there can be no pretest-related effects.

The second difference concerns the superiority of the pretest-posttest design in determining change. Only through such a design can one measure the amount of change occurring. Pretest and posttest measures must both be available in order to calculate the differences between them. The difference then is a measure of change.

In sum, the pretest-posttest design permits determination of change, but incurs the risk of a pretest effect. The posttest design eliminates the risk of a pretest effect but prohibits determining the amount of change. These two problems can be resolved through the use of a *Solomon Four Group Design*.

The Solomon Four Group Design results from a combination of the pretest-posttest and the posttest control-group design. The logic of this design appears in Table 22-3.

One may carry out additional calculations to obtain pretest and other effects.

Table 22-3. The Logic of the Solomon Four Group Design.

RANDOM ASSIGNMENT OF UNAWARE SUBJECTS TO EITHER:	OBSERVATION	INTRODUCE EXPERIMENTAL VARIABLE	POSTTEST OBSERVATION
Group 1 Experimental group (*R*)	0_1	*X*	0_2
Group 2 Control group (*R*)	0_3		0_4
Group 3 Experimental group (*R*)		*X*	0_5
Group 4 Control group (*R*)			0_6

Random assignment (*R*) creates groups which differ only by chance on all relevant variables.

The following effects now can be calculated:

	TERM
1. The effect of all variables equals $0_2 - 0_1$.	Y_1
2. The effect of all variables except the experimental variable and independent variable interaction equals $0_4 - 0_3$.	Y_2
3. The average pretest value equals $\frac{0_1 + 0_3}{2}$.	$\bar{0}$
4. The effect of all variables except the pretest effect and pretest interaction effect equals $0_5 - \bar{0}$.	Y_3
5. The effect of all variables except the experimental variable, pretest, and related interactions equal $0_6 - \bar{0}$.	Y_4
6. The effect of the experimental variable equals $Y_3 - Y_4$.	Y_5

KEY IDEAS AND CONCEPTS

control group
dependent variable
experimental group
history effect
independent variable
instrumentation effect
interaction effect
manipulating the treatment variable

maturation effect
mortality effect
posttest control-group-only design
posttest measurement
pretest effect
pretest-independent variable effect
pretest measurement
reactivity effect
regression effect
sampling effect
selection effect
Solomon Four Group Design
treatment variable

ISSUES AND PROBLEMS

1. Specify the general requirements of a posttest control-group design.
2. List the advantages of varying the magnitude or value of the independent variable in an experimental design. Contrast these with the advantages encountered in a correlational design.
3. Discuss the major weaknesses of a posttest control-group design.
4. Describe the logic of the Solomon Four Group Design.
5. Using the posttest control-group design, reevaluate the pretest-posttest experimental design created for problem 6, Chapter 21. Specify the advantages and disadvantages of these two alternative designs for measuring the effects of institutionalization on self-esteem.

RECOMMENDED READINGS

The Logic of Experimental Designs

Campbell, Donald T., and Julian C. Stanley
1963 *Experimental and Quasi-Experimental Designs for Research.* Chicago: Rand McNally.

A highly readable discussion of alternative designs in social research. Well worth pursuing.

Ross, John, and Perry Smith
1968 "Orthodox Experimental Designs," in Hubert M. Blalock and Ann B. Blalock (eds.), *Methodology in Social Research.* New York: McGraw-Hill.

A highly readable discussion of alternative designs in social research. Well worth pursuing.

Statistical Analysis and Experimental Designs

Edwards, Allen L.
1968 *Experimental Design in Psychological Research.* 3d ed. New York: Holt, Rinehart and Winston.

A highly readable introduction to the logic of experimental designs and the usefulness of various statistical procedures for analysis.

Wood, Gordon
1974 *Fundamentals of Psychological Research.* Boston: Little, Brown.

Integrates the logic of research, experimental designs, and statistical procedures in a highly readable manner.

23

NATURAL PRETEST-POSTTEST DESIGNS: THE EFFECT OF LAW ON PHYSICIANS' ATTITUDES AND BEHAVIORS

GENERAL ISSUE

Most experimental designs, whether in the laboratory or the field, occur under situations where the researcher can manipulate the independent variable. However, there is a second class of experimental designs known as *natural experiments*, where the researcher cannot manipulate such variables. Natural experiments involve phenomena which are activated by natural causes rather than by a researcher. Their occurrence provides an opportunity to apply some variant of an experimental design.

In natural experiments, control groups are not possible when the natural phenomenon affects the entire population. To be more specific, researchers could not use a control group to study the impact on American voters of a presidential assassination. Nor could they employ control groups to study such phenomena as economic depressions or specific governmental programs like Medicare. Control groups are possible only when a portion of the population under study is affected by the natural phenomenon and a portion is unaffected.

Of course, it is always possible that either by luck or foresight, the researcher might have already obtained measures of the dependent variable before the experimental treatment occurred. For example, a thoughtful or fortunate researcher, anticipating the passage of Medicare/Medicaid, might well have measured physicians' attitudes about these proposals before they became law.

To recapitulate, natural experiments take advantage of uncontrolled phenomena by applying some variant of an experimental design to them. This chapter will report on an experimental design which examined the impact of the 1965 Medicare law on physicians' attitudes and behavior.

THEORETICAL PROBLEM

"There ought to be a law" summarizes the belief of those persons who argue that legislation can be a positive instrument for social change. According to proponents of this view, laws have the capacity to compel individuals to engage in desired behavior and to forego behavior which has legally been defined as undesirable. Opponents believe that law has either little capacity for modifying behavior or that such modifications can come only with dramatically increased law enforcement costs. Opponents, for instance, point to the classic failure of prohibition to alter the drinking habits of Americans, and to the more current issue of the "decriminalization" of marijuana as evidence of the failure of governmental enactments to alter the drug habits of young Americans.

Of course, these are oversimplified views of law. They entail a belief in either the complete success or failure of legislation to change behavior. More appropriately, the issue should be addressed in terms of the conditions under which law may be an instrument of social change. Furthermore, it is necessary to distinguish between the effects of law on attitudes and their effect on behavior.

THE MEDICARE LAW

The Medicare bill, which was signed into law on July 30, 1965, and implemented July 1, 1966, represents a significant piece of social legislation. It is sometimes compared in importance to the original Social Security Act of 1935. The Medicare bill established a federal program of health insurance for people sixty-five years old or over. Part A automatically provides hospital insurance for almost all citizens in that category. Part B provides coverage for physicians' services whether furnished in hospital, office, or home.

During the 1940s, 1950s, and mid-1960s, the American Medical Association fought this type of legislation bitterly. The AMA spent millions lobbying against the development of a government-subsidized program of health insurance. After the passage of the bill, however, the important social issue narrowed down to the manner in which individual physicians reacted in their attitudes and behavior to Medicare.

THE RESEARCH DESIGN

In 1964, John Colombotos initiated a study of physician attitudes on political, medical, and other issues.* He was concerned to relate these attitudes to each other and to the personal and professional characteristics of the doctors. Thus, a number of questions on many topics were asked. Among the questions asked was one on what came to be known as Part A of Medicare, which was being widely discussed in 1964. Part B was not included in the interviews because it was not included in the legislation or widely discussed until shortly before the Medicare bill was passed.

The passage and implementation of Medicare made it possible for Colombotos to capitalize on the data he already had collected by devising a research design which incorporated the logic of a Time 1–Time 2 experiment. The experimental variable would be the Medicare Act, and the dependent variables would be the attitudes and behavior of physicians. Physicians had been interviewed before the passage of Medicare, would be interviewed after passage but before implementation, and again after implementation. Although experimental designs frequently seek to incorporate control groups in order to establish baseline comparisons between exposure to the experimental variable and nonexposure, it was impossible to do so in this case because all physicians would be exposed to the prospects and reality of Medicare. As a result, certain special features were incorporated into the design. They are discussed below.

The Sample

The intent of the research reported here was to provide generalizations about the effectiveness of law as inferred from its effects on the attitudes and behavior of physicians. However, it was not feasible to study all physicians or even a nationwide sample. Consequently, the population consisted of all physicians engaged in private practice in the state of New York. The choice of New York was related to the history of the research and the fact that Colombotos was himself located in the state. He recognized, however, that New York state physicians are more liberal than the population of American physicians. Even a study of all New York physicians, however, would have been expensive and inefficient. Consequently, Colombotos drew a random sample of physicians from the list of private physicians licensed by New York State.

Data Collection

A comparison of personal interview data with that obtained by telephone using a small random sample of physicians revealed that the quality of

* John Colombotos, "Physicians and Medicare: A Before-After Study of the Effects of Legislation on Attitudes," *American Sociological Review*, 34(1969):318–334.

information obtained by phone did not differ markedly from that obtained by face-to-face interview. As a result, cost, ease, and efficiency dictated that the information would be obtained by telephone.

Prior to the passage of the Medicare bill on July 30, 1965, telephone interviews were successfully conducted with 1,205 physicians out of an original sample of 1,500. An additional 472 physicians were sampled later in order to assess the possibility of an interview effect. Of this second group, 330 were eventually interviewed. The total of 1,535 physicians interviewed represented about 78 percent of the total sample of 1,972.

Figure 23-1. Research Design.

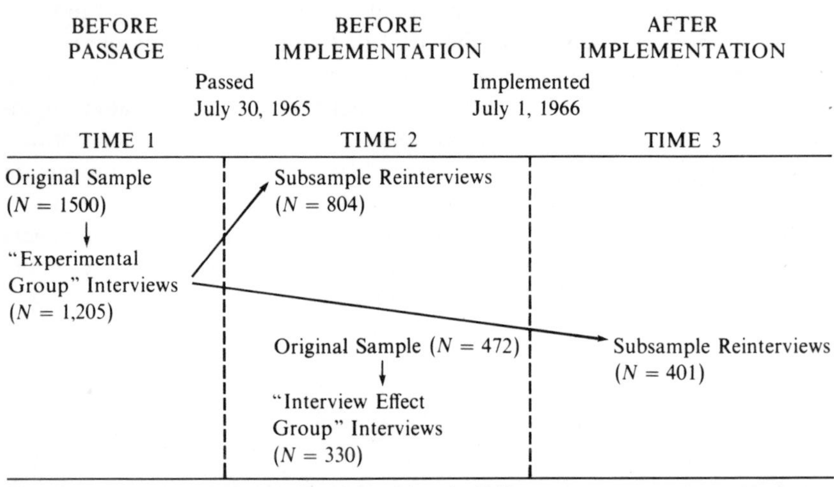

Time 1 interviews conducted during 1964 and early 1965
Time 2 interviews conducted during May 1966 and June 1966
Time 3 interviews conducted during early 1967

Actual subsample reinterviews somewhat less due to sample loss.

The first wave of interviews, Time 1, ascertained physicians' social and medical backgrounds as well as their general attitudes about the impending Medicare bill. Data obtained from these interviews permitted the grouping (stratification) of physicians by initial attitudes (favored or opposed) and by their geographic locations, religious backgrounds, and political ideologies. The 1,205 interviewed physicians then were assigned randomly to two subsamples. The first consisted of 804 physicians who were to be reinterviewed at Time 2, after passage of the Medicare bill but prior to its implementation. The second, consisting of the remaining 401 physicians, were to be reinterviewed at Time 3, after implementation of the Medicare bill.

The research design with respect to the collection of data appears in Figure 23-1. To summarize: 1,205 physicians were interviewed at Time 1,

804 of the 1,205 were to be reinterviewed at Time 2, and the remaining 401 were to be reinterviewed at Time 3. An additional 330 were interviewed at Time 2 only.

DATA ANALYSIS

Attitudes of Physicians Toward Medicare

During the first wave of interviews (Time 1), physicians were asked: "What is your opinion about the bill which would provide for compulsory health insurance through Social Security to cover hospital costs for those over sixty-five—are you personally in favor of such a plan or are you opposed to it?" The majority of physicians held negative attitudes toward the forthcoming bill: 54 percent were opposed to the bill, 38 percent favored it, and 8 percent held no opinion.

During the second wave of interviews (Time 2), when 676 of the 804 physicians were contacted, the majority of physicians interviewed supported the recently passed Medicare bill: 70 percent favored it, 26 percent were opposed, and 5 percent held no opinion.

During the third wave of interviews (Time 3), when 331 of the 401 physicians were contacted, the majority supported the bill, which had been recently implemented: 81 percent favored, 19 percent were opposed, and less than 0.5 percent held no opinion. These results are reported in Table 23-1.

Table 23-1 indicates that the proportion of physicians who favored the Medicare bill increased from Time 1 (before passage) to Time 2 (after passage) to Time 3 (after implementation). These data suggest an important

Table 23-1. Attitudes of Physicians Toward Medicare at Time 1, Time 2, and Time 3.

ATTITUDE	TIME 1	TIME 2	TIME 3
	%	%	%
Favor	38	70	81
Oppose	54	26	19
No opinion	8	5	[a]
Total	100	101 [b]	100
N =	(1,205)	(676)	(331)

SOURCE: Colombotos, "Physicians and Medicare," p. 326, Table 2.

[a] Computed percent less than 0.5.

[b] Column greater than 100 due to rounding.

impact of the law on physicians' attitudes. Since the data refer to proportions (essentially group "averages"), Tables 23-2 and 23-3 were constructed to reflect the changing positions of specific physicians.

Table 23-2. Physician Attitudes at Time 2 Cross-Tabulated with Physician Attitudes Held at Time 1.

CURRENT ATTITUDE TIME 2	PREVIOUSLY HELD ATTITUDE TIME 1 (IN PERCENTAGES)[a]	
	Favor	Oppose
Favor	90	59
Oppose	11	40
Total	101	99

SOURCE: Colombotos, "Physicians and Medicare," p. 327, Table 3.
[a] Due to rounding columns do not add to 100.

Table 23-2 indicates that between Time 1 and Time 2 there was a remarkable shift of opinion among physicians who originally opposed the Medicare bill. Fifty-nine percent of those who originally opposed the legislation had come to support it; only 40 percent of those who originally opposed the bill continued to oppose it. Ninety percent of those who favored the bill at Time 1 continued to support the bill, but 11 percent of those who originally favored it now opposed it. The dramatic shift of 59 percent of the original opponents of the bill lends credence to the argument that law is an effective component of changing attitudes.

Table 23-3 records the change in attitudes between Time 1 and Time 3. It indicates that there has also been a remarkable shift of opinion among the second group, which originally opposed the Medicare bill. Seventy percent of those who originally opposed the bill came to support it, and only 30 percent of those who originally opposed it continued to do so.

Table 23-3. Physician Attitudes at Time 3 Cross-tabulated with Physician Attitudes Held at Time 1.

CURRENT ATTITUDE TIME 3	PREVIOUSLY HELD ATTITUDE TIME 1 (IN PERCENTAGES)	
	Favor	Oppose
Favor	98	70
Oppose	2	30
Total	100	100

SOURCE: Colombotos, "Physicians and Medicare," p. 327, Table 3.

Ninety-eight percent of those who favored the bill at Time 1 continued to support it, and only 2 percent of those who originally favored it decided to oppose it. The shift of 70 percent of the original opponents lends further credence to the argument that the law is an effective component of changing attitudes.

The Behavior of Physicians and Medicare

Prior to the enactment of Medicare, physicians, through the American Medical Association (AMA), strongly resisted a federal health insurance program. In June 1965, the *New York Times* reported that the House of Delegates for the AMA proposed the possibility of a "boycott" when Medicare was passed. One month after the passage of Medicare, the president of AMA predicted that "quite a few" physicians throughout the

Table 23-4. Intended Compliance and Opposition to Medicare at Time 2 and Time 3.

INTERVIEW ITEM[a]	TIME 2	TIME 3
	%	%
(If the physician had been asked to serve on a utilization review committee for Medicare, the question was asked:) *Have you agreed to serve?*		
Yes	87	94
No	10	6
Not decided	4	0
Total	101[b]	100
(If the physician had not been asked to serve on a utilization review committee, the question was asked:) *If you were asked, would you agree to serve?*		
Yes	66	71
No	27	26
Don't know	7	3
Total	100	100
According to your present thinking, do you plan to accept patients who get benefits under Medicare or not?		
Accept (have treated)	93	93
Will not accept (have not treated)	4	6
Don't know	4	1
Total	101[b]	100

SOURCE: Colombotos, "Physicians and Medicare," p. 324, Table 1.
[a] The precise wording of these items varied from Time 2 to Time 3; however, the substance of the questions are identical.
[b] Column greater than 100 due to rounding.

United States would refuse to participate in the program. Despite such discussion of intended boycotts or noncooperation, there was no concerted, large-scale effort to block implementation of the program.

Additional evidence of changes in intended behavior was provided by the surveys conducted both after the passage of Medicare (Time 2) and after its initial implementation (Time 3). This evidence appears in Table 23-4.

An examination of the intended or actual behavior of physicians with respect to compliance or noncompliance with the goals of Medicare reveals clearly that the stated opposition to the health insurance program had evaporated. Despite the discussion of "boycotts" and other means of noncompliance, practically all physicians complied with the features of Medicare after it became law.

THREATS TO THE INFERENCE THAT LAW PRODUCED CHANGES IN THE ATTITUDES AND BEHAVIOR OF PHYSICIANS

1. Maturation Effect

Inferences from this research about the effectiveness of law might be challenged on the grounds that physicians' attitudes about Medicare were changing before enactment of the Medicare bill. According to this view, there might have been a long-term liberalization of physicians' attitudes, and acceptance of Medicare was simply one aspect of this change. Two pieces of evidence refute this interpretation.

First, the change in attitudes about Medicare over the three-year period was dramatic enough to cast doubt on the long-term hypothesis. After all, only 38 percent favored Medicare at Time 1, but that number increased to 70 percent and 81 percent within a relatively short period of time.

Second, there is evidence that the change in physicians' attitudes was specifically due to Medicare. Data about their attitudes toward economic-welfare issues, political party preference, and colleague controls indicated no concomitant liberalization over the three-year time period. Yet these attitudes were highly correlated with views about Medicare at Time 1. Thus, something stimulated a change concerning insured medical care without affecting attitudes in other areas. It is reasonable to infer that this something was the success of Medicare.

2. History Effect

Parallel to the enactment of Medicare was the passage of Title 19, commonly called Medicaid. This program provided matching federal funds to states for care of the medically indigent. The state of New York's plan for implementing its version of Medicaid met intense physician opposition. It could be argued that the state version of Medicaid was so unattractive as to produce a *contrast effect* which made Medicare a more attractive component of a federal health insurance program. Consequently, physicians' attitudes toward Medicare could have become more favorable as a result of their opposition to Medicaid and not as a result of the impact of law.

If this were true, those physicians who opposed Medicaid would have been more likely to change their thinking about Medicare than those who favored Medicaid. The data provide no support for this supposition. In fact, among those who opposed Medicare at Time 1, those who favored Medicaid at Times 2 and 3 were more likely to favor Medicare after its enactment than those who opposed Medicaid. Thus, there was no evidence of a history effect.

3. Pretest Effect

It could be argued that the results of the reinterviews at Times 2 and 3 were influenced by the initial interviews at Time 1. Perhaps the Time 1 interviews generated an interest in Medicare which caused increasingly favorable attitudes. However, the control sample of 330 physicians interviewed at Time 2, but not at Time 1, responded similarly to physicians who had been pretested at Time 1. Thus, there is no evidence for a pretest effect.

4. Instrument Effect

The items preceding the instrument at Time 2 were different than those in the Time 1 interview. Is it possible that alterations in the instrument affected the pattern of responses? To check on this possibility, two versions of the instrument were used in the Time 2 interviews. The first version mixed new questions with the repeat questions from Time 1, while the second version asked the repeat questions first, followed by new questions. There was no evidence of differences in response obtained from the two versions. Thus, there was no evidence of an instrument effect.

5. Mortality Effect

The initial sample of 1,205 physicians who were to be reinterviewed at either Time 2 or Time 3 suffered some case loss during the study. It is possible that the loss was not random but biased; that is, those physicians who could not be recontacted differed systematically from those who responded to the instrument in the reinterview phases. A comparison of backgrounds and attitudes of those physicians who participated in all phases of the research with those who participated only in phase 1 revealed no differences. Thus, there is no evidence to support the argument of a mortality effect.

23.1 TREND DATA

Interpretations which suggest that changes in a dependent variable between Time 1 and Time 2 are caused by an experimental variable, when the researcher lacked control over the experiment, contain an element of risk. Studies of changing crime rates illustrate this problem. For instance, Figure A represents the hypothetical measurement of the crime rate for Time 1 (January, 1970) and for Time 2 (January, 1971). Between Time 1 and Time 2, a law enforcement program (X) had been established. A natural tendency would be to infer that the law enforcement program "caused" a decrease in the crime rate.

Figure A. Crime Rates in Time 1 and Time 2.

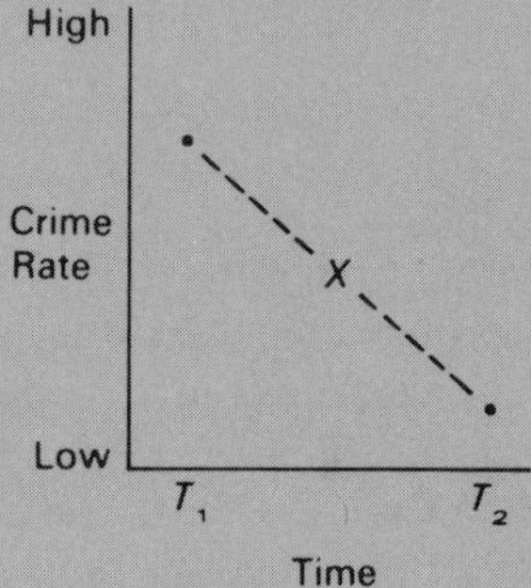

Figures B1-3 hypothetically extend the time span for Figure A, and lend themselves to differing interpretations. Figure B-1 prompts the inference that the decreased crime rate from Time 1 to Time 2 was

6. Selection Effect

There seems little basis for assuming there was a selection effect. Colombotos deliberately used random sampling procedures to draw the initial sample of physicians from the population of physicians in New York State. Following procedures used to stratify the sample, he employed random procedures to designate Time 2 and Time 3 groups. Consequently, the possibility of a selection effect in the creation of the experimental and control groups was small.

SUMMARY

The introduction of Medicare provided an opportunity for conducting a natural experiment on the relationship of a specific law to attitudes and behavior. The research began with telephone interviews of a sample of

part of a long-run decline and hence unrelated to the law enforcement program. Figure B-2 suggests that the Time 1 to Time 2 decrease was just one small change in the undulating pattern of crime rates. Finally, Figure B-3 appears consistent with the interpretation that the introduction

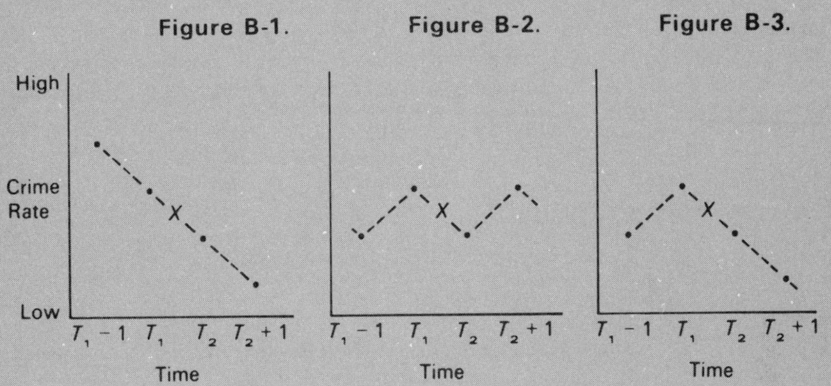

of the experimental variable (law enforcement program) was related to a decline in the dependent variable (crime rate).

Of course, the possibility remains that a still longer time span could change any of these interpretations once again. Such risks often exist in interpreting trend data.

physicians before passage of the legislation. Members of the sample were then reinterviewed at either of two times after passage. An additional sample was interviewed to test for pretest effects.

The resulting data suggested that in this case the law had indeed changed attitudes and behavior. A number of alternative explanations of the change were considered, but none appeared to successfully challenge the interpretation. The passage of Medicare therefore appears to have had a strong effect on physicians.

KEY IDEAS AND CONCEPTS

baseline
contrast effect
history effect
instrumentation effect
maturation effect
mortality effect
natural experiment
personal interview data
pretest effect
sample
selection effect
subsample
telephone interview data
trend data

ISSUES AND PROBLEMS

1. Describe two social phenomena in your community which would be amenable to study as a natural experiment.
2. Design an experiment to study one of these phenomena. List and discuss the strengths and weaknesses of the design.
3. Trends are often established using only two points in time. Discuss the strengths and weaknesses of using only two points for determining trends. Provide alternative explanations for any trend established using only two points in time.
4. Identify two trends which have been discussed recently in the newspapers. Discuss the evidence for and against the acceptance of these data to indicate a trend.

RECOMMENDED READINGS

The Logic of Experimental Designs

Campbell, Donald T., and Julian C. Stanley
1963 *Experimental and Quasi-Experimental Designs for Research.* Chicago: Rand McNally.

A highly readable discussion of alternative designs in social research. Well worth pursuing.

Ross, John, and Perry Smith
1968 "Orthodox Experimental Designs," in Hubert M. Blalock and Ann B. Blalock (eds.), *Methodology in Social Research.* Chicago: Rand McNally.

A highly readable discussion of alternative designs in social research. Well worth pursuing.

Statistical Analysis and Experimental Designs

Edwards, Allen L.
1968 *Experimental Design in Psychological Research.* 3d ed. New York: Holt, Rinehart and Winston.

A highly readable introduction to the logic of experimental designs and the usefulness of various statistical procedures for analysis.

Wood, Gordon
1974 *Fundamentals of Psychological Research.* Boston: Little, Brown.

Integrates the logic of research, experimental designs, and statistical procedures in a highly readable manner.

Causal Analysis in Nonexperimental Designs

Blalock, Hubert M., Jr.
1964 *Causal Inferences in Nonexperimental Research.* Chapel Hill: Univ. of North Carolina Press.

A stimulating discussion of the search for causality in nonexperimentally based research designs.

PART TEN

Values, Ethics, and the Responsibility of Scientists

24

SOCIAL SCIENCE RESEARCH AND ISSUES OF VALUES AND ETHICS

Throughout this text we have attempted to demonstrate that the research process consists of a series of decisions and procedures which interact with one another in subtle ways. Decisions made early in the course of the research were shown to influence decisions many steps removed in intended and unintended ways; decisions made later were shown to modify earlier decisions and to provide continuity and cohesiveness to the total effort. The end result, hopefully, has been a presentation of research as a complex process involving an interaction of theory and method devoid of the overly rational, ordered, and ritualistic characteristics often attributed to it.

In equally complex ways, social research generates value and ethical issues which have received increased attention in recent years. Private individuals and organizations have praised, criticized, and condemned the practices and accomplishments of social research, and government agencies have sought to establish guidelines and policies for its proper implementation.* Professional and scientific associations likewise have responded to

* U.S. Department of Health, Education, and Welfare, *The Institutional Guide to DHEW Policy on Protection of Human Subjects.* DHEW Publication No. (NIH) 72–102 (Washington: Government Printing Office, 1971). Two later statements by the Department of Health, Education, and Welfare appear in the *Federal Register*, November 16, 1973, 38(221), 31738–31749; and May 30, 1974, 39(10) 18914–18920. See also Herbert C. Kelman, "The Rights of the Subject in Social Research: An Analysis in Terms of Relative Power and Legitimacy," *American Psychologist*, 27(11): 989–1016.

these issues by providing a forum for discussion, forming review committees, developing guidelines, and formulating codes of ethics to guide researchers.*

The increasing number and complexity of these guidelines reflect the inherent tension between the professional responsibility of scientists to develop knowledge and their civic responsibility to enhance what might be termed the general welfare. The problem is made even more complex by the difficulty of determining what, if anything, serves the *general* welfare.

Knowledge is power. It is a resource which may be put to many purposes. Some theorists have argued that knowledge inevitably benefits some individuals and groups at the expense of others. Others have argued that knowledge is a general resource and therefore in the long run advances the general welfare of society. It is nonetheless true that a decision to generate knowledge can be used to advance one interest at the expense of another. A decision not to generate knowledge, however, foregoes the opportunity to develop information which might on balance have produced more benefits than costs. Thus, decisions to undertake—or not to undertake—research raise issues of values and ethics.

The issue of knowledge as power and the related ethical implications are aggravated by the tension between the requirements of research procedures and the needs of the subjects of research. The former often appear to depend for their success on the deception, coercion, and manipulation of human behavior and therefore are violations of basic ethical values. A decision not to use such procedures, however, may result in the weakening of research and the potential benefits that might flow from it.

Consequently, there appears to be a natural and inevitable tension between science as a knowledge-producing activity and as an activity guided by human values and ethics. Below we discuss these tensions in connection with three phases of the research process: (1) problem selection, (2) investigation procedures, and (3) dissemination of research results.

PROBLEM SELECTION

One of the most important components of problem selection is the choice of a theoretical perspective. There are many competing perspectives to be found within the purview of social science. Each has its adherents and opponents. Some social scientists perceive society as a collection of individuals and groups, each seeking to advance its special interests at the expense of others. Others view it as a system of interdependent parts, each of which contributes to the performance of the whole. Still others regard society as a mental configuration of images and meanings subject to

*See, for example, American Psychological Association, *Ethical Principles in the Conduct of Research with Human Participants* (Washington, D.C.: The Association, 1973).

change as selves and others subtly construct and chart courses of action. This list, of course, is not exhaustive, but it does illustrate that empirical reality can be—and is—conceptualized in various ways. Research problems receive their definition and meaning in terms of these conceptualizations. This, in turn, means that our understanding of a problem bears a direct relationship to the theoretical manner in which it was conceived.

There is a kind of principle of uncertainty in science. When a perspective is applied to a phenomenon, knowledge of that phenomenon is necessarily constrained by the perspective applied. For example, if community decision making is viewed in terms of a conflict perspective, understanding of that phenomenon will be in terms of conflict. However, if the same phenomenon is viewed in terms of a system perspective, understanding of it will be in terms of system performance. This argument applies to all social phenomena.

Because social scientists (and others) must perforce adopt *some* perspective, they must also accept the responsibility of making clear the terms of the perspective within which they view a research problem. While this does not solve the dilemma, it acknowledges the nature of social theory and research, and permits the reader to better evaluate subsequent research steps.

The value implications of problem selection and definition are complicated by the conditions of employment and class position of most social scientists. Generally, social research is conducted in academic, governmental, or foundational settings with data-collection forays into the larger society. Social scientists therefore occupy positions which have tended to align them with middle-class perspectives and values. From this vantage point, many of the problems selected for research have been cast in the direction of phenomena deemed problematic for societal management.

Thus, much research has focused on groups which are in some sense weak or deviant: children and old people, the poor, welfare recipients, ethnic minorities, juvenile delinquents and criminals, alcoholics and drug addicts, patients and prisoners, college students and military personnel. As groups which are viewed as problematic (i.e., weak, dependent, deserving special consideration, etc.), they have been especially vulnerable to social science research. Lacking either knowlege, power, or will to resist, such segments have been extensively researched for theoretical and practical reasons.

It should be noted, however, that social scientists do not generally investigate these groups with Machiavellian intent; rather it is usually with the noblest of intentions. They are generally seeking to simultaneously advance the state of their discipline while producing what is believed to be socially useful information. The vulnerability and ease of isolating the aforementioned groups make them doubly attractive as research targets. However, at least three consequences flow from the tendency to choose "problematic" issues as research problems.

First, there is the consequence of perspective. The same social phenomenon can be approached from several different points of view, and research procedures and findings will be shaped accordingly. High rates of unemployment among minorities, for instance, can be approached as a research problem from several different vantages, some of which may implicitly blame the individual while others may implicitly blame society. It is incumbent upon social scientists to entertain and support competing perspectives so as to provide a forum for as thorough and enlightened discussion as possible.

Second, there is the consequence of limited knowledge. Insofar as social scientists constrain their research to issues defined as problematic by middle-class perspectives, their ability to contribute intellectually to a discussion of issues and problems defined in terms of other group or class viewpoints will be limited. They, therefore, should research advantaged and powerful groups with the same range of perspectives that can be applied to less advantaged or powerless groups. This strategy should promote a fuller understanding of human behavior and social life.

Third, there is the consequence of knowledge use. Problems selected and defined in terms of middle-class values rooted in societal management deny the very development of knowledge which may be used by disadvantaged groups to influence their own life chances. Restricting investigation to one side of a power relationship tends to permit the manipulation of one group by another. Social scientists should seek to produce knowledge usable in a wide range of societal groups.

PROCEDURES OF INVESTIGATION

It is unfortunate that research procedures often appear to require for their success the deception, coercion, and manipulation of subject-participants. Again, however, it is not Machiavellian intent which produces violations of human and ethical values but rather the current nature of scientific research. For convenience, we discuss these issues in terms of the procedures used in (1) survey research, (2) field observation research, and (3) experimental research. Generally, however, the issues discussed cut across all research procedures and only an examination of a specific project will reveal which value and ethical issues are most important.

Survey Research

Survey research often depends upon the willingness of individuals to complete a questionnaire or submit to an interview. The voluntary character of most such research may seem to ameliorate many value and ethical issues involved in data collection, but in subtle ways this seemingly voluntary character of survey research generates important value and ethical dilemmas.

To obtain respondent cooperation, researchers often seek to legitimate a project through emphasizing its importance and sponsorship. Thus, potential respondents are informed that the research is undertaken with a government grant or is sponsored by a research foundation or prestigious college or university. Respondents are also informed that the project has important positive implications for the individual or larger society. While such claims may be true, they are nonetheless a subtle form of coercion. Individuals are thereby made less free in deciding whether to participate. If respondents are drawn from disadvantaged or parochial groups (e.g., ethnic minorities or college students), degrees of freedom may be reduced even further because members of such groups may be too uninformed, acquiescent, or powerless to inquire as to the real benefits or costs of participation.

Surveys also impose upon the time and privacy of respondents. Respondents may be informed that a survey will "only take a few minutes" when indeed a half-hour to an hour is required. Respondent privacy is invaded through even the most seemingly innocuous questions designed to determine an individual's age, marital status, education, or ethnic background. More serious invasions of privacy may occur with questions intended to measure racial attitudes, candidate preference, or birth control beliefs. Further invasions occur when respondents are asked to report on such behavior as illness symptoms, law violations, or intercourse frequency.

To secure data which can be conveniently analyzed, respondents are often provided with fixed-choice questions that subtly compel them to crystallize their thoughts on matters and issues which may raise new anxieties and concerns. If open-ended questions are used, subtle coercion is applied in the form of neutral probes which pressure respondents to recall additional information or draw potentially disturbing conclusions. If respondents fail to return questionnaires or are reluctant to participate in interviews, sequential follow-up mailings or contacts with more experienced interviewers may be used to secure the desired voluntary cooperation, thereby introducing a subtle form of harassment and coercion.

These are but a few of the ethical issues raised by survey research procedures.

Field Observation Research

For the social scientist using field observation techniques, a key problem is to gain access to social situations while simultaneously minimizing any influence his presence may have on the behavior being observed. By disclosing his identity and the purposes of the research, he potentially alters the research phenomenon. In concealing his identity, he engages in deception. Thus, research and ethical dilemmas are often joined in field observation studies.

As in the case of survey research, field observers seek to legitimate their projects in terms of sponsorship, importance, and presumed benefits.

If the purpose of the research is disclosed, subtle coercion is used. If it is concealed, various forms of deception may be used to explain the researchers' presence and objectives. These include posing as a bona fide neighborhood resident with similar problems and concerns or blandly passing oneself off as "writing a book" or engaged in some other seemingly innocuous but relevant task. Dilemmas of privacy are raised as individuals display potentially sanctionable behavior or inner thoughts and opinions. Researchers may promise anonymity, confidentialty, and protection from research results which, under some circumstances cannot be fulfilled, and participants may incur risks unknowingly and unanticipated by researchers.

As in survey research, field observation projects are often undertaken among groups which lack the will, knowledge, or power to resist. Institutional studies of mental patients and prisoners, field observations of delinquent groups, and observational studies of play and work groups pose additional ethical issues because the research may proceed with the permission, support, and interests of institutional controllers paramount. Rarely are patients, prisoners, delinquents, children, or workers in a position to permit or support studies of doctors, wardens, social workers, teachers, or managers. Therefore, it is not surprising that research procedures may violate the rights of the former in the course of serving the latter.

Experimental Research

Most experiments attempt to motivate participants to behave in as natural and unself-conscious manner as possible, while investigators manipulate and control experimental conditions. To implement this strategy, researchers often feel it is necessary to deceive participants about the true nature of the experiment. Rarely are participants informed as to the true nature of details of the experiment. Such deception is carried further during the conduct of the experiment itself.

Subjects may be deceived regarding the purpose of their behavior, or they may be misled about their performance (e.g., misinterpretation of personality or self-perception scores), and they may be asked to engage in behavior which is monotonous, distasteful, or physically and mentally discomforting. Such experiments pose obvious dangers to the mental health and well-being of participants, and it is clear that the interests of the participant must be placed ahead of the interest of the researcher.

The use of control and experimental subjects raises further issues of deception and potential harm to participants. Often, subjects will be deceived regarding their status in the experiment, and either the manipulation or denial of experimental stimuli introduces value and ethical dilemmas.

When experiments are carried out in natural settings, researchers may dupe unwitting participants into revealing behavior which otherwise might never be exhibited. Thus, field experiments in which researchers pose as potential employers, victims of crime, or homosexuals raise serious value and ethical issues.

RESEARCH PRODUCTS

We have already suggested that the choice of a research topic carries with it the potential of benefiting the interests of some group at the expense of others. Similarly, although science is a public enterprise, some members of the public have more access to research findings than others. Scientists tend to report their findings in media which are accessible primarily to those trained by profession or occupation to consume such information.

Thus, scientists may file research results with societal managers (e.g., government agencies) or may publish their work in professional journals. Neither medium is readily available to the general public or to weak or deviant social groups. The usual consumers of research are either professional colleagues or societal managers. Seldom do the subjects of research themselves review, debate, discuss, and interpret the findings obtained by social scientists. Consequently, the capacity of all groups to equally negotiate their own welfare is constrained not only by the character of the research but by its form of distribution. Research products, therefore, like research topics and research procedures, may serve some groups at the expense of others. Not surprisingly, they tend to serve those who fund and otherwise reward research efforts.

SUMMARY AND CONCLUSIONS

In this chapter we have taken the perspective that society is a collection of individuals and groups, each seeking to advance its own special interests. The advancement of some interests was seen as often being at the expense of others. This view applies equally well to the scientific effort.

Social scientists admittedly seek to advance their interests, which consist partly of developing knowledge. However, in their efforts to produce knowledge, problem selection, procedures of investigation, and the dissemination of results often conflict with the interests of the individuals and groups being studied. Thus, there is a natural tension between the professional responsibility of scientists to develop knowledge and their civic responsibility to individuals, groups, and the larger society. There is no evident solution to this dilemma.

The ethical implications of selection of a research problem, its definition, procedures of investigation, and dissemination of research results remain the responsibility of each researcher to consider. Policies, guidelines, and codes of ethics may serve to orient and sensitize researchers to value and ethical issues; however, they are not a substitute for conscious decision making in the conduct of research. Each researcher must judge the potential benefits and costs in human terms.

To illustrate the guidelines currently available for aiding researchers, we reproduce in the following appendix documents outlining the human subjects policy at the institution where the authors currently teach.

APPENDIX TO CHAPTER 24

HUMAN SUBJECT GUIDELINES AT THE UNIVERSITY OF DELAWARE

March 26, 1975

MEMORANDUM

TO: Deans and Heads of Departments and Divisions

FROM: Arnold L. Lippert
Associate Provost for Research
and Dean of the College of Graduate Studies

SUBJECT: Review of Research Involving Human Subjects

The present University research policy on human subjects states that every research proposal involving human subjects must be reviewed in accordance with the guidelines of the policy and officially approved before the proposal leaves the University or before research is initiated. The major part of the research in some departments and colleges is affected by this policy and therefore the time and effort required for compliance should be minimized. In order to expedite the work of the University Human Subjects Committee, a departmental committee, or the head of the department, should review each proposal to ensure that it complies with the University policy. The proposal should then be forwarded to the Coordinator of Research accompanied by the departmental review report.

For internally funded proposals, where the human subjects apparently will not be exposed to any physical or mental hazard, the short procedure can be used and only one copy need be forwarded. When there is some possible hazard or when the proposal is to be sent to an outside sponsor, nine copies should be forwarded. The information to be forwarded in either case is given by the research protocol of the University policy. (See page 2.) The protocol should be as brief as possible but should include the following information:

1. The procedure for selecting subjects which guarantees that the subject is able to exercise free power of choice without undue inducement or any element of force, fraud, deceit, duress, or any other form of constraint or coercion.
2. The explanation that the subjects will be given before they sign the informed consent statement.
3. A copy of the Certificate of Informed Consent that will be used and kept on file. The attached form is suitable for most cases.
4. The procedures that will be used to keep the data confidential. In general there should be no direct link between the data and the subject. The data should only be identified by a key or a letter and the identifying key kept in a locked file.
5. A copy of any questionnaire that will be used.

At least three weeks should be allowed for approval by the full committee. When the short procedure is used the department and principal investigator will be notified of the outcome within one week. . . .

UNIVERSITY OF DELAWARE POLICY ON THE INVOLVEMENT OF HUMAN SUBJECTS IN RESEARCH AND RESEARCH-RELATED ACTIVITIES

I. University Responsibility

The protection of the individual as a research subject is an obligation recognized and assumed by this University. Therefore, any study which involves human subjects must be performed under conditions which insure the rights and welfare of the subjects through adequate safeguards and the informed consent of those involved. Such consent is valid, however, only if the individual is first given a fair explanation of the procedures to be followed, their possible benefits and attendant hazards and discomforts, and the reasons for pursuing the research and its general objectives. This is particularly important when the experimentation or research is not for the direct benefit of the subject. Safeguards should be especially stringent when the subject is legally or physically unable to give personal consent, as in the case of minors.

In order to assure a uniform implementation of the foregoing principles, it is the policy of this University to require review and approval of individual projects by an appropriate Review Board to assure that:

1. The risks to the subject are so outweighed by the sum of the benefits to the subject and the importance of the knowledge to be gained as to warrant a decision to allow the subject to accept these risks;
2. The rights and welfare of any such subjects will be adequately protected;
3. Legally effective informed consent will be obtained by adequate and appropriate methods; and
4. The conduct of the activity will be reviewed at timely intervals.

II. Investigator Responsibility

Each university investigator who is planning a project which will involve the use of human subjects in research is expected to: 1) make available to the Review Board the plans for anticipated research prior to beginning the project and in sufficient time to allow the committee to take action; 2) make clearly evident in the written research plan, or through any further information which may be needed, precisely how the rights and welfare of the research subjects are to be protected, how informed consent of human subjects is to be obtained, and whether written consent forms are to be utilized; and 3) during the course of the project make known to the Board any changes in protocol or any emerging problems of investigation which may significantly alter the original concept.

III. Definition of Human Subject

A human subject is considered to be any individual who may be exposed to the possibility of injury, including physical, psychological, or social injury as a consequence of participation as a subject in any research, development, training or related activity which departs from the application of those established and accepted methods necessary to meet the subject's needs, or increases the ordinary risks of daily life, including the recognized risks inherent in a chosen field of service. Subjects also may include persons involved in environmental or epidemiological studies; donors of services; and living donors of body fluids, organs or tissues.

IV. Applicability

This policy applies to every project which includes research procedures that go beyond the diagnostic and therapeutic needs of the subject as determined by the Review Board. Such projects may involve the procurement of human materials or services and may be categorized as research, training, development, or related activities; and may be internally supported by University funds or externally supported through a grant, contract, fellowship, or traineeship. The applicability of this policy is most obvious in medical and behavorial science research involving procedures that may induce a potentially harmful altered state or condition. Surgical procedures; the removal of organs or tissues for biopsy, transplantation or banking; the administration of drugs or radiation; the use of indwelling catheters or electrodes; the requirement of strenuous physical exertion; subjection to deceit, public embarrassment, or humiliation are all examples of procedures which require thorough scrutiny by the University Review Board. (See also Section E, Procedure.)

There is a wide range of medical, social and behavioral research in which no immediate risk to the subject is involved. However, some of these may impose varying degrees of discomfort, irritation, and harassment. In addition, there may be substantial potential injury to the subject's rights if attention is not given to maintenance of the confidentiality of information obtained from the subject and the protection of the subject from misuse of findings. In this category are projects which may involve the use of data obtained previously for purposes other than the research in question.

There is also research concerned solely with discarded human materials obtained at surgery or in the course of diagnosis or treatment. The use of these materials involves no possible element of risk to the subject. In such instances, the only requirement that need be considered is a review of the circumstances under which the materials are to be procured.

The final determination of what constitutes human involvement is the proper concern of the University Review Board.

V. Implementation

A. The University Review Board

The Review Board will have responsibility for the final review and approval of projects involving human subjects. One member must not be a University employee but the other members will ordinarily be from the University community. Memberships will be made up of:

Group I A Sociologist
An Anthropologist
A Psychologist

Group II A University Employed Medical Doctor
A Nurse with Graduate Degree
The Director of Health Sciences

Group III The Coordinator of Research
The Associate Provost for Research, Chairperson
The Dean of Students
Outside Member (Executive Secretary, Health Planning Council)

A quorum will consist of six members and include a member from each of the three groups. A majority vote of members present is required to render decisions.

Whenever it is deemed advisable, independent consultants may be called upon to assist the Review Board.

B. Information Required for Board Consideration

The proposal in its final form, together with a brief protocol describing human subject protection, shall be submitted to the Board (9 copies). In the event that the final draft of the proposal has not been completed in time to meet the deadline for Board review, rough drafts (9) may be submitted with the protocol. The final draft must conform to the original protocol and one copy must be submitted to the Coordinator of Research as soon as possible.

The following information is required in the protocol:

1. The title of the project and the investigator's name.
2. Research objectives.
3. A description of the study with particular respect to methodology and plan of action, including information on the following:
   a. The manner and the extent to which human subjects will be involved.
   b. The procedures, tools, etc. to be employed. Include examples and a description of all questionnaires. Copies of the questionnaires must be submitted to the Board for review before use.
   c. What the subjects will be told about their involvement in the study.
   d. How informed consent will be obtained and recorded.
   e. Whether there will be any potential risks to the subject.
   f. What measures will be taken to safeguard the welfare of the subjects, their rights of privacy and the confidentiality of information being handled.
   g. Whether minors will be involved.
   h. Whether personality tests or inventories will be used.
   i. What inducements, if any, will be offered the subject.
4. Current statement of ethics for the discipline. (If not already on file in the Research Office.)

C. Informed Consent

Informed consent means the knowing consent of an individual or the individual's legally authorized representative, so situated as to be able to exercise free power of choice without undue inducement or any element of force, fraud, deceit, duress, or other form of constraint or coercion. The basic elements of information necessary to such consent include:

1. An explanation of the procedures to be followed, and their purposes, including identification of any procedures which are experimental;
2. A description of any attendant discomforts and risks reasonably to be expected;
3. A description of any benefits reasonably to be expected;
4. A disclosure of any appropriate alternative procedures that might be advantageous for the subject;

5. An offer to answer any inquiries concerning the procedures;
6. An instruction that the person is free to withdraw consent and to discontinue participation in the project or activity at any time without prejudice to the subject; and
7. In the case of minors the consent of a legally authorized representative is required.

The University is obligated to obtain and document legally effective informed consent when any research proposes to place any subject at risk. No such informed consent, oral or written, shall include any exculpatory language. The consent will be documented in one of the three following forms:

1. A written consent document embodying all of the basic elements of informed consent which is signed by the subject after being given adequate opportunity to read it.
2. A short written consent form document indicating that the basic elements of informed consent have been presented orally to the subject. The short form must be signed by the subject and by an auditor witness to the oral presentation and to the subject's signature.
3. A modification of either procedures 1 or 2 that is approved by the Review Board. Such a modification must establish 1) that the risk to any subject is minimal; 2) that use of either of the primary procedures for obtaining informed consent would surely invalidate objectives of considerable immediate importance and 3) that any reasonable alternative means for attaining these objectives would be less advantageous to the subjects.

D. Confidentiality

The identity of a human subject shall not be revealed without the prior consent of the subject. If the data are used in connection with additional research, the consent of the subject must be obtained before the subject is identified with the additional research. The records identifying the subject with the research must be kept apart from the experimental data and must be kept under security conditions equivalent to "confidential data" regulations.

E. Procedure

Every proposal involving human subjects must be reviewed prior to the start of the project or submission of it to an outside sponsor. The proposal and explanatory protocol should first be submitted to the departmental chairperson for approval. If there is a departmental review committee, the chairperson will take the responsibility for transmitting the proposal to that committee. After departmental approval, the proposal and protocol are sent to the Office of the Coordinator of Research for transmittal to the University Review Board. (Nine copies are required.) In order to allow for any modifications, the proposal must be submitted to the Board at least fifteen (15) working days prior to any deadline date. The Board will review the proposal and respond within ten (10) working days.

Since the review process may involve either individual consideration of proposals by Board members or a formal Board meeting, questions or reservations concerning the proposal project may be communicated to the author of the proposal by either the Board chairperson or by an individual Board member. It is anticipated that many questions will be resolved through such communication prior to final approval by all members of the Board. After completion of Board review, the chairperson will communicate the results of the review to the author of the proposal with copies to the Department and the Research Office.

Decision of the Board will be on the basis of a majority of those voting. A minority report is required from those dissenting from the majority opinion.

On-going projects will be reviewed on an annual basis unless a significant change in protocol dictates more frequent reviews. The Board is responsible for initiating a review of protocols on a more frequent than annual basis when the Board determines this action is advisable.

The preparation of files relating to the review of each project, including letters and memoranda pertaining to the resolution of problems, copies of consent forms, approvals and disapprovals, etc. will be the responsibility of the Board chairperson. After a decision has been reached by the Board, the file will be sent to the Research Office where it will be retained.

F. Special Short Procedure

When there are no stipulations by a sponsoring agency and when the subject runs no apparent risk of physical, psychological or social injury, research may be carried out after approval by the Department Review Committee with the concurrence of the Coordinator of Research. An informational copy of the research protocol and the departmental approval will be sent to the chairperson of the University Review Board in all such cases.

August 1, 1975

(University of Delaware Sample Form)

CERTIFICATE OF INFORMED CONSENT

The project in which I am about to participate has been explained to me and all of my questions have been answered satisfactorily. I voluntarily agree to participate in this project. I understand that I can withdraw from the project at any time and that I can decline to participate in any part of it or decline to answer any questions without prejudice to me.

____

Name (Print or type)

____

Signature

____

Date

A copy of any written explanation must be attached. If the information is presented orally, a witness is required.

____

Witness:

____

Name (Print or type)

____

Signature

____

Date

APPENDIXES

APPENDIX 1

GUIDELINES IN WRITING A RESEARCH REPORT

Selecting a problem and then executing the research according to sound procedures represent the first two steps in research. The third step consists of writing up the research results. Research can make significant contributions only if it is communicated effectively to its chosen audience. Therefore, the first requirement of a research report is that it be clearly and concisely written.

The burden of effective communication falls on the researcher. A reader usually will have some difficulty understanding a report simply because the reader did not participate in the actual research. Consequently the report must provide information in a readily understandable manner. The report should avoid burdening the reader with unnecessarily abstract language, jargon, convoluted sentences, and a dense style. Research reports should crisply convey the nature and results of research to an intended audience and still make lively (or at least interesting) reading.

Research reports, however, are not constructed like detective stories. They do not build to a climax. Rather, they prepare the reader for what is to come, then present the research, and finally summarize what has been said. The *Title* and *Abstract* prepare the reader by providing an orientation. Statements of the *Perspective* and *Problem* inform the reader of the research intent. The *Methods* and *Findings* sections tell what the researcher has to report. And the *Conclusion* summarizes what has already been said. Research reports are often stylized in this manner: *title*, *abstract*, *perspective*, *problem*, *methods*, *findings*, and *conclusions*.

Each of these sections will now be reviewed in detail.

I. TITLE

The title of a report should be clear and concise. It communicates to potential readers what information they can expect to find. Titles which promise more than they deliver deceive the reader and justifiably are severely criticized.

A title can be created either before or after the research report is written. Creating a title before the report is written may guide in the writing of the report. It may assist in deciding what contents to include and what to exclude. Since a research project may investigate several problems simultaneously, selecting a title in advance of writing the report assists in separating the relevant from the irrelevant. On the other hand, a title can also be prepared afterward. This increases the likelihood that it will correspond to the report's content. Frequently, researchers create a tentative title before writing the report and then revise it afterward. In this way, they gain the advantages of both approaches.

Titles vary with the medium of the report and the intended audience. An examination of reports written on topics similar to yours and with a similar audience will provide clues as to proper title construction and format. Basically, there are two types of audiences: academic and non-academic. Titles vary with the type of audience you are trying to catch.

If your audience is academic, you should create a title which generalizes the nature of the problem you investigated and the findings you obtained. This will assist potential readers in locating your research among that of thousands of others which are competing for their attention. It will also assist prospective readers in bridging the connection between your research and others on related topics.

If your audience is nonacademic, you should avoid abstract professional language both in the title and elsewhere in the report. There are two reasons for this. First, such language is more likely to serve as an obstacle than an aid to communication to readers outside the profession. Second, nonacademic readers are more likely to be interested in the specific problem and findings of the research than in its implications for theory or broader problems.

Often, the generality and specificity of your research can be combined in a single title. Several examples of projects and potential titles follow.

Project 1

The research consisted of an analysis of the relationship between dormitory residence and dating patterns on a college campus. The purpose was to investigate the effects of spatial location on social interaction.

Suggested Academic Title: Ecological Determinants of Social Interaction: Dormitory Location and Dating Patterns

Suggested Nonacademic Title: A Study of Dormitory Location and Dating Patterns on a College Campus

Project 2

The research focused on the social characteristics of individuals who actively protested busing desegregation. The purpose of the research was to investigate the effects of structural variables on resistance to social change.

Suggested Academic Title: Structural Determinants of Resistance to Social Change: Busing Protesters

Suggested Nonacademic Title: Social Characteristics of Busing Protesters in a Medium-Sized City

II. ABSTRACT

Literally hundreds of articles and reports to private and public agencies are competing for reader attention each month. Readers use titles as a first step in locating research of possible interest. Next, they often review the abstract or executive summary which follows the title.

If a research report is being prepared as a journal article it usually contains a brief abstract of fifty to one hundred words. If the report is being prepared for a private or public agency, it usually contains an executive summary consisting of five or more typewritten pages. The objectives of an abstract and executive summary are identical. Both describe the research problem, the methods used, and the findings obtained. However, they vary as to length and detail.

On the basis of the abstract or executive summary, readers will determine if the reported research deserves their closer attention. Consequently, the abstract or summary should pithily describe the essentials of the research. The choice of language should be governed by its communicative power. In academic reports, the careful selection of professional terms permits effective communication in terse language. In nonacademic reports, professional terms should be avoided when possible. In this case, the language of intended readers should be used in order to communicate effectively.

III. PERSPECTIVE

For academic audiences, a research write-up normally begins with a review of the literature. This is designed to locate the problem within a research tradition. For readers unfamiliar with the literature, the review serves an educational function. For those familiar with past literature, it provides an overview on how the researcher perceives the issues. For all readers, the review legitimates the research; that is, it serves to justify why the problem was important and worth investigating.

A review is necessarily selective. It cannot encompass the hundreds of past reports, articles, and books which have been published on the problem you may have investigated. There are three criteria often used in selecting which literature to incorporate in a review. First, it is important to select only those works which significantly bear on the research problem. Those which are of marginal relevance can be ignored. Second, it is important to include references to supporting and contradictory literature. Although a review is selective, it should not seek to bias the reader. Past research should be reviewed fairly and impartially. Third, a review should incorporate something old and something new. Usually, it includes references to classical writings of persons of unusual importance to the discipline, and then references to the most recent significant writings. In documenting previous literature, it is important to cite specific chapters or passages. This assists readers in locating the material which has a significant bearing on the problem.

If your report is written for a nonacademic audience, an extensive literature review may be unnecessary. If such a review is desired, it often cites only the current and relevant works. Nonacademic audiences are seldom interested in the linkage between your work and previous writings or in the historical context within which your research falls. They are interested in recent work which directly bears on the research problem you investigated. Consequently, if a review of literature is included in a report for a nonacademic audience, it is important that a direct link between the literature and the problem you are reporting on be specified.

IV. PROBLEM

If your review has been thorough, a statement of the problem should flow naturally from the previous discussion. Readers should be given a succinct but clear idea of the research problem as you perceived and structured it. This is very important because readers will eventually judge whether the conduct of the research and its findings measure up to your presentation of the problem. Since the literature review may have discussed different theoretical perspectives, the problem must be stated clearly if readers are to interpret the problem in the manner in which you intended.

V. METHOD

In this, as in other sections of the report, you must be selective. It is impossible and undesirable to inform readers about every step in the research process. There is consensus that the methods section should cover: *sources of data*, *procedures of data collection*, *techniques of variable measurement*, and *intended analysis procedures*.

A. Sources of Data

Sources of data provide information about the scope and generality of the research. For example, research may focus on data which apply to a nation (e.g., U.S. census data), to a community (e.g., a small midwestern town), or to a small group (e.g., a religious sect). Except where public information is involved, the identity of sources is usually not revealed. This honors any pledge of anonymity and confidentiality that may have been made in collecting data. Often such pledges are not formally stated but are taken for granted in the research setting. Only if participants are forewarned that information provided will become public should such a pledge (formal or informal) be violated. While the concealment of sources protects individuals, organizations, and communities, it has the disadvantage of compelling readers to accept your account of the reliability and validity of data. It also has the disadvantage of discouraging or prohibiting replicative research. At this junction, it is necessary to ethically decide how much information can be released without potential harm to your data sources.

B. Methods of Data Collection

Methods of data collection provide readers with specific information about data-collection techniques. For instance, they explain whether random or nonrandom sampling techniques were employed, whether the research used questionnaires or interviews, what conditions existed when data were collected, whether certain dimensions of the research design had to be compromised, whether the research experienced data loss from its beginnings to completion, and so on. A detailed statement of data-collection techniques is essential if readers are to develop confidence in the study. Researchers must disclose known defects as well as positive aspects of the data-collection procedures used.

C. Techniques of Variable Measurement

Techniques of variable measurement explain specific procedures used. For example, they explain if a Likert or Guttman scale was employed, what procedures and decision rules were used for grouping subjects into categories, which theoretical and operational definitions were used, and so on. Researchers must discuss any known biases or compromises which were made with respect to specific variable measurements.

D. Analysis Techniques

Your description of analysis techniques provides readers with information about specific techniques you intend to use. For example, your analysis may involve using percentages, ratios, cross-tabulations, measures of association, or chi-squares. If you intend to use a complicated or unfamiliar technique of analysis, readers should be informed as to literature sources so they may consult these for clarification. This permits them to review or learn more about the techniques you will employ.

VI. FINDINGS

The Findings section of the report provides what most readers are reading to find out—the results of the research. This section therefore must provide a focused description of what has been found with regard to the questions and expectations raised by the title, the statement of the problem, and earlier sections of the report. Hence, it must be selective.

The Findings section should not contain all that has been found in the course of the research. Many interesting observations and tables must be excluded because they are not sufficiently relevant to the thrust of the report. The Findings section should contain, in an orderly fashion, as many answers as possible to the questions previously raised in the reader's mind without his becoming bogged down in details.

A number of conventions and rules facilitate this goal. In presentations featuring tables, the first of these usually gives an overview of the data. Often this consists of a tabular presentation of the characteristics of the population or a sample if sampling was used. It provides data in a form that allows the reader to develop an orientation for the analysis which is to follow. Subsequent tables focus on the results of the analysis itself, presenting more limited aspects of the research. Because the tables which are finally presented to the reader may have resulted from a combination of ones that were constructed by the researcher during the analysis, it is essential that readers be provided as much information as possible for interpreting the data. Not all readers will draw the same inferences from data. Consequently, it is essential that sufficient information be provided so that readers may reexamine the data in this way. When possible, data should permit readers to make their own calculations. Furthermore, whenever appropriate, tables should provide measures of association and statistical significance. These are but a few of the conventional rules for presenting data in the Findings section.

Many other conventions apply, each specific to particular forms of research. Examining previous studies similar in method and appealing to a kindred audience will give an indication of what your readership expects from the report you are preparing. For the novice writer especially, it is usually best to provide information according to the most familiar and tested format.

Researchers are obligated in the Findings section to report data which contradict as well as support any hypotheses or ideas which were investigated. Only by reporting such information can scientific knowledge grow. Contradictory evidence may lead to important insights for future investigation. The researcher must also report data that are inconclusive. The Findings section therefore will often contain a number of highly tentative and qualified findings, reflecting the efforts of the researcher to neither overinterpret nor underinterpret the meaningfulness of the data.

VII. SUMMARY AND CONCLUSIONS

This is usually a brief section designed to serve three functions. First, it refocuses the reader's attention on the main issues and findings and away from the myriad details which have been presented. Second, when appropriate, it qualifies some of the findings by stressing methodological limitations or alternative interpretations of the research. Third, it may suggest promising directions for future research based upon the experience of the researcher. Such suggestions should not be broad statements that more research would be useful (which is invariably the case), but specific statements about the types and strategies of research that appear most promising.

IMPLICATIONS OF A RESEARCH REPORT

The preceding discussion attempted to provide guidelines for writing a research report. It assumed that, in influencing the beliefs of others, you would attempt to provide an honest and valid view of your research. However, within the framework of honesty, which constitutes the first canon of scientific reporting, there are many other variables which will consciously and subconsciously influence your report.

First, as hinted, a research report is selective. It reports only information you wanted your readers to read. Scientific norms dictate that you report certain information such as that regarding data sources and data collection; but having discharged this responsibility, you have considerable flexibility in deciding what other information to include. By selecting some information and ignoring some other, your report will necessarily contain some bias. The latter may not be personally recognized and therefore may influence your report in unknown ways. Discussion with colleagues and self-reflection may curb biased reporting.

Second, the document is personal. It is testimony to your competence as a researcher. Since it may influence your self-esteem or even your career mobility, there may be a natural tendency to emphasize the strengths of the research while underplaying its weaknesses. Again, this may not be a conscious decision. You may honestly believe that some of the weaknesses of the research are unimportant. However, this conclusion should be reached by your colleagues, and consequently it is important to include a discussion of strategies and procedures employed in sufficient detail so that readers can judge the merits of the research.

Third, the document is persuasive. Although the proper stance of a scientist is unflinching skepticism, it is difficult to be skeptical of one's own work. Therefore, research is usually presented in terms of arguments designed to support hypotheses rather than disprove them. This tendency to argue for the support of hypotheses may result in overlooking contradictory evidence. To curb this tendency, researchers should focus on negative as well as positive evidence and provide sufficient data for readers to draw their own conclusions.

Fourth, the report represents reconstructed history. It does not usually reflect how you engaged in all phases of the research nor does it necessarily reflect the order in which you engaged in them. To aid readers in comprehending your research, you will have portrayed it in a logical fashion, beginning with the perspective and ending with the findings and conclusions. This may provide a false image of your interaction with your data. The logical and stylized presentation is necessary for effective communication of research; however, in the process the empirical reality of false starts, dead ends, and premature decisions may be lost.

In sum, research reporting—despite its impersonal and logical format—cannot be divorced from its social setting. As writer and reader these elements must be considered in judging the scientific merits of reported research.

A1.1 STYLE GUIDELINES FOR REPORTS

Proper citations, footnotes, references, and bibliography are important in constructing any research report. A number of guidelines are available for use. These include:

Menzel, Donald H., Howard Mumford Jones, and Lyle G. Boyd
1961 *Writing a Technical Paper,* New York: McGraw-Hill.

Traces the writing of papers through various drafts that should improve communication. Includes discussions of grammar, style, jargon, and the final typed report.

Strunk, William, Jr., and E. B. White
1962 *The Elements of Style.* New York: Macmillan.

A worthy attempt to "cut the vast tangle of English rhetoric down to size and write its rules and principles on the head of a pin." The rules are useful for anyone wishing to write clearly and concisely.

Turabian, Kate L.
1967 *A Manual for Writers of Term Papers, Theses, and Dissertations.* 3d ed. Chicago: Univ. of Chicago Press.

A standard reference for the appropriate use and form of footnotes, quotations, bibliographies, tables, illustrations, text, and other items in the final preparation of a paper.

Before preparing a report for submission to a professional journal, an organization, or a government agency, researchers should determine if there are specific guidelines to be followed. The guidelines vary in a number of ways. Reproduced below are the guidelines specified by the American Sociological Association for publication in the *American Sociological Review.*

NOTICE TO CONTRIBUTORS

The maximum length of an *ASR* paper is typically ten (10) printed pages or thirty (30) typed manuscript pages including space for tables, figures and references. Due to space limitations, we must request contributors to conform to this norm as closely as possible.

To permit anonymity in the review of manuscripts, keep identifying material out of the manuscript. Attach a cover page giving authorship, institutional affiliation and acknowledgments, and provide only the title as identification on the manuscript and abstract.

ASA Multiple Submissions Policy: Submission of a manuscript to a professional journal clearly implies commitment to publish in that journal. The competition for journal space requires a great deal of time and effort on the part of editorial readers whose main compensation for this service is the opportunity to read papers prior to publication and the gratification associated with discharge of professional obligation. For these reasons, *the American Sociological Association regards submission of a manuscript to a professional journal while that paper is under review by another journal as unacceptable.*

(continued)

SUBMISSION AND PREPARATION OF MANUSCRIPTS

1. Submit four (4) copies and retain the original for your files. Copies may be Xerox, mimeograph or multilith, but not carbons.
2. Enclose a stamped self-addressed postcard for acknowledgment of manuscript receipt. *Manuscripts will not be returned.* Please do not send your original copy.
3. All copy must be typed, doublespaced (including indented material, footnotes, and references) on $8\frac{1}{2}$ by 11 inch white opaque paper. Lines must not exceed six (6) inches. Margins must be a minimum of one inch.
4. Include three (3) copies of an abstract of no more than 150 words.
5. Type each table on a separate page. Insert a location note at the appropriate place in the text, e.g., "Table 2 about here." Send copies, retain originals.
6. Figures must be drawn in India ink on white paper. Send copies, retain originals.
7. Clarify all symbols with notes in the margins of the manuscript. Circle these and all other explanatory notes not intended for printing.
8. Footnotes should not be placed in the body of the text. Type them (doublespaced) and attach them as a separate appendix to the text. Number them consecutively throughout the text.

   Footnotes are to be kept to a minimum and used only for substantive observations. Source citations are made within the text rather than in footnotes.
9. Acknowledgments, credits and grant numbers are placed on the title page with an asterisk.

REFERENCE FORMAT

A. *In the text:* All source references are to be identified at the appropriate point in the text by the last name of the author, year of publication and pagination where needed. Identify subsequent citations of the same source in the same way as the first, not using *"ibid.," "op. cit.,"* or *"loc. cit."* Examples follow:
   1. If author's name is in the text, follow it with year in parentheses. [". . . Duncan (1959) . . ."]
   2. If author's name is not in the text, insert in parentheses, the last name and year, separated by a comma. [". . . (cf. Gouldner, 1963) . . ."]
   3. Pagination (without "p." or "pp.") follows year of publication after a colon. [". . . Kuhn (1970:71)."]
   4. Give both last names for dual authors: for more than two use "et al." in the text. When two authors have the same last name, use identifying initials in the text. For institutional authorship, supply minimum identification from the beginning of the complete citation. [". . . (U.S. Bureau of the Census, 1963:117) . . ."]

(continued)

5. Separate a series of references with semicolons and enclose them within a single pair of parentheses. [". . . (Burgess, 1968; Marwell et al., 1971; Cohen, 1962) . . ."]

B. *In the appendix:* List all source citations by author, and within author by year of publication, in an appendix titled "References." The reference appendix must be complete and include all references in the text. The use of "et al." is not acceptable in the appendix; list the names of all authors. (See A. 4. for text format.)
If there is more than one reference to the same author and year, distinguish them by the letters, a, b, etc. added to the year. [". . . Levy (1965a:331) . . ."] Give the publisher's name in as brief a form as is fully intelligible. For example, John A. Wiley and Sons should be "Wiley."
If the cited material is unpublished, use "forthcoming" with name of journal or publisher; otherwise use "unpublished."
Use no underlining, italics or abbreviations.
Examples follow:

1. *Books:* Jud, Gerald J., Edgar W. Mills, Jr. and Genevieve Walters Burch
   1970 Ex-Pastors. Philadelphia: Pilgrim Press.

   U.S. Bureau of the Census.
   1960 Characteristics of Population. Volume I. Washington, D.C.: U.S. Government Printing Office.

   Bernard, Claude
   [1865] 1957 An Introduction to the Study of Experimental Medicine. Tr. Henry Copley Greene. New York: Dover.

2. *Periodicals:* Conger, Rand
   Forth-coming "The effects of positive feedback on direction and amount of verbalization in a social setting." Pacific Sociological Review.

   Merton, Robert K.
   1963a "The ambivalence of scientists." Bulletin of The Johns Hopkins Hospital 112:77–97.
   1963b "Resistance to the systematic study of multiple discoveries in science." European Journal of Sociology 4:237–82.

3. *Collections:* Davie, M.
   1938 "The pattern of urban growth." Pp. 133–61 in G. Murdock (ed.), Studies in the Science of Society. New Haven: Yale University Press.

See recent issues for further examples. Revised 1975 ASR

APPENDIX 2
USING THE LIBRARY TO LOCATE DATA

A literature review is basic to all types of research in order to determine what work has already been done on a research problem. In some cases, in fact, a research paper may be based solely on such a review. In other cases, the review of literature summarizes current findings. This appendix begins with a discussion of strategies for gathering the materials needed in a review, followed by a discussion of the sources of data available to most students.

Social scientists divide data into two main categories: *primary* and *secondary*. The distinction lies in the purpose for which the data were collected. If they were collected to address a specific research problem and are being analyzed for that purpose, they are referred to as primary. If, on the other hand, they were originally collected for purposes other than those for which they are being used, they are referred to as secondary. Because issues of primary data collection are discussed extensively in the text, this appendix will discuss only secondary data sources.

LITERATURE REVIEW

A literature review is a library-based project. Therefore, effective use of the library can make an important contribution to the success of any research paper. A library is usually a large organization and time spent learning its basic features will be rewarded. If the library prepares a pamphlet on its organization, cataloging system, department structure, special collections, and so on, you should study this information. If the facility does not provide such written information, ask a staff member to explain its features.

When initiating a research project, the most important place in the library is the reference room. The latter contains abstracts, indexes, and other materials useful for identifying and locating previously published information. The breadth and depth of sources available in the reference room are truly incredible. Begin the literature search in the reference room, not in the card catalog.

In initiating the bibliographic search, start with one of the indexes focused at the appropriate research level of your topic. Listed at the beginning of each index are the journals covered by that publication. It is useful to consult this list in order to determine if the journals you wish to review are included in the list. Additionally, the abbreviations used in each citation are explained. If you experience problems, ask a librarian for assistance. Titles of some of the important social science indexes are listed below. These vary as to level of specialization. Perhaps the most important general work to initially consult is the *Social Sciences Index* (previously published as the *Social Sciences and Humanities Index*). (*Reader's Guide* usually is not useful because its journals are oriented to the interested layman rather than to the researcher.) As your topic becomes more defined, the more specialized indexes will become useful. Some of the most useful of these are listed below. By concisely defining your topic and selecting an appropriate index, you will avoid the distraction of irrelevant citations. Your librarian can direct you to the sources that best meet your needs.

Governmental Indexes and Abstracts

American Statistics Index
Crime and Delinquency Abstracts
Current Index to Journals in Education
Index Medicus
Mental Retardation Abstracts
Research in Education

Nongovernmental Indexes and Abstracts

Abstracts of Criminology and Penology
Education Index
International Bibliography of the Social Sciences—Political Science
International Bibliography of the Social Sciences—Sociology
Psychological Abstracts
Public Affairs Information Service Bulletin
Social Sciences Index
Sociological Abstracts

A2.1 EXAMPLES OF INDEXES AND ABSTRACTS

Aids for locating previous research are in two basic forms: indexes and abstracts. Indexes consist primarily of the titles and other bibliographic information on published works, listed alphabetically by topic or author. A sample page from the *Social Sciences Index* illustrates the kinds of listing in an index (Figure A2-1).

Abstracts provide similar types of information, but in addition present brief summary descriptions of the work in question. Thus, rather than locating the complete article to determine if the article is relevant, a check of the abstract provides some assistance in selecting the most worthwhile works. A sample page from *Sociological Abstracts* illustrates the summaries reported in an abstract (Figure A2-2).

(continued)

Figure A2-1. Sample Page from *Social Sciences Index*.

678 SOCIAL SCIENCES INDEX

Power resources —United States —*cont.*
Some possible effects of energy shortages on residential preferences. F. M. Henderson and M. P. Voiland, jr. Prof Geog 27:323-6 Ag '75
Statement of the Executive committee of the Scientists' institute for public information. Environment 17:6-7 Je '75
Technology, prices, and the derived demand for energy. E. R. Berndt and D. O. Wood. bibl R Econ Statistics 57:259-68 Ag '75
Thinking big. Economist 256:67 S 27 '75
U.S. taxes on energy resources [with discussion] G. M. Brannon. bibl Am Econ R Pa & Proc 65:397-405 My '75
United States environmental legislation and energy resources: a review. D. P. Beard. Geog R 65:229-44 Ap '75
Who benefits? R. Nader. Center Mag 8:32-7 Mr '75

Power transmission, Electric. See Electric lines

Powers, Pauline S. See Coombs, R. H. jt. auth.

Powers, Ronald C. See Heltsley, M. E. jt. auth.

Powers, Separation of. See Separation of powers

Powesland, Peter and Giles, Howard
Persuasiveness and accent-message incompatibility. bibl Hum Relat 28:85-93 F '75

Poznanski, Elva O. See Awad, G. A. jt. auth.

Prachowny, Martin F. J. and Richardson, J. David
Testing a life-cycle hypothesis of the balance-of-payments effects of multinational corporations. Econ Inquiry 13:81-98 Mr '75

Practice (psychology)
Affectivity of task, rehearsal time, and physiological response. W. M. Baker and others. bibl J Abn Psychol 84:539-44 O '75
Analysis of the relation between conservation of large and small quantities. G. A. Winer. Psychol Rept 36:379-82 Ap '75
Buildup of proactive inhibition as a cue-overload effect. O. C. Watkins and M. J. Watkins. bibl J Exp Psychol (Hum Learn Mem) 104:442-52 Jl '75
Control processes in short-term memory: use of retention interval information. J. V. Hinrichs and M. E. Grunke. J Exp Psychol (Hum Learn Mem) 104:229-37 My '75
Effect of imagery on rehearsal strategies in verbal-discrimination learning. E. J. Rowe. bibl Am J Psychol 88:431-42 S '75
Effect of orienting tasks and cue timing on the free recall of remember- and forget-cued words. C. D. Wetzel. bibl J Exp Psychol (Hum Learn Mem) 1:556-66 S '75
Effects of rehearsal and serial list position on recall. C. F. Darley and A. L. Glass. J Exp Psychol (Hum Learn Mem) 104:453-8 Jl '75
Effects of rehearsal strategy on memory for spacing and frequency. R. W. Proctor and B. A. Ambler. J Exp Psychol (Hum Learn Mem) 1:640-7 S '75
Enduring visual memory despite forced verbal rehearsal [Posner effect]. T. E. Parks and N. E. A. Kroll. J Exp Psychol (Hum Learn Mem) 1:648-54 S '75
Eye movements under different rehearsal strategies. F. S. Bellezza and others. bibl J Exp Psychol (Hum Learn Mem) 1:673-9 N '75
Free recall after self-paced study: a test of the attention explanation of the spacing effect. J. Zimmerman. Am J Psychol 88:277-91 Je '75
Free recall curves: nothing but rehearsing some items more or recalling them sooner? D. A. Brodie and L. S. Prytulak. bibl J Verb Learn 14:549-63 O '75
Interaction of encoding and rehearsal processes in the recall of repeated and nonrepeated items. D. G. Elmes and R. A. Bjork. J Verb Learn 14:30-42 F '75
Long-term recognition and recall following directed forgetting. C. M. MacLeod. J Exp Psychol (Hum Learn Mem) 104:271-9 My '75
Multiple-list specific and nonspecific transfer. E. D. Smith. Am J Psychol 87:159-71 Mr/Je '74
On the influence of pretraining on recognition thresholds for English words. L. G. Richards and D. M. Platnick. Am J Psychol 87:579-92 D '74
Output order and rehearsal in multi-trial free recall. D. Rundus. bibl J Verb Learn 13:656-63 D '74
Plans to resist distraction. C. J. Patterson and W. Mischel. bibl Develop Psychol 11:369-78 My '75
Primacy effects in short-term memory with the mentally retarded. D. K. Detterman. Child Develop 45:1077-82 D '74
Rehearsal of visual and auditory stimuli while shadowing. N. E. A. Kroll and others. bibl J Exp Psychol (Hum Learn Mem) 104:215-22 Mr '75
Rehearsal strategy effects in children's discrimination learning: confronting the crucible. E. S. Ghatala and others. bibl J Verb Learn 14:398-407 Ag '75
Search of list structures stored in long-term memory. I. B. Appelman and R. C. Atkinson. bibl J Verb Learn 14:82-8 F '75
Sex differences in the comprehension of spatial orientation. J. W. Maxwell and others. J Psychol 91:127-31 S '75
Solving anagrams as a function of word frequency, imagery and distribution of practice. R. P. Stratton and others. Can J Psychol 29:22-31 Mr '75
Total time and learning to learn in paired-associate and verbal-discrimination tasks. J. H. Mueller and others. bibl Am J Psychol 87:107-16 Mr/Je '74

Practice of law
See also
Law offices

Practicum programs. See Field work (educational method)

Prager, Jonas
Central bank policy-making in Israel: the Horowitz governorship (1954-1971). Int J Mid E Stud 6:46-69 Ja '75

Prairie dogs
See also
Animal behavior (psychology)—Prairie dogs

Prairie ecology
Prairies without much grass. J. G. Nelson. il map Geog Mag 47:614-20 Jl '75

Prairie provinces
Prairies without much grass. J. G. Nelson. il map Geog Mag 47:614-20 Jl '75

Prais, Zmira
Real money balances as a variable in the production function. bibl J Money Cred Bank 7:535-43 N '75

Praise
Effects of an audio cueing system on the rate of teacher praise. R. Van Houten and K. Sullivan. bibl J App Behav Anal 8:197-201 Summ '75
Feedback and therapist praise during treatment of phobia. H. Leitenberg and others. bibl J Consult Clin Psychol 43:396-404 Je '75
Generalization of teacher behavior as a function of subject matter specific discrimination training. G. O. Horton. J App Behav Anal 8:311-19 Fall '75

Prakash, Aditya. See Sharma, R. jt. auth.

Pramoj, Mom Rachawongsee Seni. See Seni Pramoj

Prather, Dirk C. and others
Extinction and spontaneous recovery in positive reinforcement and avoidance learning. J Gen Psychol 92:211-15 Ap '75

Pratt, Arthur D. jr
Mandatory treatment program for skid row alcoholics; its implication for the uniform alcoholism and intoxication treatment act [Municipal court alcoholic rehabilitation program, Indianapolis]. J Stud Alcohol 36:166-70 Ja '75

Pratt, Henry J.
Organizational stress and adaptation to changing political status; the case of the National council of churches of Christ in the United States. bibl Am Behav Sci 17:856-83 Jl '74

Pratt, J. G.
Some notes for the future Einstein for parapsychology. Am Soc Psychical Res J 68:133-55, 442-3 Ap, O '74

Pratt, J. G. and others
Computer studies of the ESP process in card guessing; displacement effects in the C.J. records from the Colorado series. bibl Am Soc Psychical Res J 68:357-84 O '74

Pratt, Larry
Politics of Syncrude: selling out. Can Forum 55:4-10+ N '75

Pratt, Theodore C.
Psychological effects of structural integration. Psychol Rept 35:856 O '74

Prattis, J. I.
Discontinuities in priorities and policies in the development of a regional fishery in Scotland. Hum Org 34:404-7 Wint '75

Pravdin, A.
Inside the CPSU central committee; interview by M. Matthews. Survey 20:94-104 Aut '74

Prawat, Richard S. See Warden, P. G. jt. auth.

Prazsky, Jan
Détente and its opponents. World Marx R 18:134-8 Ag '75
Problem of crisis and war today. World Marx R 18:85-90 Mr '75
Victory of reason and relapses of recklessness. World Marx R 18:81-6 O '75

Preadolescent psychology. See Adolescent psychology

Precious, Ralph W.
Michigan/county-wide wastewater treatment facility. Pub Mgt 57:11-12 Ap '75

Precious stones
See also
Gems

Collectors and collecting

Our beautiful, little known gemstones. H. R. Steacy. il map Can Geog J 89:4-13 D '74

Precipitation (meteorology)
See also
Snow

Precoda, Norman
Left behind—Soviet mine wastes. il map Environment 17:14-19 N '75

Precognition
Note on precognition of the percipient's calls as an alternative hypothesis to telepathy. C. B. Nash. J Parapsychol 39:21-3 Mr '75

SOURCE: *Social Sciences Index,* 2(April 1975–March 1976): 678.

Figure A2-2. Sample Page from *Sociological Abstracts*.

Sociological Abstracts — *SOCIAL PROBLEMS & SOCIAL WELFARE* — 75H2284–H2287

2100 social problems and social welfare

43 social gerontology

75H2284

Cohen, Margery G. (Levindale Hebrew Geriatric Center & Hospital, Baltimore MD 21215), **Alternative to Institutional Care of the Aged,** *Social Casework,* 1973, 54, 8, Oct, 447–452.

¶ The Levindale Day Care Program is a 5-day-a-week program for those elderly people who need services ranging from emotional support to a complete custodial facility (though not bed-bound), but wish to remain in the community. Besides support of individuals, the goals are relief for families, prevention or postponement of institutionalization, & provision of a program to maximize physical & emotional functioning. The program has a maximum of 35 participants. Staff consists of a registered nurse, a M & a F aide, & a half-time social worker. Casework services are offered to enhance the individual's social functioning. In the process of aging, the important changes are those in attitudes, values, & personality changes as expressed in interaction with others. The disengagement theory describes a mutual withdrawal & decreased interaction between the aging person & others in his social system. The elderly in the day care program have the advantage of sharing recreation & workshop facilities. Formal group meetings once a week produce an identification of the individual with the group & create an environment of peer support. Once a month, families of participants are included in the meetings to assure the family's involvement & to receive their suggestions. General problems of aging & illness & specific problems encountered are discussed. H. Dorian

75H2285

Tsargorodtsev, G. I., V. D. Shapiro & A. T. Shatalov, Problemy Sotsialnoi Gerontologii (Problems of Social Gerontology), *Voprosy Filosofii,* 1973, 27, 3, Mar, 161–167. (Rus)

¶ The 9th International Congress of Gerontologists met in Kiev in Jul 1972. Research in many problems of biology, medicine, & the social sciences came up in the discussions of the various aspects of aging & old age. Special attention was paid to the problems of the aging society. The social & economic problems of the aged received considerable attention. The contrast between how such problems are handled in the USSR & in capitalist countries is pointed out, noting that capitalist societies merely offer palliatives, rather than solutions. The Soviet sociologists N. Ya. Solovoyov & A. Ye. Petrichenko presented a multiple factor model of the position of the elderly person in society & in the family. Speakers from Western countries, especially the US, stressed generational conflicts & economic & emotional problems of the aged. Other contributors to the Congress are noted. M. Mackler

75H2286

Wershow, Harold J. (U Alabama, Birmingham 35294), **Aging in the Israeli Kibbutz: Growing Old in a Mini-Socialist Society,** *Jewish Social Studies,* 1973, 35, 2, Apr, 141–148.

¶ Part of an ongoing study of aging in the kibbutz is presented ("Aging in the Israeli Kibbutz," *The Gerontologist,* 1969, 9, 300-304). S's were aged members of 5 long-established kibbutzim, 45% of the aged residents (N = 77 M's & 60 F's). S's were believed to be better integrated, more secure geronts. They are a remarkable group, healthy & very well educated for their generation, speaking several languages & are a prototype of kibbutz aged, as kibbutzim age & attain larger proportions of aged. A highly structured interview schedule was employed, based on the work of Bernard Kutner et al in 500 OVER 60 (New York, NY: Russell Sage, 1956). The R's were generally alert & vigorous; only 2% are fully retired, though they have been downgraded from agricultural (the highest status vocation) & managerial functions to kibbutz services (ie, maintenance, clothing fabrication & repair, laundry, etc). Large proportions of lonely people with rather superficial interpersonal relationships were noted. The causes are probably the independence & individuality of pioneers (even in a collectivist society) exacerbated by the politicization of everyday matters of eg, childrearing & hiring of peak work-load laborers. Some differences in the awareness & extent of aging problems in different kibbutzim are noted. The kibbutz collectivity attenuates much of the problems of aging that cannot be absorbed in the nuclear family. Even in the kibbutz, however, aging brings with it illness, loss of status, & children who may not remain "down on the farm" following their military service. In any case, it is better to be old & rich than old & poor, & kibbutz aged are rich—in material security, in the building of a new way of life, & if children remain "at home," in a rewarding old age. AA

47 social disorganization (crime)

75H2287

Becker, Georgeann & Karen I. Ward (*Wisconsin Law Review,* 975 Bascom Mall Madison 53706), **Alcoholism Treatment in Wisconsin: The Need for Legislative Reform,** *Wisconsin Law Review,* 1973, 1, 133–171.

¶ The nature & scope of the contacts that the alcoholic has with the law are explored, as well as the existing criminal & civil structure used by Wisc to deal with alcoholics, & some of the proposed alternatives to the existing structure. In Wisc, the statutes & ordinances which empower the police to take an intoxicated person into custody are characteristically broad, & contain no requirement of any type of intentional behavior. The arresting police are aware that the problem of public drunkenness is social rather than criminal, & they are limited to a very few alternative methods of disposing of the drunken offenders. Present police arrest procedure is nothing more than a form of social emergency care, emergency hospitalization, & not a deterrent of the prohibited conduct. Taking Dane County as representative of Wisc as a whole, samplings & interviewing were restricted to facilities, administrators, policemen, judges, & counselors in the County. Treatment alternatives were found to range from Alcoholics Anonymous to the professionally staffed Alcoholic Treatment Center at Mendota State Hospital. These were reviewed in brief. The only existing alcoholic treatment

243

SOURCE: *Sociological Abstract,* 23 (1975), p. 243.

There are alternatives to indexes and abstracts available for beginning your library search. For instance, useful handbooks are frequently published in specific areas. Examples are *The Handbook of Medical Sociology*, *The Handbook of Social Psychology*, and *The Handbook of Modern Sociology*. Chapters in these are written with the dual purpose of summarizing information and of aiding the reader in identifying published literature. Additional help in the form of an overview of many topics is available in the *International Encyclopedia of the Social Sciences*, which provides excellent summaries of current knowledge on topics within its scope.

If these sources do not yield needed materials, consult the card catalog under headings used in the various indexes. You may also find help in special bibliographies of all sorts. Finally, do not overlook references that are contained in the works you have already found.

These indexes, abstracts, bibliographies, handbooks, and other sources are just a fraction of the library materials that are available in gathering existing literature on your topic. The problems remaining for you are to choose among the available sources and select the most useful headings. For this, the best advice we can give—and this is important—is to *consult the reference librarians*. They are trained people who have an excellent grasp of the alternative sources and strategies, and it is their job to help you. Most are exceedingly helpful and pleasant.

SECONDARY DATA

Researchers often reanalyze data that has been collected and made available by others. Such secondary data may include statistical information collected and published by a state or the federal government, as well as national survey information collected and made available by Gallup, Roper, and other polling organizations.

The vast resources of the federal government, as well as its ability to command information that others could not obtain, make it a promising data source for many research projects. Government data are extensive and diverse. Printed materials include an enormous amount of census bureau data as well as a wide range of information appropriate to the functions of all departments of government. The mere vastness of these materials makes expert assistance invaluable in identifying and locating desired data. For the most efficient use of such data, consult the librarian in charge of government documents.

For more independent searching, there are also a number of guides to government publications, including general guides and bibliographies to all government publications and summary publications such as *The Statistical Abstracts of the United States* and the Bureau of Labor Statistics *Employment and Earnings Statistics for the United States*. Each of these publications provides leads to appropriate types of government data. There are also governmental indexes to assist in locating data published by the federal government, among the best being the *American Statistics Index.*

A major source of government data is the Bureau of the Census. In fact, more than thirty guides exist to assist researchers in using census data. These guides are summarized in an annotated bibliography by Ann D. Casey entitled *General Reference Sources for Accessing Census Bureau Data* (Bureau of the Census, Washington, D.C., 1976).

The United Nations publishes many volumes of data useful for researchers interested in international research. Such statistics usually consist of cross-national comparisons for which an attempt is made to keep the data standard to some common base and therefore comparable.

Of increasing importance are centers of data storage for information collected by nongovernmental researchers. The Roper Library is one such center. Additionally, data may be obtained through membership in the Interuniversity Consortium for Political Research at the University of Michigan. Similar data centers exist at the University of California at Berkeley, the University of Wisconsin, and other major universities. Faculty can generally be of assistance in providing information about these data centers, how one obtains information, and costs of acquisition.

The library reference room also contains a number of useful guides for locating secondary data. For instance, *Directory of Data Bases in the Social and Behavioral Sciences** contains well-indexed information on sources of secondary data including topics, subject, original source of data, and identification of collecting organization. These and similar publications can be useful in locating unpublished material suitable for secondary analysis.

* Vivian S. Sessions (ed.) (New York: Science Associates/International, 1974).

A2.2 NATIONAL CENTER FOR HEALTH STATISTICS: AN EXAMPLE OF GOVERNMENTAL PUBLICATIONS

The following list contains descriptions of the various series of publications containing health data published by the National Center for Health Statistics, which is a component of the Department of Health, Education, and Welfare. Within each series are publications that come out regularly in pamphlet form, containing basic data on specific topics. For instance, Series Three contains titles such as "Selected Family Characteristics and Health Measures" and "Infant Loss in the Netherlands." Series Ten contains topics such as "Selected Health Characteristics by Occupation" and "Family Out-of-Pocket Health Expenditures."

Similarly detailed secondary data are available from other governmental agencies.

Figure A2-3. Series of Data Published by the National Center for Health Statistics.

VITAL AND HEALTH STATISTICS PUBLICATIONS SERIES

Formerly Public Health Service Publication No. 1000

Series 1. *Programs and Collection Procedures.*—Reports which describe the general programs of the National Center for Health Statistics and its offices and divisions, data collection methods used, definitions, and other material necessary for understanding the data.

Series 2. *Data Evaluation and Methods Research.*—Studies of new statistical methodology including experimental tests of new survey methods, studies of vital statistics collection methods, new analytical techniques, objective evaluations of reliability of collected data, contributions to statistical theory.

Series 3. *Analytical Studies.*—Reports presenting analytical or interpretive studies based on vital and health statistics, carrying the analysis further than the expository types of reports in the other series.

Series 4. *Documents and Committee Reports.*—Final reports of major committees concerned with vital and health statistics, and documents such as recommended model vital registration laws and revised birth and death certificates.

Series 10. *Data from the Health Interview Survey.*—Statistics on illness; accidental injuries; disability; use of hospital, medical, dental, and other services; and other health-related topics, based on data collected in a continuing national household interview survey.

Series 11. *Data from the Health Examination Survey.*—Data from direct examination, testing, and measurement of national samples of the civilian, noninstitutionalized population provide the basis for two types of reports: (1) estimates of the medically defined prevalence of specific diseases in the United States and the distributions of the population with respect to physical, physiological, and psychological characteristics; and (2) analysis of relationships among the various measurements without reference to an explicit finite universe of persons.

Series 12. *Data from the Institutionalized Population Surveys.*—Discontinued effective 1975. Future reports from these surveys will be in Series 13.

Series 13. *Data on Health Resources Utilization.*—Statistics on the utilization of health manpower and facilities providing long-term care, ambulatory care, hospital care, and family planning services.

Series 14. *Data on Health Resources: Manpower and Facilities.*—Statistics on the numbers, geographic distribution, and characteristics of health resources including physicians, dentists, nurses, other health occupations, hospitals, nursing homes, and outpatient facilities.

Series 20. *Data on Mortality.*—Various statistics on mortality other than as included in regular annual or monthly reports. Special analyses by cause of death, age, and other demographic variables; geographic and time series analyses; and statistics on characteristics of deaths not available from the vital records, based on sample surveys of those records.

Series 21. *Data on Natality, Marriage, and Divorce.*—Various statistics on natality, marriage, and divorce other than as included in regular annual or monthly reports. Special analyses by demographic variables; geographic and time series analyses; studies of fertility; and statistics on characteristics of births not available from the vital records, based on sample surveys of those records.

Series 22. *Data from the National Mortality and Natality Surveys.*—Discontinued effective 1975. Future reports from these sample surveys based on vital records will be included in Series 20 and 21, respectively.

Series 23. *Data from the National Survey of Family Growth.*—Statistics on fertility, family formation and dissolution, family planning, and related maternal and infant health topics derived from a biennial survey of a nationwide probability sample of ever-married women 15-44 years of age.

For a list of titles of reports published in these series, write to:

Scientific and Technical Information Branch
National Center for Health Statistics
Public Health Service, HRA
Rockville, Md. 20852

RECOMMENDED READINGS

The Schenkman Publishing Company (Cambridge, Mass.) publishes a series of student handbooks that provide detailed descriptions of a wide range of library resources and secondary data. These are relatively inexpensive guides that can be a useful supplement to the aid provided by librarians. The series includes

Bart, Pauline, and Linda Frankel
1976 *The Student Sociologist's Handbook*

Frantz, Charles
1972 *The Student Anthropologist's Handbook*

Merritt, Richard L., and Gloria J. Pyszka
1969 *The Student Political Scientist's Handbook*

Sarbin, Theodore R., and William C. Coe
1969 *The Student Psychologist's Handbook*

Also consult the following:

Freides, Thelma
1973 *Literature and Bibliography of the Social Sciences* (Los Angeles: Melville).

Detailed descriptions of a wide range of library resources and secondary data.

White, Carl M., et al.
1973 *Sources of Information on the Social Sciences* (Chicago: American Library Assoc.).

Descriptions of social science disciplines and subdisciplines, with five to ten of the most influential books in each.

APPENDIX 3

TABLES

Table A3-1. Proportions of Area Under the Normal Curve

The Use of Table A3-1. The use of Table A3-1 requires that the raw score be transformed into a z-score and that the variable be normally distributed.

The values in Table A3-1 represent the proportion of area in the standard normal curve which has a mean of 0, a standard deviation of 1.00, and a total area also equal to 1.00.

Since the normal curve is symmetrical, it is sufficient to indicate only the areas corresponding to positive z-values. Negative z-values will have precisely the same proportions of area as their positive counterparts.

Column B represents the proportion of area between the mean and a given z.

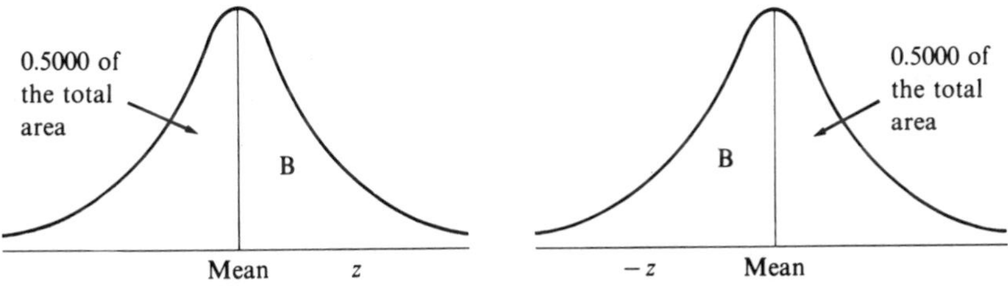

Column C represents the proportion of area beyond a given z.

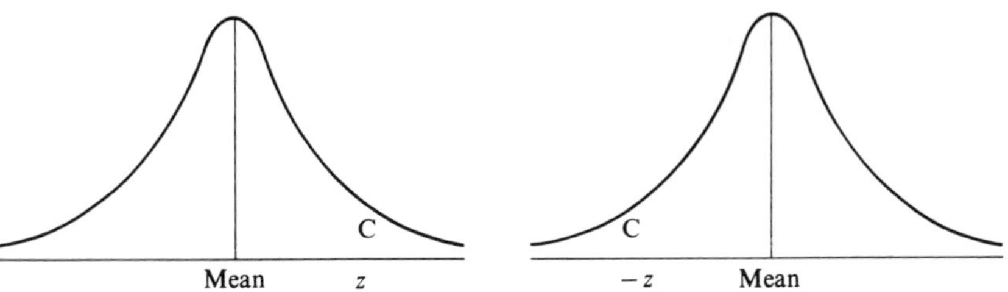

Example. Assume you have a population of student scores which are normally distributed with a mean of 75.0 and a standard deviation of 6.0. You wish to determine the percentage of students who scored below and above a given grade. To use Table A3-1, convert the grade score you are interested in to a z score. This is accomplished with the following formula:

$$z = \frac{x - \overline{X}}{\sigma}$$

Table A3-1. Projections of Area Under the Normal Curve

(A) z (STANDARD DEVIATION UNITS)	(B) AREA BETWEEN MEAN AND z	(C) AREA BEYOND z	(A) z (STANDARD DEVIATION UNITS)	(B) AREA BETWEEN MEAN AND z	(C) AREA BEYOND z
0.00	.0000	.5000	0.45	.1736	.3264
0.01	.0040	.4960	0.46	.1772	.3228
0.02	.0080	.4920	0.47	.1808	.3192
0.03	.0120	.4880	0.48	.1844	.3156
0.04	.0160	.4840	0.49	.1879	.3121
0.05	.0199	.4801	0.50	.1915	.3085
0.06	.0239	.4761	0.51	.1950	.3050
0.07	.0279	.4721	0.52	.1985	.3015
0.08	.0319	.4681	0.53	.2019	.2981
0.09	.0359	.4641	0.54	.2054	.2946
0.10	.0393	.4602	0.55	.2088	.2912
0.11	.0438	.4562	0.56	.2123	.2877
0.12	.0478	.4522	0.57	.2157	.2843
0.13	.0517	.4483	0.58	.2190	.2810
0.14	.0557	.4443	0.59	.2224	.2776
0.15	.0596	.4404	0.60	.2257	.2743
0.16	.0636	.4364	0.61	.2291	.2709
0.17	.0675	.4325	0.62	.2324	.2676
0.18	.0714	.4286	0.63	.2357	.2643
0.19	.0753	.4247	0.64	.2389	.2611
0.20	.0793	.4207	0.65	.2422	.2578
0.21	.0832	.4168	0.66	.2454	.2546
0.22	.0871	.4129	0.67	.2486	.2514
0.23	.0910	.4090	0.68	.2517	.2483
0.24	.0948	.4052	0.69	.2549	.2451
0.25	.0987	.4013	0.70	.2580	.2420
0.26	.1026	.3974	0.71	.2611	.2389
0.27	.1064	.3936	0.72	.2642	.2358
0.28	.1103	.3897	0.73	.2673	.2327
0.29	.1141	.3859	0.74	.2704	.2296
0.30	.1179	.3821	0.75	.2734	.2266
0.31	.1217	.3783	0.76	.2764	.2236
0.32	.1255	.3745	0.77	.2794	.2206
0.33	.1293	.3707	0.78	.2823	.2177
0.34	.1331	.3669	0.79	.2852	.2148
0.35	.1368	.3632	0.80	.2881	.2119
0.36	.1406	.3594	0.81	.2910	.2090
0.37	.1443	.3557	0.82	.2939	.2061
0.38	.1480	.3520	0.83	.2967	.2033
0.39	.1517	.3483	0.84	.2995	.2005
0.40	.1554	.3446	0.85	.3023	.1977
0.41	.1591	.3409	0.86	.3051	.1949
0.42	.1628	.3372	0.87	.3078	.1922
0.43	.1664	.3336	0.88	.3106	.1894
0.44	.1700	.3300	0.89	.3133	.1867

Table A3-1 (*Continued*)

(A) z (STANDARD DEVIATION UNITS)	(B) AREA BETWEEN MEAN AND z	(C) AREA BEYOND z
0.90	.3159	.1841
0.91	.3186	.1814
0.92	.3212	.1788
0.93	.3238	.1762
0.94	.3264	.1736
0.95	.3289	.1711
0.96	.3315	.1685
0.97	.3340	.1660
0.98	.3365	.1635
0.99	.3389	.1611
1.00	.3413	.1587
1.01	.3438	.1562
1.02	.3461	.1539
1.03	.3485	.1515
1.04	.3508	.1492
1.05	.3531	.1469
1.06	.3554	.1446
1.07	.3577	.1423
1.08	.3599	.1401
1.09	.3621	.1379
1.10	.3643	.1357
1.11	.3665	.1335
1.12	.3686	.1314
1.13	.3708	.1292
1.14	.3729	.1271
1.15	.3749	.1251
1.16	.3770	.1230
1.17	.3790	.1210
1.18	.3810	.1190
1.19	.3830	.1170
1.20	.3849	.1151
1.21	.3869	.1131
1.22	.3888	.1112
1.23	.3907	.1093
1.24	.3925	.1075
1.25	.3944	.1056
1.26	.3962	.1038
1.27	.3980	.1020
1.28	.3997	.1003
1.29	.4015	.0985
1.30	.4032	.0968
1.31	.4049	.0951
1.32	.4066	.0934
1.33	.4082	.0918
1.34	.4099	.0901

(A) z (STANDARD DEVIATION UNITS)	(B) AREA BETWEEN MEAN AND z	(C) AREA BEYOND z
1.35	.4115	.0885
1.36	.4131	.0869
1.37	.4147	.0853
1.38	.4162	.0838
1.39	.4177	.0823
1.40	.4192	.0808
1.41	.4207	.0793
1.42	.4222	.0778
1.43	.4236	.0764
1.44	.4251	.0749
1.45	.4265	.0735
1.46	.4279	.0721
1.47	.4292	.0708
1.48	.4306	.0694
1.49	.4319	.0681
1.50	.4332	.0668
1.51	.4345	.0655
1.52	.4357	.0643
1.53	.4370	.0630
1.54	.4382	.0618
1.55	.4394	.0606
1.56	.4406	.0594
1.57	.4418	.0582
1.58	.4429	.0571
1.59	.4441	.0559
1.60	.4452	.0548
1.61	.4463	.0537
1.62	.4474	.0526
1.63	.4484	.0516
1.64	.4495	.0505
1.65	.4505	.0495
1.66	.4515	.0485
1.67	.4525	.0475
1.68	.4535	.0465
1.69	.4545	.0455
1.70	.4554	.0446
1.71	.4564	.0436
1.72	.4573	.0427
1.73	.4582	.0418
1.74	.4591	.0409
1.75	.4599	.0401
1.76	.4608	.0392
1.77	.4616	.0384
1.78	.4625	.0375
1.79	.4633	.0367

Table A3-1 (*Continued*)

(A) z (STANDARD DEVIATION UNITS)	(B) AREA BETWEEN MEAN AND z	(C) AREA BEYOND z
1.80	.4641	.0359
1.81	.4649	.0351
1.82	.4656	.0344
1.83	.4664	.0336
1.84	.4671	.0329
1.85	.4678	.0322
1.86	.4686	.0314
1.87	.4693	.0307
1.88	.4699	.0301
1.89	.4706	.0294
1.90	.4713	.0287
1.91	.4719	.0281
1.92	.4726	.0274
1.93	.4732	.0268
1.94	.4738	.0262
1.95	.4744	.0256
1.96	.4750	.0250
1.97	.4756	.0244
1.98	.4761	.0239
1.99	.4767	.0233
2.00	.4772	.0228
2.01	.4778	.0222
2.02	.4783	.0217
2.03	.4788	.0212
2.04	.4793	.0207
2.05	.4798	.0202
2.06	.4803	.0197
2.07	.4808	.0192
2.08	.4812	.0188
2.09	.4817	.0183
2.10	.4821	.0179
2.11	.4826	.0174
2.12	.4830	.0170
2.13	.4834	.0166
2.14	.4838	.0162
2.15	.4842	.0158
2.16	.4846	.0154
2.17	.4850	.0150
2.18	.4854	.0146
2.19	.4857	.0143
2.20	.4861	.0139
2.21	.4864	.0136
2.22	.4868	.0132
2.23	.4871	.0129
2.24	.4875	.0125
2.25	.4878	.0122
2.26	.4881	.0119
2.27	.4884	.0116
2.28	.4887	.0113
2.29	.4890	.0110
2.30	.4893	.0107
2.31	.4896	.0104
2.32	.4898	.0102
2.33	.4901	.0099
2.34	.4904	.0096
2.35	.4906	.0094
2.36	.4909	.0091
2.37	.4911	.0089
2.38	.4913	.0087
2.39	.4916	.0084
2.40	.4918	.0082
2.41	.4920	.0080
2.42	.4922	.0078
2.43	.4925	.0075
2.44	.4927	.0073
2.45	.4929	.0071
2.46	.4931	.0069
2.47	.4932	.0068
2.48	.4934	.0066
2.49	.4936	.0064
2.50	.4938	.0062
2.51	.4940	.0060
2.52	.4941	.0059
2.53	.4943	.0057
2.54	.4945	.0055
2.55	.4946	.0054
2.56	.4948	.0052
2.57	.4949	.0051
2.58	.4951	.0049
2.59	.4952	.0048
2.60	.4953	.0047
2.61	.4955	.0045
2.62	.4956	.0044
2.63	.4957	.0043
2.64	.4959	.0041
2.65	.4960	.0040
2.66	.4961	.0039
2.67	.4962	.0038
2.68	.4963	.0037
2.69	.4964	.0036

Table A3-1 (*Continued*)

(A) z (STANDARD DEVIATION UNITS)	(B) AREA BETWEEN MEAN AND z	(C) AREA BEYOND z	(A) z (STANDARD DEVIATION UNITS)	(B) AREA BETWEEN MEAN AND z	(C) AREA BEYOND z
2.70	.4965	.0035	3.05	.4989	.0011
2.71	.4966	.0034	3.06	.4989	.0011
2.72	.4967	.0033	3.07	.4989	.0011
2.73	.4968	.0032	3.08	.4990	.0010
2.74	.4969	.0031	3.09	.4990	.0010
2.75	.4970	.0030	3.10	.4990	.0010
2.76	.4971	.0029	3.11	.4991	.0009
2.77	.4972	.0028	3.12	.4991	.0009
2.78	.4973	.0027	3.13	.4991	.0009
2.79	.4974	.0026	3.14	.4992	.0008
2.80	.4974	.0026	3.15	.4992	.0008
2.81	.4975	.0025	3.16	.4992	.0008
2.82	.4976	.0024	3.17	.4992	.0008
2.83	.4977	.0023	3.18	.4993	.0007
2.84	.4977	.0023	3.19	.4993	.0007
2.85	.4978	.0022	3.20	.4993	.0007
2.86	.4979	.0021	3.21	.4993	.0007
2.87	.4979	.0021	3.22	.4994	.0006
2.88	.4980	.0020	3.23	.4994	.0006
2.89	.4981	.0019	3.24	.4994	.0006
2.90	.4981	.0019	3.25	.4994	.0006
2.91	.4982	.0018	3.30	.4995	.0005
2.92	.4982	.0018	3.35	.4996	.0004
2.93	.4983	.0017	3.40	.4997	.0003
2.94	.4984	.0016	3.45	.4997	.0003
2.95	.4984	.0016	3.50	.4998	.0002
2.96	.4985	.0015	3.60	.4998	.0002
2.97	.4985	.0015	3.70	.4999	.0001
2.98	.4986	.0014	3.80	.4999	.0001
2.99	.4986	.0014	3.90	.49995	.00005
3.00	.4987	.0013	4.00	.49997	.00003
3.01	.4987	.0013			
3.02	.4987	.0013			
3.03	.4988	.0012			
3.04	.4988	.0012			

SOURCE: Richard P. Runyon and Audrey Haber, *Fundamentals of Behavioral Statistics* (Reading, Mass.: Addison-Wesley, 1967), pp. 290–291.

The grade score you are interested in is 83.0. Therefore,

$$z = \frac{83.0 - 75.0}{6.0}$$

$$z = 1.33$$

Locate 1.33 in column A and read across to the values in columns B and C. Column B indicates that .4082 (or 40.82%) of the total area is between the mean and z. Since 50% of the total area is below the mean, this means that 90.82% (50.00% + 40.82%) of student scores are below 83.0. Column C confirms this observation, since .0918 or 9.18% of the total area is above 83.0.

Table A3-2. Centile Values of the Chi-Square Statistic

The Use of Table A3-2. To use Table A3-2, first find the degrees of freedom (*df*) in the column at the left. The minimum chi-square values for the several alpha levels are given in the columns to the right of the *df* column. The subscript values for each chi-square column indicate the probability of a real difference existing. If you wish to find the probability that the obtained difference is due to chance, simply subtract the given subscript value from 1.00, e.g., 1.00 − .95 = .05.

To demonstrate the use of this table, assume that a computed chi-square of 3.8 was obtained with 1 *df*. Entering the table at the row headed by 1 *df*, read to the right. The value of 3.8 is listed in the .95 column. Thus, it is concluded that the probability is .95 that the difference is real, or that the probability is .05 that the difference is due to chance alone.

Table A3-3. Random Digits

The Use of Table A3-3. To use Table A3-3 (p. 384), first number every member of the population from which you wish to draw a random sample from zero to *N*, with *N* being the last member of the population. For instance, assume that you have a population of 2,050 members from which you wish to draw a 1 percent sample. Number the first member of the population 0000, the second 0001, the third 0002, etc., until you have numbered the last member of the population, i.e., 2,049.

Enter the table randomly and by reading the first four digits in any direction (usually by row or column), select the first twenty members of the population whose identifying numbers you read.

Table A3-2. Centile Values of the Chi-Square Statistic

df	$\chi^2_{.005}$	$\chi^2_{.01}$	$\chi^2_{.025}$	$\chi^2_{.05}$	$\chi^2_{.10}$	$\chi^2_{.25}$	$\chi^2_{.50}$	$\chi^2_{.75}$	$\chi^2_{.90}$	$\chi^2_{.95}$	$\chi^2_{.975}$	$\chi^2_{.99}$	$\chi^2_{.995}$	$\chi^2_{.999}$
1	—	—	—	—	.02	.10	.45	1.3	2.7	3.8	5.0	6.6	7.9	10.8
2	.01	.02	.05	.10	.21	.58	1.4	2.8	4.6	6.0	7.4	9.2	10.6	13.8
3	.07	.11	.22	.35	.58	1.21	2.4	4.1	6.3	7.8	9.4	11.3	12.8	16.3
4	.21	.30	.48	.71	1.1	1.92	3.4	5.4	7.8	9.5	11.1	13.3	14.9	18.5
5	.41	.55	.83	1.1	1.6	2.7	4.4	6.6	9.2	11.1	12.8	15.1	16.7	20.5
6	.68	.87	1.2	1.6	2.2	3.5	5.4	7.8	10.6	12.6	14.4	16.8	18.5	22.5
7	.99	1.24	1.7	2.2	2.8	4.3	6.4	9.0	12.0	14.1	16.0	18.5	20.3	24.3
8	1.3	1.65	2.2	2.7	3.5	5.1	7.3	10.2	13.4	15.5	17.5	20.1	22.0	26.1
9	1.7	2.09	2.7	3.3	4.2	5.9	8.3	11.4	14.7	16.9	19.0	21.7	23.6	27.9
10	2.2	2.56	3.2	3.9	4.9	6.7	9.3	12.5	16.0	18.3	20.5	23.2	25.2	29.6
11	2.6	3.05	3.8	4.6	5.6	7.6	10.3	13.7	17.3	19.7	21.9	24.7	26.8	31.3
12	3.1	3.57	4.4	5.2	6.3	8.4	11.3	14.8	18.5	21.0	23.3	26.2	28.3	32.9
13	3.6	4.11	5.0	5.9	7.0	9.3	12.3	16.0	19.8	22.4	24.7	27.7	29.8	34.5
14	4.1	4.66	5.6	6.6	7.8	10.2	13.3	17.1	21.1	23.7	26.1	29.1	31.3	36.1
15	4.6	5.23	6.3	7.3	8.5	11.0	14.3	18.2	22.3	25.0	27.5	30.6	32.8	37.7
16	5.1	5.81	6.9	8.0	9.3	11.9	15.3	19.4	23.5	26.3	28.8	32.0	34.3	39.3
17	5.7	6.41	7.6	8.7	10.1	12.8	16.3	20.5	24.8	27.6	30.2	33.4	35.7	40.8
18	6.3	7.01	8.2	9.4	10.9	13.7	17.3	21.6	26.0	28.9	31.5	34.8	37.2	42.3
19	6.8	7.63	8.9	10.1	11.7	14.6	18.3	22.7	27.2	30.1	32.9	36.2	38.6	43.8
20	7.4	8.26	9.6	10.9	12.4	15.5	19.3	23.8	28.4	31.4	34.2	37.6	40.0	45.3
21	8.0	8.9	10.3	11.6	13.2	16.3	20.3	24.9	29.6	32.7	35.5	38.9	41.4	46.8
22	8.6	9.5	11.0	12.3	14.0	17.2	21.3	26.0	30.8	33.9	36.8	40.3	42.8	48.3
23	9.3	10.2	11.7	13.1	14.8	18.1	22.3	27.1	32.0	35.2	38.1	41.6	44.2	49.7
24	9.9	10.9	12.4	13.8	15.7	19.0	23.3	28.2	33.2	36.4	39.4	43.0	45.6	51.2
25	10.5	11.5	13.1	14.6	16.5	19.9	24.3	29.3	34.4	37.7	40.6	44.3	46.9	52.6
26	11.2	12.2	13.8	15.4	17.3	20.8	25.3	30.4	35.6	38.9	41.9	45.6	48.3	54.0
27	11.8	12.9	14.6	16.2	18.1	21.7	26.3	31.5	36.7	40.1	43.2	47.0	49.6	55.5
28	12.5	13.6	15.3	16.9	18.9	22.7	27.3	32.6	37.9	41.3	44.5	48.3	51.0	56.9
29	13.1	14.3	16.0	17.7	19.8	23.6	28.3	33.7	39.1	42.6	45.7	49.6	52.3	58.3
30	13.8	15.0	16.8	18.5	20.6	24.5	29.3	34.8	40.3	43.8	47.0	50.9	53.3	59.7

SOURCE: Abridged from Table 8 of E. S. Pearson and H. O. Hartley, *Biometrika Tables for Statisticians,* Vol. 1, 2nd ed., 1958, published by the Syndics of the Cambridge University Press, London; used by permission of the authors and publishers. This abridgment is reproduced from John G. Peatman, *Introduction to Applied Statistics* (New York: Harper & Row, Publishers, 1953), pp. 402–403.

Note that median values of chi-square are in $\chi^2_{.50}$ column.

For instance, assume you began with the first four numbers in row 00026. Reading down the column, you would observe the following numbers:

1547
9455
4248
2352

0449
0054
3596
5980
4605

⋮

Since a member of the population has number 1547, include that member in your sample. Ignore 9455 (no member has that number), ignore 4248 (no member has that number), include 2352, include 0449, 0054, and so on, until you have drawn 20 members for your sample. In this manner, Table A3-3 can be used for drawing a random sample from a larger population.

Table A3-3. Random Digits

ROW NUMBER										
00000	10097	32533	76520	13586	34673	54876	80959	09117	39292	74945
00001	37542	04805	64894	74296	24805	24037	20636	10402	00822	91665
00002	08422	68953	19645	09303	23209	02560	15953	34764	35080	33606
00003	99019	02529	09376	70715	38311	31165	88676	74397	04436	27659
00004	12807	99970	80157	36147	64032	36653	98951	16877	12171	76833
00005	66065	74717	34072	76850	36697	36170	65813	39885	11199	29170
00006	31060	10805	45571	82406	35303	42614	86799	07439	23403	09732
00007	85269	77602	02051	65692	68665	74818	73053	85247	18623	88579
00008	63573	32135	05325	47048	90553	57548	28468	28709	83491	25624
00009	73796	45753	03529	64778	35808	34282	60935	20344	35273	88435
00010	98520	17767	14905	68607	22109	40558	60970	93433	50500	73998
00011	11805	05431	39808	27732	50725	68248	29405	24201	52775	67851
00012	83452	99634	06288	98083	13746	70078	18475	40610	68711	77817
00013	88685	40200	86507	58401	36766	67951	90364	76493	29609	11062
00014	99594	67348	87517	64969	91826	08928	93785	61368	23478	34113
00015	65481	17674	17468	50950	58047	76974	73039	57186	40218	16544
00016	80124	35635	17727	08015	45318	22374	21115	78253	14385	53763
00017	74350	99817	77402	77214	43236	00210	45521	64237	96286	02655
00018	69916	26803	66252	29148	36936	87203	76621	13990	94400	56418
00019	09893	20505	14225	68514	46427	56788	96297	78822	54382	14598
00020	91499	14523	68479	27686	46162	83554	94750	89923	37089	20048
00021	80336	94598	26940	36858	70297	34135	53140	33340	42050	82341
00022	44104	81949	85157	47954	32979	26575	57600	40881	22222	06413
00023	12550	73742	11100	02040	12860	74697	96644	89439	28707	25815
00024	63606	49329	16505	34484	40219	52563	43651	77082	07207	31790

Table A3-3 (*Continued*)

ROW NUMBER					
00025	61196 90446	26457 47774	51924 33729	65394 59593	42582 60527
00026	15474 45266	95270 79953	59367 83848	82396 10118	33211 59466
00027	94557 28573	67897 54387	54622 44431	91190 42592	92927 45973
00028	42481 16213	97344 08721	16868 48767	03071 12059	25701 46670
00029	23523 78317	73208 89837	68935 91416	26252 29663	05522 82562
00030	04493 52494	75246 33824	45862 51025	61962 79335	65337 12472
00031	00549 97654	64051 88159	96119 63896	54692 82391	23287 29529
00032	35963 15307	26898 09354	33351 35462	77974 50024	90103 39333
00033	59808 08391	45427 26842	83609 49700	13021 24892	78565 20106
00034	46058 85236	01390 92286	77281 44077	93910 83647	70617 42941
00035	32179 00597	87379 25241	05567 07007	86743 17157	85394 11838
00036	69234 61406	20117 45204	15956 60000	18743 92423	97118 96338
00037	19565 41430	01758 75379	40419 21585	66674 36806	84962 85207
00038	45155 14938	19476 07246	43667 94543	59047 90033	20826 69541
00039	94864 31994	36168 10851	34888 81553	01540 35456	05014 51176
00040	98086 24826	45240 28404	44999 08896	39094 73407	35441 31880
00041	33185 16232	41941 50949	89435 48581	88695 41994	37548 73048
00042	80951 00406	96382 70774	20151 23387	25016 25298	94624 61171
00043	79752 49140	71961 28296	69861 02591	74852 20539	00387 59579
00044	18633 32537	98145 06571	31010 24674	05455 61427	77938 91936
00045	74029 43902	77557 32270	97790 17119	52527 58021	80814 51748
00046	54178 45611	80993 37143	05335 12969	56127 19255	36040 90324
00047	11664 49883	52079 84827	59381 71539	09973 33440	88461 23356
00048	48324 77928	31249 64710	02295 36870	32307 57546	15020 09994
00049	69074 94138	87637 91976	35584 04401	10518 21615	01848 76938
00050	09188 20097	32825 39527	04220 86304	83389 87374	64278 58044
00051	90045 85497	51981 50654	94938 81997	91870 76150	68476 64659
00052	73189 50207	47677 26269	62290 64464	27124 67018	41361 82760
00053	75768 76490	20971 87749	90429 12272	95375 05871	93823 43178
00054	54016 44056	66281 31003	00682 27398	20714 53295	07706 17813
00055	08358 69910	78542 42785	13661 58873	04618 97553	31223 08420
00056	28306 03264	81333 10591	40510 07893	32604 60475	94119 01840
00057	53840 86233	81594 13628	51215 90290	28466 68795	77762 20791
00058	91757 53741	61613 62269	50263 90212	55781 76514	83483 47055
00059	89415 92694	00397 58391	12607 17646	48949 72306	94541 37408
00060	77513 03820	86864 29901	68414 82774	51908 13980	72893 55507
00061	19502 37174	69979 20288	55210 29773	74287 75251	65344 67415
00062	21818 59313	93278 81757	05686 73156	07082 85046	31853 38452
00063	51474 66499	68107 23621	94049 91345	42836 09191	08007 45449
00064	99559 68331	62535 24170	69777 12830	74819 78142	43860 72834
00065	33713 48007	93584 72869	51926 64721	58303 29822	93174 93972
00066	85274 86893	11303 22970	28834 34137	73515 90400	71148 43643
00067	84133 89640	44035 52166	73852 70091	61222 60561	62327 18423
00068	56732 16234	17395 96131	10123 91622	85496 57560	81604 18880
00069	65138 56806	87648 85261	34313 65861	45875 21069	85644 47277
00070	38001 02176	81719 11711	71602 92937	74219 64049	65584 49698
00071	37402 96397	01304 77586	56271 10086	47324 62605	40030 37438

Table A3-3 ***(Continued)***

ROW NUMBER					
00072	97125 40348	87083 31417	21815 39250	75237 62047	15501 29578
00073	21826 41134	47143 34072	64638 85902	49139 06441	03856 54552
00074	73135 42742	95719 09035	85794 74296	08789 88156	64691 19202
00075	07638 77929	03061 18072	96207 44156	23821 99538	04713 66994
00076	60528 83441	07954 19814	59175 20695	05533 52139	61212 06455
00077	83596 35655	06958 92983	05128 09719	77433 53783	92301 50498
00078	10850 62746	99599 10507	13499 06319	53075 71839	06410 19362
00079	39820 98952	43622 63147	64421 80814	43800 09351	31024 73167
00080	59580 06478	75569 78800	88835 54486	23768 06156	04111 08408
00081	38508 07341	23793 48763	90822 97022	17719 04207	95954 49953
00082	30692 70668	94688 16127	56196 80091	82067 63400	05462 69200
00083	65443 95659	18288 27437	49632 24041	08337 65676	96299 90836
00084	27267 50264	13192 72294	07477 44606	17985 48911	97341 30358
00085	91307 06991	19072 24210	36699 53728	28825 35793	28976 66252
00086	68434 94688	84473 13622	62126 98408	12843 82590	09815 93146
00087	48908 15877	54745 24591	35700 04754	83824 52692	54130 55160
00088	06913 45197	42672 78601	11883 09528	63011 98901	14974 40344
00089	10455 16019	14210 33712	91342 37821	88325 80851	43667 70883
00090	12883 97343	65027 61184	04285 01392	17974 15077	90712 26769
00091	21778 30976	38807 36961	31649 42096	63281 02023	08816 47449
00092	19523 59515	65122 59659	86283 68258	69572 13798	16435 91529
00093	67245 52670	35583 16563	79246 86686	76463 34222	26655 90802
00094	60584 47377	07500 37992	45134 26529	26760 83637	41326 44344
00095	53853 41377	36066 94850	58838 73859	49364 73331	96240 43642
00096	24637 38736	74384 89342	52623 07992	12369 18601	03742 83873
00097	83080 12451	38992 22815	07759 51777	97377 27585	51972 37867
00098	16444 24334	36151 99073	27493 70939	85130 32552	54846 54759
00099	60790 18157	57178 65762	11161 78576	45819 52979	65130 04860
00100	03991 10461	93716 16894	66083 24653	84609 58232	88618 19161
00101	38555 95554	32886 59780	08355 60860	29735 47762	71299 23853
00102	17546 73704	92052 46215	55121 29281	59076 07936	27954 58909
00103	32643 52861	95819 06831	00911 98936	76355 93779	80863 00514
00104	69572 68777	39510 35905	14060 40619	29549 69616	33564 60780
00105	24122 66591	27699 06494	14845 46672	61958 77100	90899 75754
00106	61196 30231	92962 61773	41839 55382	17267 70943	78038 70267
00107	30532 21704	10274 12202	39685 23309	10061 68829	55986 66485
00108	03788 97599	75867 20717	74416 53166	35208 33374	87539 08823
00109	48228 63379	85783 47619	53152 67433	35663 52972	16818 60311
00110	60365 94653	35075 33949	42614 29297	01918 28316	98953 73231
00111	83799 42402	56623 34442	34994 41374	70071 14736	09958 18065
00112	32960 07405	36409 83232	99385 41600	11133 07586	15917 06253
00113	19322 53845	57620 52606	66497 68646	78138 66559	19640 99413
00114	11220 94747	07399 37408	48509 23929	27482 45476	85244 35159
00115	31751 57260	68980 05339	15470 48355	88651 22596	03152 19121
00116	88492 99382	14454 04504	20094 98977	74843 93413	22109 78508
00117	30934 47744	07481 83828	73788 06533	28597 20405	94205 20380
00118	22888 48893	27499 98748	60530 45128	74022 84617	82037 10268
00119	78212 16993	35902 91386	44372 15486	65741 14014	87481 37220

Table A3-3 ***(Continued)***

ROW NUMBER					
00120	41849 84547	46850 52326	34677 58300	74910 64345	19325 81549
00121	46352 33049	69248 93460	45305 07521	61318 31855	14413 70951
00122	11087 96294	14013 31792	59747 67277	76503 34513	39663 77544
00123	52701 08337	56303 87315	16520 69676	11654 99893	02181 68161
00124	57275 36898	81304 48585	68652 27376	92852 55866	88448 03584
00125	20857 73156	70284 24326	79375 95220	01159 63267	10622 48391
00126	15633 84924	90415 93614	33521 26665	55823 47641	86225 31704
00127	92694 48297	39904 02115	59589 49067	66821 41575	49767 04037
00128	77613 19019	88152 00080	20554 91409	96277 48257	50816 97616
00129	38688 32486	45134 63545	59404 72059	43947 51680	43852 59693
00130	25163 01889	70014 15021	41290 67312	71857 15957	68971 11403
00131	65251 07629	37239 33295	05870 01119	92784 26340	18477 65622
00132	36815 43625	18637 37509	82444 99005	04921 73701	14707 93997
00133	64397 11692	05327 82162	20247 81759	45197 25332	83745 22567
00134	04515 25624	95096 67946	48460 85558	15191 18782	16930 33361
00135	83761 60873	43253 84145	60833 25983	01291 41349	20368 07126
00136	14387 06345	80854 09279	43529 06318	38384 74761	41196 37480
00137	51321 92246	80088 77074	88722 56736	66164 49431	66919 31678
00138	72472 00008	80890 18002	94813 31900	54155 83436	35352 54131
00139	05466 55306	93128 18464	74457 90561	72848 11834	79982 68416
00140	39528 72484	82474 25593	48545 35247	18619 13674	18611 19241
00141	81616 18711	53342 44276	75122 11724	74627 73707	58319 15997
00142	07586 16120	82641 22820	92904 13141	32392 19763	61199 67940
00143	90767 04235	13574 17200	69902 63742	78464 22501	18627 90872
00144	40188 28193	29593 88627	94972 11598	62095 36787	00441 58997
00145	34414 82157	86887 55087	19152 00023	12302 80783	32624 68691
00146	63439 75363	44989 16822	36024 00867	76378 41605	65961 73488
00147	67049 09070	93399 45547	94458 74284	05041 49807	20288 34060
00148	79495 04146	52162 90286	54158 34243	46978 35482	59362 95938
00149	91704 30552	04737 21031	75051 93029	47665 64382	99782 93478
00150	94015 46874	32444 48277	59820 96163	64654 25843	41145 42820
00151	74108 88222	88570 74015	25704 91035	01755 14750	48968 38603
00152	62880 87873	95160 59221	22304 90314	72877 17334	39283 04149
00153	11748 12102	80580 41867	17710 59621	06554 07850	73950 79552
00154	17944 05600	60478 03343	25852 58905	57216 39618	49856 99326
00155	66067 42792	95043 52680	46780 56487	09971 59481	37006 22186
00156	54244 91030	45547 70818	59849 96169	61459 21647	87417 17198
00157	30945 57589	31732 57260	47670 07654	46376 25366	94746 49580
00158	69170 37403	86995 90307	94304 71803	26825 05511	12459 91314
00159	08345 88975	35841 85771	08105 59987	87112 21476	14713 71181
00160	27767 43584	85301 88977	29490 69714	73035 41207	74699 09310
00161	13025 14338	54066 15243	47724 66733	47431 43905	31048 56699
00162	80217 36292	98525 24335	24432 24896	43277 58874	11466 16082
00163	10875 62004	90391 61105	57411 06368	53856 30743	08670 84741
00164	54127 57326	26629 19087	24472 88779	30540 27886	61732 75454
00165	60311 42824	37301 42678	45990 43242	17374 52003	70707 70214
00166	49739 71484	92003 98086	76668 73209	59202 11973	02902 33250
00167	78626 51594	16453 94614	39014 97066	83012 09832	25571 77628

Table A3-3 ***(Continued)***

ROW NUMBER					
00168	66692 13986	99837 00582	81232 44987	09504 96412	90193 79568
00169	44071 28091	07362 97703	76447 42537	98524 97831	65704 09514
00170	41468 85149	49554 17994	14924 39650	95294 00556	70481 06905
00171	94559 37559	49678 53119	70312 05682	66986 34099	74474 20740
00172	41615 70360	64114 58660	90850 64618	80620 51790	11436 38072
00173	50273 93113	41794 86861	24781 89683	55411 85667	77535 99892
00174	41396 80504	90670 08289	40902 05069	95083 06783	28102 57816
00175	25807 24260	71529 78920	72682 07385	90726 57166	98884 08583
00176	06170 97965	88302 98041	21443 41808	68984 83620	89747 98882
00177	60808 54444	74412 81105	01176 28838	36421 16489	18059 51061
00178	80940 44893	10408 36222	80582 71944	92638 40333	67054 16067
00179	19516 90120	46759 71643	13177 55292	21036 82808	77501 97427
00180	49386 54480	23604 23554	21785 41101	91178 10174	29420 90438
00181	06312 88940	15995 69321	47458 64809	98189 81851	29651 84215
00182	60942 00307	11897 92674	40405 68032	96717 54244	10701 41393
00183	92329 98932	78284 46347	71209 92061	39448 93136	25722 08564
00184	77936 63574	31384 51924	85561 29671	58137 17820	22751 36518
00185	38101 77756	11657 13897	95889 57067	47648 13885	70669 93406
00186	39641 69457	91339 22502	92613 89719	11947 56203	19324 20504
00187	84054 40455	99396 63680	67667 60631	69181 96845	38525 11600
00188	47468 03577	57649 63266	24700 71594	14004 23153	69249 05747
00189	43321 31370	28977 23896	76479 68562	62342 07589	08899 05985
00190	64281 61826	18555 64937	13173 33365	78851 16499	87064 13075
00191	66847 70495	32350 02985	86716 38746	26313 77463	55387 72681
00192	72461 33230	21529 53424	92581 02262	78438 66276	18396 73538
00193	21032 91050	13058 16218	12470 56500	15292 76139	59526 52113
00194	95362 67011	06651 16136	01016 00857	55018 56374	35824 71708
00195	49712 97380	10404 55452	34030 60726	75211 10271	36633 68424
00196	58275 61764	97586 54716	50259 46345	87195 46092	26787 60939
00197	89514 11788	68224 23417	73959 76145	30342 40277	11049 72049
00198	15472 50669	48139 36732	46874 37088	73465 09819	58869 35220
00199	12120 86124	51247 44302	60883 52109	21437 36786	49226 77837

SOURCE: Rand Corporation, *A Million Random Digits* (Glencoe, Ill.: Free Press, 1955).

Table A3-4. Squares, Square Roots, and Reciprocals of Numbers from 1 to 1,000

The Use of Table A3-4. Three pieces of information are provided in Table A3-4: a number squared, the square root of the number, and the reciprocal of the number.

The first column lists the number, the second column gives the value of the number when squared, the third column gives the square root of the number, and the fourth column gives the reciprocal of the number, i.e., the decimal value obtained when 1 is divided by the number.

Table A3-4. Squares, Square Roots, and Reciprocals

N	N²	$\sqrt{N}$	1/N	N	N²	$\sqrt{N}$	1/N
1	1	1.0000	1.000000	51	2601	7.1414	.019608
2	4	1.4142	.500000	52	2704	7.2111	.019231
3	9	1.7321	.333333	53	2809	7.2801	.018868
4	16	2.0000	.250000	54	2916	7.3485	.018519
5	25	2.2361	.200000	55	3025	7.4162	.018182
6	36	2.4495	.166667	56	3136	7.4833	.017857
7	49	2.6458	.142857	57	3249	7.5498	.017544
8	64	2.8284	.125000	58	3364	7.6158	.017241
9	81	3.0000	.111111	59	3481	7.6811	.016949
10	100	3.1623	.100000	60	3600	7.7460	.016667
11	121	3.3166	.090909	61	3721	7.8102	.016393
12	144	3.4641	.083333	62	3844	7.8740	.016129
13	169	3.6056	.076923	63	3969	7.9373	.015873
14	196	3.7417	.071429	64	4096	8.0000	.015625
15	225	3.8730	.066667	65	4225	8.0623	.015385
16	256	4.0000	.062500	66	4356	8.1240	.015152
17	289	4.1231	.058824	67	4489	8.1854	.014925
18	324	4.2426	.055556	68	4624	8.2462	.014706
19	361	4.3589	.052632	69	4761	8.3066	.014493
20	400	4.4721	.050000	70	4900	8.3666	.014286
21	441	4.5826	.047619	71	5041	8.4261	.014085
22	484	4.6904	.045455	72	5184	8.4853	.013889
23	529	4.7958	.043478	73	5329	8.5440	.013699
24	576	4.8990	.041667	74	5476	8.6023	.013514
25	625	5.0000	.040000	75	5625	8.6603	.013333
26	676	5.0990	.038462	76	5776	8.7178	.013158
27	729	5.1962	.037037	77	5929	8.7750	.012987
28	784	5.2915	.035714	78	6084	8.8318	.012821
29	841	5.3852	.034483	79	6241	8.8882	.012658
30	900	5.4772	.033333	80	6400	8.9443	.012500
31	961	5.5678	.032258	81	6561	9.0000	.012346
32	1024	5.6569	.031250	82	6724	9.0554	.012195
33	1089	5.7446	.030303	83	6889	9.1104	.012048
34	1156	5.8310	.029412	84	7056	9.1652	.011905
35	1225	5.9161	.028571	85	7225	9.2195	.011765
36	1296	6.0000	.027778	86	7396	9.2736	.011628
37	1369	6.0828	.027027	87	7569	9.3274	.011494
38	1444	6.1644	.026316	88	7744	9.3808	.011364
39	1521	6.2450	.025641	89	7921	9.4340	.011236
40	1600	6.3246	.025000	90	8100	9.4868	.011111
41	1681	6.4031	.024390	91	8231	9.5394	.010989
42	1764	6.4807	.023810	92	8464	9.5917	.010870
43	1849	6.5574	.023256	93	8649	9.6437	.010753
44	1936	6.6332	.022727	94	8836	9.6954	.010638
45	2025	6.7082	.022222	95	9025	9.7468	.010526
46	2116	6.7823	.021739	96	9216	9.7980	.010417
47	2209	6.8557	.021277	97	9409	9.8489	.010309
48	2304	6.9282	.020833	98	9604	9.8995	.010204
49	2401	7.0000	.020408	99	9801	9.9499	.010101
50	2500	7.0711	.020000	100	10000	10.0000	.010000

Table A3-4 *(Continued)*

N	N²	√N	1/N	N	N²	√N	1/N
101	10201	10.0499	.00990099	151	22801	12.2882	.00662252
102	10404	10.0995	.00980392	152	23104	12.3288	.00657895
103	10609	10.1489	.00970874	153	23409	12.3693	.00653595
104	10816	10.1980	.00961538	154	23716	12.4097	.00649351
105	11025	10.2470	.00952381	155	24025	12.4499	.00645161
106	11236	10.2956	.00943396	156	24336	12.4900	.00641026
107	11449	10.3441	.00934579	157	24649	12.5300	.00636943
108	11664	10.3923	.00925926	158	24964	12.5698	.00632911
109	11881	10.4403	.00917431	159	25281	12.6095	.00628931
110	12100	10.4881	.00909091	160	25600	12.6491	.00625000
111	12321	10.5357	.00900901	161	25921	12.6886	.00621118
112	12544	10.5830	.00892857	162	26244	12.7279	.00617284
113	12769	10.6301	.00884956	163	26569	12.7671	.00613497
114	12996	10.6771	.00877193	164	26896	12.8062	.00609756
115	13225	10.7238	.00869565	165	27225	12.8452	.00606061
116	13456	10.7703	.00862069	166	27556	12.8841	.00602410
117	13689	10.8167	.00854701	167	27889	12.9228	.00598802
118	13924	10.8628	.00847458	168	28224	12.9615	.00595238
119	14161	10.9087	.00840336	169	28561	13.0000	.00591716
120	14400	10.9545	.00833333	170	28900	13.0384	.00588235
121	14641	11.0000	.00826446	171	29241	13.0767	.00584795
122	14884	11.0454	.00819672	172	29584	13.1149	.00581395
123	15129	11.0905	.00813008	173	29929	13.1529	.00578035
124	15376	11.1355	.00800452	174	30276	13.1909	.00574713
125	15625	11.1803	.00800000	175	30625	13.2288	.00571429
126	15876	11.2250	.00793651	176	30976	13.2665	.00568182
127	16129	11.2694	.00787402	177	31329	13.3041	.00564972
128	16384	11.3137	.00781250	178	31684	13.3417	.00561798
129	16641	11.3578	.00775194	179	32041	13.3791	.00558659
130	16900	11.4018	.00769231	180	32400	13.4164	.00555556
131	17161	11.4455	.00763359	181	32751	13.4536	.00552486
132	17424	11.4891	.00757576	182	33124	13.4907	.00549451
133	17689	11.5326	.00751880	183	33489	13.5277	.00546448
134	17956	11.5758	.00746269	184	33856	13.5647	.00543478
135	18225	11.6190	.00740741	185	34225	13.6015	.00540541
136	18496	11.6619	.00735294	186	34596	13.6382	.00537634
137	18769	11.7047	.00729927	187	34969	13.6748	.00534759
138	19044	11.7473	.00724638	188	35344	13.7113	.00531915
139	19321	11.7898	.00719424	189	35721	13.7477	.00529101
140	19600	11.8322	.00714286	190	36100	13.7840	.00526316
141	19881	11.8743	.00709220	191	36481	13.8203	.00523560
142	20164	11.9164	.00704225	192	36864	13.8564	.00520833
143	20449	11.9583	.00699301	193	37249	13.8924	.00518135
144	20736	12.0000	.00694444	194	37636	13.9284	.00515464
145	21025	12.0416	.00689655	195	38025	13.9642	.00512821
146	21316	12.0830	.00684932	196	38416	14.0000	.00510204
147	21609	12.1244	.00680272	197	38809	14.0357	.00507614
148	21904	12.1655	.00675676	198	39204	14.0712	.00505051
149	22201	12.2066	.00671141	199	39601	14.1067	.00502513
150	22500	12.2474	.00666667	200	40000	14.1421	.00500000

Table A3-4 ***(Continued)***

N	N^2	$\sqrt{N}$	1/N	N	N^2	$\sqrt{N}$	1/N
201	40401	14.1774	.00497512	251	63001	15.8430	.00398406
202	40804	14.2127	.00495050	252	63504	15.8745	.00396825
203	41209	14.2478	.00492611	253	64009	15.9060	.00395257
204	41616	14.2829	.00490196	254	64516	15.9374	.00393701
205	42025	14.3178	.00487805	255	65025	15.9687	.00392157
206	42436	14.3527	.00485437	256	65536	16.0000	.00390625
207	42849	14.3875	.00483092	257	66049	16.0312	.00389105
208	43264	14.4222	.00480769	258	66564	16.0624	.00387597
209	43681	14.4568	.00478469	259	67081	16.0935	.00386100
210	44100	14.4914	.00476190	260	67600	16.1245	.00384615
211	44521	14.5258	.00473934	261	68121	16.1555	.00383142
212	44944	14.5602	.00471698	262	68644	16.1864	.00381679
213	45369	14.5945	.00469484	263	69169	16.2173	.00380228
214	45796	14.6287	.00467290	264	69696	16.2481	.00378788
215	46225	14.6629	.00465116	265	70225	16.2788	.00377358
216	46656	14.6969	.00462963	266	70756	16.3095	.00375940
217	47089	14.7309	.00460829	267	71289	16.3401	.00374532
218	47524	14.7648	.00458716	268	71824	16.3707	.00373134
219	47961	14.7986	.00456621	269	72361	16.4012	.00371747
220	48400	14.8324	.00454545	270	72900	16.4317	.00370370
221	48841	14.8661	.00452489	271	73441	16.4621	.00369004
222	49284	14.8997	.00450450	272	73984	16.4924	.00367647
223	49729	14.9332	.00448430	273	74529	16.5227	.00366300
224	50176	14.9666	.00446429	274	75076	16.5529	.00364964
225	50625	15.0000	.00444444	275	75625	16.5831	.00363636
226	51076	15.0333	.00442478	276	76176	16.6132	.00362319
227	51529	15.0665	.00440529	277	76729	16.6433	.00361011
228	51984	15.0997	.00438596	278	77284	16.6733	.00359712
229	52441	15.1327	.00436681	279	77841	16.7033	.00358423
230	52900	15.1658	.00434783	280	78400	16.7332	.00357143
231	53361	15.1987	.00432900	281	78961	16.7631	.00355872
232	53824	15.2315	.00431034	282	79524	16.7929	.00354610
233	54289	15.2643	.00429185	283	80089	16.8226	.00353357
234	54756	19.2971	.00427350	284	80656	16.8523	.00352113
235	55225	15.3297	.00425532	285	81225	16.8819	.00350877
236	55696	15.3623	.00423729	286	81796	16.9115	.00349650
237	56169	15.3943	.00421941	287	82369	16.9411	.00348432
238	56644	15.4272	.00420168	288	82944	16.9706	.00347222
239	57121	15.4596	.00418410	289	83521	17.0000	.00346021
240	57600	15.4919	.00416667	290	84100	17.0294	.00344828
241	58081	15.5242	.00414938	291	84681	17.0587	.00343643
242	58564	15.5563	.00413223	292	85264	17.0880	.00342466
243	59049	15.5885	.00411523	293	85849	17.1172	.00341297
244	59536	15.6205	.00409836	294	86436	17.1464	.00340136
245	60025	15.6525	.00408163	295	87025	17.1756	.00338983
246	60516	15.6844	.00406504	296	87616	17.2047	.00337838
247	61009	15.7162	.00404858	297	88209	17.2337	.00336700
248	61504	15.7480	.00403226	298	88804	17.2627	.00335570
249	62001	15.7797	.00401606	299	89401	17.2916	.00334448
250	62500	15.8114	.00400000	300	90000	17.3205	.00333333

Table A3-4 *(Continued)*

N	N²	√N	1/N	N	N²	√N	1/N
301	90601	17.3494	.00332226	351	123201	18.7350	.00284900
302	91204	17.3781	.00331126	352	123904	18.7617	.00284091
303	91809	17.4069	.00330033	353	124609	18.7883	.00283286
304	92416	17.4356	.00328047	354	125316	18.8149	.00282486
305	93025	17.4642	.00328947	355	126025	18.8414	.00281690
306	93636	17.4929	.00326797	356	126736	18.8680	.00280899
307	94249	17.5214	.00325733	357	127449	18.8944	.00280112
308	94864	17.5499	.00321675	358	128164	18.9209	.00279330
309	95481	17.5784	.00323625	359	128881	18.9473	.00278552
310	96100	17.6068	.00322581	360	129600	18.9737	.00277778
311	96721	17.6352	.00321543	361	130321	19.0000	.00277008
312	97344	17.6635	.00320513	362	131044	19.0263	.00276243
313	97969	17.6918	.00319489	363	131769	19.0526	.00275482
314	98596	17.7200	.00318471	364	132496	19.0788	.00274725
315	99225	17.7482	.00317460	365	133225	19.1050	.00273973
316	99856	17.7764	.00316456	366	133956	19.1311	.00273224
317	100489	17.8045	.00315457	367	134689	19.1572	.00272480
318	101124	17.8326	.00314465	368	135424	19.1833	.00271739
319	101761	17.8606	.00313480	369	136161	19.2094	.00271003
320	102400	17.8885	.00312500	370	136900	19.2354	.00270270
321	103041	17.9165	.00311526	371	137641	19.2614	.00269542
322	103684	17.9444	.00310559	372	138384	19.2873	.00268817
323	104329	17.9722	.00309598	373	139129	19.3132	.00268097
324	104976	18.0000	.00308642	374	139876	19.3391	.00267380
325	105625	18.0278	.00307692	375	140625	19.3649	.00266667
326	106276	18.0555	.00306748	376	141376	19.3907	.00265957
327	106929	18.0831	.00305810	377	142129	19.4165	.00265252
328	107584	18.1108	.00304878	378	142884	19.4422	.00264550
329	108241	18.1384	.00303951	379	143641	19.4679	.00263852
330	108900	18.1659	.00303030	380	144400	19.4936	.00263158
331	109561	18.1934	.00302115	381	145161	19.5192	.00262467
332	110224	18.2209	.00301205	382	145924	19.5448	.00261780
333	110889	18.2483	.00300300	383	146689	19.5704	.00261097
334	111556	18.2757	.00299401	384	147456	19.5959	.00260417
335	112225	18.3030	.00298507	385	148225	19.6214	.00259740
336	112896	18.3303	.00297619	386	148996	19.6469	.00259067
337	113569	18.3576	.00296736	387	149769	19.6723	.00258398
338	114244	18.3848	.00295858	388	150544	19.6977	.00257732
339	114921	18.4120	.00294985	389	151321	19.7231	.00257069
340	115600	18.4391	.00294118	390	152100	19.7484	.00256410
341	116281	18.4662	.00293255	391	152881	19.7737	.00255754
342	116964	18.4932	.00292398	392	153664	19.7990	.00255102
343	117649	18.5203	.00291545	393	154449	19.8242	.00254453
344	118336	18.5472	.00290698	394	155236	19.8494	.00253807
345	119025	18.5742	.00289855	395	156025	19.8746	.00253165
346	119716	18.6011	.00289017	396	156816	19.8897	.00252525
347	120409	18.6279	.00288184	397	157609	19.9249	.00251889
348	121104	18.6548	.00287356	398	158404	19.9499	.00251256
349	121801	18.6815	.00286533	399	159201	19.9750	.00250627
350	122500	18.7083	.00285714	400	160000	20.0000	.00250000

Table A3-4 *(Continued)*

N	N^2	$\sqrt{N}$	1/N	N	N^2	$\sqrt{N}$	1/N
401	160801	20.0250	.00249377	451	203401	21.2368	.00221729
402	161604	20.0499	.00248756	452	204304	21.2603	.00221239
403	162409	20.0749	.00248139	453	205209	21.2838	.00220751
404	163216	20.0998	.00247525	454	206116	21.3073	.00220264
405	164025	20.1246	.00246914	455	207025	21.3307	.00219870
406	164836	20.1494	.00246805	456	207936	21.3542	.00219298
407	165649	20.1742	.00245700	457	208849	21.3776	.00218818
408	166464	20.1990	.00245098	458	209764	21.4009	.00218341
409	167281	20.2237	.00244499	459	210681	21.4243	.00217865
410	168100	20.2485	.00243902	460	211600	21.4476	.00217391
411	168921	20.2731	.00243309	461	212521	21.4709	.00216920
412	169744	20.2978	.00242718	462	213444	21.4942	.00216450
413	170569	20.3224	.00242131	463	214369	21.5174	.00215983
414	171396	20.3470	.00241546	464	215296	21.5407	.00215517
415	172225	20.3715	.00240964	465	216225	21.5639	.00215054
416	173056	20.3961	.00240385	466	217156	21.5870	.00214592
417	173889	20.4206	.00239808	467	218089	21.6102	.00214133
418	174724	20.4450	.00239234	468	219024	21.6333	.00213675
419	175561	20.4695	.00238663	469	219961	21.6564	.00213220
420	176400	20.4939	.00238095	470	220900	21.6795	.00212766
421	177241	20.5183	.00237580	471	221841	21.7025	.00212314
422	178084	20.5426	.00236967	472	222784	21.7256	.00211864
423	178929	20.5670	.00236407	473	223729	21.7486	.00211416
424	179776	20.5913	.00235849	474	224676	21.7715	.00210970
425	180625	20.6155	.00235294	475	225625	21.7945	.00210526
426	181476	20.6398	.00234742	476	226576	21.8174	.00210084
427	182329	20.6640	.00234192	477	227529	21.8403	.00209644
428	183184	20.6882	.00233645	478	228484	21.8632	.00209205
429	184041	20.7123	.00233100	479	229441	21.8861	.00208768
430	184900	20.7364	.00232558	480	230400	21.9089	.00208333
431	185761	20.7605	.00232019	481	231361	21.9317	.00207900
432	186624	20.7846	.00231481	482	232324	21.9545	.00207469
433	187489	20.8087	.00230947	483	233289	21.9773	.00207039
434	188356	20.8327	.00230415	484	234256	22.0000	.00206612
435	189225	20.8567	.00229885	485	235225	22.0227	.00206186
436	190096	20.8806	.00229358	486	236196	22.0454	.00205761
437	190969	20.9045	.00228833	487	237169	22.0681	.00205339
438	191844	20.9284	.00228311	488	238144	22.0907	.00204918
439	192721	20.9523	.00227790	489	239121	22.1133	.00204499
440	193600	20.9762	.00227273	490	240100	22.1359	.00204082
441	194481	21.0000	.00226757	491	241081	22.1585	.00203666
442	195364	21.0238	.00226244	492	242064	22.1811	.00203252
443	196249	21.0476	.00225734	493	243049	22.2036	.00202840
444	197136	21.0713	.00225225	494	244036	22.2261	.00202429
445	198025	21.0950	.00224719	495	245025	22.2486	.00202020
446	198916	21.1187	.00224215	496	246016	22.2711	.00201613
447	199809	21.1424	.00223714	497	247009	22.2935	.00201207
448	200704	21.1660	.00223214	498	248004	22.3159	.00200803
449	201601	21.1896	.00222717	499	249001	22.3383	.00200401
450	202500	21.2132	.00222222	500	250000	22.3607	.00200000

Table A3-4 *(Continued)*

N	N^2	$\sqrt{N}$	1/N	N	N^2	$\sqrt{N}$	1/N
501	251001	22.3830	.00199601	551	303601	23.4734	.00181488
502	252004	22.4054	.00199203	552	304704	23.4947	.00181159
503	253009	22.4277	.00198807	553	305809	23.5160	.00180832
504	254016	22.4499	.00198413	554	306916	23.5372	.00180505
505	255025	22.4722	.00198020	555	308025	23.5584	.00180180
506	256036	22.4944	.00197628	556	309136	23.5797	.00179856
507	257049	22.5167	.00197239	557	310249	23.6003	.00179533
508	258064	22.5389	.00196850	558	311364	23.6220	.00179211
509	259081	22.5610	.00196464	559	312481	23.6432	.00178891
510	260100	22.5832	.00196078	560	313600	23.6643	.00178571
511	261121	22.6053	.00195695	561	314721	23.6854	.00178253
512	262144	22.6274	.00195312	562	315844	23.7065	.00177936
513	263169	22.6495	.00194932	563	316969	23.7276	.00177620
514	264196	22.6716	.00194553	564	318096	23.7487	.00177305
515	265225	22.6936	.00194175	565	319225	23.7697	.00176991
516	266256	22.7156	.00193798	566	320356	23.7908	.00176678
517	267289	22.7376	.00193424	567	321489	23.8118	.00176367
518	268324	22.7569	.00193050	568	322624	23.8328	.00176056
519	269361	22.7816	.00192678	569	323761	23.8537	.00175747
520	270400	22.8035	.00192308	570	324900	23.8747	.00175439
521	271441	22.8254	.00191939	571	326041	23.8956	.00175131
522	272484	22.8473	.00191571	572	327184	23.9165	.00174825
523	273529	22.8692	.00191205	573	328329	23.9374	.00174520
524	274576	22.8910	.00190840	574	329476	23.9583	.00174216
525	275625	22.9129	.00190476	575	330625	23.9792	.00173913
526	276676	22.9347	.00190114	576	331776	24.0000	.00173611
527	277729	22.9565	.00189753	577	332929	24.0208	.00173310
528	278784	22.9783	.00189394	578	334084	24.0416	.00173010
529	279841	23.0000	.00189036	579	335241	24.0624	.00172712
530	280900	23.0217	.00188679	580	336400	24.0832	.00172414
531	281961	23.0434	.00188324	581	337561	24.1039	.00172117
532	283024	23.0651	.00187970	582	338724	24.1247	.00171821
533	284089	23.0868	.00187617	583	339889	24.1454	.00171527
534	285156	23.1084	.00187266	584	341056	24.1661	.00171233
535	286225	23.1301	.00186916	585	342225	24.1863	.00170940
536	287296	23.1517	.00186567	586	343396	24.2074	.00170648
537	288369	23.1733	.00186220	587	344569	24.2281	.00170358
538	289444	23.1948	.00185874	588	345744	24.2487	.00170068
539	290521	23.2164	.00185529	589	346921	24.2693	.00169779
540	291600	23.2379	.00185185	590	348100	24.2899	.00169492
541	292681	23.2594	.00184843	591	349281	24.3105	.00169205
542	293764	23.2809	.00184502	592	350454	24.3311	.00168919
543	294849	23.3024	.00184162	593	351649	24.3516	.00168634
544	295936	23.3238	.00183824	594	352836	24.3721	.00168350
545	297025	23.3452	.00183486	595	354025	24.3926	.00168067
546	298116	23.3666	.00183150	596	355216	24.4131	.00167785
547	299209	23.3880	.00182815	597	356409	24.4336	.00167504
548	300304	23.4094	.00182482	598	357604	24.4540	.00167224
549	301401	23.4307	.00182149	599	358801	24.4745	.00166945
550	302500	23.4521	.00181818	600	360000	24.4949	.00166667

Table A3-4 ***(Continued)***

N	N^2	$\sqrt{N}$	1/N	N	N^2	$\sqrt{N}$	1/N
601	361201	24.5153	.00166389	651	423801	25.5147	.00153610
602	362404	24.5357	.00166113	652	425104	25.5343	.00153374
603	363609	24.5561	.00165837	653	426409	25.5539	.00153139
604	364816	24.5764	.00165563	654	427716	25.5734	.00152905
605	366025	24.5967	.00165289	655	429025	25.5930	.00152672
606	367236	24.6171	.00165017	656	430336	25.6125	.00152439
607	368449	24.6374	.00164745	657	431649	25.6320	.00152207
608	369664	24.6577	.00164474	658	432964	25.6515	.00151976
609	370881	24.6779	.00164204	659	434281	25.6710	.00151745
610	372100	24.6982	.00163934	660	435600	25.6905	.00151515
611	373321	24.7184	.00163666	661	436921	25.7099	.00151286
612	374544	24.7386	.00163399	662	438244	25.7294	.00151057
613	375769	24.7588	.00163132	663	439569	25.7488	.00150830
614	376996	24.7790	.00162866	664	440896	25.7682	.00150602
615	378225	24.7992	.00162602	665	442225	25.7876	.00150376
616	379456	24.8193	.00162338	666	443556	25.8070	.00150150
617	380689	24.8395	.00162075	667	444889	25.8263	.00149925
618	381924	24.8596	.00161812	668	446224	25.8457	.00149701
619	383161	24.8797	.00161551	669	447561	25.8650	.00149477
620	384400	24.8998	.00161290	670	448900	25.8844	.00149254
621	385641	24.9199	.00161031	671	450241	25.9037	.00149031
622	386884	24.9399	.00160772	672	451584	25.9230	.00148810
623	388129	24.9600	.00160514	673	452929	25.9422	.00148588
624	389376	24.9800	.00160256	674	454276	25.9615	.00148368
625	390625	25.0000	.00160000	675	455625	25.9808	.00148148
626	391876	25.0200	.00159744	676	456976	26.0000	.00147929
627	393129	25.0400	.00159490	677	458329	26.0192	.00147710
628	394384	25.0599	.00159236	678	459684	26.0384	.00147493
629	395641	25.0799	.00158983	679	461041	26.0576	.00147275
630	396900	25.0998	.00158730	680	462400	26.0768	.00147059
631	398161	25.1197	.00158479	681	463761	26.0960	.00146843
632	399424	25.1396	.00158228	682	465124	26.1151	.00146628
633	400689	25.1595	.00157978	683	466489	26.1343	.00146413
634	401956	25.1794	.00157729	684	467856	26.1534	.00146199
635	403225	25.1992	.00157480	685	469225	26.1725	.00145985
636	404496	25.2190	.00157233	686	470596	26.1916	.00145773
637	405769	25.2389	.00156986	687	471969	26.2107	.00145560
638	407044	25.2587	.00156740	688	473344	26.2298	.00145349
639	408321	25.2784	.00156495	689	474721	26.2488	.00145138
640	409600	25.2982	.00156250	690	476100	26.2679	.00144928
641	410881	25.3180	.00156006	691	477481	26.2869	.00144718
642	412164	25.3377	.00155763	692	478864	26.3059	.00144509
643	413449	25.3574	.00155521	693	480249	26.3249	.00144300
644	414736	25.3772	.00155230	694	481636	26.3439	.00144092
645	416025	25.3969	.00155039	695	483025	26.3629	.00143885
646	417316	25.4165	.00154799	696	484416	26.3818	.00143678
647	418609	25.4362	.00154560	697	485809	26.4008	.00143472
648	419904	25.4558	.00154321	698	487204	26.4197	.00143266
649	421201	25.4755	.00154083	699	488601	26.4386	.00143062
650	422500	25.4951	.00153846	700	490000	26.4575	.00142857

Table A3-4 ***(Continued)***

N	N^2	$\sqrt{N}$	1/N	N	N^2	$\sqrt{N}$	1/N
701	491401	26.4764	.00142653	751	564001	27.4044	.00133156
702	492804	26.4953	.00142450	752	565504	27.4226	.00132979
703	494209	26.5141	.00142248	753	567009	27.4408	.00132802
704	495616	26.5330	.00142045	754	568516	27.4591	.00132626
705	497025	26.5518	.00141844	755	570025	27.4773	.00132450
706	498436	26.5707	.00141643	756	571536	27.4955	.00132275
707	499849	26.5895	.00141443	757	573049	27.5136	.00132100
708	501264	26.6083	.00141243	758	574564	27.5318	.00131926
709	502681	26.6271	.00141044	759	576081	27.5500	.00131752
710	504100	26.6458	.00140845	760	577600	27.5681	.00131579
711	505521	26.6646	.00140647	761	579121	27.5862	.00131406
712	506944	26.6833	.00140449	762	580644	27.6043	.00131234
713	508369	26.7021	.00140252	763	582169	27.6225	.00131062
714	509796	26.7208	.00140056	764	583696	27.6405	.00130890
715	511225	26.7395	.00139860	765	585225	27.6586	.00130719
716	512656	26.7582	.00139665	766	586756	27.6767	.00130548
717	514089	26.7769	.00139470	767	588289	27.6948	.00130378
718	515524	26.7955	.00139276	768	589824	27.7128	.00130208
719	516961	26.8142	.00139082	769	591361	27.7308	.00130039
720	518400	26.8328	.00138889	770	592900	27.7489	.00129870
721	519841	26.8514	.00138696	771	594441	27.7669	.00129702
722	521284	26.8701	.00138504	772	595984	27.7849	.00129534
723	522729	26.8887	.00138313	773	597529	27.8029	.00129366
724	524176	26.9072	.00138122	774	599076	27.8209	.00129199
725	523625	26.9258	.00137931	775	600625	27.8388	.00129032
726	527076	26.9444	.00137741	776	602176	27.8568	.00128866
727	528529	26.9629	.00137552	777	603729	27.8747	.00128700
728	529984	26.9815	.00137363	778	606284	27.8927	.00128535
729	531441	27.0000	.00137174	779	606341	27.9106	.00128370
730	532900	27.0185	.00136986	780	608400	27.9285	.00128205
731	534361	27.0370	.00136799	781	609961	27.9464	.00128041
732	535824	27.0555	.00136612	782	611524	27.9643	.00127877
733	537289	27.0740	.00136426	783	613089	27.9821	.00127714
734	538756	27.0924	.00136240	784	614656	28.0000	.00127551
735	540225	27.1109	.00136054	785	616225	28.0179	.00127389
736	541696	27.1293	.00135870	786	617796	28.0357	.00127226
737	543169	27.1477	.00135685	787	619369	28.0535	.00127065
738	544644	27.1662	.00135501	788	620944	28.0713	.00126904
739	546121	27.1846	.00135318	789	622521	28.0891	.00126743
740	547600	27.2029	.00135135	790	624100	28.1069	.00126582
741	549081	27.2213	.00134953	791	625681	28.1247	.00126422
742	550564	27.2397	.00134771	792	627264	28.1425	.00126263
743	552049	27.2580	.00134590	793	628849	28.1603	.00126103
744	553536	27.2764	.00134409	794	630436	28.1780	.00125945
745	555025	27.2947	.00134228	795	632025	28.1957	.00125786
746	556516	27.3130	.00134048	796	633616	28.2135	.00125628
747	558009	27.3313	.00133869	797	635209	28.2312	.00125471
748	559504	27.3496	.00133690	798	636804	28.2489	.00125313
749	561001	27.3679	.00133511	799	638401	28.2666	.00125156
750	562500	27.3861	.00133333	800	640000	28.2843	.00125000

Table A3-4 *(Continued)*

N	N^2	$\sqrt{N}$	1/N	N	N^2	$\sqrt{N}$	1/N
801	641601	28.3019	.00124844	851	724201	29.1719	.00117509
802	643204	28.3196	.00124688	852	725904	29.1890	.00117371
803	644809	28.3373	.00124533	853	727609	29.2062	.00117233
804	646416	28.3549	.00124378	854	729316	29.2233	.00117096
805	648025	28.3725	.00124224	855	731025	29.2404	.00116959
806	649636	28.3901	.00124069	856	732736	29.2575	.00116822
807	651249	28.4077	.00123916	857	734449	29.2746	.00116686
808	625864	28.4253	.00123762	858	736164	29.2916	.00116550
809	654481	28.4429	.00123609	859	737881	29.3087	.00116414
810	656100	28.4605	.00123457	860	739600	29.3258	.00116279
811	657721	28.4781	.00123305	861	741321	29.3428	.00116144
812	659344	28.4956	.00123153	862	743044	29.3598	.00116009
813	660969	28.5132	.00123001	863	744769	29.3769	.00115875
814	662596	28.5307	.00122850	864	746496	29.3939	.00115741
815	664225	28.5482	.00122699	865	748225	29.4109	.00115607
816	665856	28.5657	.00122549	866	749956	29.4279	.00115473
817	667489	28.5832	.00122399	867	751689	29.4449	.00115340
818	669124	28.6007	.00122249	868	753424	29.4618	.00115207
819	670761	28.6182	.00122100	869	755161	29.4788	.00115075
820	672400	28.6356	.00121951	870	756900	29.4958	.00114943
821	674041	28.6531	.00121803	871	758641	29.5127	.00114811
822	675684	28.6705	.00121655	872	760384	29.5296	.00114679
823	677329	28.6880	.00121507	873	762129	29.5466	.00114548
824	678976	28.7054	.00121359	874	763876	29.5635	.00114416
825	680625	28.7228	.00121212	875	765625	29.5804	.00114286
826	682276	28.7402	.00121065	876	767376	29.5973	.00114155
827	683929	28.7576	.00120919	877	769129	29.6142	.00114025
828	685584	28.7750	.00120773	878	770884	29.6311	.00113895
829	687241	28.7924	.00120627	879	772641	29.6479	.00113766
830	688900	28.8097	.00120482	880	774400	29.6848	.00113636
831	690561	28.8271	.00120337	881	776161	29.6816	.00113507
832	692224	28.8444	.00120192	882	777924	29.6985	.00113379
833	693889	28.8617	.00120048	883	779689	29.7153	.00113250
834	695556	28.8791	.00119904	884	781456	29.7321	.00113122
835	697225	28.8964	.00119760	885	783225	29.7489	.00112994
836	698896	28.9137	.00119617	886	784996	29.7658	.00112867
837	700569	28.9310	.00119474	887	786769	29.7825	.00112740
838	702244	28.9482	.00119332	888	788544	29.7993	.00112613
839	703921	28.9655	.00119190	889	790321	29.8161	.00112486
840	705600	28.9828	.00119048	890	792100	29.8329	.00112360
841	707281	29.0000	.00118906	891	793881	29.8496	.00112233
842	708964	29.0172	.00118765	892	795664	29.8664	.00112108
843	710649	29.0345	.00118624	893	797449	29.8831	.00111982
844	712336	29.0517	.00118483	894	799236	29.8998	.00111857
845	714025	29.0689	.00118343	895	801025	29.9166	.00111732
846	715716	29.0861	.00118203	896	802816	29.9333	.00111607
847	717409	29.1033	.00118064	897	804609	29.9500	.00111483
848	719104	29.1204	.00117925	898	806404	29.9666	.00111359
849	720801	29.1376	.00117786	899	808201	29.9833	.00111235
850	722500	29.1548	.00117647	900	810000	30.0000	.00111111

Table A3-4 ***(Continued)***

N	N^2	$\sqrt{N}$	1/N	N	N^2	$\sqrt{N}$	1/N
901	811801	30.0167	.00110988	951	904401	30.8383	.00105152
902	813604	30.0333	.00110865	952	906304	30.8545	.00105042
903	815409	30.0500	.00110742	953	908209	30.8707	.00104932
904	817216	30.0666	.00110619	954	910116	30.8869	.00104822
905	819025	30.0832	.00110497	955	912025	30.9031	.00104712
906	820836	30.0998	.00110375	956	913936	30.9192	.00104603
907	822649	30.1164	.00110254	957	915849	30.9354	.00104493
908	824464	30.1330	.00110132	958	917764	30.9516	.00104384
909	826281	30.1496	.00110011	959	919681	30.9677	.00104275
910	828100	30.1662	.00109890	960	921600	30.9839	.00104167
911	829921	30.1828	.00109769	961	923521	31.0000	.00104058
912	831744	30.1993	.00109649	962	925444	31.0161	.00103950
913	833569	30.2159	.00109529	963	927369	31.0322	.00103842
914	835396	30.2324	.00109409	964	929296	31.0483	.00103734
915	837225	30.2490	.00109290	965	931225	31.0644	.00103627
916	839056	30.2653	.00109170	966	933156	31.0805	.00103520
917	840889	30.2820	.00109051	967	935089	31.0966	.00103413
918	842724	30.2985	.00108932	968	937024	31.1127	.00103306
919	844561	30.3150	.00108814	969	938961	31.1288	.00103199
920	846400	30.3315	.00108696	970	940900	31.1448	.00103093
921	848241	30.3480	.00108578	971	942841	31.1609	.00102987
922	850084	30.3645	.00108460	972	944784	31.1769	.00102881
923	851929	30.3809	.00108342	973	946729	31.1929	.00102775
924	853776	30.3974	.00108225	974	948676	31.2090	.00102669
925	855625	30.4138	.00108108	975	950625	31.2250	.00102564
926	857476	30.4302	.00107991	976	952576	31.2410	.00102459
927	859329	30.4467	.00107875	977	954529	31.2570	.00102354
928	861184	30.4631	.00107759	978	956484	31.2730	.00102249
929	863041	30.4795	.00107643	979	958441	31.2890	.00102145
930	864900	30.4959	.00107527	980	960400	31.3050	.00102041
931	866761	30.5123	.00107411	981	962361	31.3209	.00101937
932	868624	30.5287	.00107296	982	964324	31.3369	.00101833
933	870489	30.5450	.00107181	983	966289	31.3528	.00101729
934	872356	30.5614	.00107066	984	968256	31.3688	.00101626
935	874225	30.5778	.00106952	985	970225	31.3847	.00101523
936	876096	30.5941	.00106838	986	972196	31.4006	.00101420
937	877969	30.6105	.00106724	987	974169	31.4166	.00101317
938	879844	30.6268	.00106610	988	976144	31.4325	.00101215
939	881721	30.6431	.00106496	989	978121	31.4484	.00101112
940	883600	30.6594	.00106383	990	980100	31.4643	.00101010
941	885481	30.6757	.00106270	991	982081	31.4802	.00100908
942	887364	30.6920	.00106157	992	984064	31.4960	.00100806
943	889249	30.7083	.00106045	993	986049	31.5119	.00100705
944	891136	30.7246	.00105932	994	988036	31.5278	.00100604
945	893025	30.7409	.00105820	995	990025	31.5436	.00100503
946	894916	30.7571	.00105708	996	992016	31.5595	.00100402
947	896809	30.7734	.00105597	997	994009	31.5753	.00103842
948	898704	30.7896	.00105485	998	996004	31.5911	.00100200
949	900601	30.8058	.00105374	999	998001	31.6070	.00100100
950	902500	30.8221	.00105263	1000	1000000	31.6228	.00100000

SOURCE: Jack W. Dunlap and Albert K. Kurtz, *Handbook of Statistical Nomographs, Tables, and Formulas* (New York: World Book, 1932), pp. 72–81.

Tables A3-5 and A3-6. Sample Size for Specified Confidence Limits and Precision When Sampling Attributes in Percentages

Researchers often specify a sample size prior to drawing it. This is done in order to achieve a desired level of precision and confidence in their results. To accomplish this, researchers solve the following equation:

$$\text{Desired precision} = (\text{Desired confidence level}) \left[\frac{\text{Standard deviation of population}}{\sqrt{N}} \right]$$

Precision and confidence level are determined in advance by the researcher. Standard deviation is estimated using whatever information is available. Thus, to obtain needed sample size the equation has only to be solved for N.

For instance, assume that a researcher wished to draw a random sample of community residents for purposes of estimating mean educational level. The desired confidence is 95 percent (1.96) and desired precision is to be within $\pm.1$ years. Guessing the standard deviation of the population to be 2.5 years, the sample size needed to achieve these results can then be calculated using basic algebra:

$$.1 = 1.96 \frac{Sd}{\sqrt{N}}$$

$$.1 = 1.96 \frac{2.5}{\sqrt{N}}$$

$$\sqrt{N} = \frac{1.96\,(2.5)}{.1} = 49$$

$$N = (49)^2 = 2401$$

This procedure must be independently applied in every research situation according to the needs of the particular problem.

When sampling attributes can be stated in proportions or percents rather than interval or ratio values, it is possible to use tables which have been constructed for purposes of determining sample size. Tables A3-5 and A3-6 have been constructed for this purpose.

The Use of Table A3-5. Table A3-5 is constructed for researchers who wish to obtain 95 percent confidence in their results. The table is constructed for maximum standard deviation. Needed sample size is determined by locating the size of the population (in column 1) and reading across to the column with the desired precision level. The intersection of the appropriate row and column indicates the needed sample size.

Thus, if your population has 10,000 members and you wish to have 95 percent confidence in your estimate of the population percentage having a specified attribute with a precision level of ± 5 percent, you will need a sample of 385.

Table A3-5. Sample Size for Specified Confidence Limits and Precision When Sampling Attributes, in Percentages

95% confidence interval ($p = 0.5$)[a]

POPULATION SIZE	SAMPLE SIZE FOR PRECISION OF					
	±1%	±2%	±3%	±4%	±5%	±10%
500	[b]	[b]	[b]	[b]	222	83
1,000	[b]	[b]	[b]	385	286	91
1,500	[b]	[b]	638	441	316	94
2,000	[b]	[b]	714	476	333	95
2,500	[b]	1,250	769	500	345	96
3,000	[b]	1,364	811	517	353	97
3,500	[b]	1,458	843	530	359	97
4,000	[b]	1,538	870	541	364	98
4,500	[b]	1,607	891	549	367	98
5,000	[b]	1,667	909	556	370	98
6,000	[b]	1,765	938	566	375	98
7,000	[b]	1,842	959	574	378	99
8,000	[b]	1,905	976	580	381	99
9,000	[b]	1,957	989	584	383	99
10,000	5,000	2,000	1,000	588	385	99
15,000	6,000	2,143	1,034	600	390	99
20,000	6,667	2,222	1.053	606	392	100
25,000	7,143	2,273	1,064	610	394	100
50,000	8,333	2,381	1,087	617	397	100
100,000	9,091	2,439	1,099	621	398	100
$\rightarrow \infty$	10,000	2,500	1,111	625	400	100

SOURCE: Taro Yamane, *Elementary Sampling Theory* (Englewood Cliffs, N.J.: Prentice-Hall, 1967), p. 398.

[a] p—Proportion of units in sample possessing characteristic being measured; for other values of p, the required sample size will be smaller.

[b] In these cases 50% of the universe in the sample will give more than the required accuracy. Since the normal distribution is a poor approximation of the hypergeometrical distribution when n is more than 50% of N, the formula used in this calculation does not apply.

The Use of Table A3-6. Table A3-6 is constructed in the same manner as Table A3-5 with one difference. The former should be used when the desired level of confidence is 99 percent rather than 95 percent.

Table A3-6. Sample Size for Specified Confidence Limits and Precision When Sampling Attributes, in Percentages

99.7% confidence interval ($p = 0.5$)[a]

POPULATION SIZE	SAMPLE SIZE FOR PRECISION OF				
	±1%	±2%	±3%	±4%	±5%
500	[b]	[b]	[b]	[b]	[b]
1,000	[b]	[b]	[b]	[b]	474
1,500	[b]	[b]	[b]	726	563
2,000	[b]	[b]	[b]	826	621
2,500	[b]	[b]	[b]	900	662
3,000	[b]	[b]	1,364	958	692
3,500	[b]	[b]	1,458	1,003	716
4,000	[b]	[b]	1,530	1,041	735
4,500	[b]	[b]	1,607	1,071	750
5,000	[b]	[b]	1,667	1,098	763
6,000	[b]	2,903	1,765	1,139	783
7,000	[b]	3,119	1,842	1,171	798
8,000	[b]	3,303	1,905	1,196	809
9,000	[b]	3,462	1,957	1,216	818
10,000	[b]	3,600	2,000	1,233	826
15,000	[b]	4,091	2,143	1,286	849
20,000	[b]	4,390	2,222	1,314	861
25,000	11,842	4,592	2,273	1,331	869
50,000	15,517	5,056	2,381	1,368	884
100,000	18,367	5,325	2,439	1,387	892
$\rightarrow\infty$	22,500	5,625	2,500	1,406	900

SOURCE: Taro Yamane, *Elementary Sampling Theory* (Englewood Cliffs, N.J.: Prentice-Hall, 1967), p. 399.

[a] *p*—Proportion of units in sample possessing characteristic being measured; for other values of *p*, the required sample size will be smaller.

[b] In these cases 50% of the universe in the sample will give more than the required accuracy. Since the normal distribution is a poor approximation of the hypergeometrical distribution when *n* is more than 50% of *N*, the formula used in this calculation does not apply.

APPENDIX 4

ESTIMATING YULE'S *Q* OF A POPULATION AND DETERMINING CONFIDENCE LIMITS

In Chapter 9, Yule's Q was used to measure the relationship of socioeconomic characteristics to drunken driving convictions for a group of Los Angeles County drivers. In Chapter 10, it was used to measure the relationship of reference groups, attitudes, and behavior for a group of university students. In both cases, the groups studied were treated as samples of larger populations. The goals scientists have when they use samples is to describe the populations that would likely produce such samples. That is, they study samples, but their goals are to describe populations.

Thus, finding Yule's Q measures of association shown in Chapters 9 and 10 was not the ultimate goal of the researchers. The measures shown describe the relationships among variables found in the *samples*, but the researchers wished to know the relationships in the *populations* from which the samples were drawn.

When a sample has been selected by random procedures, statistical techniques can be used to estimate the kind of relationship in populations that might produce the relationship found in the sample. That is, the relationship in the sample can be used to estimate the relationship in the population. The logic of the procedure is similar to that of the chi-square test in Chapter 11, and many of the same concepts (e.g., standard error, confidence limit) are used. The *standard error* is a measure of the theoretical distribution of the dispersion of values which would have been obtained if repeated random samples of a fixed size had been drawn from the population. *Confidence limits* are those values within which the true value of the population is likely to fall for a given level of confidence.

A formula for calculating the standard error of Yule's Q has been devised, but the background for this formula is beyond the scope of this book.* The formula provides the theoretical distribution of Yule's Q if a series of samples were to be randomly drawn, and a Yule's Q calculated for each sample. The formula is as follows:

$$Q_{se} = \left(\frac{1 - Q^2}{2}\right)\sqrt{\frac{1}{a} + \frac{1}{b} + \frac{1}{c} + \frac{1}{d}}$$

In this formula, Q is the value of the relationship actually found by the researcher in the sample that happened to be drawn; and a, b, c, and d are the values found in the researcher's contingency table for the actual sample. Q_{se} is the standard error of Q for the hypothetical population.

* See M. J. Moroney, *Facts from Figures* (London: Penguin Books, 1974 printing), p. 264. See also Maurice G. Kendall and Alan Stuart, *The Advanced Theory of Statistics*, 2d ed. (New York: Hafner, 1967), Vol. 2, p. 540.

Example: In investigating the relationship between political party membership and political participation, the following results were obtained for a random sample of adults.

Political Party Membership | **Last Presidential Election**

	Voted	Did Not Vote
Member	72	18
Not a member	26	52

$N = 168$

Yule's Q, based on this contingency table, can be calculated as follows:

a	b
c	d

$$Q = \frac{ad - bc}{ad + bc}$$

$$Q = \frac{(72)(52) - (18)(26)}{(72)(52) + (18)(26)}$$

$$Q = .864$$

Using the Yule's Q just calculated, the standard error of Q (Q_{se}) can now be calculated:

$$Q_{se} = \left(\frac{1 - Q^2}{2}\right)\sqrt{\frac{1}{a} + \frac{1}{b} + \frac{1}{c} + \frac{1}{d}}$$

$$Q_{se} = \left(\frac{1 - (.864)^2}{2}\right)\sqrt{\frac{1}{72} + \frac{1}{18} + \frac{1}{26} + \frac{1}{52}}$$

$$Q_{se} = (.1268)\sqrt{.1271} = .0451$$

Now, since certain minimum criteria were met (e.g., a random sample greater than 30 was used) the indicated calculations provide a basis for determining the confidence limits of Q. For this, the normal curve table is used. (The normal curve is an approximation for the sampling distribution of the statistic Q.)

As explained in Chapter 11, there is 95.44 percent confidence that the true population value will fall within plus or minus two standard errors of the sample. Thus, there is 95.44 percent confidence that the true population value for Q is greater than $Q - 2Q_{se}$ and less than $Q + 2Q_{se}$. In the example used here, there is therefore 95.44 percent that Q is greater than

.864 − 2 (.0451) and less than .864 + 2 (.0451). Completing the calculations indicates that there is 95.44 percent confidence that the Q value of the *population* lies between .9542 and .7738.

Let us return now to the original data and assume that the researcher hypothesized a relationship between the variables. Therefore, he would have established a null hypothesis to the opposite effect. His test then takes the form of assuming there is no relationship between the variables in the population. That is, his null hypothesis would state that the value of Q for the population is zero. If he accepted a confidence level of 95.44 percent, he would therefore hypothesize that the confidence interval would include zero. This allows for sampling error. In fact, it did not include zero. Hence, he can say that the probability is less than 5 in 100 that the population has a Yule's Q equal to zero. The chances are less than 5 in 100 that there is no relationship between the variables in the population.*

* It should be noted that Yule's Q is a special case of gamma which is a more generalized measure of association. Yule's Q is applicable only to 2 by 2 tables whereas gamma is applicable to 2 by 3 tables or larger. An excellent discussion of gamma as well as Yule's Q can be found in John H. Mueller, Karl F. Schuessler, and Herbert L. Costner, *Statistical Reasoning in Sociology*, 2d ed. (Boston: Houghton Mifflin, 1970), pp. 279–292. Although the standard error of gamma is not calculated directly, an approach to this problem is presented in two works: Linton C. Freeman, *Applied Statistics* (New York: Wiley, 1965), pp. 162–175, and Robert S. Weiss, *Statistics in Social Research* (New York: Wiley, 1968), pp. 269–274.

INDEX

About the Authors

Kenneth W. Eckhardt, associate professor of sociology at the University of Delaware, received his B.A. from Beloit College (1955) and his M.A. and Ph.D. from the University of Wisconsin (1960, 1965). Prior to his affiliation with the University of Delaware, he was Senior Research Sociologist at Battelle Columbus Laboratories. He previously held academic appointments at the College of Wooster and at Alma College. His teaching interests are in research methods and in social organization. He is a member of numerous professional societies and has contributed methodological and substantive articles to the *American Journal of Sociology, Social Problems, Journal of Social Psychology, Behavior Science Notes, Public Opinion Quarterly, Sociological Quarterly, Journal of Marriage and the Family, Journal for the Review of Religious Research, American Sociologist*, and *Rural Sociology.*

M. David Ermann, assistant professor of sociology at the University of Delaware, received his B.S. from the University of Pennsylvania (1963) and his M.A. and Ph.D. from the University of Michigan (1969, 1973). While at the University of Michigan, he was a teaching fellow and conducted research under a grant from the National Center for Health Services Research. His current methodological interests are focused on the analysis of complex organizations. In addition to papers presented at national meetings, he has contributed a chapter on control of organizations in *Cost Control in Hospitals* and has written for *Milbank Memorial Fund Quarterly/Health and Society.*